MCSE Windows® 2000 Net...
Infrastructure For Dumm...

C000132192

New Since Windows NT 4

These networking infrastructure features are new since Windows NT 4.0, making them likely candidates for exam questions:

- **Active Directory:** Windows 2000's enterprise directory service
- **Dynamic DNS:** Lets clients and DHCP servers update DNS database
- **Routing and Remote Access:** Combines two NT tools
- **IPSec:** For encrypted communications
- **Encrypting File System (EFS):** For NTFS file encryption
- **Certificate Service:** Manages public key infrastructure
- **Internet Authentication Service (IAS):** Centralizes remote access authentication
- **L2TP (Layer 2 Tunneling Protocol):** Works with IPSec for secure Virtual Private Networking
- **EAP (Extensible Authentication Protocol):** For smart cards and so on
- **Bandwidth Allocation Protocol (BAP):** For multilink connections

WINS

- WINS = NetBIOS-to-IP mapping database
- NetBIOS node types: B-node (broadcast), P-node (direct query), H-node (first P, then B), M-node (first B, then P)
- Static mappings let Windows PCs find non-WINS clients
- WINS proxy listens for broadcasts, enabling non-WINS clients to resolve NetBIOS names
- Pull replication over slow links; push replication over fast links
- Configure replication on both sides for bi-directional updating

DHCP

- You must authorize DHCP in Active Directory before it works.
- Relay Agent needed if DHCP server is remote and router doesn't forward DHCP broadcasts.
- Can automatically update DNS database for Windows and non-Windows clients.
- A reservation guarantees a specific client the same IP address.
- User classes enable tuning lease duration for local versus dial-up clients.

For Dummies®: Bestselling Book Series for Beginners

DNS

- Queries can be *recursive* (need full answer) or *iterative* (partial info okay).
- Forward lookups: You have hostname, and you need IP (A record).
- Reverse lookups: You have IP, and you need hostname (PTR record).
- Active Directory uses SRV resource records.
- Caching-only server has no zone database.
- Three zone replication types: Active Directory-integrated, standard primary, standard secondary.

RRAS

- Active Directory account allows dial-in, denies dial-in, or lets remote access policy govern in native mode network.
- Remote access policy (local to server) includes conditions for connection.
- Remote access profile (local to server) part of policy, specifies nature of connection.
- First matching policy in list gets applied; sequence matters.
- Encryption options: none, basic (40-bit), strong (56-bit).
- IAS (Internet Authentication Server) is RADIUS server for centralized authentication and accounting.

Test-Taking Tips

- For a nonadaptive test: Answer easy questions first; mark long or tough ones to come back to later; and answer every question.
- For an adaptive test: Do your level best on each question before proceeding.
- Get lots of paper to draw diagrams, and at least two pencils.
- Take every last minute coming to you.
- Tile exhibit windows with question windows to make a split screen.
- Watch out for the number of answers requested ("best answer," "all that apply," and so on).

For Dummies®: *Bestselling Book Series for Beginners*

 ™

References for the Rest of Us ®

BESTSELLING BOOK SERIES

Are you intimidated and confused by computers? Do you find that traditional manuals are overloaded with technical details you'll never use? Do your friends and family always call you to fix simple problems on their PCs? Then the ...*For Dummies*® computer book series from IDG Books Worldwide is for you.

...*For Dummies* books are written for those frustrated computer users who know they aren't really dumb but find that PC hardware, software, and indeed the unique vocabulary of computing make them feel helpless. ...*For Dummies* books use a lighthearted approach, a down-to-earth style, and even cartoons and humorous icons to dispel computer novices' fears and build their confidence. Lighthearted but not lightweight, these books are a perfect survival guide for anyone forced to use a computer.

> **"I like my copy so much I told friends; now they bought copies."**
>
> **— Irene C., Orwell, Ohio**

> **"Quick, concise, nontechnical, and humorous."**
>
> **— Jay A., Elburn, Illinois**

> **"Thanks, I needed this book. Now I can sleep at night."**
>
> **— Robin F., British Columbia, Canada**

Already, millions of satisfied readers agree. They have made ...*For Dummies* books the #1 introductory level computer book series and have written asking for more. So, if you're looking for the most fun and easy way to learn about computers, look to ...*For Dummies* books to give you a helping hand.

IDG BOOKS WORLDWIDE ®

MCSE Windows 2000 Network Infrastructure

FOR

DUMMIES®

MCSE Windows® 2000 Network Infrastructure

FOR DUMMIES®

by Glenn Weadock

IDG
BOOKS
WORLDWIDE

IDG Books Worldwide, Inc.
An International Data Group Company

Foster City, CA ◆ Chicago, IL ◆ Indianapolis, IN ◆ New York, NY

MCSE Windows® 2000 Network Infrastructure For Dummies®

Published by
IDG Books Worldwide, Inc.
An International Data Group Company
919 E. Hillsdale Blvd.
Suite 300
Foster City, CA 94404
www.idgbooks.com (IDG Books Worldwide Web Site)
www.dummies.com (Dummies Press Web Site)

Library of Congress Control Number: 00-105687

ISBN: 0-7645-0711-7

Printed in the United States of America

10 9 8 7 6 5 4 3 2 1

1B/QV/RS/QQ/IN

Distributed in the United States by IDG Books Worldwide, Inc.

Distributed by CDG Books Canada Inc. for Canada; by Transworld Publishers Limited in the United Kingdom; by IDG Norge Books for Norway; by IDG Sweden Books for Sweden; by IDG Books Australia Publishing Corporation Pty. Ltd. for Australia and New Zealand; by TransQuest Publishers Pte Ltd. for Singapore, Malaysia, Thailand, Indonesia, and Hong Kong; by Gotop Information Inc. for Taiwan; by ICG Muse, Inc. for Japan; by Intersoft for South Africa; by Eyrolles for France; by International Thomson Publishing for Germany, Austria and Switzerland; by Distribuidora Cuspide for Argentina; by LR International for Brazil; by Galileo Libros for Chile; by Ediciones ZETA S.C.R. Ltda. for Peru; by WS Computer Publishing Corporation, Inc., for the Philippines; by Contemporanea de Ediciones for Venezuela; by Express Computer Distributors for the Caribbean and West Indies; by Micronesia Media Distributor, Inc. for Micronesia; by Chips Computadoras S.A. de C.V. for Mexico; by Editorial Norma de Panama S.A. for Panama; by American Bookshops for Finland.

For general information on IDG Books Worldwide's books in the U.S., please call our Consumer Customer Service department at 800-762-2974. For reseller information, including discounts and premium sales, please call our Reseller Customer Service department at 800-434-3422.

For information on where to purchase IDG Books Worldwide's books outside the U.S., please contact our International Sales department at 317-572-3993 or fax 317-572-4002.

For consumer information on foreign language translations, please contact our Customer Service department at 1-800-434-3422, fax 317-572-4002, or e-mail rights@idgbooks.com.

For information on licensing foreign or domestic rights, please phone +1-650-653-7098.

For sales inquiries and special prices for bulk quantities, please contact our Order Services department at 800-434-3422 or write to the address above.

For information on using IDG Books Worldwide's books in the classroom or for ordering examination copies, please contact our Educational Sales department at 800-434-2086 or fax 317-572-4005.

For press review copies, author interviews, or other publicity information, please contact our Public Relations department at 650-653-7000 or fax 650-653-7500.

For authorization to photocopy items for corporate, personal, or educational use, please contact Copyright Clearance Center, 222 Rosewood Drive, Danvers, MA 01923, or fax 978-750-4470.

Use of the Microsoft Approved Study Guide Logo on this product signifies that it has been independently reviewed and approved in complying with the following standards: acceptable coverage of all content related to Microsoft exam number 70-216, entitled Implementing and Administering a Microsoft Windows 2000 Network Infrastructure; sufficient performance-based exercises that relate closely to all required content; and technically accurate content, based on sampling of text.

is a registered trademark under exclusive license to IDG Books Worldwide, Inc., from International Data Group, Inc.

About the Author

Glenn Weadock is president of Independent Software, Inc., a consulting firm he founded in 1982 after graduating from Stanford University's engineering school. One of the country's most popular technical trainers, Glenn has taught Windows to thousands of students in the United States, United Kingdom, and Canada in more than 200 seminars since 1988. He testified as an expert witness in the Microsoft antitrust trial and was actually on CNN for about two seconds.

Glenn is the author of *MCSE Windows 2000 Professional For Dummies*, *Windows 2000 Registry For Dummies*, *MCSE Windows 98 For Dummies*, and ten other computer books. He is a member of the Association for Computing Machinery, the American Society for Training and Development, and the Society of People Who Mistakenly Thought They'd Never Have to Take Another Exam After They Got Their Degree.

ABOUT IDG BOOKS WORLDWIDE

Welcome to the world of IDG Books Worldwide.

IDG Books Worldwide, Inc., is a subsidiary of International Data Group, the world's largest publisher of computer-related information and the leading global provider of information services on information technology. IDG was founded more than 30 years ago by Patrick J. McGovern and now employs more than 9,000 people worldwide. IDG publishes more than 290 computer publications in over 75 countries. More than 90 million people read one or more IDG publications each month.

Launched in 1990, IDG Books Worldwide is today the #1 publisher of best-selling computer books in the United States. We are proud to have received eight awards from the Computer Press Association in recognition of editorial excellence and three from Computer Currents' First Annual Readers' Choice Awards. Our best-selling ...*For Dummies®* series has more than 50 million copies in print with translations in 31 languages. IDG Books Worldwide, through a joint venture with IDG's Hi-Tech Beijing, became the first U.S. publisher to publish a computer book in the People's Republic of China. In record time, IDG Books Worldwide has become the first choice for millions of readers around the world who want to learn how to better manage their businesses.

Our mission is simple: Every one of our books is designed to bring extra value and skill-building instructions to the reader. Our books are written by experts who understand and care about our readers. The knowledge base of our editorial staff comes from years of experience in publishing, education, and journalism — experience we use to produce books to carry us into the new millennium. In short, we care about books, so we attract the best people. We devote special attention to details such as audience, interior design, use of icons, and illustrations. And because we use an efficient process of authoring, editing, and desktop publishing our books electronically, we can spend more time ensuring superior content and less time on the technicalities of making books.

You can count on our commitment to deliver high-quality books at competitive prices on topics you want to read about. At IDG Books Worldwide, we continue in the IDG tradition of delivering quality for more than 30 years. You'll find no better book on a subject than one from IDG Books Worldwide.

John Kilcullen
Chairman and CEO
IDG Books Worldwide, Inc.

*Eighth Annual
Computer Press
Awards ≥1992*

*Ninth Annual
Computer Press
Awards ≥1993*

*Tenth Annual
Computer Press
Awards ≥1994*

*Eleventh Annual
Computer Press
Awards ≥1995*

IDG is the world's leading IT media, research and exposition company. Founded in 1964, IDG had 1997 revenues of $2.05 billion and has more than 9,000 employees worldwide. IDG offers the widest range of media options that reach IT buyers in 75 countries representing 95% of worldwide IT spending. IDG's diverse product and services portfolio spans six key areas including print publishing, online publishing, expositions and conferences, market research, education and training, and global marketing services. More than 90 million people read one or more of IDG's 290 magazines and newspapers, including IDG's leading global brands — Computerworld, PC World, Network World, Macworld and the Channel World family of publications. IDG Books Worldwide is one of the fastest-growing computer book publishers in the world, with more than 700 titles in 36 languages. The "...For Dummies®" series alone has more than 50 million copies in print. IDG offers online users the largest network of technology-specific Web sites around the world through IDG.net (http://www.idg.net), which comprises more than 225 targeted Web sites in 55 countries worldwide. International Data Corporation (IDC) is the world's largest provider of information technology data, analysis and consulting, with research centers in over 41 countries and more than 400 research analysts worldwide. IDG World Expo is a leading producer of more than 168 globally branded conferences and expositions in 35 countries including E3 (Electronic Entertainment Expo), Macworld Expo, ComNet, Windows World Expo, ICE (Internet Commerce Expo), Agenda, DEMO, and Spotlight. IDG's training subsidiary, ExecuTrain, is the world's largest computer training company, with more than 230 locations worldwide and 785 training courses. IDG Marketing Services helps industry-leading IT companies build international brand recognition by developing global integrated marketing programs via IDG's print, online and exposition products worldwide. Further information about the company can be found at www.idg.com.   1/26/00

Dedication

To whoever invented coffee.

Author's Acknowledgments

Thanks to Emily, Carina, and Cecily, for lending me to IDG for the summer; to my agent, Mike Snell, for special ops; to my colleague, Brett Hill, for technical assistance; at IDG, to everyone who contributed time and effort to this project, especially Kyle Looper and John Pont, editors *sine qua non*;to our sharp-eyed technical editor, Bassam Alameddine; and at Microsoft, to Amy and Megan Stuhlberg, for assistance with research materials.

Publisher's Acknowledgments

We're proud of this book; please register your comments through our IDG Books Worldwide Online Registration Form located at http://my2cents.dummies.com.

Some of the people who helped bring this book to market include the following:

Acquisitions, Editorial, and Media Development

Project Editor: John W. Pont

Acquisitions Manager: Judy Brief

Proof Editor: Teresa Artman

Technical Editor: Bassam Alameddine, MCSE+Internet, MCT, CCNA

Permissions Editor: Carmen Krikorian

Media Development Specialist: Brock Bigard

Media Development Coordinator: Marisa E. Pearman

Editorial Manager: Constance Carlisle

Media Development Manager: Laura Carpenter

Media Development Supervisor: Richard Graves

Editorial Assistant: Candace Nicholson, Amanda Foxworth, Jean Rogers

Production

Project Coordinator: Maridee Ennis

Layout and Graphics: Amy Adrian, Jacque Schneider, Julie Trippetti, Jeremey Unger, Erin Zeltner

Proofreaders: Vickie Broyles, Linda Quigley, Dwight Ramsey, Charles Spencer, York Production Services, Inc.

Indexer: York Production Services, Inc.

General and Administrative

IDG Books Worldwide, Inc.: John Kilcullen, CEO; Bill Barry, President and COO; John Ball, Executive VP, Operations & Administration; John Harris, CFO

IDG Books Technology Publishing Group: Richard Swadley, Senior Vice President and Publisher; Mary Bednarek, Vice President and Publisher; Walter R. Bruce III, Vice President and Publisher; Joseph Wikert, Vice President and Publisher; Mary C. Corder, Editorial Director; Andy Cummings, Publishing Director, General User Group; Barry Pruett, Publishing Director

IDG Books Manufacturing: Ivor Parker, Vice President, Manufacturing

IDG Books Marketing: John Helmus, Assistant Vice President, Director of Marketing

IDG Books Online Management: Brenda McLaughlin, Executive Vice President, Chief Internet Officer; Gary Millrood, Executive Vice President of Business Development, Sales and Marketing

IDG Books Packaging: Marc J. Mikulich, Vice President, Brand Strategy and Research

IDG Books Production for Branded Press: Debbie Stailey, Production Director

IDG Books Sales: Roland Elgey, Senior Vice President, Sales and Marketing; Michael Violano, Vice President, International Sales and Sub Rights

◆

The publisher would like to give special thanks to Patrick J. McGovern, without whom this book would not have been possible.

◆

Contents at a Glance

Cartoons at a Glance

By Rich Tennant

page 311

page 327

page 11

page 45

page 257

page 171

Fax: 978-546-7747
E-mail: richtennant@the5thwave.com
World Wide Web: www.the5thwave.com

Table of Contents

Introduction

· ·

*W*elcome! You're reading the introduction to a quick, no-nonsense guide to passing the Windows 2000 Network Infrastructure MCP/MCSE test number 70-216. (One other network infrastructure exam exists: 70-221, Designing a Windows 2000 Network Infrastructure. This book doesn't deal with that exam.) This introduction covers the book's purpose, style, and organization, and describes the icons I use to guide you through the text.

About This Book

The computer industry is inching its way toward an organized system of credentials for technical professionals, but we're not there yet. The lack of any independent, comprehensive certification authority makes life needlessly difficult for managers and job seekers alike. Managers have a hard time qualifying job applicants, and applicants have a hard time explaining just what it is that they know without getting overly technical.

Businesses looking to hire technical consultants face similar problems. As the computer business grows exponentially in importance with each passing year, the need for some system of credentials has increased dramatically. The computer industry has failed (well, it hasn't even really tried) to get together on a single, industry-wide certification program for software expertise, so the larger individual vendors (most notably Microsoft, Novell, and Cisco) offer their own programs.

Several certifications now exist for computer professionals, such as the Certified NetWare Engineer (CNE) from Novell and the "A+" designation for hardware technicians. As Microsoft has increased its dominance on the desktop and has made inroads in the server market, the MCSE (Microsoft Certified Systems Engineer) certification has grown in importance, making it one of the more desired professional certifications in today's PC industry.

"Test #70-216, Implementing and Administering a Microsoft Windows 2000 Network Infrastructure" — catchy name! — is one of the required tests in the Windows 2000 track that computer professionals can pursue toward obtaining MCSE certification. The Windows NT 4.0 track remains an option as I write this, but it is slated for expiration at the end of calendar 2001. So, many aspiring MCSEs will follow the newer Windows 2000 track in order to enjoy the MCSE credential for the longest possible time.

Test 70-216 also conveys the somewhat less exalted certification of MCP, or Microsoft Certified Professional. For those who want to put three letters after their names instead of four, this is the test to take if you already use Windows 2000 at home or at work.

What this book is

My goal in writing this book is simple: to help you pass the Windows 2000 Network Infrastructure certification test while investing as little study time as possible. (Time is of the essence; pass this test, and you've got six more to go to get your MCSE.) As a result, this book isn't as chatty as other ...*For Dummies* books you may have read. The style is get-to-the-point. Although I do throw in the occasional zinger or chuckle to enliven the (we may as well admit it) often-dry material, the jokes stay out of your way.

Because of the time factor, I personally don't like the approach in which you first read a 1,500-page tome covering the material (much of it irrelevant) in excruciating detail, then also buy and read and learn by rote a 200-page collection of bullet items to use for "cramming" right before the exam. That approach is inefficient if your primary goal is to get certified, although book publishers love it because they get to sell twice as many books.

MCSE Windows 2000 Network Infrastructure For Dummies is designed to be the only book you need to read on the subject if you want to pass the test. Of course, you need more than just a book to pass this exam. You also need lots of hands-on experience in a medium- to very large-sized networking environment. And in the process of acquiring the experience and expertise that you need to pass exam 70-216, you need to tap all the resources that can help you to become an effective network administrator — Microsoft's resource kits, Windows 2000 online help, TechNet, and so on.

This book does three things:

- ✔ It gives you enough technical explanation so that you can understand the various key technology concepts.
- ✔ It gives you enough sample questions in each chapter so that you can assess your own readiness and identify areas that need more work.
- ✔ It lets you do some "cramming" right before the test by providing a sample test in print and hundreds of sample questions on the enclosed CD.

Don't get me wrong. By all means consult other books to supplement this one if you want to increase your odds still further, or if you need to know more about Windows 2000 networking than the exam covers.

The famous ..._For Dummies_ series has grown beyond introducing computer basics to rank novices. Titles like the one you now have in front of you are clearly designed for a professional readership. I can explain the apparent contradiction (I'd _better_ be able to!). The hallmarks of the ..._For Dummies_ book series are clear writing, good organization, lighthearted irreverence, respect for the reader, and value for the dollar. Those are important attributes for a test-prep book.

The publisher and I are adding an extra dollop of accuracy for the MCSE series. For example, because few of my consulting clients have "pure" Windows 2000 networks for me to play with (heck, the operating system just came out a few months ago as I write this), I built a test network. That network consists of four PCs running various versions of Windows, including Windows 2000 Professional and Windows 2000 Server, so that I could test everything in this book against reality (or at least a "lab" version of reality!).

Your friends may rib you about buying one of these yellow-and-black titles, but let me encourage you to zing them back when you get your MCSE many weeks (and dollars) before they do.

I hope you'll tell me how you like this book, and how I can make it better for the next edition. You can reach me through my company's Web site, which is at www.i-sw.com.

What this book isn't

This book isn't an encyclopedia of Windows 2000 networking information. It only contains stuff that I think you'll need to know on the exam, based on what I saw when I took it. Therefore, this book is not, or at least should not be, your last stop on the way to Windows 2000 mastery. Passing the test is the first milestone en route to Windows 2000 guru-hood, not the last. You'll need to read other materials, work (and experiment) with the products, and converse with other Windows 2000 experts (for example, on public Internet newsgroups), to gain true practical expertise.

This book isn't a rehash of a text on the old "Networking Essentials" exam, or any other exam, for that matter. I wrote this book from the ground up to be 100 percent specific to Windows 2000 and 100 percent relevant to Microsoft's published objective list. (Yes, the objective list may change, but that happens fairly rarely, and it's a risk that you and I both must take.)

Finally, this book is not a guarantee. If you read it carefully in conjunction with some hands-on time on a Windows 2000 network, you should pass the first time you take the test. If you don't, you may not. If Microsoft rewrites the test the day this book hits the streets, you may not. All any test-prep book can shoot for is to do a good job presenting the material you'll need to know in a clear and concise way, and that's been my goal.

Who you are

MCSE Windows 2000 Network Infrastructure For Dummies is for actual or aspiring computer professionals. I don't make a lot of assumptions in these pages about you or your business, but the few assumptions I do make are as follows:

- You have some prior experience with computers, and you've logged some hours in the air flying Windows 98, 95, or NT 4.0.
- You have better things to do than to read a thousand-page epic on any Windows 2000 certification test.
- You want to pass the certification test on the first try.
- You'd like to pick up some tips in the course of studying for the exam that you'll actually be able to use in real life.

If this sounds like you, read on!

Who I am

The value of any book depends on the experience of the author, so you should want to know just who the heck is writing this book. I've run a computer consulting business, Independent Software, Inc., since 1982, and I've been a seminar developer and instructor since 1988. As a consultant, I normally work with large organizations on rolling out and supporting Windows technologies, although for a change of pace I provided consulting services and testimony in the Microsoft antitrust trial for about a year. My seminars target the professional technical market, and have included intensive two-day courses on Windows 3.0, 3.1, 95, 98, and (now) 2000.

An MCSE myself, I've taken more Microsoft exams than I care to remember. I've received MCP status for all versions of Windows since 3.1, and I've also passed various weird limited-time Microsoft tests, such as "Windows 95 Migration Specialist." In addition, I've been a Windows 2000 beta tester for about the last 20 years. (OK, it only seemed that long!)

I've written a few other books on Windows before this one. *MCSE Windows 2000 Professional For Dummies* focuses on test 70-210. *Windows 2000 Registry For Dummies, Windows 98 Registry For Dummies,* and *Windows 95 Registry For*

Dummies make the inscrutable Registry database at least moderately scrutable. *Bulletproofing Windows 98, Bulletproofing Windows 95,* and *Bulletproofing NetWare* are more technical books in the McGraw-Hill series that I created, focusing on reliability.

How This Book Is Organized

Microsoft publishes a list of *objectives,* or *skills,* for each test in the MCSE series. (You can find them, at this writing, at www.microsoft.com/ trainingandservices/exams/examasearch.asp?PageID=70-216.) I've designed this book to follow that list. (In a few cases, I've juggled topics so they fit where they make a bit more sense, and in other cases, I've added material that does not appear on the objective list but that shows up on the exam.)

As with most *...For Dummies* books, you can dip in and out of specific chapters according to where you are in your studies and what level of knowledge you already have about particular subjects. You can certainly read this book cover to cover, but each chapter is designed to give you all the information you need on a specific topic and not leave you hanging if you haven't read the entire book up to that point.

Part I: The Backdrop

Part I answers the following burning questions: 1) What's the Windows 2000 Network Infrastructure test all about? and 2) What are the basics of Windows 2000 that you must know to profitably study the rest of the book?

I recommend that everyone read Chapter 1. If you already have a fair amount of hands-on experience with Windows 2000, skim Chapter 2, and if you see anything that looks new or unfamiliar, read it.

Part II: Protocols and Services: Alphabet Soup

Part II is where you should start if you already have a reasonable familiarity with Windows 2000 and you want to get to the meat of exam topics right away. Chapter 3 deals with configuring the two network protocols you're most likely to see on the exam: TCP/IP and NWLink (Microsoft's name for IPX/SPX). Chapter 4 covers the installation and configuration of Domain Name System, or DNS, the service that correlates domain names with numerical IP addresses.

Chapter 5 covers the Dynamic Host Configuration Protocol service (DHCP), which assigns IP addresses (and other TCP/IP settings) to clients automatically when they connect to the network. Finally, Chapter 6 deals with Windows Internet Name Service (WINS), which manages those older-style Microsoft "computer names" in the IP environment.

Part III: LAN/WAN Infrastructure: Connecting the Dots

Where Part II concerns itself mainly with Local Area Network (LAN) issues, Part III looks at remote access and Wide Area Network (WAN) issues. Chapter 7 deals with configuring, securing, and monitoring remote access — for example, via dial-up connections. Chapter 8 covers how to set up Windows 2000 Server as a *router,* linking different physical subnets to each other. Chapter 9 focuses on linking your LAN to the Internet for both inbound and outbound communications.

Part IV: Security Infrastructure

In Part IV, I walk you through the essentials of securing a Windows 2000 network. Chapter 10 covers IPsec and packet filtering. Chapter 11 explores the various aspects of security certificates and how a Windows 2000 network uses them, including a discussion of the new Encrypting File System (EFS).

Part V: The Part of Tens

The Part of Tens is a venerable and standard feature of *...For Dummies* books, including this one. (I have lobbied for a "Part of Twos" that would be more in the spirit of digital computing, but so far with no success.) Chapter 12 offers ten test-taking tips that have nothing to do with Windows 2000 but everything to do with passing the exam. Chapter 13 presents ten sources for additional information if you want to beef up your understanding of any subject area.

Part VI: Appendixes

This book has four appendixes. The first is a practice test that you can take shortly before the actual exam, to refresh the main points, fill in any gaps in your knowledge, and get you comfortable with the probable format of the actual test questions. Appendix B explains details of MCSE and MCP certification, how you can benefit from it, and the specific requirements for the different certifications. Appendix C is a glossary of terms for those occasions when the main text uses words you don't know; I also recommend that you scan Appendix C prior to the exam, to make sure you understand all the words that the exam may use. Finally, Appendix D is a description of the software goodies on the enclosed CD-ROM, which contains a practice exam, a self-assessment exam, and some commercial test-prep software demos, among other gems.

Chapter Structure

Although you may have read books in the ...*For Dummies* series, the MCSE books share some design features that don't appear in non-MCSE titles. You'll appreciate their usefulness as you work your way through the chapters, but here's a capsule description of those features.

Page one

Page one of each chapter presents the exam objectives covered by the chapter, along with a brief two- or three-paragraph introduction to the subject matter. You can therefore use each chapter's first page as a guide to focusing your attention on the subjects you know least well, and skipping chapters covering material you already know.

Quick assessment

Right after the first page is a quick assessment test covering the exam objectives for that chapter. If you get every question right, you may not even need to read the chapter; you should jump to the end and take the Prep Test (which I describe in a moment). If you miss a few of the quick assessment questions, you can flag the chapter sections that you should focus on with particular zeal. Little "sticky notes" appear next to the quick assessment questions to help you match the questions with their associated objectives.

Labs, tables, and graphics

Throughout the main part of each chapter are various labs, tables, and graphics to help you study. *Labs* are simply sequences of numbered steps that you can perform on an actual Windows 2000 network (assuming you have access to one) in order to grasp a subject more fully. *Tables* are columnar lists of information that would be awkward if presented in paragraph form. *Graphics* are either screen snapshots of actual Windows 2000 systems or line drawings that illustrate specific points.

Prep test

Each chapter of exam material ends with a "prep test" consisting of questions that are designed to look and feel like the actual exam. Of course, there's no guarantee that the prep test questions will actually appear on the test, but they're great for double-checking that you really understand the chapter material. They also have value in preparing you for the format of questions that Microsoft likes to use in the real test.

Icons Used in This Book

Several graphical icons highlight certain kinds of material:

This icon points out a bit of knowledge that's worth committing to your long-term memory because it's likely to appear in the test.

This icon identifies a core concept that you may already know, but that you should understand thoroughly before taking the exam.

These are tips to save you time when preparing for, or actually taking, the certification exam.

Short suggestions, hints, and bits of useful information appear next to this icon.

Use this icon to avoid a *gotcha* — a common trap or pitfall, either in test-taking technique or in understanding some aspect of Windows 2000.

Conventions Used in This Book

If you're aware of the following typographical conventions, this book makes more sense:

- Commands that you would type appear in boldface. For example: Type **CMD** in the Run dialog box.

- File paths appear in monofont, like this: `C:\WINNT\SYSTEM32`.

- When a command, file path, or Registry location includes a replaceable parameter that can vary depending on circumstances, the replaceable value appears in italics and enclosed within angle brackets, like this: `C:\Documents and Settings\<username>`.

Where to Go from Here

Now that you've come to the end of this Introduction, I would like to offer you a special congratulations. The fact that you looked over this section and didn't skip immediately to Chapter 1 indicates that you're thorough-minded and therefore extra likely to do well on this (and any other) exam. So pat yourself on the back for a brief second, take a deep breath, and proceed to Part I. It's time to get ready for the test.

Part I
The Backdrop

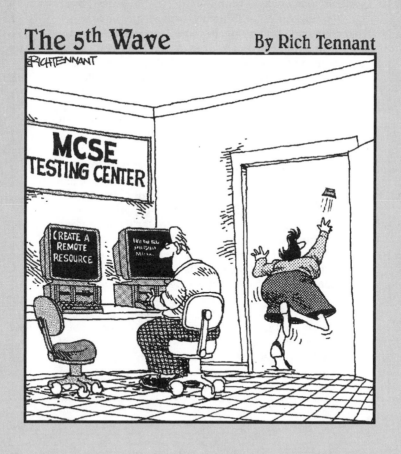

In this part . . .

"Implementing and Administering a Microsoft Windows 2000 Network Infrastructure." What on earth does that mean?

Well, *implementing* — perhaps the most overused buzzword in the computer industry — generally means installing and configuring. In other words, implementing is everything that comes after designing. This exam deals with some network design issues, but it doesn't focus on them nearly as much as the implementation details.

The word *administering* is a synonym for "housekeeping." Fixing things when they break, performing regular maintenance, keeping the network updated, that sort of thing.

Finally, *infrastructure*. Infrastructure is every network component that makes useful work possible, but isn't useful in and of itself. If productivity is the end, infrastructure is the means. And it's generally invisible, if properly implemented (that word again). The computer users in your organization may never know what DNS does, any more than they know the thickness of the concrete on the roads they drive over. Infrastructure is concrete. It is plumbing, wiring, and drywall. You don't see it, but you use it daily.

Now that we have that cleared up, a word or two about this Part. In Part I, this book gives you an overview of what you can expect from exam 70-216 — its format, types of questions, topics it covers, and so on. This Part also offers a backgrounder on Windows 2000 in case it's new to you.

Chapter 1

The Network Infrastructure Implementation Test

. . . .

In This Chapter

▶ Finding out how test 70-216 fits into the Microsoft certification scheme

▶ Getting familiar with testing procedures

▶ Understanding the test's style and format

▶ Discovering the list of skills Microsoft says you need to know in order to pass the test

▶ Picking up a few hints about test-taking

. . . .

*T*his chapter introduces the Microsoft certification system, test-taking procedure, and specific objectives for the 70-216 exam, with cross-references to the main body of the book. When you're done here, you may want to check out Chapter 12 for more test-prep advice. I recommend re-reading both this chapter and Chapter 12 fairly close to exam time.

The Test's Role in Certification

Microsoft exam 70-216, which has the catchy name *Implementing and Administering a Microsoft Windows 2000 Network Infrastructure,* helps fulfill certification requirements for the following "degrees:"

- ✔ Microsoft Certified Professional (MCP)
- ✔ Microsoft Certified Professional + Internet
- ✔ Microsoft Certified Trainer (MCT)
- ✔ Microsoft Certified Systems Engineer (MCSE)
- ✔ Microsoft Certified Systems Engineer + Internet

You can read a lot more detail on these (and other) Microsoft certification programs in Appendix B. For now, just know that by passing one test, you not only gain the right to add the MCP certification to your résumé, you also pass a core requirement of the MCSE certification's Windows 2000 track.

The Windows 2000 MCSE track does not include the Networking Essentials exam, which was part of the core requirements for the NT 4.0 MCSE track. Exam 70-216 is the nearest thing to the old Networking Essentials test, but it covers more Windows-specific material than that test. It's also harder. A *lot* harder.

You may have bought this book because the Windows 2000 Network Infrastructure exam is the only one you want to take: An MCP is good enough for your needs. That's fine, and 99 percent of this book remains relevant for you despite the "MCSE" in the title. Your MCP designation will have a longer life if you achieve it with a Windows 2000 Professional exam as opposed to a Windows 98 or Windows NT 4.0 exam.

This exam is probably not the first one you should take in the MCSE Windows 2000 track unless you have some experience with Windows networking. I suggest you "warm up" to exam 70-216 by taking exam 70-210 first; that's the one on Windows 2000 Professional. On the other hand, if you're an experienced networking hand, you may prefer to take 70-216 first. Just remember Glenn's Rule Of Test Sequencing (GROTS): Take first the tests that cover the topics you know best. By doing so, you build confidence while getting a feel for the style of Microsoft exams.

About the Exam

If you hope to pass MCSE exams, you have to master *both* the style and substance aspects of the tests. This section lays out the key points in both categories. But first, a few words on procedure.

Procedure

You should know about a few formalities and procedural issues before diving into the exam.

Signing up

Microsoft exams are delivered by two organizations: Sylvan Prometric and Virtual University Enterprises (VUE). The usual procedure is to get in touch with one of these organizations (either by phone or Web site) at least one day in advance of the test, make payment arrangements (credit cards are okay), and set up a time and a place. Here's some contact information:

✔ **Sylvan Prometric** (www.prometric.com, www.2test.com): 800-755-EXAM (from the U.S. and Canada), 410-843-8000 (from anywhere)

✔ **NCS Virtual University Enterprises** (www.vue.com/ms): 888-837-8616 (from the U.S. and Canada), 612-995-8800 (from anywhere)

I recommend that you provide a zip code or postal code and let the customer representative find the testing location nearest you. The shorter the drive, the fresher you'll be when you walk into the testing center. Calling the testing center directly for detailed directions is also smart.

Plan to arrive about 15 minutes before test time. At Sylvan Prometric centers, you must normally present two forms of identification — at least one with a photograph on it. You also have to sign a form and a sign-in sheet, which takes a few minutes. However, if you're late, don't fret; depending on how busy the testing center is, you may still be able to slide on in and take your test.

After you sign in, you receive a few sheets of scratch paper and a couple of pencils, and the proctor asks to see your forearms and palms to make sure you haven't made a body part into a human cheat sheet with a Rapidograph technical pen. Okay, nobody really asks to see your skin. And anyway, scribbling on your epidermis or hiding papers down your pants wouldn't help you, because most test sites have TV cameras watching your every move. Don't be offended by this; video monitoring is a good way to ensure that someone else doesn't gain an unfair advantage over you by cheating.

Agree or go home

As your session at the testing center starts, you have to agree to a statement written by Microsoft that says things like "I agree not to use my belt-buckle spy camera to make screen shots of this test, which I will then sell on the Internet for big bucks." As an honest, upright citizen, you will most likely click the Agree button and move on. (If you want to actually read the agreement, go ahead; doing so takes no time off the actual exam clock.)

Easy questions that (alas) don't count

You're likely to see a timed questionnaire before the graded test questions. Your answers provide various marketing data to Microsoft. The "exam time" meter isn't running during this questionnaire, but the "total elapsed time" meter is. So don't dawdle here; it's better to blast through the questionnaire quickly. Save your brain cells for the questions that count. (In my opinion Microsoft should pay you if it wants marketing data, not the other way around. I sometimes check box "A" on every answer as a form of protest.)

Call for comments

At the end of your exam, after you click the Finish button, you have an opportunity to comment on the test. I always feel that this part is premature; I'd like to know whether I passed before telling Microsoft whether its test is excellent or terrible. If you feel really strongly about some aspect of the test, then by all means, let your feelings be known. Otherwise, skip this part. You want to get out of the room as quickly as possible, for reasons I'll explain in a minute.

Signing off

At the end of the test, you get instant feedback as to whether you passed. The two bars at the top of the page indicate the required score and your score.

On some MCSE tests, the report breaks down your performance by category, so you can spend a little time reviewing where you did well and where you could have done better. That information may be useful as you study for other exams, if you're en route to your MCSE, or if you need to take the Windows 2000 test again in order to pass. Unfortunately, Microsoft seems to be moving away from this practice; both times that I took the Network Infrastructure exam, my report included no such helpful information. If the report does not break down your performance by category, and if you failed, then you need to read the next section, "Rerun readiness."

After the test, you can either click Exit or Print another report. (One report prints automatically.) Printing one or two extra reports as file copies isn't a bad idea; you can give one to your boss, keep one for your own file, frame another, and so on. You'll most likely have to get the printouts from an administrator after you leave the test room.

Rerun readiness

After you leave the test center, if you have to take the exam again, increase your odds of success by finding the nearest desk, plonking yourself down into a chair, whipping out a pen and notebook (or notebook computer), and writing down as much as you can remember about the questions you just faced — especially the tough ones. Do this while the material is still fresh in your mind.

You're not likely to see all the same questions again next time, but you are almost certain to see *some* of them. If you make some post-mortem notes, you can focus your study time and increase your odds of passing next time.

Style

Knowing something about an exam's design can help get you comfortable with the format in advance, so here are a few words on what you can expect to see after you sign in at the test center.

Microsoft is free to modify the exam format whenever and however it wants. As I write this, Microsoft uses two styles: classic multiple choice and adaptive, so this section discusses both. Don't make the assumption that the exam will be one style or the other, despite what you may see on various MCSE-related Web sites. Microsoft has been known to change a test's style midway through its life cycle. I can tell you that when I took the Network Infrastructure exam most recently, its format was classic multiple choice, with 55 questions, 140 minutes, and a minimum passing score of 62 percent.

Choose from multiples

The "classic" MCSE test is a closed-book, multiple-choice exam (no bringing your well-worn copy of this book, and no essay questions such as "Describe the probable impact of Windows 2000 on world history, in 500 words or less"). Computers are well suited for grading multiple-choice tests, and it *is* nice to get your grade right away.

Just because the exam is multiple choice doesn't mean that you can ignore the question format. A common pitfall is giving only one answer when the question calls for multiple answers. Be very aware as to whether the question is calling for the best answer, two answers, three answers, "all that apply," or whatever the case may be. (You can usually tell the question format by the graphical element next to the answers: Circles — technically, radio buttons — mean the question has only one correct answer. Squares — that is, check boxes — indicate that the question may have more than one correct answer choice.) I recommend marking questions that expect more than one answer for later review (see "Skipping to success" later in this chapter) because of their inherent trickiness. (Bear in mind that if your test is the adaptive type, you can't mark questions for review. See the section "Adapting to adaptive tests" later in this chapter.)

Some questions are pretty long, and they sometimes give you more information than you really need. I'm in favor of reading through these long paragraphs once and only once, noting the key facts (and maybe even drawing a picture) on your scratch paper. This way, you won't have to read those long spiels multiple times.

A graphic example

Some of the questions involve a graphical screen, either as part of the question (in which the screen is called an *exhibit*) or as the way to provide the answer (in which the screen is called a *simulation*).

When a graphic is an exhibit, don't skip over it! You can click a button at the question's main screen to show the exhibit, but overlooking the button is possible. Most often, an exhibit shows a simplified network diagram illustrating the hypothetical setup you're being quizzed about.

Consider looking at the exhibit before even reading the question. That way, you already have a mental picture of the question's premise. You can look at the exhibit as often as you like. I prefer tiling the two windows, so I can read the question while glancing down at the exhibit instead of having to click back and forth between the two.

When a graphic is the vehicle for *providing* an answer, it's normally a screen shot of a dialog box or property sheet. The cursor turns into a rifle sight icon, and you must point-and-click at the check box(es) or radio button(s) on the dialog box in order to answer the question. (The inclusion of such dialog boxes and property sheets on the test is one big reason I include a fair number of screen shots in this book.)

In some situations, you see a network diagram with some empty squares, and a separate area over to the right or left with some labeled computers ("DHCP Server," "DNS Server," and so on). You have to drag and drop one or more of the labeled computers over to one or more empty squares in order to complete the diagram. You may also see questions in which you must click one or more computer icons in a network diagram in order to convey your answer. In another variation on the drag-and-drop answer, the exam asks you to put choices in a particular sequence — for example, remote access policies, which Windows processes from top to bottom (see Chapter 7).

Although no one who can talk about it really knows how accurate you have to be in order for your answer to register with the test engine, take your time and click right in the middle of the check box or radio button. No point losing points for poor pointing, and it's dumb to be dunned when your "drag" doesn't "drop."

So, although most of the exam questions and answers don't involve pictures, know how to deal with those that do. By the time you take the test, Microsoft may cook up some other clever graphical exam elements, but at least you'll be aware of the ones in this section, if you encounter them.

Skipping to success

In the classical multiple-choice test style, you can skip any questions you don't immediately understand, and come back to them later. That practice is actually a very good thing to do. Because your grade in a classical style test depends solely on the percentage of questions you get right, you need to make sure that you answer as many questions as you can. An unanswered question may as well be wrong; you only get points for questions you answer, and answer correctly.

So, if a question stumps you, go ahead and make your best guess, but mark the question for later review by clicking the Mark button on the test screen. Then move on to the next question. When you're done with the first pass through all the questions, you get a review screen that shows the questions you've marked. A click of the mouse takes you back to ponder further on those knotty problems. You may run out of time before you can study them all, but at least you're not missing the opportunity to score on questions that you can quickly answer correctly.

If your test uses the classic style, *use every last minute you have coming to you.* You may very well finish in less than the allotted 140 minutes (or whatever the length is when you take the exam), especially if you've done a great job preparing by studying this book carefully. Take the time to go back and review questions that you marked, especially those asking for multiple answers. Look for keywords in the test questions that may offer a clue that you missed on first glance. Draw diagrams. For questions that you don't understand well, use the process of elimination to improve your odds.

Adapting to adaptive tests

Adaptive, or "hybrid" tests, have two parts: a regular, what-percent-did-you-get-right part, and an adaptive part. Unfortunately, you don't necessarily know where the dividing line is between the two parts, so you may have to treat the whole test as if it is adaptive, unless Microsoft gives you some clues in the testing instructions.

Okay, so what does "adaptive" mean? An adaptive exam grades you based on the hardest question you can answer on the subject matter of the test. You encounter a series of questions of increasing difficulty. Each question is, in a sense, based on the previous answer: If you got the previous answer correct, you get a harder question, but if you got it wrong, you get an easier question. The questions "adapt" to your answers.

Pace yourself using the onscreen clock. Adaptive tests don't have as many questions, so you can allow yourself more time per question than on a classic style test. However, you typically don't know in advance how many questions you'll receive. I usually take the average of the maximum and minimum number of questions (the test tells you this information) and calculate the approximate amount of time I should spend per question using that number.

In an adaptive test, or in the adaptive part of a hybrid test, the key is to *go slowly and carefully and do your best on each question, skipping none of them.* You don't have the luxury of marking and reviewing questions on an adaptive exam: You have one shot at each question. So the test-taking style is very different indeed from the "classic" test in which your grade depends solely on the percentage of questions you answer correctly.

Substance

This section deals in more detail with exam content. First, I present the formal Microsoft test objectives, and then I offer a few subjective comments.

Testing by objectives

The exam questions test your knowledge in a wide variety of areas. Microsoft publishes objectives, or "skill areas," for each MCP exam on its Web site under `www.microsoft.com/mcp`. (These objectives appear elsewhere, too, sometimes in somewhat different form, as in the *Microsoft Windows 2000 Network Infrastructure MCSE Training Kit,* which you do not need to buy now that you have this book.) In this section, I provide Microsoft's list of objectives for exam 70-216, Implementing and Administering a Windows 2000 Network Infrastructure, along with a cross-reference linking each objective to the relevant chapter in this book.

You may notice that the organization of this book varies somewhat from the organization of the Microsoft objective list. Although you can use this book as a reference, dipping in and out of chapters *ad hoc* and as needed, some of you will read it front to back. For those readers, I've tried to put the topics in a more logical order. (For example, you have to get TCP/IP installed and configured to some extent before you can configure the DNS service, so I treat TCP/IP before DNS, unlike the Microsoft list.)

The formal list is subject to change at any time, so you may want to see if Microsoft has added or removed topics by checking the MCP Web site. However, don't take the list of objectives as gospel. Some exam questions don't relate to the stated objectives, and, conversely, any given exam session may not cover every stated objective.

At this writing, Microsoft's published list of objectives for the Network Infrastructure exam comprises the tasks that I list in the following sections.

Installing, configuring, managing, monitoring, and troubleshooting DNS (Domain Name System) in a Windows 2000 network infrastructure

✔ Install, configure, and troubleshoot DNS (see Chapter 4):

- Install the DNS Server service.
- Configure a root name server.
- Configure zones.
- Configure a caching-only server.
- Configure a DNS client.
- Configure zones for dynamic updates.
- Test the DNS Server service.
- Implement a delegated zone for DNS.
- Manually create DNS resource records.

✔ Manage and monitor DNS (see Chapter 4).

Installing, configuring, managing, monitoring, and troubleshooting DHCP (Dynamic Host Configuration Protocol) in a Windows 2000 network infrastructure

✔ Install, configure, and troubleshoot DHCP(see Chapter 5):

- Install the DHCP Server service.
- Create and manage DHCP scopes, superscopes, and multicast scopes.
- Configure DHCP for DNS integration.
- Authorize a DHCP server in Active Directory.

✔ Manage and monitor DHCP (see Chapter 5).

Configuring, managing, monitoring, and troubleshooting remote access in a Windows 2000 network infrastructure

✔ Configure and troubleshoot remote access (see Chapter 7):

- Configure inbound connections.
- Create a remote access policy.
- Configure a remote access profile.
- Configure a virtual private network (VPN).
- Configure multilink connections.
- Configure Routing and Remote Access for DHCP integration.

✔ Manage and monitor remote access (see Chapter 7).

✔ Configure remote access security (see Chapter 7):

- Configure authentication protocols.
- Configure encryption protocols.
- Create a remote access policy.

Installing, configuring, managing, monitoring, and troubleshooting network protocols in a Windows 2000 network infrastructure

✔ Install, configure, and troubleshoot network protocols (see Chapter 3):

- Install and configure TCP/IP.
- Install the NWLink protocol.
- Configure network bindings.

✔ Configure TCP/IP packet filters (see Chapter 10).

✔ Configure and troubleshoot network protocol security (see Chapter 10).

✔ Manage and monitor network traffic (see Chapter 3).

✔ Configure and troubleshoot IPSec (see Chapter 10):

- Enable IPSec.

- Configure IPSec for transport mode.

- Configure IPSec for tunnel mode.

- Customize IPSec policies and rules.

- Manage and monitor IPSec.

Installing, configuring, managing, monitoring, and troubleshooting WINS (Windows Internet Name Service) in a Windows 2000 network infrastructure

✔ Install, configure, and troubleshoot WINS (see Chapter 6).

✔ Configure WINS replication (see Chapter 6).

✔ Configure NetBIOS name resolution (see Chapter 6).

✔ Manage and monitor WINS (see Chapter 6).

Installing, configuring, managing, monitoring, and troubleshooting IP (Internet Protocol) routing in a Windows 2000 network infrastructure

✔ Install, configure, and troubleshoot IP routing protocols (see Chapter 8):

- Update a Windows 2000-based routing table by means of static routes.

- Implement demand-dial routing.

✔ Manage and monitor IP routing (see Chapter 8):

- Manage and monitor border routing.

- Manage and monitor internal routing.

- Manage and monitor IP routing protocols.

Installing, configuring, and troubleshooting Network Address Translation (NAT)

✔ Install Internet Connection Sharing (see Chapter 9).

✔ Install NAT (see Chapter 9).

✔ Configure NAT properties (see Chapter 9).

✔ Configure NAT interfaces (see Chapter 9).

Installing, configuring, managing, monitoring, and
troubleshooting Certificate Services

> ✔ Install and configure Certificate Authority (see Chapter 11).
>
> ✔ Issue and revoke certificates (see Chapter 11).
>
> ✔ Remove the Encrypting File System (EFS) recovery keys (see Chapter 11).

Hints that may help

Although the formal list of objectives is incredibly wide-ranging, expect a heavy focus on features that are new since Windows NT 4.0. For example, you can bet the exam will include many more questions on dynamic DNS (Chapter 4), given its importance as the Active Directory naming scheme. For another example, the new Routing and Remote Access management console receives a great deal of attention (Chapters 7 and 8). Interoperability with Windows 2000 Professional clients is important, too. (The exam doesn't spend a lot of time covering interoperability with Windows 9x clients.)

Although exam 70-216 is by its nature server-oriented, I suggest that you gain a basic familiarity with Windows 2000 Professional features before taking the Network Infrastructure test. You should have a fundamental understanding of how to configure a networking client, including using the Network and Dial-Up Connections folder to install and set up protocols, clients, and services.

Most people learn best by doing. Therefore, if at all possible, set yourself up a little test network consisting of at least one Windows 2000 Professional PC and one Windows 2000 Server PC. You can use an old and slow "leftover" computer for the workstation PC if you're just using it for educational purposes (but don't go slower than a Pentium 200 with 64MB of RAM). This way, you can actually play around with the various networking concepts.

By the way: After you pass the test, reward yourself! Buy that CD you've been wanting, go to the movies, pick up some real French champagne — do whatever you do for fun. Passing a Microsoft exam is cause for celebration and for forgetting, temporarily, that more exams may be waiting for you down the road.

From a psychological standpoint, if you reward yourself for passing each test, you give yourself positive reinforcement that will help you gear up for the next test that much more enthusiastically. But that's not why you should do it. You should do it because good work always deserves celebration.

Chapter 2

Exam Prep Roadmap: Windows 2000 Basics

● ●

In This Chapter

▶ Familiarizing yourself with the Windows family tree

▶ Discovering the underpinnings of the Windows 2000 architecture

▶ Finding out what sets Windows 2000 apart from Windows NT 4.0

● ●

*W*hen I was an engineering student in college, several lifetimes ago, I worked part time at the student union bowling alley. That was a great job because I could study in between spraying disinfectant on rented shoes and freeing up jammed pinsetting machines. One day, Cheryl, another part-time employee, was having lunch with me at the counter. She looked at my three textbooks, thought for a second, and then said, "*Fundamentals of Nuclear Physics, Fundamentals of Materials Science, Fundamentals of Computer Science.* Don't you ever take any *advanced* classes?" At that moment, purely by accident, I disinfected her sandwich.

Hey, a budding engineer has to start somewhere, and so does a budding MCSE. You need a good basic understanding of the Windows 2000 history and architecture in order to deal with some of the detailed questions that presume such an understanding. For example, you may encounter a question that expects you to know that the concept of primary domain controllers and backup domain controllers no longer exists in Windows 2000 Server. Or Microsoft may expect you to understand some of the dependencies in the Windows 2000 network architecture, such as the fact that Active Directory requires TCP/IP.

I suggest that you get comfortable with the information in this chapter before you read the rest of the book. I promise to keep it brief and avoid arcane topics that probably won't surface on the exam. Later chapters address (in much greater detail) many of the concepts that this chapter introduces, but you should start with the big picture and then focus on the details. Even if it does mean reading a chapter that has the word *Basics* in the title.

Climbing the Windows Family Tree

This section explains where Windows 2000 falls within the Windows product family. Windows 2000 combines many of the benefits of both its ancestors, Windows 98 and Windows NT 4.0. (You're unlikely to see Windows 3.*x* questions on the exam, so that section is very short.)

Windows 3.x

Windows 3.*x* (that is, Windows 3.0, Windows 3.1, Windows for Workgroups 3.1, and Windows for Workgroups 3.11) is still in use worldwide. So you may encounter Windows 3.*x* at some point — if only as a desktop client for which you must provide some level of network connectivity.

Microsoft describes all Windows 3.*x* products as operating *environments* rather than operating systems, because Windows doesn't entirely replace MS-DOS. Windows 3.*x* is 16-bit software, and application programs written for Windows 3.*x* are (with rare exceptions) also 16-bit software.

Windows 3.1 (early 1992) brought the PC user a graphical user interface, the ability for applications to use more memory than 640K, the ability to run multiple applications simultaneously and to rapidly switch between loaded applications, an environment in which all programs use a single set of print and screen drivers, and a structure for exchanging data between programs.

Windows for Workgroups 3.1 (late 1992) introduced peer networking — a concept that LAN administrators were (and are still) somewhat leery of, and it didn't bring any compelling reasons to upgrade. Its successor, Version 3.11 (late 1993), was a much more stable and versatile network client than its predecessors. Windows for Workgroups added file and printer sharing, faster performance, dial-in access to NT Server machines, support for two concurrent networks, and better (although not airtight by any means) security.

Windows 9x

Windows 95 and its successors, Windows 98 and Windows ME, bring 32-bit capabilities to the Intel-and-compatible PC, along with a heavily revised user interface. Windows 9*x* (as the exam may refer to Versions 98 and 95 collectively) focuses on compatibility, whereas Windows NT and Windows 2000 Professional focus on security and reliability.

Design goals

The nine key goals of the Windows 9*x* design team tell you nearly all you need to know about where Windows 9*x* fits in regard to Windows 3.*x,* NT, and 2000. The goals are

- ✔ **Compatibility:** If you have an old DOS device driver that loads in CONFIG.SYS or AUTOEXEC.BAT, chances are excellent that you can use that device with Windows 9*x*. Need to run an old 16-bit Windows 3.1 application? It probably runs fine under Windows 9*x*, too.

- ✔ **Performance:** Windows 9*x* was designed to perform well under low memory conditions, so its designers had to forego the extra layers of memory protection that make NT and 2000 more reliable.

- ✔ **Robustness:** Windows 9*x* is more reliable than Windows 3.*x,* and less reliable than NT or 2000.

- ✔ **Better setup and configuration:** Windows 9*x* autodetects a wide variety of hardware during setup, in large part thanks to the Plug and Play standard. You can install Windows 9*x* from a network server as well as aCD-ROM, and the Batch Setup tool helps you script LAN-based installations. Windows 9*x* control panels use the Registry database for most system settings, centralizing such settings but adding to system complexity.

- ✔ **Better user interface:** The Start button, taskbar, and property sheet made their debut in Windows 95, along with dozens of other user interface (UI) changes and a new emphasis on the right mouse button. Windows 98 makes few changes to the core UI of Windows 95, although the Web View of folders and the Active Desktop add a new Internet look.

- ✔ **Protected mode design:** Nearly everything in Windows 9*x* runs in the Intel processor's protected mode, which affords better reliability, as opposed to the real mode that DOS software uses.

- ✔ **Support for 32-bit applications:** Windows 9*x* can run 32-bit applications, conferring upon them goodies such as a private memory space, preemptive multitasking, and multithreaded execution. However, Windows 9*x* does not use 32-bit software through and through.

- ✔ **Better client and workgroup functionality:** Windows 9*x* contains the peer-to-peer networking capabilities introduced by Windows for Workgroups, adding peer services for Novell networks, too. Windows 9*x* also provides better support for multiple concurrent networks, 32-bit network components, a more modular design, and better speed.

- ✔ **Better mobile computing support:** From Dial-Up Networking to the Direct Cable Connection and Briefcase, Windows 9*x* makes life easier on road warriors who need to connect to office and public networks.

Versions

The important distinctions that you should know for the exam, and for real life, are between the original Windows 95, Windows 95 OSR2, Windows 98, and Windows 98 Second Edition. (You can check the version number for all Windows 9*x* products by right-clicking the My Computer icon, choosing Properties, and looking at the version on the General tab.)

- The original Windows 95 product has the version number 4.00.950 or, if patched by Service Pack 1 (which corrected mostly minor bugs), 4.00.950a. This version only supports the FAT file system.

- OSR2, or OEM Service Release 2, has the version number 4.00.950B or 4.00.950C. This variant started shipping in late 1996 and added the FAT32 file system, most of the Plus! enhancements, and various device support improvements.

- Windows 98 (original version) has the version number 4.10.1998. It supports both FAT and FAT32.

- Windows 98 Second Edition has the version number 4.10.2222A. It, too, supports both FAT and FAT32.

Windows NT/2000

Windows NT and Windows 2000 can both function as workstation operating systems or as server operating systems. In either case, Microsoft recommends these products for situations in which reliability and security take precedence over maximum hardware and software compatibility.

Reliability and security

Reliability in the NT platform is achieved through various architectural characteristics, including the following:

- No support for 16-bit device drivers or Windows 9*x*-style VxDs (virtual device drivers), only 32-bit device drivers. (Older, 16-bit drivers are a major source of Windows 9*x* and 3.*x* crashes.)

- Total hardware protection via a Hardware Abstraction Layer, or HAL. (Software is never allowed to communicate directly with a device.)

- Restricted list of approved hardware devices compared to Windows 9*x*. (See HCL.TXT in the SUPPORT directory of the Windows 2000 CD-ROM for the Hardware Compatibility List.)

Windows 2000 and NT have their own self-contained security system (users, passwords, permissions, rights, and so on). This is in sharp contrast to Windows 9*x*, which offers only relatively weak share-level security or which can leverage the security capabilities of NT or NetWare.

The price of progress

Windows NT and its successor, Windows 2000 (formerly Windows NT 5.0!), have not made Windows 9*x* obsolete on the desktop, nor are they likely to do so anytime soon. The main reason, aside from a significant cost disparity, is that for some customers, a move to Windows 2000 means abandoning some older software and hardware. In order to provide enhanced reliability and security, the NT/2000 product line sacrifices compatibility with some legacy devices and programs. These flagship operating systems don't support DOS-style device drivers, and they don't support all 16-bit Windows programs.

What NT4 and 2000 have in common

You should understand the basic differences between the NT/2000 products and the Windows 9*x* products. To that end, here are some of the key features of NT/2000:

- ✔ Full 32-bit operating system

- ✔ High reliability, largely because all applications and the operating system itself run in protected memory areas

- ✔ Preemptive multitasking for all applications, providing generally better performance running 32-bit software (Windows 9*x* uses the less sophisticated *cooperative* multitasking for 16-bit applications)

- ✔ Support for *symmetrical multiprocessing* — that is, multiple CPUs in the same box (the number of processors allowed varies with the version; Server supports up to 4, Advanced Server up to 8, Datacenter Server up to 32)

- ✔ High-performance file system (NTFS) with transaction logging and file-level security (Windows 9*x* offers only folder-level security)

- ✔ Incompatibility with real-mode device drivers and with software that tries to "speak" directly to hardware devices

The ways in which Windows 2000 improves on the Windows NT 4.0 platform are important enough to warrant their own big section (coming up next).

What's New about Windows 2000?

What's new with Windows 2000? That's a hugely important question, because the MCSE exams tend to focus on these new features.

First, the family tree has some new (and renamed) leaves. Windows 2000 isn't really one product, it's two: Windows 2000 Professional (what we used to call "Windows NT Workstation"), and Windows 2000 Server. The Server product is available in three flavors: regular *Windows 2000 Server, Windows 2000 Advanced Server* (formerly "Windows NT Server, Enterprise Edition"), and *Windows 2000 Datacenter Server* (a product with no immediate ancestor).

Here are the key distinguishing characteristics of the different server products:

- **Windows 2000 Server** supports up to four processors and up to 4GB of RAM. It's a general-purpose business operating system that can function as a file, print, Web, or application server.

- **Windows 2000 Advanced Server** supports up to eight processors and up to 8GB of RAM and provides network load balancing and two-way clustering. It's for applications that require more horsepower and higher availability than Windows 2000 Server, such as e-commerce.

- **Windows 2000 Datacenter Server** supports up to 32 processors and up to 64GB of RAM on Intel machines (32GB on Alpha machines). It also does four-way server clustering. This operating system is for data warehousing, online transaction processing (OLTP), and intensive Web server duties.

Windows 2000 has been described as Windows NT 4.0 plus Plug and Play, power management, and directory services (Active Directory). That's reasonably accurate for a one-sentence description, but Windows 2000 offers a lot more than that. (Weighing in at over 600MB of disk space, it had better!)

Windows 2000 represents a combination of the Windows 9*x* and NT product lines in the following ways:

- Tight security is available but you don't have to use all the security features.

- Reliability is very good but ease of use approaches that of Windows 9*x*.

- Workgroup networking and client/server networking are both supported.

- Windows 2000 works on more hardware than NT4 but less than Windows 9*x*.

Without question, Windows 2000 is more nearly Windows NT 5.0 than it is Windows 99, but the new operating system borrows much of the user interface and hardware support technology from Windows 98.

The remainder of this section compares Windows 2000 Server to its nearest cousin, Windows NT 4.0 Server. The new goodies break out into the following categories:

- Active Directory
- IntelliMirror
- Active Desktop and Internet software

- TCP/IP protocol enhancements

- TCP/IP service enhancements (DNS, DHCP, WINS, RRAS)

- Security

- Usability

- Hardware

- Deployment

- Management

Take a look at each area in the following sections. And don't forget that whereas the network infrastructure exam tends to focus on new features, it doesn't omit features that migrate to Windows 2000 essentially unchanged, such as the Gateway Service for NetWare (GSNW). (That service, by the way, lets workstations on a Windows 2000 network access NetWare servers without having the NetWare client installed on each workstation.)

Active Directory

One of the more important new features of Windows 2000, at least for network users, is Active Directory (AD). AD is supposed to act like a master phone book for your whole network: It contains details on all network resources, from users and groups to printers and programs. Actually, AD is a bit more like a security guard holding a master phone book, because AD also handles access control. AD uses constructs such as *forests, trees, domains, organizational units,* and *groups* to organize the network. Organizational units are especially valuable because they enable domain administrators to delegate network management tasks to physical or logical subsets of the domain.

The Active Directory model simplifies the earlier Windows NT 4.0 networking model in some ways:

- The concept of primary and backup domain controllers is gone; all domain controllers are peers.

- Trust relationships are now *transitive* (that is, if domain A trusts domain B, and domain B trusts domain C, then A trusts C), simplifying network design and administration.

- A single database contains the entire network directory, instead of a collection of databases.

- The network naming system is DNS, which Active Directory requires, enabling (forcing?) organizations to unify their public and private network namespaces.

- The network directory data itself moves out of the Registry and into a more extensible, scalable, and speedy structure.

Many of the benefits of Windows 2000 only become possible when a combination of Windows 2000 Servers and Windows 2000 Professional clients interact in the context of Active Directory (a "native mode" network). Also, many of the topics in exam 70-216 center on network services that integrate with Active Directory, such as DNS and remote access.

IntelliMirror

"IntelliMirror" is a marketing term for a collection of technologies designed to let users move more freely around the network and on the road while maintaining their own settings, preferences, applications, and documents. This includes the inclusion of My Documents in user profiles and the ability for users to designate folders as available offline.

Offline folders and frequent synchronization can have a significant impact on a network, so the various performance enhancements in TCP/IP and TCP/IP services become important — as does the need to design a network infrastructure that wastes as little network bandwidth as possible.

Active Desktop and Internet software

Windows 2000 includes the Internet Explorer 5 Web browser with the operating system and also provides a Web view option for folders and for the desktop itself. The Web view feature lets you specify an HTML file, with whatever objects you want to include (ActiveX, Java, and so on), to appear as the desktop or folder background. The Web objects occupy a layer underneath the typical desktop and folder icons.

Web view also enables you to specify that

- ✔ Selectable objects should appear underlined, as they would on a Web page.
- ✔ Moving a cursor over an object highlights it.
- ✔ Single-clicking a highlighted object activates it, instead of double-clicking.

Web view folders can also show thumbnails of selected data files in a separate windowpane. Active Desktop lets you plop an entire Web page onto the desktop as well, in which case you can tell Windows 2000 how often you want it updated. Finally, Active Desktop includes numerous enhancements not related in any functional way to Internet technologies, such as new support for drag-and-drop operations on the taskbar.

The "single Explorer" aspect of Windows 2000 means that you can invoke a Web browsing window from a Windows Explorer screen by typing the URL (Uniform Resource Locator) into the address bar. You can also move back and forth between the local view and the browser view using the Back and Forward buttons, although most of the menu bar buttons change between the two environments (which is why I put "single Explorer" in quotes at the start of this paragraph).

Microsoft has brought Internet technology into the help system, too, by making HTML documents the starting point instead of RTF (Rich Text Format) documents. *HTML Help* functions similarly to the Windows 98 help engine, and it lets application vendors add graphics to their help files somewhat more easily and flexibly than before.

Windows 2000 Server comes with a variety of other Internet-related software: Outlook Express, NetMeeting, Internet Information Server (IIS) Version 5.0, Indexing service, and so on. IIS figures into exam 70-216 in that it must be present to allow users to request digital certificates via Internet Explorer.

TCP/IP protocol enhancements

Although Windows 2000 also supports NWLink, NetBEUI, and AppleTalk, TCP/IP is now clearly the network language of choice for Windows 2000 networking. Flexible, routable, fault tolerant, and compatible with the Internet, TCP/IP is a prerequisite for Active Directory, which in turn is a prerequisite for lots of other Windows 2000 features (such as group policies).

Microsoft has made a number of enhancements to the TCP/IP protocol stack since the days of NT 4:

- **Better speed:** Support for dynamically recalculating the TCP/IP window size means fewer acknowledgments and more throughput. Better round-trip time estimation means less time wasted when a receiving computer requests a retransmission of a packet that just hasn't arrived yet from a sending computer. And selective acknowledgment means that a receiving computer can request retransmission of selected packets only, instead of all packets that came after a corrupted one.

- **New capabilities:** For example, Quality of Service (QoS) features mean that network managers can reserve connection bandwidth for applications that need it, such as streaming multimedia.

- **Better security:** For example, IPsec provides for secure encryption of data transmitted between computers. The Windows 2000 *group policy system* lets administrators govern how IPsec is implemented in a given network; administrators can also set IPsec options on individual PCs.

TCP/IP service enhancements

TCP/IP is famous for the "acronymania" it has spawned — a whole bowl full of alphabet soup. Most of these acronyms refer to TCP/IP *services* — that is, operating system programs that perform useful functions on a TCP/IP network. Much of the time you will spend studying for exam 70-216 will be spent on these services. Here are a few quick introductory notes on each:

- ✓ **DNS:** Domain Name System (or, as you sometimes see it, Domain Name Service) lets network users specify computers using friendly host names (www.microsoft.com) instead of unfriendly, numeric IP addresses. DNS is the naming system for Microsoft's enterprise-wide directory service, Active Directory. The big news here is that DNS has become *dynamic* — that is, Windows can automatically update client configuration changes into the DNS database. You can also integrate the DNS database with the Active Directory database for easier administration.

- ✓ **DHCP:** Dynamic Host Configuration Protocol is a service that automatically assigns IP addresses (and other TCP/IP configuration details) to users as they log on to the network. In Windows 2000, DHCP integrates with DNS and Active Directory.

- ✓ **WINS:** Windows Internet Naming Service lets network users specify computers using *computer names* (also called *NetBIOS names*), the common naming system for computers running previous Microsoft operating systems. You need WINS on a Windows 2000 network if you have any machines running versions of Windows prior to Windows 2000 and you have more than one physical subnet. Windows 2000 DNS servers can use WINS lookups as a last resort for name resolution.

- ✓ **NAT:** Network Address Translation lets you connect your LAN users to the public Internet with greater security and lower costs. It translates hidden, private IP addresses within the LAN to a smaller number of public IP addresses that communicate with the outside world. A variant of NAT, Internet Connection Sharing (ICS), is less flexible but easier to set up.

- ✓ **RRAS:** Routing and Remote Access Service lets remote users connect to a specific machine or to the network itself, using either a "regular" dial-up link or a virtual private network (VPN) link that tunnels through the public Internet. Microsoft has combined the routing and remote access functions into a single management console, largely because both remote access and demand-dial routing depend on the Point-to-Point Protocol (PPP). Active Directory figures into the remote access game by enabling you to allow or deny remote access to users on an account-by-account basis.

Security

The big news in security is Windows 2000's support of the MIT-developed Kerberos security protocol instead of the older, slower NTLM mechanism for LAN communications. However, that's not the only important addition to your security arsenal:

- ✔ **Encryption** makes its way into the NTFS file system, enabling a user to encrypt data files so that only he or she can view, open, and modify those files.

- ✔ Windows 2000 makes some improvements to the TCP/IP protocol that underlies Internet applications. New support for **IPSec** (Internet Protocol Security) and **L2TP** (Layer 2 Tunneling Protocol) make communications more secure, even when they cross public networks.

- ✔ The default **access control** restrictions for the file system and the Registry are stricter for Windows 2000 than they are for Windows NT Server 4.0.

- ✔ Windows 2000 supports **authentication devices,** such as smart cards, which have been around for awhile in the military and are now becoming popular in the corporate world.

- ✔ New and improved **authentication protocols**, such as MS-CHAP (Microsoft Challenge/Handshake Authentication Protocol) Version 2, increase the security of dial-up and VPN links. The Extensible Authentication Protocol (EAP) supports the smart cards mentioned in the previous item.

- ✔ **Certificate Services** let you set up and manage Certificate Authorities (CAs) which, in turn, issue digital certificates that (like birth certificates or passports) guarantee the identity of users, computers, and organizations.

Usability

Windows 2000 makes a number of strides forward (and one or two in the opposite direction) compared to the NT 4.0 platform when it comes to usability, but the user interface isn't much different from that of Windows 98 — just a few evolutionary improvements.

Dialog boxes

Various dialog boxes have been refined in Windows 2000, such as the Open, Save As, Logon, and Shut Down dialog boxes. These improvements are generally of the incremental, evolutionary nature.

New wizards

A *wizard* is a guided sequence of steps that helps the user accomplish a common task. Windows 2000 Server has lots and lots of new wizards, as you'll see when we examine the various network services.

AutoComplete and MRU (Most Recently Used) lists

Many Windows 2000 dialog boxes automatically complete fields as the user begins typing them, creating convenience for some and security holes for others. The list of Most Recently Used (MRU) lists has grown very long indeed, including even individual fields on Web site forms. Where the security and privacy of user computing are of low importance, AutoComplete and the proliferation of MRU lists can save users time going about daily tasks.

Personalized menus

Here is another feature that some users love and others hate: After a period of time, Windows 2000 begins hiding menu selections that users have not chosen. The Start menu and its cascading submenus only show recently used choices, hiding others beneath a chevron character which, if clicked, shows (after a delay) all the menu options.

Although reducing clutter is generally considered a plus for user interface design, making users take extra steps in order to activate programs (even seldom-used ones) is not. Organizations must weigh the potential convenience of disappearing menu options against the potential confusion and delays it can introduce. In any case, you can easily disable personalized menus via a dialog box, policy setting, or Registry setting.

Device Manager

One of the better additions to Windows 2000 since NT 4.0 is the user-friendly Device Manager utility from Windows 9*x*. Get to Device Manager via a button on the System control panel's Hardware tab. It's a great central point from which to examine and change hardware settings.

Hardware

The big news in Windows 2000 hardware support involves Plug and Play and power management — two longstanding bugbears with Windows NT 4.0. However, new device and bus support is significant also, and driver signing could go a long way toward improving hardware reliability.

Plug and Play

Windows 2000 builds on the Plug-and-Play support in Windows 98 and puts to shame the limited add-in Plug-and-Play support that you could retrofit to Windows NT 4.0. Windows 2000 does a pretty good job of detecting and configuring most Plug-and-Play hardware (modems and COM ports are an unhappy exception), and should make those Windows NT 4.0 resource assignment spreadsheets a thing of the past. Plug and Play also reduces the likelihood that the operating system won't be able to boot because of a hardware problem.

Note that PCs designed to the ACPI specification (see next section) work *much* better with Plug and Play.

Power management

Windows 2000 manages PC power much differently from Windows NT 4.0. In fact, power management is tied very closely to Plug and Play. Two abbreviations come into play here:

- ✔ **APM,** or Advanced Power Management, is an older standard that was less than rigorous and therefore inconsistently implemented. Most PCs built before 1999 use APM if they offer any power management features at all.

- ✔ **ACPI,** or Advanced Configuration and Power Interface, is a newer standard that is more completely defined. Windows 2000 much prefers ACPI to APM. ACPI is a better-defined standard which gives more control to the operating system and less to the BIOS.

Although you can run Windows 2000 Server on APM machines, the operating system doesn't support power management on those systems, and they will run in an "always on" state. Not to sound like a Microsoft technical document, but "this behavior is by design" because you sure don't want a server going down at the wrong time because of a bug or inconsistency in the power management BIOS.

New devices and buses

Windows 2000 supports a variety of new devices and buses, including the following:

- ✔ **Universal Serial Bus (USB)** uses a single daisy-chained cable to connect keyboards, speakers, scanners, mice, monitors, and other devices to a PC port. The port uses only one interrupt.

- ✔ **FireWire (IEEE 1394)** offers transfer rates high enough to handle consumer electronic devices such as camcorders and VCRs.

- ✔ **DVD (short for Digital VideoDisc or Digital Versatile Disc)** devices now receive Windows support, at least in the standardized read-only flavor. DVDs can hold video, audio, and computer data on the same disc.

- ✔ **Digital scanners and cameras** also receive Windows support, even to the extent of getting their own special Control Panel icon.

- ✔ **Multiple displays** running at the same time are a boon to network administrators, but the feature is limited to AGP and PCI adapters and even then, not all models work.

With respect to disk drive management, Windows 2000 brings three new items to the table:

- ✔ The space-saving **FAT32** file system from Windows 95 OSR2 comes with Windows 2000, along with a one-directional conversion utility. FAT32 also lets you create much larger disk partitions than FAT16 but remains less secure and reliable than NTFS and is not recommended for servers. (In fact, Active Directory *requires* NTFS for servers that are domain controllers.) Windows 2000 supports FAT32 on any partition, including the boot partition.

- ✔ Windows 2000 introduces **Version 5 of NTFS**, the NT File System. This is the recommended file system for Windows 2000 and it provides the following features: file-and-folder security, extensible volumes, support for multiple-disk stripe sets, encryption (but not simultaneously with compression), and compression (but not simultaneously with encryption).

- ✔ Windows 2000 now includes a basic **disk defragmenter.**

Driver signing

Windows 2000 provides a new level of authentication called *driver signing*. Microsoft brands a *digital signature* into the core operating system files and drivers that it ships with Windows 2000. That way, Windows 2000 can tell when a program installation tries to replace one of those core files with a version not "signed" by Microsoft. Administrators can control whether any given PC can accept unsigned drivers.

On a related note, a background program watches system files and replaces them if necessary with known-good versions from a special "hip pocket" folder named DLLCACHE. This feature goes by the name *Windows File Protection.*

Deployment

Windows 2000 makes several changes to installation and deployment.

Interactive installations

In some ways, the Windows 2000 installation process offers improvements over that for Windows NT 4.0 and Windows 9*x*, and in other ways, it regresses. Here are some positive aspects of the new installation procedure:

- ✔ Fewer reboots
- ✔ Better (although not perfect) "clumping" of question-and-answer screens
- ✔ Better overall hardware detection than Windows NT 4.0
- ✔ More wizards to ease setup chores (especially valuable in Server)

On the minus side, Windows 2000 Setup gives customers less choice than ever about which accessories, applets, and options should be installed. The familiar typical, custom, and minimal installation options are gone, and the only area in which a user can interactively choose components to install is in the networking area. The lack of flexibility afforded to customers in this area is one reason the hardware requirements are dramatically higher for Windows 2000 than for Windows 98 or even NT 4.

Automated installations

Microsoft has introduced two new options for automated deployment of the operating system: **Remote Installation Service,** or RIS, which lets a server install Windows 2000 onto a PC that doesn't even have to have an operating system on it already, and **SysPrep,** which you use in conjunction with disk cloning software such as Ghost or Drive Image. The usual scripted installation options using answer files are still available, too.

New migration paths

You can now upgrade a Windows 95 or 98 system to Windows 2000. A direct upgrade path from the 9x platform to Windows NT 4.0 never existed. Having said that, the upgrade path from Windows NT 4.0 to Windows 2000 is likely to be smoother, due to the greater similarities between the two operating systems.

Management

Microsoft says that it is focusing on TCO (Total Cost of Ownership) these days, and administrators may be able to reduce TCO with certain new Windows 2000 features.

Group Policy

Policies, which can be local or network-based (or both), are really more of a mechanism for implementing and controlling the various other types of Windows 2000 security than a new type of security themselves. You can think of policies as the "rules of the house" that set forth all the security restrictions you've chosen to implement from the areas discussed so far.

Policies work differently depending on whether you're running a standalone machine, a computer in a pure Windows 2000 network, or a computer in a mixed-mode network with Windows NT 4.0 clients. However, although the details vary, the concept is basically the same: After an administrator sets them, policies automatically modify the Registry (applying security, user interface consistency, or both) at boot time, logon time, and periodic refresh intervals.

Winning the award for most awkward name for a software utility, Microsoft calls the Windows 2000 implementation of policies "Group Policy." You use the Local Group Policy utility on a local workstation, and the Group Policy property sheets in the various Active Directory administrative tools on a server (or on a workstation on which you have installed the Server administrative tools).

Automatic Private IP Addressing

Automatic Private IP Addressing (APIPA) enables Windows 2000 PCs to assign themselves IP addresses from a special, private address range if no address server exists on the network. (Windows 98 also offers this capability.) That's handy for computers on purely private networks — that is, networks that don't need to connect to the public Internet. Note that the address range used for APIPA differs from the three "normal" private IP address ranges; Chapter 9 goes into the details.

Microsoft Management Console

Windows 2000 uses a new kind of control panel in addition to the older *.CPL files. This new variation is called *Microsoft Management Console,* or *MMC* for short. Microsoft used MMCs in a few products (such as its Internet server software) prior to Windows 2000, and it seems to be the way the company is moving. At a minimum, you need to become intimately familiar with the DNS, DHCP, WINS, Routing and Remote Access, and Certification Authority consoles in order to pass exam 70-216.

MMC is a little like a standard car chassis within which software developers can put whatever engine they want. That is, the framework has some consistent elements, but the contents of any given MMC window may vary greatly. One nice feature is the ability for administrators to build their own customized consoles with whatever snap-ins they find most useful. Custom-built consoles with access control enable administrators to delegate specific administrative tasks to others, without having to give those delegates access to *all* administrative capabilities.

Windows Update

Windows 98's Windows Update feature migrates intact to Windows 2000. This feature enables a user to connect to a Microsoft Web site that downloads ActiveX controls to the PC. Those programs then scan the software environment, consult a central Microsoft server, and present recommended downloads to the user, even organizing them by priority (critical, nice-to-have, and so on).

The problem that many organizations have found with this capability is its tendency to introduce fragmentation — that is, the opposite of standardization — into the network community. With users free to run Windows Update at random times and free to choose whichever updates they deem appropriate, administrators, technicians, and troubleshooters can't know in advance just what updates any given PC may contain. The more variables in a PC's setup, the harder administration and trouble-shooting become. You can disable Windows Update through the Group Policy tool.

Windows Installer

The new Windows Installer model attempts to bring some order to the chaos of application installation. Here are some key elements of Windows Installer technology:

- ✔ Organized "package" file format that lists application actions in a structured and organized manner
- ✔ One-click installation repair capability
- ✔ Full uninstall capability (including Registry entries)

Understanding the Windows 2000 Architecture

This section presents a very concise overview of the Windows 2000 architecture for those of you unfamiliar with Windows NT 4.0. (The underlying architecture is very similar between the two operating systems.)

The three multis: multitasking, multithreading, and multiprocessing

Multitasking is running multiple programs at the same time. Actually, the computer *seems* to be doing multiple things at once but is really slicing up CPU (Central Processing Unit) time into tiny amounts and distributing it to multiple activities.

Windows 3.*x* can multitask, but only in a fairly unsophisticated manner known as *cooperative* multitasking. In that model, programs are expected to be good citizens, periodically yielding control of the computer to other programs. Windows 3.*x* has no way of giving the hook to a program that's hogging the stage. Windows 9*x*, NT, and 2000, on the other hand, use a cleverer system called *preemptive* multitasking. The operating system can jump in and suspend a piggish application instead of waiting for it to yield control. Further, the operating system figures out in advance how much CPU time each program gets when its turn comes around (that job is handled by the scheduler).

Multithreading sounds similar, but it's not exactly the same as multitasking. Multithreading means that a single program can create (or *spawn*) several threads of execution that proceed simultaneously. For example, a word processor may spawn a spell-check task in a separate, independent thread, while another thread performs document repagination at the same time. Again, Windows 9*x*, NT, and 2000 all support multithreading.

Multiprocessing means that the operating system can use more than one CPU. Windows 2000 and NT support multiprocessing, but Windows 9*x* does not. Windows 2000 Professional supports up to two CPUs, while Windows 2000 Server supports up to four CPUs (more with vendor-specific support). Note that the type of multiprocessing supported by Windows 2000 is *symmetric* (SMP) — that is, each CPU is the same type and has access to the same memory. Note also that many operating system tasks still run only on the first CPU in a multi-CPU system.

User mode and kernel mode

Any given program or thread in Windows 2000 runs in either *user mode* or *kernel mode*. User mode is safer, slower, and further removed from the underlying hardware; applications run in user mode. Kernel mode is riskier, faster, and closer to the hardware; core operating system functions such as memory management, file system management, and device driver management run in kernel mode.

Virtual memory

Every loaded 32-bit program in a Windows 2000 environment thinks that it has access to a 4GB address space, half of which it can use for its own code, and half of which is reserved for operating system code (the API). However, Windows 2000 and all Windows applications can only use a maximum of 4GB physical memory on the entire PC. Windows lets multiple programs think that they can each see the entire 4GB through *memory mapping.*

At any given moment, Program X isn't using its entire 4GB memory space, so Windows can present to Program X only the memory that it's using at that moment. Think of an analogy: Most banks couldn't pay all depositors their entire balance at the same moment, but each depositor could withdraw a portion of his or her balance over the span of a typical day. So, in a sense, your bank accounts are virtual money. No wonder people still hide cash in coffee cans or under the mattress.

Even after parceling out physical memory on an as-needed basis in this elaborate shell game of memory mapping, sometimes physical memory (RAM) becomes exhausted. (That's likely to occur faster with Windows 2000 than with Windows NT 4.0, partly because Windows 2000 needs more RAM to hold all the extra Internet software that loads at startup.) When an application demands more memory than Windows can find in physical RAM, Windows 2000 grabs a chunk of disk space to use as *virtual memory,* also known as the *pagefile.* Disks are much slower than RAM, but a system that runs slowly is better than one that stops entirely. (The effect of using the pagefile can impair your ability to run the Network Monitor utility; see Chapter 3 for details. Also, many of the network services that exam 70-216 covers require much more memory than a simple file-and-print server requires.)

Windows 2000 manages the swapfile size automatically, shrinking and expanding it as needed, in the default configuration. However, you can specify a minimum pagefile size yourself in order to reduce Windows 2000 overhead. You can also place the pagefile on an alternate local hard drive for better speed — for example, if your D: drive is faster than your C: drive.

Dynamic link libraries

Dynamic link libraries, or *DLLs,* are files that (typically) contain program code. A program or the Windows 2000 operating system itself can load a DLL into memory on an as-needed basis. The DLL concept lets you run programs with less RAM than would be required if all programs loaded every bit of code they needed, every time they started.

Much of Windows 2000 itself is in the form of DLLs, and most Windows applications use DLLs, too. Many Windows programs call upon DLLs in Windows to accomplish certain tasks; such DLLs go by the name of *system DLLs.*

The DLL model has presented some problems in the past. Microsoft often updates and modifies system DLL files between version releases of Windows. Application software developers sometimes "redistribute" specific versions of system DLLs, under license from Microsoft, so that the application knows that the PC is using a recent-enough version of the system DLLs for the application to work correctly. However, application installation routines sometimes overwrite newer DLLs with older ones, which can cause other applications to break. Other times, a newer DLL may not work with an older program.

The new System File Checker utility, Windows File Protection, and the Windows Installer model have features designed to reduce DLL problems. Make sure you understand their respective purposes!

Hardware abstraction

The layer of Windows 2000 that communicates directly with the PC's hardware is called the *HAL,* or *Hardware Abstraction Layer.* Windows 2000 chooses an appropriate HAL for a given PC during the early stages of the installation program, based on factors such as CPU type, number of CPUs, and power management support in the BIOS.

The HAL design, which "abstracts" the underlying hardware from the rest of the Windows 2000 operating system, enables Windows 2000 to run on non-Intel processors. Windows 9*x* never had that capability. However, the economics of the market (and perhaps some strained relations between Microsoft and Compaq) have led Microsoft to all but drop support for the Alpha processor. Microsoft dropped NT 4.0 support for the Mips processors some time ago. So, Windows 2000's ability to run on non-Intel processors has become much less of a factor than it might have been. Therefore:

You probably won't see any exam questions having to do with Windows 2000 Server running on non-Intel processors.

You can't change the HAL without reinstalling Windows 2000.

If you're comfortable with the basics that this chapter presents, it's time to introduce the major topics that will get you through the Windows 2000 network infrastructure exam with flying colors. If not, then before continuing, you may want to spend a little time with the Windows 2000 help system or Microsoft Technet (www.microsoft.com/technet), targeting the areas that seem a little fuzzy, and perhaps re-read some sections of this chapter as necessary.

Part II
Protocols and Services: Alphabet Soup

The 5th Wave   By Rich Tennant

"I DON'T KNOW – SOME PARTS OF THE NETWORK SEEM JUST FINE, AND OTHER PARTS SEEM TO BE COMPLETELY OUT OF CONTROL."

In this part . . .

*B*ecause I secretly wish I were Dave Barry, I tell lots of jokes in my seminars for computer support technicians. One area that's fun to play around with is industry acronyms. PCMCIA doesn't really stand for Personal Computer Memory Card Industry Association; it stands for People Can't Memorize Computer Industry Acronyms. TWAIN (the scanner interface standard) stands for Toolkit Without An Interesting Name (that one's true). APL, a programming language, stands for — well, you figure it out! (That one's true, too.)

All the material in Part II has two unifying characteristics: It deals with plumbing issues that matter whether your network has a single location or a hundred, and it's chock-full of acronyms: TCP/IP, DNS, DHCP, WINS, and so on.

It's a shame that our industry can't come up with better acronyms than these. *Other* industries get to use cool acronyms, like the travel industry's SABRE and APOLLO. Computer acronyms are not only uncool, they're counter-productive, too. Think of how much time is wasted by computer geniuses having to slow their thought processes and say "Tee See Pee Eye Pee" a hundred times a day. Or "doubleyou doubleyou doubleyou."

Anyway, on with the show. Here I am editorializing, when you need to get your W2K MCSE ASAP.

Chapter 3

Installing and Configuring TCP/IP and NWLink

· ·

Exam Objectives

▶ Install and configure TCP/IP

▶ Install the NWLink protocol

▶ Configure network bindings

▶ Manage and monitor network traffic

· ·

*J*ust about everything in this book (and on the exam) depends on the TCP/IP network protocol. Microsoft has anointed TCP/IP as its networking language of choice — after many millions of Internet users had made *that* decision a no-brainer. NetBEUI, which was Microsoft's networking language of choice a few years ago, may merit only a single question on exam 70-216.

This chapter goes through a brief discussion of what TCP/IP is, how it fits into the Department of Defense network architecture model, how to install it, and how you should configure its basic settings on both Windows 2000 Server and Windows 2000 Professional. And, because Microsoft gives lip service to NWLink, the protocol that lets Windows boxes communicate with NetWare boxes, this chapter takes a look at that protocol as well (although not in as much detail). NetBEUI and other secondary network protocols receive brief mention here, and the chapter wraps up with a look at Network Monitor, an old friend from the NT 4.0 world.

Quick Assessment

Install and configure TCP/IP

1 The Department of Defense network architecture model has a layer called Transport, which corresponds to the _____ layer in the OSI network architecture model.

2 The subnet mask divides out the _____ ID part of the IP address from the _____ ID part.

3 The IP address 10.0.0.3 is a Class _____ address.

4 To configure a Windows 2000 TCP/IP client to use DHCP, you must click the radio button labeled _____.

5 The network feature that automatically assigns Windows 2000 IP addresses without a DHCP server present is called _____.

6 The network ID used for local system diagnostics is _____.

Install the NWLink protocol

7 NWLink is required for the following NetWare connectivity utilities: _____ and _____.

8 If you use GSNW, you must set up a group named _____ on the NetWare server.

Configure network bindings

9 Network adapters bind to _____.

Manage and monitor network traffic

10 You can view a subset of captured IP traffic in Network Monitor with a(n) _____.

Answers

1   *Transport.* They won't all be this easy to guess. See the section titled "The Department of Defense model" for more.

2   *Network; host.* See "The IP address and subnet mask" if this is news to you.

3   *A.* See "IP address classes" for a lot of details which, cruelly, the exam expects you to memorize.

4   *Obtain an IP Address Automatically.* Yes, the test does expect you to know stuff like this. See the "DHCP" section.

5   *Automatic Private IP Addressing.* The "DHCP" section holds forth on this new-to-the-NT-platform feature.

6   *127.* See the "IP address classes" section for more.

7   *Client Service for NetWare; Gateway Service for NetWare.* See the section "NWLink and related components" for details on these services.

8   *NTGATEWAY.* The "Gateway Service for NetWare (GSNW)" section explains the why and wherefore.

9   *Protocols.* The "Legally Binding" section explains what *binding* means.

10 *Display filter.* See "Big Network Brother" for details.

Network Architecture

Years ago, when vendors other than IBM got into the computer networking act, the industry realized the importance of defining a standard interface between different layers of the network *stack* (the software levels through which data travels, on both sending and receiving machines). Thus was born the famous seven-layer OSI (Open Systems Interconnect) model.

The OSI model

In case you see a question about the OSI model on the exam, the layers from top to bottom are

- ✔ Application
- ✔ Presentation
- ✔ Session
- ✔ Transport
- ✔ Network
- ✔ Datalink
- ✔ Physical

The interfaces between each layer are published and standardized, so that you can use, say, a transport protocol from one vendor with a network card driver from another vendor, as long as both vendors follow the model.

For the exam, you probably won't need to know exactly what each layer does, but you may need to remember the layer order. Use a memory aid. The phrases "**P**lease **D**o **N**ot **T**hrow **S**ausage **P**izza **A**way" (bottom to top) or "**A**ll **P**eople **S**eem **T**o **N**eed **D**ata **P**rocessing" (top to bottom) can jog your memory by providing the first letter of each layer.

The Department of Defense model

The OSI model isn't for everybody, and the USA Department of Defense decided it wanted its own network stack model, thank you very much. The good news is that the DoD model has only four layers; the bad news is, you should memorize it as well as the OSI model.

The following list concisely defines the DoD model and gives examples of how it applies to TCP/IP (Transmission Control Protocol/Internet Protocol), Windows 2000's network language of choice:

✔ **Application:** This layer is roughly equivalent to the top three layers of the OSI model. TCP/IP applications running on Windows 2000 may use either NetBIOS (older) or WinSock (newer) to communicate with lower layers. Programs that run at this layer include DNS, FTP, HTTP, SMTP, SNMP, and Telnet. (If you're not familiar with these abbreviations yet, don't worry; I describe them all in detail elsewhere in the book.)

✔ **Transport:** This layer is roughly equivalent to the Transport layer in the OSI model, and is where Windows establishes computer-to-computer communication sessions. In the TCP/IP world, the transport layer is either TCP or UDP (User Datagram Protocol). TCP guarantees data delivery (it's *connection-oriented*) and is suited for large data transfers; UDP doesn't guarantee delivery (it's *connectionless*) and is suited for small data transfers.

✔ **Internet:** The Internet layer is roughly equivalent to the OSI model's Network layer, and is where Windows 2000 assembles, addresses, and routes network packets. The main resident of this layer is IP, but ARP (Address Resolution Protocol), ICMP (Internet Control Message Protocol), and IGMP (Internet Group Management Protocol) also live here.

✔ **Network Interface:** Corresponding to the lower two layers of the OSI model, here's where computers send and receive frames over links such as Ethernet, Token Ring, FDDI (Fiber Distributed Data Interface), dial-up, ATM (Asynchronous Transfer Mode), frame relay, and so on.

A mnemonic device for the DoD model is ATIN, or **A**ll **T**hat **I**nternet **N**onsense.

Microsoft modules

Microsoft designed Windows 2000 in a modular fashion, including the networking bits, which correlate fairly closely to the OSI and DoD models. Some of the OSI layers are fixed in Windows 2000, such as the Win32 network API (application programming interface) that programmers use when writing applications. Some other OSI layers combine to form a single software component that you can add, replace, or delete in Windows 2000. The end result is that in Windows 2000, user-installable networking modules fall into the following four categories:

✔ **Adapter:** The network interface card (NIC) adapter requires a software device driver so that the upper layers of network software can communicate across the physical medium (copper cable, fiber-optic cable, and so on). You must have at least one adapter to participate in a network.

✓ **Protocol:** The "network language," or transport protocol, defines how Windows 2000 packages information. Two computers must speak the same protocol in order to communicate across a network. You must have at least one protocol to participate in a network. In the Microsoft scheme of things, the protocol layer spans several layers of the OSI or DoD models.

✓ **Client:** The network client enables Windows 2000 to communicate with specific network operating systems, such as Windows 2000 Server and Novell NetWare. You must have at least one client to participate in a network.

✓ **Service:** Network services provide specialized capabilities, such as resource sharing (File and Printer Sharing for Microsoft Networks). You don't necessarily have to have any services loaded to participate in a network, but services are necessary to perform certain network functions.

You can see evidence of this four-level structure when you right-click a local area connection in the Network and Dial-Up Connections folder and choose Properties, displaying a dialog box such as Figure 3-1. The adapter for the specific LAN connection appears at the top in its own little area, whereas clients, protocols, and services are in the main components list. (This layout differs from that in Windows 9*x*, where all adapter drivers appear in the same list with all the other components, in the Network control panel.)

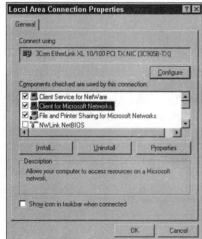

Figure 3-1:
The LAN
link's
property
sheet.

The fact that these four modular pieces are separately installable means that you can mix and match pieces to some extent. For example, a single adapter can support two protocols; you can run two or more clients over a single protocol; you can run a specific client over one protocol, or over a different one; and so on. You can also get modules from manufacturers other than Microsoft. The freedom to mix and match components provides flexibility, but it also begets a certain amount of complexity for the system designer.

Focus on network protocols

The *protocol,* or, more properly, *transport protocol,* describes how network clients and servers package information for delivery and unpackage it upon receipt. The protocol communicates downward with the adapter driver, and upward with both client and service software. Protocol setup ranges from pleasingly simple (NetBEUI) to pretty darned complicated (TCP/IP).

Two computers must "speak" the same protocol in order to communicate across a network.

Windows 2000 supports three main protocols: NetBEUI, IPX/SPX, and TCP/IP. The operating system also supports several secondary protocols, namely, DLC, AppleTalk, and a pseudo-protocol called Network Monitor Driver. You can install all of them via the local area network connection's Properties dialog box by clicking the Install button and then selecting Protocol, as shown in Figure 3-2. Note that when you install a protocol for one network adapter, that protocol becomes available for all other network adapters, too.

Figure 3-2:
Installing a
network
protocol.

Old Windows hands should note that in Windows 2000, you activate network protocols on a *per-connection basis,* by opening the Network and Dial-Up Connections folder, right-clicking the connection of interest, and choosing Properties. For example, if you have two network cards in one PC, you can run TCP/IP on one card and NetBEUI on the other. In previous versions of Windows, you configured all connections in one big catch-all control panel window that could get pretty confusing.

NetBEUI

NetBIOS Extended User Interface, or NetBEUI for short (pronounced Net-BOOie), is a great network protocol for a small local area network (Microsoft says 20 to 200 computers) that doesn't need to connect to the Internet and isn't likely to grow beyond a single physical location.

Remember the following points about NetBEUI:

✔ NetBEUI works with a wide variety of operating systems, including Windows 9*x*, NT, Windows for Workgroups, and (now we're *really* going back in time) LAN Manager and MS-DOS.

✔ The NetBEUI addressing scheme is very simple: NetBEUI uses the computer name on the property sheet that you access via the System control panel's Network Identification tab. Figure 3-3 shows this property sheet.

✔ Managing a NetBEUI network is a piece of cake. All you have to do is make sure all computer names are unique. This protocol may be the only object in the entire Windows 2000 operating system without a property sheet.

Figure 3-3:
Viewing the old-style NetBIOS computer name.

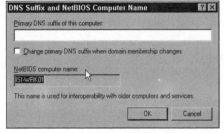

The main reason more large networks don't use this protocol is that, unlike IPX/SPX and TCP/IP, NetBEUI is not *routable.* That is, it can't communicate across routers, the traffic management devices that link subnetworks together. A secondary reason is that NetBEUI puts more broadcast traffic onto the network than other protocols.

Use NetBEUI for troubleshooting network connections. This simple, bullet-proof protocol is a great tool for verifying that you have a continuous physical connection between two PCs. Just add the protocol to the two PCs that you're troubleshooting, and see if the machines can see each other in My Network Places.

NWLink

Novell developed the IPX/SPX protocol (Internet packet exchange/sequenced packet exchange) for use in its popular NetWare network. You can use this network protocol so that Microsoft servers and workstations can communicate with NetWare servers, or you can use it in a Microsoft-only environment (although by doing so, you give up the benefits of Active Directory, which requires TCP/IP).

NWLink basics

Microsoft's version of IPX/SPX now goes by the name IPX/SPX/NetBIOS-compatible protocol or *NWLink* for short. NWLink, which comes with all flavors of Windows 2000, is a workalike for Novell's network protocol in all key respects:

- NWLink is routable, so you can use it in large networks.
- NWLink runs programs that use Winsock or NetBIOS-over-IPX to communicate with the network.
- For computer addressing purposes, this protocol uses a unique identifier (the MAC address, where *MAC* stands for Media Access Control) that is burned into a chip on the network interface card.
- This protocol is relatively easy to manage, because NIC manufacturers worry about ensuring unique MAC addresses on every adapter.
- IPX/SPX grew out of the PC DOS environment, which means support for other platforms (notably, UNIX) is not strong.

NWLink and related components

If you use NWLink, you probably also use at least one related networking component from the following list:

- Client Service for NetWare (CSNW)
- Gateway Service for NetWare (GSNW)
- File and Print Services for NetWare (FPSN)

Remember, though, that you don't have to use any NetWare connectivity products. You can use NWLink as the sole transport protocol in an all-Microsoft network. You just can't set up that network for Active Directory. Normally, you'd only use NWLink if you need NetWare connectivity.

Client Service for NetWare (CSNW)

The *Client Service for NetWare* lets a Windows 2000 Professional client access NetWare 2.*x*, 3.*x*, or 4.*x* servers. If you install the Client Service for NetWare, Windows 2000 installs NWLink automatically, because CSNW requires it.

Client Service for NetWare doesn't support NetWare 5.*x* servers running IP. If you want to use CSNW, you must install IPX/SPX on the NetWare server or servers.

The Client Service for NetWare supports NDS (NetWare Directory Services) without additional components. NDS is software for NetWare Versions 4.*x* and later that organizes network resources into a single, hierarchical structure. This method is an advance over the bindery method in NetWare 3.*x*, because the bindery is a server-centric database of users and groups. In other words, if you want to use a resource on a bindery-based server other than the bindery-based server you're logged onto already, you must log on to the other server. When a user logs on to an NDS "tree," however, all the network resources that the user has rights to access become available, regardless of where those resources live. Microsoft's Active Directory is a direct response to the success of NDS in large organizations.

When you configure Client Service for NetWare (and, oddly, you must do this via the CSNW control panel because the client's Properties button in the Network and Dial-Up Connections folder doesn't work), you can either set a *preferred server* (for bindery-based networks) or a *preferred tree and context* (for NDS-based networks), but you shouldn't set both. The "context" is the tree location of the user's NetWare user object. You shouldn't have to know any details about the NDS structure or about Novell's NDS object naming conventions for the Windows 2000 Network Infrastructure exam.

If you only need to connect to client/server applications (such as SQL Server) running on a NetWare server, NWLink is all you need. You don't have to have the Client Service for NetWare, unless you also need connectivity to NetWare file and print services.

Gateway Service for NetWare (GSNW)

Gateway Service for NetWare (GSNW) comes with all flavors of Windows 2000 Server. This product's most common use is to permit network clients running some version of Windows to access shared files and printers on a NetWare server, without having NetWare client software installed locally on each client PC. That is, GSNW translates requests from Microsoft network clients into requests that a Novell NetWare server can understand. GSNW is therefore a classic "gateway" product, acting like an interpreter between two different networking worlds.

GSNW requires NWLink, and installs NWLink if it's not already there. GSNW also automatically installs the Client Service for NetWare.

You wouldn't use GSNW for heavy duty NetWare access, because of the performance penalty the gateway imposes. For clients who need to access NetWare servers frequently, you're better off installing Client Service for NetWare (CSNW) on the clients.

Installing GSNW is a piece of cake:

1. **Log on as an administrator and open the Network and Dial-Up Connections folder.**

2. **Right-click the icon for your local area connection, choose Properties, and click the Install button.**

3. **Choose Client as the network component type and click the Add button; Gateway (And Client) Service For NetWare appears in the list.**

As is the case with CSNW, you configure GSNW to use either a preferred server or default tree-and-context, but not both. Set the preferred server in a Novell bindery environment, or the default tree and context in an NDS environment. Windows 2000 Server asks you to make this choice the first time you log on after installing GSNW; you can change the setting later via the GSNW control panel.

You have to set up a NetWare group named NTGATEWAY, and a NetWare user account that belongs to that group, in order to actually use GSNW. Give the user account privileges to whatever resources you want your Windows clients to be able to use. What happens is that Windows 2000 Server "logs on" to the NetWare server with the user account that you define under NetWare. GSNW then uses that connection to the NetWare server as the pipeline for serving up shared NetWare resources to Windows clients on the Windows 2000 Server side.

In addition to providing gateway services, GSNW acts like CSNW for interactive users of a Windows 2000 Server machine. That is, such users can log on to NetWare servers via GSNW.

File and Print Services for NetWare (FPSN)

File and Print Services for NetWare (FPSN) only works with Windows 2000 Server. It lets NetWare clients access file and print services on a Windows 2000 Server machine, and is sort of the flip side of GSNW. FPSN does not come with Windows 2000 Server and, as I write this, its details of operation are not a likely subject for exam 70-216.

Configuring NWLink

Configuring NWLink is pretty simple. This section covers the three variables you can set: frame type, network number, and internal network number. Set these via the NWLink property sheet (see Figure 3-4).

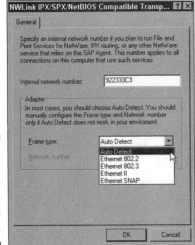

Figure 3-4:
NWLink
properties
for a spe-
cific LAN
connection.

Frame type

One of the more common reasons for a failure to connect in an NWLink network is a *frame type* mismatch.

Don't worry about the details of what a frame type is. Just know that it affects how Windows packages network data, and that the frame type must match the frame type that your server uses in order for you to connect to that server.

The default setting of Auto Detect means that Windows 2000 tries to sense the correct frame type at the time you install NWLink. However, if it can't, then on an Ethernet network, it defaults to 802.2, the frame type used by NetWare 3.12 and above. (The 802.3 frame type is an older version in less common use today, despite the newer number.) You can manually set the frame type and not worry about whether Windows 2000's autodetection will work properly or not.

For a client to access both 802.2 and 802.3 frames, fire up your favorite Registry editor and add both types to the multi-string value PktType in HKLM\SYSTEM\ CurrentControlSet\Services\NwlnkIPX\Parameters\Adapters\<ID>, where <ID> is the network adapter identifier. Yes, this capability should be in the user interface, but some settings still require brute force.

Network number

Computers on an NWLink network segment must all have the same network number in order to see each other. Usually, Windows 2000's autodetection capability works fine and you don't need to modify this value. (Good thing, because to change it, you must use a Registry editor.) In fact, if you enable autodetection for the frame type, you can't manually enter a network number — the field appears grayed out in the dialog box.

Internal network number

This eight-digit number is for internal routing and you normally don't need to use it unless you are running Windows 2000 Server and either File and Print Service for NetWare or IPX routing. The default value is 00000000.

TCP/IP Basics

Of the major network protocols, the exam hits TCP/IP the hardest, so this rather long section presents the details you should know. Please know that you are not expected to absorb this stuff in a single read; it may take two or three.

Why TCP/IP?

TCP/IP has become the protocol of choice in organizations large and small. Why, if it's so complicated? Part of the reason, certainly, is the popularity of the Internet. When you set up a network to use the TCP/IP protocol, you can connect PCs to the Internet without adding another protocol, because TCP/IP is the native protocol of the Net.

Another part of the reason is that TCP/IP is routable and works well over wide-area networks. Organizations that plan for growth, therefore, must consider TCP/IP favorably.

Third, TCP/IP runs on lots of operating systems: Mac, UNIX, and so on. That makes it convenient for big organizations with several different computer architectures.

Finally, TCP/IP isn't a proprietary, closed standard, but rather, a set of standards developed with public funds and not controlled by any single computer company. Consequently, any technology changes are likely to be more consensual, better documented, and more broadly compatible with a wide range of software and hardware.

How TCP/IP delivers data

One often refers to TCP/IP as a single software component, but in fact it is two. The "TCP" part runs at the Department of Defense model's Transport layer and is the part that guarantees delivery. The "IP" part runs at the DoD Internet layer and is the part that bundles and delivers data (the bundles are called *datagrams* at the IP layer). IP works with just about any kind of network nuts-and-bolts: Ethernet, Token Ring, frame relay, and so on.

An IP packet has a header containing the following information:

- Source address
- Destination address
- Checksum (for verifying that the datagram contents arrive okay)
- Protocol (should Windows use TCP or UDP for this datagram)
- Time to Live (TTL — how many seconds the datagram can spend en route before the network throws it away)

At the transport layer, the "TCP" part of this network protocol sends datagrams and requires acknowledgments from the receiving computer. TCP resends data if the receiving machine doesn't acknowledge receipt within a given window of time. TCP sends data to *port numbers* that identify the intended application; for example, port 80 corresponds to the World Wide Web application.

The IP address and subnet mask

TCP/IP uses a highly flexible addressing scheme for identifying and locating devices on a network. That scheme has two basic parts: the IP address and the subnet mask.

The IP address

In the TCP/IP scheme of things, computers find each other by means of *IP addresses:* unique 32-bit numbers having four numeric parts (called *octets*) separated by periods (like 199.174.225.101). Actually, it's more correct to say "*network cards* find each other," because two or more network cards in the same computer may have their own IP addresses (and subnet masks and default gateways, but I'll come to those later). Each Ethernet interface in a router has to have its own IP address, too, as does each TCP/IP printer.

An octet has eight bits (hence the name), although we commonly display octets in decimal form. That is, decimal 255 is the same as binary 11111111. In binary notation, instead of the ones, tens, hundreds, and thousands places, numbers have the places ones, twos, fours, eights, and so on. Decimal notation is base ten; binary notation is base two.

The good old Windows calculator is a handy tool for converting between binary and decimal. Choose View➪Scientific, and you can select radio buttons for changing the display of a number between these two formats. Microsoft lets you use the Windows calculator during the exam.

You can assign a specific, *static* IP address to a network card via the Internet Protocol (TCP/IP) Properties dialog box's Use The Following IP Address radio button and related fields, as shown in Figure 3-5. You might do that, for example, if other computers on the network need to know your computer's IP address ahead of time. Such might be the case when you're playing a multiuser Internet game, or when you're configuring a Windows 2000 Server machine that workstations must always be able to find — such as a DNS, DHCP, WINS, NAT, or Certificate Authority server.

Figure 3-5:
Windows 2000 can have a static IP address or a dynamic, automatic one.

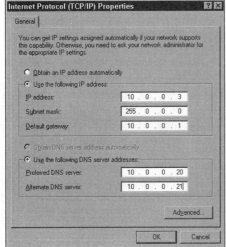

The default setup for Windows 2000 is to have Windows go fetch an IP address from another computer on the network whose job is to provide such dynamic addresses on demand. Such a computer is called a *DHCP server* (see "Configuring DHCP, WINS, and DNS" later in this chapter).

The subnet mask

The *subnet mask* is another four-octet number, but it has a very specific function. Wrapped up in the four octets of an IP address are actually two addresses: the network ID, and the computer or "host" ID. (Kind of like a street name and a house number in a physical mail address.) However, the dividing line between where the network ID ends and where the host ID begins is a flexible one; that is, it can change from one network to the next.

All computers on the same physical network, or subnet, must have the same network ID in order to communicate with each other. If the exam shows you a diagram in which two computers on the same subnet are using different network IDs, you know one of those computers is configured incorrectly.

In order to figure out what exact part of any given IP address is the network ID and what part is the host ID, you need to look at a second number that defines where the dividing line is for this particular IP address. That second number is — you guessed it — the *subnet mask*. TCP/IP uses the subnet mask to figure out, for example, whether a particular IP address is on the local network or on a remote network.

An example of a subnet mask is: 255.255.255.0. In this case, the network ID is the first three octets, and the host ID is the last octet. The reason it's called a mask is that it "masks out" the host ID part of the address by using zeroes. Think of the subnet mask's binary form: 255.255.255.0 becomes 11111111.11111111.11111111.00000000. The ones allow the network part of the IP address to filter through the mask; the zeroes block out the host part of the address.

So, if a computer needs to know whether a destination IP address is headed to the same network or a different network, it runs the address through the subnet mask, looks at the network part, and figures out whether that ID is the same as the local subnet's ID, or some other ID. If it's some other ID, the packet must be forwarded to a router, which can send it on its way to its destination network.

The bare minimum configuration information that a computer must have in order to participate in a TCP/IP network is a correct IP address and subnet mask.

If a PC's IP address and subnet mask are correctly configured, the PC should be able to connect to a server on the local network.

IP address classes

The central authority that allocates Internet addresses, the InterNIC, assigns IP addresses into various classes. Three classes are in popular use: A, B, and C. You can tell whether an IP address is a Class A, B, or C address in two ways: by looking at its first octet, or by looking at its subnet mask (see Table 3-1).

Table 3-1				IP Address Classes		
Class	Range for First Octet	Network ID Part	Host ID Part	Default Subnet Mask	Number of Networks	Number of Hosts per Network
A	1–126	a	b.c.d	255.0.0.0	126	16,777,214
B	128–191	a.b	c.d	255.255.0.0	16,384	65,534
C	192–223	a.b.c	d	255.255.255.0	2,097,152	254

Note that I left out 127 in the "Range for First Octet" column. That's because this is a reserved value. For example, 127.0.0.1 is the *loopback address* that you can use when addressing your own computer with a TCP/IP utility such as PING. Note also that Class C addresses stop at 223 for the first octet. Values between 223 and 254 are reserved for lesser-used Class D and E addresses; you probably won't need to know about these for the exam.

Table 3-1 is a bit complex at first glance, so it may help to analyze one row (the top row) in an attempt to explain how these IP address classes work:

- ✔ Class A addresses use a default subnet mask of 255.0.0.0, meaning that if the IP address of a given computer is a.b.c.d, the network ID part is "a" (the first octet) and the host ID part is "b.c.d" (the second, third, and fourth octets).

- ✔ Because the network ID part is the first octet, and because the allowable range for that number is 1 to 126, it makes sense that a Class A address permits a maximum number of 126 networks.

- ✔ Each Class A network, however, can have lots of computers (hosts). Specifically, it can have however many hosts you can identify with the three remaining octets: $256 \times 256 \times 256 = 16,777,216$. When you factor in that you're not allowed to have a host ID that is all ones or all zeroes, the number of hosts is actually 16,777,214 (16,777,216 − 2).

Installing and Configuring TCP/IP

This section looks at the nuts and bolts of adding TCP/IP to a Windows 2000 computer and setting up the common configuration choices.

Installing TCP/IP

Installing TCP/IP is a task that Windows 2000 normally handles for you when you install the operating system, or when the operating system first detects a network adapter. However, in case the protocol is not present on any given Windows 2000 machine, Lab 3-1 provides the steps for installing it.

| Lab 3-1 | Installing TCP/IP on Windows 2000 (Server or Professional) |

1. **Choose Start⇨Settings⇨Network and Dial-Up Connections.**

    Incidentally, you must be logged on as an administrator.

2. **Right-click the icon labeled Local Area Network and choose Properties from the context menu.**

3. **Click the Install button.**

4. **Select Protocol in the list of component types and then click the Add button.**

5. **Select Internet Protocol (TCP/IP) in the Network Protocol list and then click the OK button.**

6. **Click the Close button.**

Configuring the default gateway

If you want to connect to other networks, you must configure TCP/IP to look for a *gateway* — a computer that links your network with another one (such as the public Internet). In this context, a gateway is simply a *router*.

You can specify a default gateway on the General tab of the TCP/IP protocol's property sheet, and you can specify additional gateways by clicking that property sheet's Advanced button and then entering the gateway IP addresses on the IP Settings tab (see Figure 3-6). The default gateway is the one your computer will use to connect to other networks unless the default gateway isn't available, in which case Windows 2000 will try to use a gateway that appears on the supplemental list.

If you have a DHCP server on your network and you select the Obtain An IP Address Automatically radio button in Figure 3-5, the DHCP server typically assigns your Windows 2000 PC a default gateway (code "03-router") upon logon.

Figure 3-6:
You can
enter one or
more extra
gateway
addresses
here.

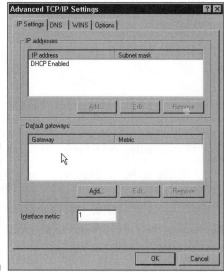

Configuring DHCP, WINS, and DNS

Here comes the alphabet soup. The programs in this section all have one overarching goal: to make managing IP addresses more automatic.

DHCP

DHCP (Dynamic Host Configuration Protocol) is a service that assigns a computer an IP address from a range of IP addresses when that computer logs on to the network. Actually, DHCP also assigns a subnet mask and (typically) a default gateway address. DHCP can run on a Windows 2000 Server, but it can also run on an NT server, a NetWare 4.11 or 5.0+ server, or a UNIX computer. DHCP does *not* run on Windows 2000 Professional.

DHCP sure beats running around from machine to machine keying in fixed, or *static,* IP addresses and subnet masks in the TCP/IP control panel. Activate it by clicking the Obtain An IP Address Automatically option on the General tab of the TCP/IP Properties dialog box. That's it!

If you've set the automatic option, but no DHCP server is available, Windows 2000 uses a new feature called *Automatic Private IP Addressing (APIPA)*. This feature makes the PC assign itself an IP address with a predefined format (169.254.x.x and a subnet mask of 255.255.0.0, but don't memorize that for the exam unless you feel the need to get an "A" instead of a mere passing grade).

The only way to turn APIPA off is to hack the Registry, but you don't need to know the specific key for the exam.

Windows 2000 PCs that have assigned themselves an IP address via Automatic Private IP Addressing can usually only communicate with other Windows 2000 or Windows 98 PCs on the same subnet that have done the same.

WINS

Prior to Windows 2000, every Windows computer has a *NetBIOS name,* or "computer name," which identifies it on a Microsoft-based network. In order for a network user to find your PC anywhere on a TCP/IP network by specifying your PC's NetBIOS name, the TCP/IP protocol must consult a lookup directory somewhere that correlates the NetBIOS name with an IP address.

That lookup is exactly what a *WINS (Windows Internet Naming Service)* server does. You set it up on the WINS tab of the Advanced TCP/IP Settings dialog box, as shown in Figure 3-7. WINS is another program that can run on a Windows 2000 or NT Server in a TCP/IP network.

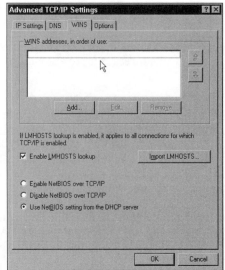

If you click the radio button Use NetBIOS Setting From The DHCP Server, Windows 2000 will get the address of a WINS server from the DHCP server. Alternatively, you can click the Enable NetBIOS Over TCP/IP radio button and key in the WINS server's IP address(es) yourself.

Without WINS, you can still browse the local subnetwork using NetBIOS names, but you can't connect to Windows PCs on a remote subnetwork. The exam may include a question describing a situation in which a user can see other PCs on the local subnet but can't find PCs on other subnets using their NetBIOS names. The answer will probably reflect the likelihood that the user's WINS configuration isn't correct, or the WINS server is down.

The exam may ask you about LMHOSTS (see the related checkbox in Figure 3-7). This text file lives on the local PC and correlates NetBIOS names with IP addresses. Because administrators must maintain LMHOSTS manually every time an IP address change or a computer name change occurs on the network, LMHOSTS is an awful pain, even though you can minimize the pain with the #INCLUDE tag (see Chapter 6). Just remember that with WINS, you don't really need LMHOSTS anymore. In fact, with DNS, one day you won't need WINS anymore, either, as the following section should help explain.

DNS

Yet another way of accessing computers on a TCP/IP network is by domain name (also called *host name*). You're already familiar with domain names such as www.dummies.com. A TCP/IP network doesn't have to use domain names, but doing so is often very convenient — for example, in a company-wide intranet. Here again, some facility must exist for domain names to be matched up with IP addresses. The typical facility is a DNS server, where DNS is short for Domain Naming Service (or, sometimes, Domain Naming System). Windows 2000 networks rely heavily on DNS, not least for the new Active Directory service.

The Microsoft DNS service itself runs only on Windows 2000 Server, but you must know how to configure a Windows 2000 Professional machine to locate a DNS server on the network. The usual approach is to leave the Obtain DNS Server Address Automatically radio button selected, in the TCP/IP properties sheet for the connection of interest. (This method uses DHCP to get the DNS server address or addresses — see earlier in this chapter.) Otherwise, you can click Use The Following DNS Server Addresses and type in a main and alternate IP address for the DNS server(s) on your network.

Troubleshooting TCP/IP

The more settings that exist for a given computer feature, the greater the likelihood that something won't work. Client configuration problems are nonexistent under NetBEUI, rare under NWLink, and very common under TCP/IP.

This section presents a four-step program for troubleshooting TCP/IP connections and illustrates the use of two utilities you may well see on the exam: *IPCONFIG* and *PING.*

1. **Make sure that the TCP/IP protocol has initialized itself on your computer. Open a command prompt by clicking StartÍRun and then typing CMD in the Run dialog box. Then, type** IPCONFIG /ALL | MORE.

   You should see a display something like Figure 3-8 if the protocol is running, including your IP address, subnet mask, and other details. If the subnet mask is 0.0.0.0, your computer has a duplicate IP address!

   Note also that IPCONFIG /ALL shows you a "physical address" that looks like 00-10-5A-CE-02-D6. That's the *MAC (Media Access Control) address,* a unique sequence burned into the network card's silicon. TCP/IP correlates a computer's IP address to the MAC address using *ARP,* or *Address Resolution Protocol.* Use the MAC address when you must to refer to a specific physical device that may have a variable IP address, such as when making a DHCP reservation (see Chapter 5).

2. **While still at the command prompt, type** PING 127.0.0.1 **in order to confirm that TCP/IP is bound to your network adapter.**

   The IP address 127.0.0.1 is known as the *loopback address.* A successful result is a "reply from" message repeated four times.

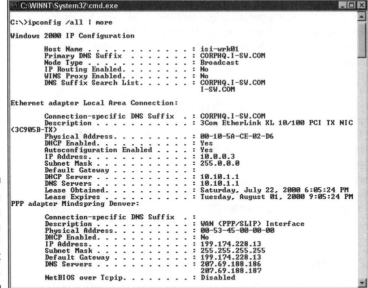

```
C:\WINNT\System32\cmd.exe                                          _ □ ✕

C:\>ipconfig /all | more

Windows 2000 IP Configuration

        Host Name . . . . . . . . . . . . . : isi-wrk01
        Primary DNS Suffix  . . . . . . . : CORPHQ.I-SW.COM
        Node Type . . . . . . . . . . . . : Broadcast
        IP Routing Enabled. . . . . . . . : No
        WINS Proxy Enabled. . . . . . . . : No
        DNS Suffix Search List. . . . . . : CORPHQ.I-SW.COM
                                            I-SW.COM

Ethernet adapter Local Area Connection:

        Connection-specific DNS Suffix  . : CORPHQ.I-SW.COM
        Description . . . . . . . . . . . : 3Com EtherLink XL 10/100 PCI TX NIC
(3C905B-TX)
        Physical Address. . . . . . . . . : 00-10-5A-CE-02-D6
        DHCP Enabled. . . . . . . . . . . : Yes
        Autoconfiguration Enabled . . . . : Yes
        IP Address. . . . . . . . . . . . : 10.0.0.3
        Subnet Mask . . . . . . . . . . . : 255.0.0.0
        Default Gateway . . . . . . . . . :
        DHCP Server . . . . . . . . . . . : 10.10.1.1
        DNS Servers . . . . . . . . . . . : 10.10.1.1
        Lease Obtained. . . . . . . . . . : Saturday, July 22, 2000 6:05:24 PM
        Lease Expires . . . . . . . . . . : Tuesday, August 01, 2000 9:05:24 PM
PPP adapter Mindspring Denver:

        Connection-specific DNS Suffix  . :
        Description . . . . . . . . . . . : WAN (PPP/SLIP) Interface
        Physical Address. . . . . . . . . : 00-53-45-00-00-00
        DHCP Enabled. . . . . . . . . . . : No
        IP Address. . . . . . . . . . . . : 199.174.228.13
        Subnet Mask . . . . . . . . . . . : 255.255.255.255
        Default Gateway . . . . . . . . . : 199.174.228.13
        DNS Servers . . . . . . . . . . . : 207.69.188.186
                                            207.69.188.187

        NetBIOS over Tcpip. . . . . . . . : Disabled
```

Figure 3-8:
Windows
2000 offers
IPCONFIG
as a text
command.

3. **Now, PING the default gateway.**

   If you get a successful result here, your computer can "see" other computers on the same subnet and (specifically) the gateway computer that is your link to computers on other subnets.

4. **Finally, PING a computer on a remote subnet, to ensure that your computer can see computers on the other side of the router.**

Other TCP/IP troubleshooting utilities include NSLOOKUP, which is helpful for fixing DNS problems; NBTSTAT, useful for WINS troubleshooting; and TRACERT (trace route), handy for chasing down router problems. I discuss these tools in the appropriate chapters.

Secondary Network Protocols

The exam may quiz you on one of the secondary network protocols that Windows 2000 supports. Thankfully, you don't need to remember a lot of details about these protocols.

Microsoft DLC

The *Data Link Control* (*DLC*) protocol is handy for connecting a Windows 2000 PC to certain types of networked printers, particularly Hewlett-Packard models with JetDirect network adapters. You would also use DLC to communicate with some IBM minicomputers and mainframes.

Know the following material for the exam:

- ✔ DLC has a "continuous mode" that locks up a networked printer until a print job transmission is complete.

- ✔ DLC need only be installed on the computer that acts as print server, not on every workstation that can submit a print job.

- ✔ You wouldn't ever use this protocol as your main protocol for communicating with Windows NT Server or Novell NetWare networks.

AppleTalk

This protocol lets Windows 2000 machines interoperate with Apple Macintosh computers. Note that Macintoshes can use TCP/IP to access shared resources on a Windows 2000 Server machine. The service that makes such sharing possible is File Services for Macintosh.

Network Monitor Driver

The Network Monitor Driver isn't a network protocol in the traditional sense. Installing it enables Windows 2000 to collect statistics about your computer's network card activity, for reporting to a Windows 2000 Server machine running either Network Monitor or Systems Management Server.

Legally Binding

A. *Binding* is simply a rather unusual word for an active connection between network layers. View bindings by opening the Network and Dial-Up Connections folder and choosing Advanced⇨Advanced Settings (see Figure 3-9). As usual, you've got to be an Administrator to make any changes here.

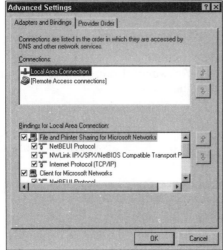

Figure 3-9:
Control
active
network
bindings
here.

The checkboxes indicate which network protocols, services, and clients you can use at this moment on the selected connection. You may very well want to modify these settings. For example, if you use your adapter solely for communicating on a NetWare network running NWLink, you would clear the TCP/IP check box.

Remember these two rules of the Adapters and Bindings tab:

✔ Disable unused adapter bindings for better speed and security and for a somewhat smaller memory footprint, by clearing the related checkboxes.

✔ Position protocols in the order that you're likely to use them, using the up and down arrows to the right of the dialog box. This improves performance over the long run, as Windows doesn't waste as much time trying to establish connections with inappropriate protocols.

Big Network Brother

The primary tool that Windows 2000 Server provides for monitoring network traffic is a familiar one to Windows NT 4.0 network administrators: Network Monitor ("NetMon" for short). This program is a *protocol analyzer,* sometimes called *sniffer.* It captures packets and lets you view them (source address, destination address, traffic type) to get a handle on network traffic.

The version you get with Windows 2000 is a "lite" variant that excludes various commands and features that come with the full version, which Microsoft supplies with System Management Server (SMS). Install the program with the Add/Remove Programs tool; it's a Windows Component under the category of Management and Monitoring Tools.

Here are the essential facts to remember for the exam:

- ✔ When you install Network Monitor, the Network Monitor driver installs automatically. (You can also load the driver separately, as a network protocol, onto other server or workstation machines — as you'd do if you had the full version of NetMon and wanted to monitor those machines' traffic.)

- ✔ Network Monitor captures packet data to a mapped area of RAM for speed. If you don't have enough RAM, or if you don't set aside enough RAM space in this *capture buffer* (the default is 1MB), you can lose packets; when Windows has to use the pagefile, performance suffers drastically.

- ✔ The "lite" Network Monitor only captures data coming into or going out from the computer on which it's running.

- ✔ Network Monitor can detect other instances of Network Monitor running on the same subnet.

- ✔ Network Monitor can detect computers on a remote subnet that are running the Network Monitor driver (not necessarily the program itself); those computers could be workstations or servers.

- ✔ Use a *capture filter* to restrict the packets that Network Monitor grabs; this reduces the program's RAM requirement but requires more CPU horsepower.

- ✔ Use a *display filter* to restrict the packets that Network Monitor displays from an existing batch of captured data.

Prep Test

1 NWLink is required by which of the following network services? (Choose all that apply.)

A ❑ Client Service for NetWare

B ❑ Novell Client for Windows 2000

C ❑ Gateway Service for NetWare

D ❑ IPX/SPX

2 You're responsible for setting up a Windows 2000 Server machine to run the Gateway Service for NetWare (GSNW). This process involves certain setup steps on the NetWare side. What are they? (Choose all that apply.)

A ❑ Create a NetWare group named GATEWAY.

B ❑ Create a NetWare group named NTGATEWAY.

C ❑ Create a NetWare group named W2KGATEWAY.

D ❑ Create a NetWare user that belongs to the group you created in A, B, or C.

E ❑ Assign rights to the NetWare group you created in A, B, or C.

F ❑ Assign rights to the NetWare user you created in D.

3 Which of the following is a possible IP address for a Windows 2000 computer using Automatic Private IP Addressing? (Choose all that apply.)

A ❑ 127.0.0.1

B ❑ 10.10.1.1

C ❑ 255.255.0.0

D ❑ 169.54.20.38

E ❑ 168.54.20.38

4 Which of the following is a valid TCP/IP address and subnet mask? (Choose all that apply.)

A ❑ 10.10.10.10, 255.0.0.0

B ❑ 128.232.14.95, 255.255.0.0

C ❑ 127.232.14.95, 255.0.0.0

D ❑ 24.40.50.60, 256.0.0.0

5 TCP operates at the Transport layer of the four-layer Department of Defense network stack. What other protocol also operates at the Transport layer?

A ○ IP

B ○ UDP

C ○ NetBIOS

D ○ ATM

6 To communicate with each other, computers on the same physical TCP/IP network (subnet) must have the same what? (Choose all that apply.)

A ❑ Network ID

B ❑ Host ID

C ❑ Subnet mask

D ❑ Time To Live

7 You're configuring a Windows 2000 PC to communicate on a TCP/IP local area network. You enter the IP address 144.44.4.14 and the subnet mask 255.255.0.0. What is the network ID for the subnet on which this computer resides?

A ○ 144

B ○ 144.44

C ○ 144.44.4

D ○ 4.14

8 What is the job of ARP?

A ○ Resolve NetBIOS names to IP addresses

B ○ Resolve domain names to IP addresses

C ○ Resolve IP addresses to MAC addresses

D ○ Resolve MAC addresses to UDP addresses

9 You are installing a new Hewlett-Packard network laser printer that has a built-in network card. Your local area network uses TCP/IP. Which of the following network protocols must you add to every client workstation that prints to this machine? (Choose all that apply.)

A ❑ DLC

B ❑ TLC

C ❑ NetBT

D ❑ UDP

E ❑ None

10 Bill comes to you complaining that he cannot communicate with computers in a separate subnet at a remote office, although he can communicate with computers in the local office. Your wide-area network runs TCP/IP. Other computer users in the local office have no trouble connecting to the remote machines. What setting on Bill's machine would you immediately suspect? (Choose the best answer.)

A ○ DHCP server address

B ○ DNS server address

C ○ Subnet mask

D ○ Default gateway

Answers

1 **A** and **C.** The Novell client comes with Novell's own implementation of IPX/SPX and also supports TCP/IP access to NetWare 5 servers. Choice D is wrong because NWLink is a lookalike replacement for IPX/SPX. *See "NWLink and related components."*

2 **B, D,** and **F.** The NetWare group must have the name NTGATEWAY, and you have to assign a user account in that group so that the user account has all the rights necessary to access the resources you want clients of GSNW to be able to use. *See "NWLink and related components."*

3 **D.** *169.54.20.38.* The allowable range is 169.54.0.1 through 169.54.255.254. This private address range is guaranteed never to be used on the public Internet. Choice C is the subnet mask for the address in choice D. *See "Configuring DHCP, WINS, and DNS."*

4 **A** and **B.** Choice A is a Class A address (first octet in the range 1 to 126); the default subnet mask for a Class A address is 255.0.0.0, meaning that the first octet is the network ID and the remaining three octets form the host ID. Choice B is a Class B address (first octet in the range 128 to 191); the default subnet mask for a Class B address is 255.255.0.0. Choice C isn't valid because its first octet is 127, a value reserved for testing and troubleshooting. Choice D isn't valid because 256 isn't allowed in the subnet mask. *See "The IP address and subnet mask."*

5 **B.** *UDP.* User Datagram Protocol is connectionless and doesn't guarantee packet delivery; it's suited for small data transfers and is used by services such as SNMP (Simple Network Management Protocol). You should just go ahead and memorize the DoD layers. *See "The Department of Defense model."*

6 **A** and **C.** Computers with different network IDs can communicate, but routers are required. Because the same network ID is required, the same subnet mask is also required; two computers cannot have the same network ID without also having the same subnet mask, because the subnet mask determines how many bits are in the network ID. The Time To Live (TTL) is part of the IP packet header, and irrelevant here. *See "The IP address and subnet mask."*

7 **B.** *144.44.* The subnet mask of 255.255.0.0 has all ones in the first two octets, meaning that the network ID comprises the first two octets, and the host ID comprises the last two octets. *See "The IP address and subnet mask."*

8 **C.** *Resolve IP addresses to MAC addresses.* Address Resolution Protocol, or ARP, matches up IP addresses with the MAC hardware addresses burned into each network adapter. The theory is that no two MAC hardware addresses are the same. *See "Troubleshooting TCP/IP."*

9 **E.** *None.* This is a bit of a trick question. The protocol that's required is DLC, but you only have to add it to the computer that is acting as the print server — not to every client workstation that may use the printer. *See "Microsoft DLC."*

10 **D.** *Default gateway.* The default gateway setting identifies a router that should link Bill to the remote office. Bill's subnet mask is probably fine, as he can "see" computers in the local office. *See "Troubleshooting TCP/IP."*

Chapter 4

Domain Name System (DNS)

• •

Exam Objectives

▶ Install the DNS Server service

▶ Configure a root name server

▶ Configure zones

▶ Configure a caching-only server

▶ Configure a DNS client

▶ Configure zones for dynamic updates

▶ Test the DNS Server service

▶ Implement a delegated zone for DNS

▶ Manually create DNS resource records

▶ Manage and monitor DNS

• •

Domain Name System (DNS) is the name service for Microsoft's new Active Directory enterprise directory service. As such, DNS is extremely important, as you probably deduced from the length of the preceding list of exam objectives. So I'll dispense with my usual bad jokes and anecdotes
and let you get right into this material, which I can assure you the exam addresses with particular zeal.

Quick Assessment

Install the DNS Server service	**1** If you plan to create an Active Directory–integrated DNS server, install DNS on a(n) _____.
Configure a root name server	**2** You must create a root name server if your corporate intranet connects to the public Internet through a(n) _____.
Configure zones	**3** A zone that returns a computer's host name when the client provides an IP address is a(n) _____.
Configure a caching-only server	**4** A caching-only server has no local _____ files.
Configure a DNS client	**5** Find the primary DNS suffix on the _____ tab of the System control panel.
Configure zones for dynamic updates	**6** If a Windows 2000 Professional client gets its IP address automatically, then the _____ updates the DNS database.
Test the DNS Server service	**7** The built-in test facility of the DNS Server lets you test both _____ and _____ queries.
Implement a delegated zone for DNS	**8** You delegate a zone using the _____ console.
Manually create DNS resource records	**9** The type of resource record used for a reverse lookup is _____.
Manage and monitor DNS	**10** The default location for the DNS debugging log is _____.

Answers

1   *Domain controller.* The "Zone types" section explains.

2   *Proxy server.* "Configuring a root zone" is the section to read if you missed this one.

3   *Reverse lookup zone.* See the "Zone types" section for more.

4   *Zone.* See "Configuring a caching-only server" if you didn't get this one right.

5   *Network Identification.* "Configuring DNS Clients" is the section where this gem of knowledge appears.

6   *DHCP server.* The "Configuring dynamic updating" section offers this and related nuggets.

7   *Iterative; recursive.* If you said "simple" instead of iterative, give yourself nine-tenths of a point. "Testing DNS" is the relevant section.

8   *DNS.* If you missed this one, laugh at yourself good-naturedly, and read "Configuring delegation."

9   *PTR.* If you said "pointer," you get full credit. See "What's a resource record?" for more.

10   `C:\WINNT\SYSTEM32\DNS\DNS.LOG.` The "Monitoring for activity" section contains details.

The DNA of DNS

Everyone by now is familiar with *domain names* such as www.acmecognac. com. Such names are much easier for actual humans to remember and use than the dotted-decimal IP address notation that Chapter 3 presents.

With Windows 2000 Active Directory, Microsoft embraces the domain name system, or DNS, as the name system for computers on internal networks as well as for computers serving up public Web sites. DNS has lots of advantages compared to older name systems, such as NetBIOS:

- ✔ DNS is hierarchical and therefore scales up better for large networks.

- ✔ DNS is already the de facto name system standard on the Internet. By using DNS internally, companies can manage one namespace instead of two. Also, many users are already familiar with DNS from their Web experiences.

- ✔ Lots of other software manufacturers and products already work well with DNS.

The DNS namespace

The DNS namespace consists of (from top to bottom) the root domain, top-level domains, second-level domains, and subdomains:

- ✔ A **root domain** is indicated by a period.

- ✔ **Top-level domains** indicate type of organization (.com for commercial, .edu for educational, .gov for nonmilitary governmental, and so on) or country (.ca for Canada).

- ✔ **Second-level domains** are owned by persons or organizations (microsoft.com, i-sw.com, acmecognac.com).

- ✔ **Subdomains** are namespace structures that subdivide second-level domains, and you can have several levels of them (sales.acmecognac. com, westcoast.sales.acmecognac.com).

You go up the hierarchy as you traverse a domain name from left to right. A domain name that is complete is called a *Fully Qualified Domain Name (FQDN)*, as opposed to a shortcut or nickname, which you may be able to use if Windows is configured to append the necessary suffixes.

Every computer in a Windows 2000 TCP/IP network has a DNS name. For example, the machine I'm using to write this book has the FQDN isi-wrk01. corphq.i-sw.com.

The FQDN of an Active Directory domain (say, `idgbooks.com`) must not exceed 64 ASCII bytes.

You may see Microsoft refer to a DNS name as a *domain name, host name,* or *computer name;* of those, host name is the most precise. *Domain name* is technically the name of the domain rather than of a computer in the domain; for example, the domain name for my computer is `corphq.i-sw.com`. *Computer name* traditionally refers to a computer's NetBIOS name, which is usually part of (but not synonymous with) its FQDN. The NetBIOS name for my computer is simply `isi-wrk01`. (For more on NetBIOS names, check out Chapter 6.)

The DNS service

The TCP/IP protocol, which constitutes the foundation layer of Windows 2000 network infrastructure, requires IP addresses for communication between clients. A network therefore must provide some way for any computer on the network to determine that a given DNS name corresponds to a particular IP address — that is, to *resolve* a DNS name to an IP address.

The famous phone book analogy

The DNS service is basically a phone book. Instead of cross-referencing names to phone numbers, it cross-references host names to IP addresses. Normally, a requesting computer presents the DNS service with a Fully Qualified Domain Name, and asks for the corresponding IP address. That's a forward lookup.

If you work in a medium to large office, you probably have several sets of phone books, both for convenience (so people don't have to walk as far) and to avoid tie-ups when one person needs to look up a phone number and some-one else is using the directory. Similarly, the DNS service in Windows 2000 uses a *distributed database* so that multiple computers on a network can pro-vide name resolution services. That database may be integrated with Active Directory, or it may be a separate mechanism based on text files. Either way, changes that occur on one DNS server *replicate* to other DNS servers, so that they all stay up to date.

In really large cities, one phone book isn't enough to contain all the listings, so you have a set of phone directories: for example, one for A through J, one for K through Z. In large organizations, you divide DNS listings up among dif-ferent *zones,* so that one DNS server handles one zone, and another DNS server handles a different zone. If a DNS server gets a request for a forward lookup that isn't in its zone of authority, the DNS server can pass the request along to the proper DNS server that does handle that zone.

How DNS is better than a phone book

So the phone book analogy is pretty good, but it only takes you so far:

- ✔ Unlike a traditional phone book, the DNS service can also operate in the reverse direction, cross-referencing IP addresses to domain names. (That's called a reverse lookup.)

- ✔ Even more unlike a phone book, the version of DNS that Microsoft built into Windows 2000 also lets computers (via the DHCP service) dynamically update their address mappings in the DNS database — sort of like letting you update your phone number whenever you move, instead of relying on the phone company to do so when it republishes the phone book.

- ✔ Phone books can't talk to other phone books, but DNS servers do talk to other DNS servers. If a DNS server doesn't have a name mapping in its own database, it can go looking for another DNS server that may, in a process called *recursion.* The DNS server that's hunting around may use *hints* that you configure and that point to likely DNS servers. (DNS is beginning to sound a bit like a television game show, so I'd better move on to the next section.)

What the DNS service replaces

In the early days of the Internet, a central file named HOSTS contained the phone book mappings. Internet sites would post changes and updates, and retrieve new versions of the HOSTS file, on a regular basis. That approach became unworkable as the Internet grew in size. However, the HOSTS file is still around; view it in `C:\WINNT\SYSTEM32\DRIVERS\ETC`.

The exam isn't likely to expect you to know much about the syntax of HOSTS files. Do know that Windows 2000 still checks the HOSTS file for a host name mapping before consulting a DNS server. Therefore, if you want, you can reduce network traffic by preloading commonly used server names and IP addresses into the HOSTS file.

Installing the DNS Server Service

Lab 4-1 walks you through the process of installing the DNS service on a Windows 2000 Server computer.

This lab assumes that you didn't install DNS during the original Windows 2000 Server installation. The lab also assumes that you didn't let Windows 2000 Server install DNS automatically, as part of installing Active Directory. (Active Directory requires DNS.) You should be aware that these two options exist, though, as they're very convenient.

You don't need to install DNS on a Windows 2000 Professional client computer. The DNS client capability is built in to TCP/IP. You may need to configure it, however. See "Configuring DNS Clients," later in this chapter.

If you haven't already configured your server's TCP/IP properties for a static IP address and subnet mask, you should do so before following the steps in Lab 4-1. You should also configure the server to use 127.0.0.1 as the Preferred DNS Server; that's the loopback address, so you're telling the server to use itself as a DNS server.

Lab 4-1	Installing the DNS Server Service on Windows 2000 Server

1. **Log on as an administrator and choose Start⇨Settings⇨Control Panel.**

2. **Double-click Add/Remove Programs.**

3. **Click the Add/Remove Windows Components button at the left edge.**

4. **Select Networking Services and then click the Details button.**

5. **Check the Domain Name System (DNS) box and click OK.**

6. **Click Next.**

7. **Supply the Windows 2000 Server CD-ROM or network location and click OK.**

If you install the DNS Server service manually, as per Lab 4-1, then you have some configuring to do afterward, as the next section discusses. However, if you let Windows 2000 Server install DNS as part of setting up Active Directory, Windows 2000 performs much of the configuration work for you automatically. (When the Active Directory wizard works, it's a great time-saver.)

Configuring the DNS Server Service

Configuring the DNS Server service consists mainly of setting up and configuring zones. This section also looks at other configuration issues, such as the caching-only DNS server and dynamic DNS updating.

Zones

A whole bunch of the configuration chores in setting up the DNS Server service has to do with creating and configuring zones. Before I get into the paint-by-numbers procedures, however, a few words are in order about zones, resource records, and zone types.

What's a zone?

A *zone* is a chunk of your DNS namespace over which a DNS server has the authority to perform name and address resolution. (You'll often see terminology such as "the DNS server is authoritative for the zone" — a grammatically unforgivable way of saying that the server is duly authorized to resolve name queries in the zone.)

One zone, one server? That concept has a certain simplistic appeal, but real life is usually more complex. One DNS server can handle multiple zones — as it would, for example, if your budget for server hardware is tight. Conversely, multiple DNS servers can handle a single zone — as they would, for example, if your budget is not so tight and you need to provide some redundancy in case a single server fails.

Zone files

Zone files are disk-based files in `C:\WINNT\SYSTEM32\DNS` that contain address mappings for a specific zone. Zone files contain *resource records,* which begs the question in the following section.

What's a resource record?

A *resource record (RR)* is just a fancy way of saying "database record." The most common RRs are associations between an IP address and a fully qualified domain name. The A (host) RR is a *forward lookup entry* — that is, a host name-to-IP address mapping. It's the most common type of RR. A PTR RR is a *reverse lookup entry* — that is, an IP-address-to-host name mapping.

Other RRs permit the use of *aliases,* or alternative names, for computers with specific host names. Still other RRs let other DNS servers obtain crucial operating facts about the DNS server. Table 4-1 lists the major resource record types and their functions; memorize it.

DNS provides for a couple dozen different types of resource record. I recommend you concentrate on the ones in Table 4-1.

Table 4-1	DNS Resource Records
Resource Record Type	*What It Does*
A (host)	Forward lookup entry; maps a host name to an IP address. You add these manually for computers that don't support DDNS.
CNAME (alias)	Adds a *canonical name* (that is, alias) to a server with an existing A (host) RR.
MX (mail exchanger)	Names the server to which applications should deliver e-mail; each such server needs an A (host) RR.

Resource Record Type	What It Does
NS (name server)	Names which DNS servers are authoritative for a zone.
PTR (pointer)	Reverse lookup entry; maps an IP address to a host name.
SOA (start of authority)	Indicates the DNS server that is authoritative for the zone; first RR in any new zone. Also contains refresh and retry intervals for secondary DNS servers to use.
SRV	An automatic operating system service registration; allows clients to find a specific service (such as logon) on a specific domain by querying DNS, which replies with applicable server names. (The DNS service running on Windows NT 4.0 Server provides support for SRV resource records as long as NT is running Service Pack 4 or higher.)

Zone types

DNS classifies zones in two ways: according to the sort of lookups they perform, and according to their place in the DNS database replication scheme.

A DNS zone may perform either forward lookups or reverse lookups.

- ✔ A **forward lookup zone** contains (among other things) A (host) resource records and provides host name-to-IP-address mappings.

- ✔ A **reverse lookup zone** contains PTR (pointer) resource records and provides IP-address-to-host name mappings. DNS didn't originally support this type of query, and the mechanism for implementing it is a bit odd looking: The network part of the IP address becomes inverted, and Windows appends the special domain suffix in-addr.arpa.

The NSLOOKUP utility reports the error that it "can't find server name for address *<suchandsuch>*" if no reverse lookup (PTR) record is available for the designated name server. (For more on NSLOOKUP, see the "Testing DNS" section later in this chapter.) The TRACERT command can fail, also, if reverse lookup records don't exist.

A DNS zone may be replicated in the following ways:

- ✔ An **Active Directory–integrated zone** becomes part of the Active Directory database, and Windows replicates the zone along with all the other AD information. This option is only available if you're installing DNS on an AD domain controller.

- ✔ A **standard primary zone** is readable and writable — that is, it's both informative and updatable. If you configure a standard primary zone, the DNS server is called a primary server. The first DNS server you configure for a zone must have a primary zone before it can have a secondary zone.

✔ A **standard secondary zone** is readable only. If you configure a standard secondary zone, the DNS server is called a secondary server. Secondary servers get all their data from *master servers* by means of *replication.* (Note that a master server can be a primary server or a secondary server that gets zone data from *its* master server.) Secondary servers exist for the twin purposes of fault tolerance and workload balancing.

Creating and configuring zones

Lab 4-2 presents a typical sequence for creating a new zone with the New Zone wizard.

| **Lab 4-2** | **Creating a DNS Zone** |

1. **Log on as an administrator.**

2. **Choose Start⇨Programs⇨Administrative Tools⇨DNS.**

3. **Right-click a DNS server in the tree pane and choose New Zone.**

   This step initiates the New Zone wizard.

4. **Choose whether you want an Active Directory–integrated zone, a standard primary zone, or a standard secondary zone.**

   You can change the choice later on by opening the zone's General property sheet and clicking Change. However, only a standard primary zone can be changed to an Active Directory–integrated zone.

5. **Choose whether you want a forward lookup zone or a reverse lookup zone.**

6. **If you specify a reverse lookup zone, enter the network ID for the network on which the DNS server is to permit reverse lookups.**

   Windows automatically inverts the network ID and appends the `in-addr.arpa` domain suffix.

7. **Give the zone a name.**

8. **If you're creating a standard secondary zone, specify the IP address of one or more DNS master servers from which to obtain zone data, as shown in Figure 4-1.**

   The master server can be a primary server or a secondary server, but if it's a secondary server, it must have a master DNS server of its own.

9. **Click Finish.**

Configuring a root zone

If your corporate intranet doesn't connect to the public Internet, or if it only connects to the Internet through a proxy server, you must create a root server that resides at the very top of the DNS namespace hierarchy. A root server hosts a root zone. (If your network does connect to the public Internet through a connection other than a proxy server, your network can use root servers on the public Internet.)

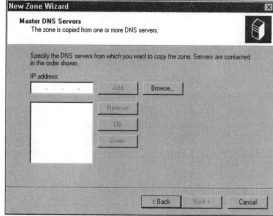

The process for creating a root zone is simple: Run the New Zone wizard, as I describe in the previous section, and give the zone a name consisting of a single period.

Configuring zone transfers

A *zone transfer* is the replication, or copying, of zone file data from a master DNS server to a secondary DNS server. Zone transfers ensure that if you've set up multiple DNS servers on your network, they all keep up-to-date. Remember that with standard zones, updates only occur on primary DNS servers; secondary DNS servers get their data from someone else.

Note that with an Active Directory-integrated zone, you don't configure zone transfers, because DNS replication occurs as part of the normal Active Directory replication.

When you set up Active Directory–integrated DNS zones, either when creating a new zone or converting an existing one, Windows 2000 deletes the text files that constitute a traditional DNS database and folds the database into the Active Directory database. Microsoft recommends this approach for several reasons, which are worth a mention here:

> ✔ Integrated zones mean less work for administrators. You don't have to worry about configuring zone transfers by editing SOA resource records, and you don't have to worry about backing up zone files separately.

✔ Because Active Directory uses a multiple-master replication model instead of the single-master model of traditional DNS, you gain fault tolerance. That is, if one AD domain controller fails, another can perform DNS updates, because each domain controller running DNS acts as a primary server for the zone.

✔ As I mention in Lab 4-3, later in this chapter, you can slap some domain security on integrated zones.

✔ AD replication may be faster than traditional DNS zone transfers because of AD's change-only replication architecture.

Zone transfers occur when a master server notifies a secondary server that the zone information has changed (push), when a secondary server asks a master server for an update (pull), and when a secondary server starts up.

You can put yourself in charge of the zone transfer schedules from either the "pull" side or the "push" side, as follows:

✔ On a secondary DNS server, open the zone's Properties dialog box and click the Start of Authority (SOA) tab, as shown in Figure 4-2. Here, you modify the SOA resource record for the zone:

• The **Serial Number** field increments any time the zone file is updated, and is how a secondary server determines if its version of the zone file is older than that of a primary server.

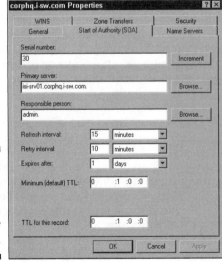

Figure 4-2: Controlling DNS replication from a secondary server.

- The **Primary Server** field shows the name of the server that hosts the primary zone file.

- The **Responsible Person** is the SMTP mail address of the person in charge of managing the zone.

- The **Refresh Interval** is the interval the secondary server waits before asking its corresponding master server for new zone data. The longer the interval, the less DNS replication traffic occurs on the network, but the greater the likelihood that a secondary server's database is out of synch.

- The **Retry Interval** is the interval the secondary server waits to try reaching its master server after a failed attempt to do so.

- The **Expires After** field is how long the secondary server continues handling name resolution queries without any response from its master server.

- The **Minimum (Default) TTL** field is the Time-To-Live interval — that is, the least amount of time the server should cache a name resolution in memory (the default is 1 hour).

✔ On a primary DNS server, open the zone's Properties dialog box and click the Zone Transfers tab, as shown in Figure 4-3. You have the following options:

- The **Allow Zone Transfers** checkbox and its associated radio buttons determine which secondary DNS servers should receive a zone transfer. Clear this box if you don't want the server to send zone transfers at all.

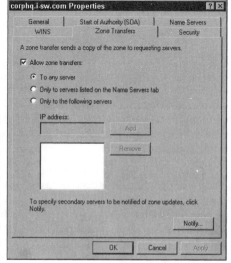

Figure 4-3:
Telling a primary server whom to notify of zone changes.

> • The **Notify** button opens a dialog box in which you specify which
> secondary servers should receive automatic notification of a zone
> change. Notified secondary servers automatically request a zone
> transfer from the primary server.

You can configure zone transfers using a combination of refresh requests
(from secondary servers) and notifications (from primary servers) that
meets your needs for keeping servers synchronized while simultaneously
keeping network traffic to a manageable level.

Older UNIX servers don't support the fast (compressed) zone transfers that
Windows 2000 uses by default. To disable fast zone transfers, right-click the
server and select the checkbox BIND Secondaries, on the Advanced tab.

Configuring delegation

You may want to create a *subdomain* in your DNS namespace. A subdomain is
a new domain that you create beneath the existing parent domain. For example, a DNS server may manage the CORPHQ.I-SW.COM domain, but you may
want a different DNS server to manage a new subdomain, ADMIN.CORPHQ.
I-SW.COM. Subdomain *delegation* can provide load balancing for the computer network as well as offload some central IS responsibilities to the
departmental level.

You can create a subdomain that's part of the same zone, without delegating
it. If so, the original zone file remains authoritative for the subdomain.

You can use the DNS management console to create a subdomain and to
delegate authority for that subdomain to another DNS server or servers:

✔ Create a subdomain by opening the DNS management console and
expanding the Forward Lookup Zones or Reverse Lookup Zones folder.
Right-click the zone name and choose New Domain. Give the new subdomain a name.

✔ Delegate authority for a subdomain by opening the DNS management
console and expanding the Forward Lookup Zones or Reverse Lookup
Zones folder. Right-click the subdomain zone and choose New
Delegation. Provide the name of the domain to which you're delegating
responsibility and then specify the name or IP address of the server or
servers you want to host the new subdomain.

✔ Add an NS (name server) resource record to the parent zone, advertising the fact that the server you delegated responsibility to is now in
charge of the delegated subdomain. You must also add an A resource
record, called a "glue record," associating the newly-responsible server's
host name with its IP address.

Configuring a caching-only server

A *caching-only server* is simply a DNS server that doesn't use a zone database of its own, and is therefore not authoritative for any zone, but instead provides address mappings that it caches (or "learns") from its own lookup activities.

You might set up a caching-only server under the following circumstances:

- You want a DNS server at a particular location, but you don't want to create a separate zone for that location.

- You want a DNS server at a particular location, but that location connects to the Internet, or to the rest of your corporate intranet, over a slow link. (Caching-only servers don't generate zone transfer traffic.)

Set up a caching-only server by installing the DNS Server service normally, but without setting up any forward or reverse lookup zones.

You can set up a caching server to forward lookup requests to another, non-caching DNS server. You might do this, for example, to reduce the amount of traffic between the DNS server and the slow WAN link. That may seem a little counterintuitive, but it turns out that forwarding name resolution queries across a WAN link generally uses less bandwidth than using the WAN link to hunt down the actual address mapping as a "normal" DNS server would. The hunting down process may require several message round trips, but the forwarded query generates only one round trip.

A DNS server that receives forwarded requests is called a *forwarder.* (It should really be called a *forwardee,* but I probably shouldn't pick nits.)

Enable a DNS server to use a forwarder by opening the DNS management console and navigating to the Forwarders tab in the server's Properties dialog box (see Figure 4-4). Check the Enable Forwarders box and enter the IP address of one or more forwarders into the IP Address field, clicking the Add button after each one.

As you can see from Figure 4-4, you can't enable forwarders if the DNS server is a root server.

If you check the box labeled Do Not Use Recursion, the DNS server relies upon forwarders *exclusively* for resolving DNS name queries. That is, the DNS server won't even try to find the requested mapping if the forwarder DNS server fails to find it. (The default behavior is just the opposite.)

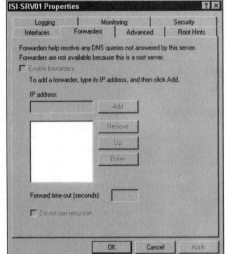

Figure 4-4:
The
Forwarders
tab in the
server's
Properties
dialog box.

Configuring dynamic updating

A new DNS feature since Windows NT 4.0 is *dynamic updating*. This feature, also called Dynamic DNS or DDNS, lets network clients automatically update their host name mappings on the DNS database. That's a great capability, especially when you use Dynamic Host Configuration Protocol (DHCP), because a given host's IP address can change from one day to the next (or even more frequently). (For more on DHCP, please see Chapter 5.)

A Windows 2000 Professional client automatically performs Dynamic DNS updating if it uses a static IP address on its TCP/IP property sheet. If a client uses a DHCP-assigned IP address, the default behavior is that the client doesn't update the DNS database, but the Windows 2000 DHCP server does.

A dynamic update occurs whenever a client's IP address information changes for any of its network connections. That includes lease renewals with a DHCP server, and lease initiations that occur when a computer starts up.

The IPCONFIG command has various applications in DDNS:

 ✔ You can force a client to update its name registration by opening a command prompt and typing **IPCONFIG /REGISTERDNS**.

 ✔ The **IPCONFIG /DISPLAYDNS** command shows the contents of the local DNS name cache, which lives in RAM.

✓ The **IPCONFIG /FLUSHDNS** command clears the local cache. You'd issue this command if a DNS database change has occurred, but your DNS name cache doesn't yet reflect the change. DNS entries have a Time-To-Live (TTL) value, meaning that the client DNS name cache doesn't immediately reflect changes that occur to the DNS database.

You can enable or disable dynamic DNS support on a per-zone basis for standard primary zones or for Active Directory–integrated zones. (The default is for DDNS support to be enabled for Active Directory–integrated zones.) Lab 4-3 goes through the procedure.

Lab 4-3	Configuring Dynamic Updating

1. **Choose Start⇨Programs⇨Administrative Tools⇨DNS.**

2. **Expand the zones in the tree pane, on the left.**

3. **In the tree pane, right-click the zone to which you want to configure and choose Properties.**

   You see the zone's Properties dialog box, as shown in Figure 4-5.

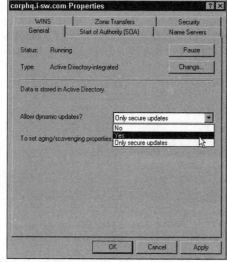

Figure 4-5: Setting DDNS options for a directory-integrated zone.

4. **In the Allow Dynamic Updates list box, choose the desired behavior.**

   If the zone is a standard primary zone, you can choose to turn DDNS on or off. If the zone is an Active Directory–integrated zone, you have those two options, plus an option for Only Secure Updates (the default). The latter option honors any Active Directory security restrictions on zones or resource records (set through the Security tab of those objects' property sheets in the DNS management console). Using secure updates increases the security of your DNS server by restricting which users can update the database.

5. **Click OK to close the Properties dialog box.**

Configuring WINS integration

Windows 2000 DNS can perform WINS lookups (both forward and reverse) as a last resort. That is, when a DNS server can't resolve a name any other way, it can try submitting the name, stripped of its DNS suffix, to a WINS server. Configuring DNS for WINS lookups also enables non-WINS clients to perform NetBIOS name resolution if they "speak" DNS.

Enable a DNS server to perform WINS lookups by clicking the WINS tab in the zone's Properties dialog box and selecting the Use WINS Forward Lookup checkbox. You must also specify the IP address of at least one WINS server.

When you enable WINS lookups, DNS creates nonstandard WINS-specific resource records in its database. Such nonstandard RRs can confuse non-Windows-2000 DNS secondary servers that may receive the resource records in a zone transfer, so you may want to configure DNS not to replicate those RRs. Just select the Do Not Replicate This Record checkbox on the WINS tab of the zone's Properties dialog box.

Configuring DNS Clients

Compared to installing and configuring the DNS Server service, configuring DNS clients is relatively simple. Lab 4-4 takes you through the procedure for a Windows 2000 Professional client — including some advanced settings that you normally wouldn't need to change.

A DNS client sometimes goes by the name *resolver*. That's a bit odd, because it's the server that really performs address resolution, but I just report the news, I don't make it.

Lab 4-4	Configuring DNS for a Windows 2000 Professional Client

1. **Right-click My Network Places and choose Properties.**

The Network and Dial-Up Connections folder opens.

2. **Right-click Local Area Connection and choose Properties.**

3. **Select Internet Protocol (TCP/IP) and click the Properties button.**

   The Internet Protocol (TCP/IP) Properties dialog box opens, as shown in Figure 4-6.

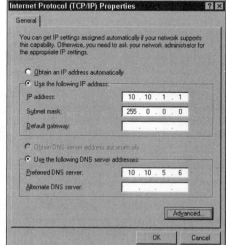

Figure 4-6:
The General tab in the Internet Protocol (TCP/IP) Properties dialog box.

4. **If you use DHCP to provide DNS server addresses, make sure both Obtain an IP Address Automatically and Obtain DNS Server Address Automatically are selected; otherwise, proceed to Step 5.**

5. **If you want to specify DNS server addresses manually, click Use the Following DNS Server Addresses and enter up to two IP addresses.**

   Click OK twice to close all windows; otherwise, proceed to Step 6.

6. **If you want to set advanced settings, click the Advanced button.**

7. **Click the DNS tab.**

   The Advanced TCP/IP Settings dialog box opens with the DNS tab displayed, as shown in Figure 4-7.

8. **If you want to configure more than two DNS servers, use the Add button to create a list.**

   Use the up- and down-arrow buttons to specify the order in which Windows 2000 should look for DNS servers.

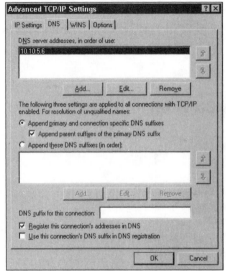

Figure 4-7:
Making
advanced
DNS client
settings.

9. **To enable proper nickname processing, click Append Primary and Connection Specific DNS Suffixes and enter a connection-specific suffix in the field DNS Suffix for This Connection.**

   This instructs Windows 2000 to concatenate your primary DNS suffix if you execute a command that specifies an unqualified host name (nickname). For example, **ping sales** on my computer would become **pingsales.corphq.i-sw.com**. (Your primary DNS suffix is visible from the System control panel's Network Identification tab: From that tab, click Properties and then More to access the dialog box shown in Figure 4-8.)

   If your primary DNS suffix doesn't work, Windows 2000 tries a DNS suffix that you can key into the field DNS Suffix for This Connection.

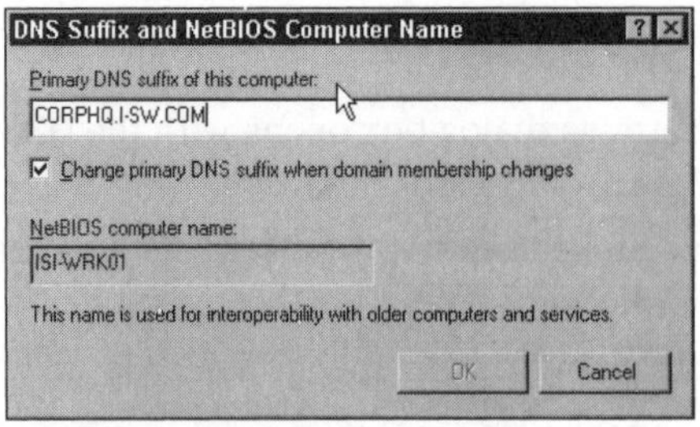

Figure 4-8:
Finding your
computer's
primary
DNS suffix.

10. **If you want to specify the suffixes that DNS uses to fill in an unqualified name, click Append These DNS Suffixes (In Order) and click the Add button to add IP addresses.**

11. **To enable the "dynamic" part of Dynamic DNS, make sure the Register This Connection's Addresses in DNS box is checked.**

   The name that Windows 2000 registers with the DNS Server is the computer name plus the primary DNS suffix.

12. **To enable dynamic updating using the connection suffix, check the Use This Connection's DNS Suffix in DNS Registration box.**

   The name that Windows 2000 registers with the DNS Server is the computer name plus the connection suffix.

13. **Click OK until you're out.**

If you want to verify that the DNS Client service is running on a given Windows 2000 computer, open the Services management console and look for a status of Started and a Startup Type of Automatic.

Managing and Monitoring DNS

This section looks at a few fairly common management tasks: creating a resource record, testing a DNS server, and monitoring a DNS server for errors, activities, and performance.

Creating a resource record

Lab 4-5 presents the procedure for manually adding a resource record (RR) to the DNS database.

Lab 4-5   Adding a Resource Record to DNS

1. **Choose Start⇨Programs⇨Administrative Tools⇨DNS.**

2. **Expand the zones in the tree pane, on the left.**

3. **In the tree pane, right-click the zone to which you want to add an RR and choose the appropriate command (New Host, for this lab).**

   Your options are New Host, to add an A (host) RR; New Alias, to add a CNAME RR; New Mail Exchanger, to add an MX RR; or Other New Records, to add an RR of any supported type.

4. **In the New Host dialog box, enter the host name and IP address (see Figure 4-9).**

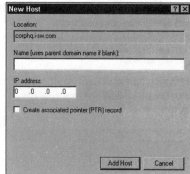

Figure 4-9:
Adding an
A (host)
resource
record.

5. **Click Create Associated Pointer (PTR) Record if you want to enable reverse lookup for this mapping.**

6. **Click the Add Host button.**

7. **Click OK at the dialog box informing you of your success.**

8. **Click the Done button if you're done.**

Sometimes, you may add a resource record in order to link the same host name to multiple IP addresses. When a Windows 2000 resolver (DNS client) gets multiple resource records from a DNS server for the same host name, the resolver performs *subnet prioritization* and orders them with local subnet addresses first.

Testing DNS

You can test the operation of a DNS server using the DNS management console. The test performs a simple DNS query and a recursive DNS query, and you can set the test to repeat at a frequency that you specify. Lab 4-6 presents the procedure.

A *simple query* (also known as an *iterative query*) is one in which a client asks the DNS server to provide the best answer it can — such as a pointer to another DNS server — without pestering any other DNS servers if the data isn't in its database. A *recursive query* is one in which a client asks the DNS server to provide the address mapping, even if the server needs to do a little legwork and get the information from another DNS server. Recursion is the default query type for the Windows 2000 DNS Client service.

Lab 4-6	Testing a DNS Server

1. **Choose Start➪Programs➪Administrative Tools➪DNS.**

2. **Right-click the server icon in the tree pane and choose Properties.**

3. **Click the Monitoring tab to see the dialog box shown in Figure 4-10.**

4. **Under Select a Test Type, check A Simple Query Against This DNS Server, and also check A Recursive Query to Other DNS Servers.**

5. **Click the Test Now button.**

   You should see the date, time, and the word PASS in the Test Results area.

6. **If you want to perform the test repeatedly, click Perform Automatic Testing at the Following Interval and enter the desired interval.**

7. **Click OK when done.**

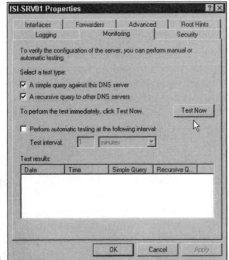

Figure 4-10:
The built-in DNS diagnostic test.

You can also test the operation of a DNS server by using the NSLOOKUP utility, either on the server itself or on a Windows 2000 Professional client. You might use NSLOOKUP after adding, removing, or changing resource records on a DNS server.

The procedure for using NSLOOKUP is to open a command prompt (Start⇨Run and type **CMD**), type **NSLOOKUP**, and press Enter. A prompt (>) appears. At that point, you can enter a computer's host name, press Enter, and NSLOOKUP returns the associated IP address. You can also enter an IP address, press Enter, and NSLOOKUP returns the associated host name. Typing **?** at the prompt gives you all the command qualifiers.

One trick is to open a command prompt at the DNS server and type **NSLOOKUP** *w.x.y.z* **127.0.0.1** where *w.x.y.z* is the server's IP address. You should get a reply including the word `localhost` if the DNS server is responding.

Monitoring DNS

You can monitor DNS for errors, activity, and performance.

Monitoring for errors

Perform error monitoring with the Event Viewer. When you install the DNS Server service, you get a new category, DNS Server, in the Event Viewer console (Start⇨Programs⇨Administrative Tools⇨Event Viewer). If your server is running smoothly, you should mainly see informational messages in the event log — for example, `The DNS server has started`.

You can view the DNS event log on a remote computer by highlighting Event Viewer (local) in the tree pane and then choosing Action⇨Connect to Another Computer. Specify either the DNS name, network path, or IP address of the remote DNS server whose events you want to view.

Monitoring for activity

If you want to monitor DNS activity, you can activate the DNS *debugging log,* but beware: You incur a significant performance penalty by doing so. The debugging log offers a dozen or so categories of events to log; choose these selectively and disable the log when you're done monitoring the server.

The debugging log options appear in the DNS console, on the Logging tab of the server's Properties dialog box, as shown in Figure 4-11. The log file itself is `C:\WINNT\SYSTEM32\DNS\DNS.LOG`.

Monitoring for performance

The Windows 2000 System Monitor program provides 62 (yes, I counted) different performance counters for the DNS object. (Open System Monitor by choosing Performance from the Administrative Tools folder.) You can use System Monitor to watch specific counters on your DNS server in real time. You can also connect to other DNS servers and monitor their performance.

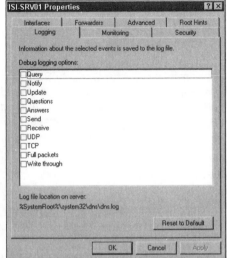

Figure 4-11:
Activating
the debug-
ging log.

Prep Test

1 You have just hired on as a network administrator for Spacely Sprockets, Ltd., and your first job is to roll out a new application on the corporate Windows 2000 network. However, the application contains code that depends on the network's ability to resolve domain host names from IP addresses. The application doesn't work. What should you do? (Choose the best answer.)

A ○ Modify the HOSTS file on every computer.

B ○ Modify the LMHOSTS file on every computer.

C ○ Add a forward lookup zone to your DNS server.

D ○ Add a reverse lookup zone to your DNS server.

E ○ Add a sideways lookup zone to your DNS server.

2 Your boss, Sam Spacely, asks you for your opinion on increasing the fault tolerance of the corporate network, which uses TCP/IP, Active Directory, and Windows 2000 computers. Specifically, Spacely is concerned that with only one DNS server on subnet #1, users may run into serious problems if that machine ever experiences downtime, or if the link between the two subnets goes down. Each subnet has its own Windows 2000 domain controller.

What would you suggest to provide fault tolerance for the network? (Choose the best answer.)

A ○ Set up a secondary DNS server on subnet #2 and configure it to request refreshes from the master DNS server on subnet #1.

B ○ Set up a secondary DNS server on subnet #2. Configure the primary DNS server on subnet #1 to send notifications of zone changes to the secondary DNS server.

C ○ Install a caching-only DNS server on subnet #2.

D ○ Configure DNS on both domain controllers using Active Directory–integrated zones.

3 How often should you manually enter SRV resource records? (Choose the best answer.)

A ○ Never

B ○ Annually

C ○ Monthly

D ○ Weekly

E ○ Daily

4 You have two DNS servers in your corporate network. You want to ensure that the two servers are synchronized as closely as possible without wasting bandwidth. One of the servers, SRV-1, is configured as a standard primary server and is the master for the other, SRV-2, a standard secondary server. Most users on the network have static IP addresses.

How should you configure database replication? (Choose the best answer.)

A ○ On the Start of Authority (SOA) tab of the zone's Properties dialog box on computer SRV-2, change the refresh interval to 1 minute.

B ○ On the Start of Authority (SOA) tab of the zone's Properties dialog box on computer SRV-1, change the refresh interval to 1 minute.

C ○ On the Zone Transfers tab of the zone's Properties dialog box on computer SRV-2, check Allow Zone Transfers, and add the SRV-1 computer to the notify list.

D ○ On the Zone Transfers tab of the zone's Properties dialog box on computer SRV-1, check Allow Zone Transfers, and add the SRV-2 computer to the notify list.

5 You just started the DNS service on a new Windows 2000 Server computer. You manually added a dozen resource records. You want to test your DNS server's name resolution capabilities from a client computer running Windows 2000 Professional. Which utility should you use? (Choose all that apply.)

A ❑ NETSTAT

B ❑ DNSMON

C ❑ NBTSTAT

D ❑ NSLOOKUP

E ❑ REGEDT32

6 What's the name of the DNS query type that expects a complete answer? (Choose the best answer.)

A ○ Iterative

B ○ Recursive

C ○ Simple

D ○ Delegated

7 Your computer name is `wrk0010` and your colleague's computer name is `wrk0019`. You suspect that DNS is not properly configured on your PC. When you open a command prompt and execute the command `ping wrk0019`, you receive an error message. However, if you execute the command `ping wrk0019.corphq.i-sw.com`, you get a successful result.

What setting is probably configured improperly on your computer? (Choose the best answer.)

A ○ FQDN

B ○ Primary DNS suffix

C ○ DNS server address

D ○ Allow dynamic updates

8 **Assuming default configurations, what machine dynamically updates the DNS database when a Windows 2000 Professional computer obtains an IP address lease from a DHCP server? (Choose the best answer.)**

A ○ The DHCP server

B ○ The Windows 2000 Professional computer

C ○ The Active Directory domain controller

D ○ The DNS server authoritative for the zone

E ○ The root name server

Answers

1 **D.** *Add a reverse lookup zone to your DNS server.* A reverse lookup zone enables the DNS server to return host names when a client presents IP addresses. Reverse lookup zones aren't always required on DNS networks, but some applications and utilities need them. As for choice A, the HOSTS file is for forward lookups. The LMHOSTS file in choice B is for NetBIOS names, not host names. I put in choice E purely to amuse myself after having written a long chapter on a very dry subject. *See "Zone types."*

2 **D.** *Configure DNS on both domain controllers using Active Directory–integrated zones.* By taking advantage of Active Directory integration, you don't have to configure DNS replication separately. Choices A and B would be okay but they're not the best choice. Choice C wouldn't give you database redundancy, because a caching-only server doesn't have a local copy of the DNS database. *See "Creating and configuring zones."*

3 **A.** *Never.* Operating system services normally add SRV records to the DNS database automatically, so you should never have to add them manually. You do have to enter A (host) records, and perhaps their associated PTR records, for clients that do not support dynamic DNS. *See "What's a resource record?"*

4 **D.** *On the Zone Transfers tab of the zone's Properties dialog box on computer SRV-1, check Allow Zone Transfers, and add the SRV-2 computer to the notify list.* As the master DNS server, SRV-1 should be configured to notify SRV-2 whenever the database changes. When SRV-2 receives such notification, it requests a database update from SRV-1. In choices A and B, setting the refresh interval to a lower value than the default (15 minutes) would improve synchronization, but it would also generate needless traffic, as this network doesn't exhibit much volatility in terms of address mappings. *See "Configuring zone transfers."*

5 **D.** *NSLOOKUP.* NSLOOKUP lets you test the DNS server's ability to perform forward and reverse lookups, so you can determine whether the resource records you entered manually are working. The other utilities mentioned don't perform DNS diagnostics. NETSTAT gives information about the TCP/IP protocol and current TCP/IP connections; NBTSTAT provides information about current NetBIOS-over-TCP/IP (NetBT) connections; REGEDT32 is one of the two Windows 2000 Registry editors; and I just made up DNSMON (sounds good though, eh?). *See "Testing DNS."*

6 **B.** *Recursive.* A recursive query asks the DNS server to recursively query other DNS servers as required to obtain a final, complete answer — that is, a name resolution. Choices A and C are synonymous and describe a query that asks the DNS server to reply with the name resolution if available, or a pointer to another DNS server, if not. Choice D doesn't describe a query type. *See "Testing DNS."*

7 **B.** *Primary DNS suffix.* The primary DNS suffix tells Windows what to append to a shorthand "nickname" in order to create a fully qualified domain name (FQDN) that Windows can submit to a DNS server. Set the primary DNS suffix via the Network Identification tab of the System control panel, or via the Network Identification command on the Advanced menu of the Network and Dial-Up Connections folder. *See "Configuring DNS Clients."*

8 **A.** *The DHCP server.* If the Windows 2000 Professional computer is configured to use DHCP, the DHCP server is responsible for providing DDNS updates to the DNS server. If the workstation is configured to use a static IP address, the workstation is responsible for providing DDNS updates. *See "Configuring dynamic updating."*

Chapter 5

Dynamic Host Configuration Protocol (DHCP)

. . . .

. . . .

*I*n the olden days of the Internet and TCP/IP, system managers throughout the land manually maintained spreadsheets listing all the static IP address assignments of networked computers. By doing so, they could feel just as organized managing their computers' identifying codes as the Human Resources people felt managing Social Security numbers. (Psychologists call this "boring number envy.")

Nowadays, most Windows network managers use *DHCP,* or *Dynamic Host Configuration Protocol,* to automate the business of configuring TCP/IP settings. This process is, of course, frowned upon by "old school" network managers, who are fond of saying things like, "When *I* was your age, I had to maintain IP addresses by hand," in much the same way that my parents are fond of saying, "We used to have to walk to school three miles every day, in the snow and ice, with no shoes or socks — heck, with no *toes* (lost 'em to frostbite), while carrying 20 large textbooks *and* a shovel to clear our path."

You can respond to the senior network managers by saying, "Oh, sure, but at least you didn't have to study for all these MCSE exams." What you say to your parents is, of course, up to you.

Quick Assessment

Install the DHCP Server service

1 In an Active Directory environment, the first Windows 2000 Server on which you install DHCP should be a(n) _____ type of server.

2 If it isn't already installed, you add the DHCP Server service by running the _____ wizard.

3 A DHCP server should always have a(n) _____ IP address.

Create and manage DHCP scopes, superscopes, and multicast scopes

4 When you create a scope for a DHCP server, you need to _____ the IP addresses for computers within the scope that have static IP addresses.

5 Superscopes are used when you have more than one _____ IP network on a single physical network segment.

6 A multicast scope uses Class _____ IP addresses.

Configure DHCP for DNS integration

7 The DNS feature that lets Windows 2000 DHCP clients dynamically update DNS servers is called _____.

8 Windows 2000 Professional clients automatically update the _____ resource record when they receive an IP address lease from a DHCP server.

Authorize a DHCP server in Active Directory

9 Normally, you only need to manually authorize a DHCP server on a(n) _____ type of computer.

Manage and monitor DHCP

10 At a DHCP client, you can immediately verify a changed scope option by issuing the command _____ at a command prompt.

Answers

1 *Domain controller.* See "Installing the DHCP service" if this answer eluded you.

2 *Add New Programs.* "Installing the DHCP service" provides the detailed procedure.

3 *Static.* Yep, "Installing the DHCP service" again.

4 *Exclude.* See the "Configuring scopes" section for this and other nuggets of wisdom.

5 *Logical.* The "Configuring superscopes" section elaborates.

6 *D.* The name of the relevant section here is "Configuring multicast scopes."

7 *Dynamic updating.* Sorry, I couldn't resist. Check out "Integrating DHCP with DNS" for more.

8 *Forward lookup.* If you said "Host (A)," you're also correct. See the section "Integrating DHCP with DNS."

9 *Member server.* See "Authorizing a DHCP server" for details.

10 *IPCONFIG /RENEW.* The section "Using IPCONFIG to check DHCP operation" tells the story.

The Role of DHCP

Before getting into the details of DHCP, you should understand what the service does and why it's important.

If terms like *static IP address* are unclear to you, please read Chapter 3 before proceeding with this one.

Drawbacks of manual TCP/IP configuration

Using static IP addresses has several drawbacks:

✔ Administrators have to make sure that no two IP addresses on the network are duplicates.

✔ Administrators have to make sure that every computer on the same subnet has an IP address and subnet mask that guarantee the computers have the same network ID. If the administrators don't set up the PCs themselves, they must ask users to do it, and errors can occur.

✔ Administrators must assign every new computer a new IP address, and free up an IP address when a computer is retired.

✔ Administrators must change a computer's IP address when the computer's physical location changes to a different subnet.

✔ Other TCP/IP settings, such as the default gateway and DNS server address, require manual configuration at the workstation, too.

✔ Administrators must assign every computer on the network its own IP address, even though it's unlikely that every computer is actively communicating on the network at the same time.

Many of the configuration tasks associated with TCP/IP are exactly the sort of brainless grundge work that computers are good at handling and that human beings find tedious. So, it was only a matter of time before network architects came up with BOOTP, or *bootstrap protocol,* which permits a basic level of automatic IP configuration (for example, by a diskless workstation). DHCP is, in essence, a somewhat more evolved version of BOOTP, although DHCP and BOOTP messages are almost identical.

What DHCP buys you

With Windows 2000 servers and clients using DHCP, Windows can assign the following TCP/IP configuration variables automatically (each one, other than the essential IP address, has an associated code that you should memorize):

- ✔ IP addresses
- ✔ Subnet masks (code 001)
- ✔ Default gateways/routers (code 003)
- ✔ DNS server addresses (code 006)
- ✔ DNS domain name (code 015)
- ✔ WINS server addresses (code 044)
- ✔ NetBIOS over TCP/IP node type (code 046)
- ✔ NetBIOS scope IDs (code 047)
- ✔ Lease duration (code 051)

The list of possible configuration variables according to the DHCP Internet standard is a lot longer than this, but Windows 2000 only supports configuration of the items listed here.

Note that DHCP treats each separate network card as a separate DHCP client to be configured. So, if you have multiple network cards in a single computer, DHCP configures them each separately.

DHCP "leases" IP addresses; it doesn't "sell" them. That is, DHCP assigns addresses for a fixed period of time only. Think of it like a motor pool in the army: If you need a Jeep, you check one out of the motor pool, for a specific time period. When you're done with it, you check it back in, and it becomes available for someone else to check out.

One big advantage of DHCP is the centralization of IP configuration data. You can manage this data in one place, instead of having to run around the network configuring each workstation with on-site visits.

With DHCP running on your network, a client doesn't even need to have an operating system installed to communicate with other computers. For example, a network PC with a blank hard drive can automatically receive an IP address for itself, and the IP address of a server from which to install Windows 2000 Professional over the wire. (Such a server goes by the name *RIS,* by the way, for *Remote Installation Service.*)

Automatic configuration is great, but it's not the only benefit. DHCP assigns IP addresses from a predefined pool. Because the likelihood of every computer using the network at the same time is small, the number of available IP addresses in the pool can be smaller than the number of physical computers. That can save the company some money, as organizations must typically pay for the IP addresses they use.

Windows 2000 Server's DHCP implementation supports the following clients, although Windows 2000 Professional clients permit the greatest flexibility:

- Windows 2000 (all varieties)
- Windows NT (all varieties)
- Windows 98
- Windows 95
- Windows for Workgroups 3.11 with the Microsoft 32-bit TCP/IP stack
- Microsoft Network Client 3.0 for MS-DOS
- Microsoft LAN Manager 2.2c

Limitations of DHCP

Some limitations of DHCP are as follows:

- You can't use DHCP for every computer on the network. Some machines, such as Windows 2000 Servers running the DHCP service itself, or the DNS service, must have static IP addresses. You must exclude these static IP addresses from use by your DHCP servers.

- You must have a DHCP server, or a DHCP Relay Agent, or a router that supports DHCP/BOOTP forwarding, on every physical subnet of your internetwork.

- DHCP servers are "standalone" and don't share information with other DHCP servers. Therefore, human beings are responsible for ensuring that the range of IP addresses that different DHCP servers can assign do not overlap.

- If a DHCP server is down, clients that depend on DHCP may have problems. You can, however, set up multiple DHCP servers on the same subnet for increased fault tolerance.

How DHCP works

Here's what happens when a Windows 2000 Professional computer boots and initializes TCP/IP, or when the computer requires a new IP address lease:

1. **The client issues a broadcast message asking for a DHCP server to lease it an IP address. This message is called DHCPDISCOVER.**

   Broadcast messages are messages that a computer sends to every other computer on the network, as opposed to messages that a computer sends to a specific computer. If you think about it, without having its own IP address yet, or knowing the address of any other computers on the network, the client can *only* issue a broadcast message at this stage. The DHCPDISCOVER message uses 0.0.0.0 for the source address and 255.255.255.255 for the destination address. The message contains the client's computer name and MAC address (hardware address burned into the network card), so the DHCP server can find the client in order to respond.

   Note that if the only available DHCP servers are on the other side of a router (that is, on a different subnet), the router must support DHCP/BOOTP broadcast forwarding, and have that feature enabled, in order for the DHCPDISCOVER message to reach a DHCP server. (Most modern routers support DHCP/BOOTP broadcast forwarding.)

   Also note that when a DHCP client restarts, it tries to re-lease the same IP address that it had when the user shut the machine down.

2. **Any DHCP server that receives the DHCPDISCOVER message responds by offering up an IP address and subnet mask, again via a broadcast message. This message is called DHCPOFFER.**

   DHCPOFFER messages also include the lease duration and the IP address of the server making the offer, so the client knows to whom to respond. This message has to be a broadcast message, too, as the client doesn't yet have an IP address. While the offer is pending, the DHCP server makes a note that it has offered the IP address, so that the server doesn't offer it to anyone else.

   If no DHCP server responds to the DHCPDISCOVER message within one second, and if X is a random fraction of a second, the client tries again after 9+X seconds, 13+X seconds, and 16+X seconds. At that point, the client tries every five minutes. If the client is Windows 2000 Professional, it uses a feature called Automatic Private IP Addressing (APIPA). The client gives itself an IP address from a Microsoft-reserved address bank (169.254.x.x), after first checking the local subnet for a conflict. The client continues to check for a DHCP server every five minutes, and if it finds one, the client discards the APIPA configuration in favor of the DHCP data. APIPA is handy for small networks that aren't likely to have a DHCP server, but that need Internet connectivity.

3. **The client takes the first offer it receives (sort of reminds me of high school) and broadcasts an IP lease request (DHCPREQUEST).**

   The DHCPREQUEST has to be a broadcast message so that any other DHCP server that may have seen the DHCPDISCOVER message, and issued a DHCPOFFER message, can take back its offer.

4. **The DHCP server gets the DHCPREQUEST message and responds to the client acknowledging the deal. This message is called DHCPACK.**

   The acknowledgment may contain more configuration details than just the IP address. After the client receives the DHCPACK message, the client's TCP/IP configuration is complete, and it can happily party with the rest of the network computers. If the DHCP server can't acknowledge the lease (for example, because a client is trying to lease its previous IP address and the address is no longer available), it sends a message called DHCPNACK, and the client starts the whole process over again.

For performance reasons, DHCP communications don't actually use TCP; they use UDP (User Datagram Protocol). The exam may also expect you to know that the UDP ports involved are 67 and 68. (If you want DHCP broadcasts to cross subnets, you may need to enable forwarding on these ports at your routers if they don't already do so.)

Installing DHCP at the Server

You can install the full-blown DHCP service, or you can install the DHCP Relay Agent service, onto a Windows 2000 Server machine. (You typically use the Relay Agent if your subnet doesn't have a DHCP server, but clients need to reach DHCP services on a remote subnet.) This section looks at both cases.

Installing the DHCP service

This section covers the steps for installing the DHCP service on a Windows 2000 Server machine. (The DHCP client always installs by default on Windows 2000 Professional computers, whether the computer actually uses the DHCP client or not.)

Microsoft recommends upgrading existing Windows NT Server 4.0 domain controllers to Windows 2000 Server before deploying DHCP, presumably because NT doesn't support the step of authorizing a DHCP server in Active Directory (see "Authorizing a DHCP server" later in this chapter).

Because a DHCP server can't also be a DHCP client, you should assign a static IP address, subnet mask, and (optionally) default gateway address to the Windows 2000 Server on which you plan to install the DHCP service.

The first DHCP server you install in an Active Directory environment should be an Active Directory domain controller.

Windows 2000 Server can install DHCP automatically when you install the operating system, and can guide you through some of the configuration steps via the Configure Your Server wizard that appears automatically after you install the operating system. Lab 5-1 assumes that you did not choose to install DHCP when you installed Windows 2000 Server.

Lab 5-1   Installing DHCP on a Windows 2000 Server

1. **Choose Start⇨Settings⇨Control Panel.**

2. **Double-click Add/Remove Programs.**

3. **In the list at the far left of the Add/Remove Programs window, click Add/Remove Windows Components.**

4. **Scroll down to the component named Networking Services and click it, as shown in Figure 5-1.**

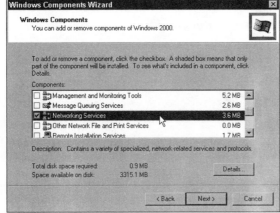

Figure 5-1:
The
Windows
Components
Wizard
dialog box.

5. **Click the Details button.**

6. **Check the box labeled Dynamic Host Configuration Protocol (DHCP).**

7. **Click the OK button.**

8. In the Windows Components Wizard dialog box, click the Next button.

9. Supply the Windows 2000 Server CD-ROM or distribution server location if asked to do so.

10. Click the Finish button.

Installing the DHCP Relay Agent

If a given subnet lacks a DHCP server, and the default gateway (router) on that subnet cannot forward DHCP/BOOTP broadcasts, but a DHCP server exists on another subnet, you can opt to install the DHCP Relay Agent. This option is a viable one on Windows NT Server 4.0 machines, as well as on Windows 2000 Server machines. Lab 5-2 shows you the procedure for installing the DHCP Relay Agent on a Windows 2000 Server computer.

Lab 5-2	Installing the DHCP Relay Agent on a Windows 2000 Server

1. Choose Start⇨Programs⇨Administrative Tools⇨Routing and Remote Access.

2. In the left window pane, navigate to the IP Routing node under the icon for the server of interest.

3. Right-click the General node under the IP Routing node, and choose New Routing Protocol.

4. Click DHCP Relay Agent to select it.

5. Click OK.

Configuring DHCP

After you install DHCP on a Windows 2000 Server, you have several configuration tasks ahead of you. The order in which you perform these tasks can vary, but a typical sequence is as follows:

1. Configure scopes.

2. Configure superscopes, if needed.

3. Configure multicast scopes, if needed.

4. Authorize the DHCP server in Active Directory.

5. Configure DHCP-to-DNS integration.

6. Perform a variety of miscellaneous configuration chores.

7. Configure DHCP at client workstations.

The following sections deal with each task in turn. Many configuration chores make use of the DHCP management console, shown in Figure 5-2.

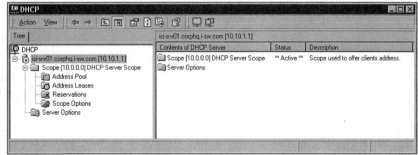

Figure 5-2:
The DHCP
manage-
ment
console.

Configuring scopes

A *scope* is simply a range of IP addresses that a DHCP server can lease to DHCP clients. When setting up DHCP, you must create a scope and configure it.

Creating a scope

Start the New Scope wizard by right-clicking a DHCP server in the DHCP management console and choosing New Scope. You then provide the following details:

- ✔ Name of the scope.
- ✔ Description (optional).
- ✔ IP address range start and end, as shown in Figure 5-3.

Figure 5-3:
Specifying
a scope for
a DHCP
server.

✔ Subnet mask (which you can specify by length, in bits, from 0 to 31, or in the more traditional form as an IP address).

✔ Exclusions (IP address ranges that you don't want the DHCP server to distribute).

If any client on the network uses a static IP address that falls within the scope of any DHCP server, you must exclude that address from the DHCP server's scope.

✔ Lease duration (which should equal the average amount of time the computer is connected to the network; the default is eight days).

Mobile computers should have a lease duration of less than eight days to increase IP address availability. Desktop computers should have a lease duration of longer than eight days to reduce network traffic from lease renewals.

DHCP clients submit a DHCPDISCOVER request to renew their IP address lease after 50 percent of the lease duration has expired. If that request fails, they try again at the 87.5 percent mark.

✔ Optional settings for DHCP to configure on clients: default gateway (router), the DNS domain name, DNS server names or IP addresses, and WINS server names or IP addresses. You can also set these scope options later by right-clicking the Scope Options node under the particular scope and choosing Configure Options. (If you want to set these options globally for the DHCP server, right-click the Server Options node under the server and choose Configure Options.)

✔ Whether to activate the scope now or delay activation. You must activate a scope before the DHCP server can begin assigning IP addresses from that scope — just like in Windows NT 4.0.

After you create a scope, you can't go back and change the IP address range or the subnet mask. You have to delete the old scope and create a new one.

Rules for creating and managing scopes

Here are some key rules for creating DHCP scopes that you should remember for the exam:

✔ Every DHCP server must have at least one scope configured.

✔ Settings that you specify for the scope apply to all DHCP client computers on the subnet, except those with locally configured settings, in which case the local settings override the scope settings.

✔ You must make sure that no two DHCP servers have overlapping addresses in their respective scopes. That would allow the possibility of two DHCP servers trying to assign the same IP address to two different clients.

✔ Only one scope may be active on a subnet at one time, unless you configure superscopes (see the next section).

✔ If you want to include some fault tolerance on your network by allowing DHCP clients to access a remote DHCP server if the local one is down, use the "75/25 rule" as follows: Assign 75 percent of the addresses in the scope to the local DHCP server, and 25 percent to the remote DHCP server.

✔ Don't deactivate a scope unless you want to retire it and remove it from a server. Deactivation begins a scope address recall process. If you need to modify a scope, change its exclusions.

✔ If you want to migrate clients from an old scope to a new one, deactivate the old one and wait 50 percent of its lease duration time before removing it, to ensure that clients have renewed their leases with the new scope.

If you're in a hurry to remove a scope, you can force clients to manually renew their leases by executing the **IPCONFIG /RENEW** command.

Configuring superscopes

A *superscope* is a scope with X-ray vision. (Forgive me, it's getting late as I write this.) Seriously, folks, a superscope is just a group of regular scopes that you may need to manage together. Let me clarify this with an example.

Sometimes, organizations set up multiple logical networks on a single physical network. (That's called a *multinet.*) For example, you could have one group of computers using IP addresses 193.54.2.1 through 193.54.2.254, and another group of computers using addresses 193.54.10.1 through 193.54.10.254. That's two different logical networks: 193.54.2.x, and 193.54.10.x. If both groups of computers — each group comprising a single logical IP network — are on the same physical network segment, you've got yourself a multinet.

Now, in this situation, a regular scope (like 193.54.2.1 to 193.54.2.254) doesn't let a DHCP server assign IP addresses to both logical networks, just one. The DHCP server can only lease addresses to clients having the same network ID as itself. If the DHCP server has address 193.54.2.2, it can only lease addresses to the 193.54.2.x logical network.

Okay, you say, why not just set up two DHCP servers? That's problematical as well. Remember how DHCP broadcasts work: The first available DHCP server to offer an IP lease gets the job. With two DHCP servers on a multinet, you have no guarantee that Bob's computer (on logical network A) would always connect with the DHCP server that you've configured with network A's scope.

Windows 2000's answer to this dilemma is the superscope. Lab 5-3 lists the simple steps for creating a superscope on a Windows 2000 Server that already has at least two regular scopes defined and configured.

Lab 5-3	Creating a Superscope

1. **On a Windows 2000 Server, choose Start⇨Programs⇨Administrative Tools⇨DHCP.**

2. **In the left window pane, right-click the server on which you want to create a superscope and choose New Superscope.**

   This starts the New Superscope wizard. I know, it sounds like a kid's toy.

3. **Select the scopes that you want to lump together into the superscope and click the Next button.**

   The individual scopes go by the name *child scope* or *member scope.*

4. **Choose to activate the superscope and click Finish to exit the wizard.**

You can add scopes to a superscope after you define the superscope.

Configuring multicast scopes

As I explain in Chapter 3, the typical classes for IP addresses are A, B, and C. However, a mysterious animal called Class D also exists. Class D addresses range from 224.0.0.0 to 239.255.255.255. These addresses are used for *multicasting*, in which datagrams flow to a group of recipients instead of to a single recipient (*unicasting*). Multicasting has applications in streaming audio and video transmission.

The DHCP service in Windows 2000 Server supports a proposed protocol standard named MADCAP (Multicast Address Dynamic Client Allocation Protocol). MADCAP specifies how the DHCP service can provide IP addresses in the Class D range.

You can configure the DHCP service with multicast scopes only, in which case it becomes a MADCAP server but not a DHCP server.

Creating a multicast scope is similar to Steps 1 and 2 in Lab 5-3 for creating a superscope, except in Step 2, you would choose New Multicast Scope instead of New Superscope. Multicast scopes don't use the same options that a regular unicast scope would use. The properties of a multicast scope include the following:

✔ **Multicast scope lifetime:** You can specify a date and time when the multicast scope expires. This option makes sense when you consider that organizations often use multicasting for sending audio or video pertaining to a special one-time event.

✔ **Time-To-Live value:** This value lets you specify how many hops (router traversals) multicast packets are allowed to pass before the network expires them. Again, think of the multimedia application: too many hops and the stream of audio or video loses too much quality to be useful.

Authorizing a DHCP server

Having a DHCP server "go live" before you've carefully checked and double-checked its various configuration settings could be a problem. Clients could receive invalid IP addresses or invalid addresses for other kinds of servers, such as DNS servers. In order to guard against such problems, Windows 2000 prevents a DHCP server from functioning unless that server has been *authorized*.

When you authorize a DHCP server, you tell the Active Directory database that the server should, indeed, appear in the list of authorized servers because you've set it up correctly and it's ready for action. This is easy to do; Lab 5-4 lists the steps.

Lab 5-4	Authorizing a DHCP Server

1. **Log on as an enterprise administrator to the DHCP server you want to authorize.**

2. **Open the DHCP console (Start⇨Programs⇨Administrative Tools⇨ DHCP).**

3. **Choose Action⇨Manage Authorized Servers.**

   You should see a dialog box such as the one in Figure 5-4. You can authorize and unauthorize specific DHCP servers here.

4. **To authorize an unlisted server, click Authorize and provide the server's IP address.**

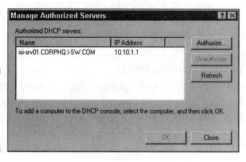

Figure 5-4:
Authorizing
a DHCP
server.

Now, whenever the DHCP service starts, it checks Active Directory to see if the computer on which the service is running is in the list of authorized DHCP servers. If it isn't, then that's that — the DHCP service does not go live and does not service client requests. (An unauthorized DHCP server sometimes goes by the name of *rogue server.*)

The process of authorizing a DHCP server is one that only makes sense in the context of Active Directory. You wouldn't have to authorize a Windows NT 4.0 Server running DHCP, for example, because NT doesn't understand about Active Directory. On both NT and Windows 2000, however, you must activate each individual scope before it can begin issuing addresses.

You only have to authorize a DHCP server manually if you're running DHCP on a member server, as opposed to a domain controller. When you install DHCP on a domain controller (which you should do for the first DHCP server on your Active Directory network), Windows 2000 automatically authorizes the server when you add it to the DHCP management console.

Integrating DHCP with DNS

One of the advances that Microsoft needed to make when it made DNS its default enterprise name service is *dynamic updating.* That's just a fancy way of saying that with Windows 2000, a DHCP client can tell a DNS server automatically when DHCP has given that client a different IP address.

If you think about it, you can see why this feature is so important. Without it, a DNS server doesn't necessarily know for sure what IP address a given computer name should be associated with. DNS servers don't have that problem (at least, not nearly as severely) in a non-DHCP environment, because every named computer has a static IP address. The address may change from time to time, such as when a particular computer moves to a different subnet, but by and large, a given computer name is associated with a constant IP address. In a DHCP environment, however, the computer `isiwrk01.corphq.i-sw.com` is likely to have a different IP address every time it boots. DNS has to find out about that IP address in order to do its job of matching "friendly" computer names with numerical IP addresses.

DNS updating with Windows 2000 clients

Windows 2000 Professional clients are compatible with Dynamic DNS updating. Therefore, after a Windows 2000 Professional machine receives an acknowledgment of lease from a DHCP server, the client sends a message to the DNS server updating its forward lookup resource record — that is, host (A) RR. The DHCP server handles the chore of sending a message to the DNS server updating the client's reverse lookup resource record (or PTR RR). At that point, the DNS server can now find the client computer's IP address given its computer name, and it can go the other way and find the client's computer name from its IP address.

So, with a Windows 2000 client, the DHCP client and the DHCP server share the chore of updating the DNS server. The client updates the host (A) RR, and the server updates the PTR RR. The division of labor makes life a bit easier on the server. You can override this behavior if you want, and have the server handle both updates, but that's entirely at your discretion.

DNS updating with older Windows clients

Older Windows clients (NT 4.0, 98, and so on) are not compatible with Dynamic DNS updating. Fortunately, the Windows 2000 Server knows this, and automatically picks up the slack. When an older Windows client receives an IP address from a Windows 2000 DHCP server, the DHCP server sends both forward lookup and reverse lookup resource records to the DNS server.

The dance of the checkboxes

To configure DHCP-to-DNS integration, right-click the server in the DHCP console and choose Properties. The various checkboxes appear on the DNS tab.

Here's what they mean:

- The Automatically Update DHCP Client Information in DNS checkbox is a prerequisite for DHCP to update DNS at all.

- You can choose either Update DNS Only If DHCP Client Requests or Always Update DNS in the dialog box. If you choose the latter, then the DHCP server updates both A and PTR records even though Windows 2000 clients update their A records by default. So the former is a better choice for keeping needless traffic down.

- The Enable Updates for DNS Clients That Do Not Support Dynamic Update checkbox instructs the server to update both A and PTR records for clients (such as Windows NT 4.0) that don't support dynamic DNS at all.

Miscellany

You can set several miscellaneous options for DHCP servers. Here are three that the exam may quiz you about.

Client reservations

A *reservation* is simply an IP address that you want DHCP always to assign to the same DHCP client (for example, a print server). Any DHCP client with a hard-coded IP address may be one you should consider reserving on your DHCP server.

When you reserve an IP address by right-clicking the Reservations icon in the left window pane of the DHCP console and choosing New Reservation, you see a dialog box (see Figure 5-5) in which you must supply the client's hard-ware address (or MAC address, for Media Access Control). The MAC address is the only fail-safe way of positively identifying a given machine on the net-work. You can see it by typing **IPCONFIG /ALL | MORE** at a command prompt on the client PC.

Figure 5-5:
Making a
client reser-
vation with
DHCP.

You should make a client reservation at every DHCP server that the client could possibly see on the network.

If a computer is already using an IP address that you need to reserve, release that lease by executing the command **IPCONFIG /RELEASE** at a command prompt window at the client computer.

You can set scope options for a reserved client, just as you can set scope options for a server or for a particular scope. Click the Reservations node in the tree pane, right-click the client entry in the details pane, and choose Configure Options. Any scope options that you set for a reserved client take precedence over global or scope-specific options.

Conflict detection

Conflict detection is off by default. If you turn it on, DHCP pings an IP address in its scope before offering it to a client in a DHCPOFFER message, reducing the likelihood that DHCP will offer an IP address that is already *occupado*. Activating conflict detection increases network traffic, so you may want to keep the number of conflict detection attempts low. As shown in Figure 5-6, you set this value on the Advanced tab of the server's Properties dialog box in the DHCP console.

Audit logging

You can have DHCP create an audit log of server activity by checking the Enable DHCP Audit Logging checkbox on the General tab of the server's Properties dialog box in the DHCP console (see Figure 5-7). For some reason known only to Microsoft, the path for the audit log file is on the Advanced tab, instead of the General tab.

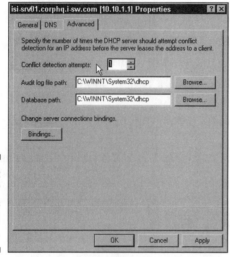

Figure 5-6:
A DHCP server's advanced properties.

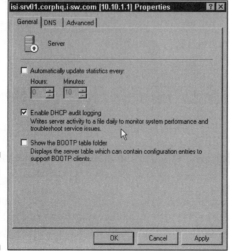

Figure 5-7:
A DHCP server's general properties.

Activating DHCP at the clients

Compared to configuring a DHCP server, configuring a DHCP client is a walk in the park. The default behavior for Windows 2000 Professional is to use DHCP for TCP/IP configuration, so the chances are good that you don't have to do anything! However, to verify that this default behavior hasn't been modified on any given computer, follow the steps in Lab 5-5.

Lab 5-5	Checking the DHCP Setting on a Windows 2000 Professional Machine

1. **Choose Start⇨Settings⇨Network and Dial-Up Connections.**

2. **Right-click the Local Area Connection and choose Properties.**

3. **Double-click the list item labeled Internet Protocol (TCP/IP).**

4. **Click the radio button Obtain an IP Address Automatically.**

   This instructs the client to use DHCP for IP address, subnet mask, and default gateway assignment.

5. **Optionally, click the radio button Obtain DNS Server Address Automatically.**

   This instructs the client to use DHCP for DNS server address assignment.

Testing, Monitoring, and Managing DHCP

After you get DHCP up and running and activated on Windows 2000 Servers and clients, you must verify that it's working, keep track of its performance, and perform occasional troubleshooting and management chores. This section presents the details you need for exam 70-216.

Using IPCONFIG to check DHCP operation

A useful TCP/IP utility that comes with Windows 2000 (all flavors) is the IP Configuration tool, IPCONFIG.EXE. (Windows 98 users get a jazzy graphical version, WINIPCFG.EXE. Windows NT 4.0 users also must use the clunky command-line version.)

This program displays details of the currently active IP connection or connections, including the data that Windows 2000 configures via DHCP. Trying out IPCONFIG on a variety of network client machines is one way to see whether DHCP is behaving the way you want it to behave. You can check out IP addresses, subnet masks, default gateways, and any other options that you configured your DHCP server to provide.

Typically, you would run IPCONFIG by choosing Start⇨Run, typing **CMD** and pressing Enter, and then typing **IPCONFIG /ALL | MORE** at the command prompt. Doing so should display a screen similar to Figure 5-8.

```
C:\WINNT\System32\cmd.exe                                              _ □ ×
Microsoft Windows 2000 [Version 5.00.2195]
(C) Copyright 1985-1999 Microsoft Corp.

C:\>ipconfig /all | more

Windows 2000 IP Configuration

        Host Name . . . . . . . . . . . . : isi-wrk01
        Primary DNS Suffix  . . . . . . . : CORPHQ.I-SW.COM
        Node Type . . . . . . . . . . . . : Broadcast
        IP Routing Enabled. . . . . . . . : No
        WINS Proxy Enabled. . . . . . . . : No
        DNS Suffix Search List. . . . . . : CORPHQ.I-SW.COM
                                            I-SW.COM

Ethernet adapter Local Area Connection:

        Connection-specific DNS Suffix  . : CORPHQ.I-SW.COM
        Description . . . . . . . . . . . : 3Com EtherLink XL 10/100 PCI TX NIC
(3C905B-TX)
        Physical Address. . . . . . . . . : 00-10-5A-CE-02-D6
        DHCP Enabled. . . . . . . . . . . : Yes
        Autoconfiguration Enabled . . . . : Yes
        IP Address. . . . . . . . . . . . : 10.0.0.3
        Subnet Mask . . . . . . . . . . . : 255.0.0.0
        Default Gateway . . . . . . . . . :
        DHCP Server . . . . . . . . . . . : 10.10.1.1
        DNS Servers . . . . . . . . . . . : 10.10.1.1
        Lease Obtained. . . . . . . . . . : Thursday, July 27, 2000 7:46:42 AM
        Lease Expires . . . . . . . . . . : Sunday, August 06, 2000 10:46:42 AM
PPP adapter Mindspring Denver:

        Connection-specific DNS Suffix  . :
        Description . . . . . . . . . . . : WAN (PPP/SLIP) Interface
        Physical Address. . . . . . . . . : 00-53-45-00-00-00
        DHCP Enabled. . . . . . . . . . . : No
        IP Address. . . . . . . . . . . . : 199.174.231.28
        Subnet Mask . . . . . . . . . . . : 255.255.255.255
        Default Gateway . . . . . . . . . : 199.174.231.28
        DNS Servers . . . . . . . . . . . : 207.69.188.186
                                            207.69.188.187
        NetBIOS over Tcpip. . . . . . . . : Disabled

C:\>
```

Figure 5-8:
The IP
Configur-
ation tool.

If you want a more concise report, you can omit the /ALL | MORE part of the command.

IPCONFIG also has command line options to renew (/RENEW) and release (/RELEASE) IP address leases. These may come in handy, for example, if you need to release an IP address that a client is presently using but that you must reserve for a new client with a hard-coded IP address. Another example is when you make a change to the configuration options that a DHCP server assigns, and you want to test the effect of the change by renewing a lease at a client workstation. Finally, if you're getting ready to move a PC to a different subnet, you should release its lease, because the present IP address and subnet mask won't work at the new location.

After you run IPCONFIG /RELEASE, the client can't communicate anymore using TCP/IP until it restarts or you run IPCONFIG /RENEW.

Starting and stopping DHCP

As is usual with Windows 2000, you can accomplish tasks through the graphical user interface (GUI) or at the command line.

To start or stop the DHCP service on a Windows 2000 Server machine using the GUI, run the DHCP console (Start⇨Programs⇨Administrative Tools⇨ DHCP) and right-click the server you want to start or stop. Scroll down to All Tasks on the context menu and choose Start, Stop, Pause, Resume, or Restart.

At the command line, use **NET START DHCPSERVER** or **NET STOP DHCPSERVER**.

Moving the DHCP database

You probably won't ever have to move the DHCP database, but the exam may expect you to know the procedure. Thankfully, it's a simple one:

1. **Stop the DHCP service on the old server.**

   You can use the DHCP console, the Services console, or the Services and Applications snap-in of the Computer Management console.

2. **Back up the Registry key** HKLM\SOFTWARE\Microsoft\DhcpServer\Configuration.

3. **Install DHCP onto the new server.**

4. **Stop the DHCP service on the new server.**

5. **Restore the Registry key from the old server onto the new server.**

6. **Delete the contents of** C:\WINNT\SYSTEM32\DHCP **on the new server.**

7. **Copy the database file DHCP.MDB from the old server onto the new server.**

   Don't copy the transaction logging (*.LOG) and checkpoint (*.CHK) files.

8. **Start the DHCP service on the new server.**

9. **Reconcile all scopes on the new server to synchronize the database with the Registry.**

That last step (right-click the server and choose Reconcile All Scopes) checks the database for inconsistencies and ensures that the database is synchronized with the data that DHCP maintains in the Registry.

Maintaining DHCP performance

DHCP isn't the most intense network service you can run on a Windows 2000 Server — Terminal Service probably holds that dubious honor — but DHCP does incur fairly significant overhead, especially when it comes to disk input and output (I/O). You should start with a high-performance disk subsystem on any DHCP server unless you expect it to be very lightly loaded. Obviously, too, you should spec out your DHCP machine so that it meets Microsoft's minimum hardware recommendations for Windows 2000 Server.

You can monitor the DHCP service's impact on performance using the System Monitor utility, which you access via the Performance icon in the Administrative Tools folder. Select the DHCP Server performance object, which has more than a dozen associated performance counters (see Figure 5-9). These counters include

- Acks/second
- Active queue length
- Conflict check queue length
- Declines/second
- Discovers/second
- Duplicates dropped/second
- Informs/second
- Milliseconds per packet (average)
- Nacks/second
- Offers/second
- Packets expired/second
- Packets received/second
- Releases/second
- Requests/second

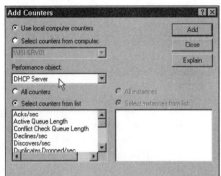

Figure 5-9:
DHCP
perfor-
mance
counters.

Checking the event log for trouble

When you install the DHCP service on a Windows 2000 Server machine, Windows 2000 enables logging of service-related events. DHCP messages go into the System event log, as shown in Figure 5-10. Most of the time, these messages are merely informational (a blue letter *i* on a white field), but if DHCP is having a problem, it can log a warning (black exclamation point on a yellow field) or an error (white X on a red field). The event log is a great place to turn early in the DHCP troubleshooting process.

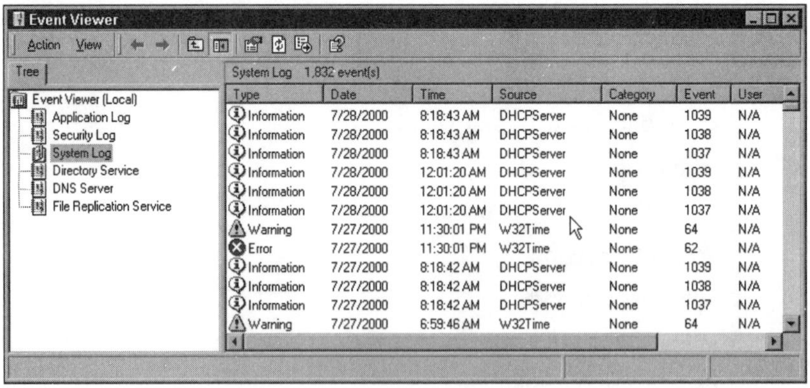

Figure 5-10:
DHCP
Server mes-
sages in the
System
event log.

Prep Test

1 You suspect that your DHCP database has become corrupted. Microsoft technical support advises you to stop the DHCP service and make a copy of the database file to send to Redmond for immediate and detailed analysis. (Your company has a very expensive support contract.) What file do you send?

A ○ DHCP.DAT

B ○ DHCP.DMB

C ○ DHCP.MDB

D ○ DHCP.DBF

2 Which of the following are valid names for DHCP messages that clients and servers send back and forth during the process of assigning TCP/IP configuration data? (Choose all that apply.)

A ❑ DHCPDISCOVER

B ❑ DHCPREQUEST

C ❑ DHCPOFFER

D ❑ DHCPDENY

3 Which of the following TCP/IP configuration options can a Windows 2000 Server running DHCP not assign? (Choose all that apply.)

A ❑ Subnet mask

B ❑ DNS server address

C ❑ Window size

D ❑ Lease duration

4 You are in charge of a small company with two locations. You have configured a Windows 2000 network so that each location has a single subnet that connects to the other subnet via a router. Subnet A has a DHCP server. Subnet B does not. What do you need so that Windows 2000 Professional clients on Subnet B can use the DHCP server on Subnet A? (Choose all that apply.)

A ❑ Routers that support DHCP/BOOTP broadcast forwarding.

B ❑ A Windows 2000 Professional PC on Subnet B running the DHCP Relay Agent.

C ❑ A Windows 2000 Server PC on Subnet B running the DHCP Relay Agent.

D ❑ A superscope configured on the DHCP server on Subnet A.

5 Jeannie is an employee at NASA, where you manage Windows 2000 networks. Major Healey gives Jeannie a promotion, and she moves her office from one building to another, taking her desktop computer with her. Jeannie discovers that she can no longer communicate on the network from her new location, although her coworkers at the new location can do so just fine. Both buildings have subnets using DHCP servers. What could be the problem? (Choose all that apply.)

A ❑ The DHCP server at the new location is down.

B ❑ Jeannie's DHCP lease has expired.

C ❑ Jeannie's computer has a static IP configuration.

D ❑ The DHCP server at the new location has an incorrect default gateway set for the subnet scope.

E ❑ Jeannie dropped the computer on the way across the campus.

6 Which of the following is a valid multicast address? (Choose all that apply.)

A ❑ 224.40.19.40

B ❑ 240.40.19.40

C ❑ 10.0.0.1

D ❑ 241.241.58.58

7 When a Windows 2000 client receives an IP address from a DHCP server, what is the default behavior for notifying DNS of the change? (Choose the best answer.)

A ○ The DHCP client sends a forward lookup resource record, and the DHCP server sends a reverse lookup resource record.

B ○ The DHCP server sends a forward lookup resource record, and the DHCP client sends a reverse lookup resource record.

C ○ The DHCP server sends both resource records.

D ○ The DHCP client sends both resource records.

8 You set up two subnets and a DHCP server on each one. Your routers support DHCP/BOOTP broadcast forwarding, and you enable that capability on each router. How should you configure the scopes for each DHCP server to provide fault tolerance?

A ❑ Each DHCP server should be set up to provide the exact same sets of IP addresses.

B ❑ Set each Windows 2000 client's TCP/IP property sheet to access the local DHCP server first and the remote DHCP server second, using the DHCP tab.

C ❑ Set up each DHCP server to provide scopes for 75 percent of the local addresses and 25 percent of the remote addresses.

D ❑ Set up each DHCP server to provide scopes for 25 percent of the local addresses and 25 percent of the remote addresses.

9 **When would you use a superscope?**

A ❑ When you have more than 255 PCs on a local subnet.

B ❑ When you have more than one physical network on a logical network.

C ❑ When you have more than one logical network on a physical network.

D ❑ When your existing mouthwash just isn't working.

10 **If a DHCP server is not authorized in Active Directory, which of the following statements is true?**

A ❑ It cannot assign any optional TCP/IP configuration details but it can assign an IP address and subnet mask.

B ❑ It cannot assign any TCP/IP configuration details at all.

C ❑ It operates normally, but creates an entry in the System event log.

D ❑ It operates normally, but sends an alert message to a designated network administrator.

Answers

1 **C.** *DHCP.MDB.* The exam may also expect you to know where that file resides: C:\WINNT\SYSTEM32\DHCP. *See "Moving the DHCP database."*

2 **A, B,** and **C.** These aren't in the right order, though. The usual sequence is DHCPDISCOVER from the client, DHCPOFFER from the server, DHCPREQUEST from the client, and finally (if all goes well) DHCPACK from the server. *See "How DHCP works."*

3 **C.** *Window size.* The TCP/IP window size is normally managed dynamically by Windows 2000 and is not configurable by DHCP. Of course, you don't need to know that in order to answer the question. *See "What DHCP buys you."*

4 **A** and **C.** Windows 2000 Professional can't run the DHCP Relay Agent, and adding a superscope to the DHCP server on Subnet A wouldn't do anything for the clients on Subnet B. Most modern routers do support DHCP/BOOTP broadcast forwarding, although you may need to enable the feature manually. *See "Installing the DHCP Relay Agent."*

5 **C** and **E.** With a static IP address, Jeannie's PC would work on the original subnet, but when she changed subnets, the old address forced her PC to try using the old network ID, which does not match the new subnet's network ID. This is the sort of problem that DHCP helps solve — although even if Jeannie's PC were a DHCP client, if she didn't run IPCONFIG /RELEASE before moving the PC, she'd need to run IPCONFIG /RENEW at the new location to force an immediate lease renewal. Choice B is wrong because if Jeannie's PC were a DHCP client, it would negotiate a new lease when the old one expired, at which point Jeannie would get a valid IP address and not have the problems she's seeing. *See "How DHCP works."*

6 **A.** *224.40.19.40.* You can bet the exam will expect you to know that multicast, or Class D, addresses range from 224.0.0.0 to 239.255.255.255. *See "Configuring multicast scopes."*

7 **A.** *The DHCP client sends a forward lookup resource record, and the DHCP server sends a reverse lookup resource record.* The implementation of Dynamic DNS in Windows 2000 permits the Windows 2000 Professional machine to send an update message directly to the DNS server. A Windows 2000 Server running DHCP acts as a proxy for down-level Windows clients, and sends both resource records to the DNS server. *See "Integrating DHCP with DNS."*

8 **C.** *Set up each DHCP server to provide scopes for 75 percent of the local addresses and 25 percent of the remote addresses.* Note that Windows 2000 Professional clients do not have a DHCP tab on their TCP/IP property sheets, so it isn't possible to configure a primary DHCP server and a secondary one. Choice A is not a correct answer because you shouldn't overlap IP addresses between DHCP servers. *See "Configuring scopes."*

9 **C.** *When you have more than one logical network on a physical network.* Normally, you can assign only one scope to a local subnet, but if you have a multinet, you need the ability to assign IP addresses from more than one scope to the local subnet. *See "Configuring superscopes."*

10 **B.** *It cannot assign any TCP/IP configuration details at all.* If it ain't authorized, it don't work. *See "Authorizing a DHCP server."*

Chapter 6

Windows Internet Name Service (WINS)

Exam Objectives

▶ Install, configure, and troubleshoot WINS

▶ Configure WINS replication

▶ Configure NetBIOS name resolution

▶ Manage and monitor WINS

A prime consideration for technical professionals implementing a network infrastructure is the fact that many networks include computers
running versions of Windows earlier than Windows 2000. Those computers
require the NetBIOS interface for computer name identification. Windows
Internet Name Service (WINS) is a network service for managing those
NetBIOS names.

NetBIOS came on the scene almost two decades ago, but it's still imposing
restrictions on network designers and giving headaches to certification candidates. The importance and inertia of decades-old technology is so perva-
sive that the industry has even come up with a euphemism for the term *old:*
legacy. A computer tech support manager I knew used to refer to his ex-wife
as his "legacy spouse." He said to me, "She's part of my past, but she's still
around, and I still have to deal with her from time to time." Well, NetBIOS is
part of the past, but it's still around, and Windows 2000 still has to deal with
it — mainly with WINS.

Quick Assessment

Install, configure, and troubleshoot WINS

1   Install WINS onto a Windows 2000 Server using the _____ option in the Add/Remove Programs wizard.

2   If your network has only a single physical subnet, you probably don't need WINS unless you have more than _____ computers.

3   You can set up a client to use WINS by manually specifying the addresses of WINS servers, or by using _____.

4   Before you install WINS onto a server, make sure it uses a(n) _____ IP address.

Configure WINS replication

5   If two WINS servers connect over a slow link, they should use _____ replication.

6   The primary and secondary WINS servers for a group of clients should normally use _____ replication.

Configure NetBIOS name resolution

7   Windows 2000 computers configured to access a WINS server use the _____ NetBIOS node type.

8   If a Windows 2000 computer can't find a WINS server, it resorts to using the _____ NetBIOS node type.

Manage and monitor WINS

9   After you've configured a backup directory, WINS creates a database backup every _____ hours.

10 The command to compact a WINS database is _____.

Answers

1 *Add/Remove Windows Components.* If you said "Windows Components Wizard," give yourself half a point. See "Installing and Activating WINS."

2 *50.* See "When do you need WINS?" if your answer was significantly different.

3 *DHCP.* See "Installing and activating WINS on a client" if you missed this one.

4 *Static.* "Installing and activating WINS on a server" provides the why and wherefore.

5 *Pull.* See "Replication (a WINS-WINS situation)" for more.

6 *Push-pull.* Ditto.

7 *H-node.* If you said "hybrid," that's worth full credit. For more information, see "Alternatives to WINS" — especially Table 6-2.

8 *B-node.* "Broadcast" also would get full credit. Again, Table 6-2 is worth memorizing.

9 *3.* The section "Backing up and restoring the database" offers details.

10 *JETPACK.* If you said "JETPACK WINS.MDB TEMP.MDB," you should give yourself a high-five (don't sprain anything). "Compacting the database" has more.

The Role of WINS

Every version of Windows before Windows 2000 requires the use of NetBIOS names, which Microsoft also sometimes calls *computer names* or *legacy computer names,* to identify computers on the network.

Now, wait a minute, I hear you thinking. Isn't that what DNS is for — to provide "friendly names" that make it easy for users to find and communicate with computers? The answer is yes, sure, but Microsoft didn't use DNS in the past. The company's conversion to Internet technologies happened fairly late in the game, at least on the computer industry time scale. And Microsoft sold many millions of copies of Windows — relying on NetBIOS names for identification — before Windows 2000 came out.

What's NetBIOS?

NetBIOS (Network Basic Input/Output System) can mean different things depending on the context, but for our purposes, think of NetBIOS as an *Application Programming Interface* (API) that presents commands for applications to use when they need to move data using the network.

For example, an application can use NetBIOS commands for network communications, without caring whether the underlying transport protocol is TCP/IP, IPX/SPX, NetBEUI, or even the old Sytec protocols used in IBM's vintage PC Network (where NetBIOS originated). NetBIOS also provides commands for name registration and verification, session establishment and termination, and data transfer for both reliable and unreliable connection-oriented sessions.

Windows operating systems have long used the NetBIOS interface regardless of the underlying network protocol, by means of the following software components:

- **NetBEUI,** which Windows bundles as a network data transport protocol along with NWLink and TCP/IP, is actually short for NetBIOS Extended User Interface. NetBEUI is nonroutable and appropriate for small networks.

- **NetBIOS-over-IPX** adds a layer that provides NetBIOS support for Novell networking clients using the IPX/SPX transport protocol, which Microsoft calls NWLink, in Windows 9*x*. The Windows 2000 version of NWLink includes NetBIOS support as an integral part of the transport protocol.

- **NetBIOS-over-TCP/IP,** or **NetBT** for short, is appropriate for larger TCP/IP networks that need NetBIOS support. NetBT is the API for which Microsoft designed the version of WINS in Windows 2000. It runs as a service on Windows 2000 computers, using the service name TCP/IP NetBIOS Helper.

The NetBIOS interface has its own naming system, or *namespace,* as described in the following section.

What's a NetBIOS name?

A *NetBIOS name* is a name that identifies a computer, service, group, or other resource on a network that uses the NetBIOS programming interface. All Windows versions before Windows 2000 must communicate with NetBIOS names.

The NetBIOS name system is not hierarchical, but flat. Note the contrast to DNS, in which a fully qualified domain name includes multiple hierarchical levels separated by periods. You can tell that the NetBIOS namespace wasn't built for really big organizations. Every NetBIOS name must be unique on the network.

NetBIOS names can't be really long, either. Specifically, they're 16 bytes long. Computer names in the Microsoft networking scheme can be only 15 bytes long, however, because the network needs the 16th byte to identify different services running on the same computer. Say, for example, the NetBIOS name of a computer is CARLSNEWPENTIUM. The File and Printer Sharing service (which appears as simply *Server* in the Services console) on that computer takes the 15-character computer name and appends the hexadecimal character 020 to it. This way, other services, such as the Workstation and Messenger services, can also register NetBIOS names for CARLSNEWPENTIUM.

NetBIOS names permit names for groups (*nonexclusive* names) as well as computers (*exclusive* names). Group names also have a 15-character limit. If you send a NetBIOS message to a group name, it goes to all the computers in that group.

Incidentally, if a computer name uses less than 15 characters, Windows adds spaces to the name until the length equals 15.

Check out local NetBIOS names by typing the following command in a command prompt window:

```
NBTSTAT -N
```

What does WINS do?

You need some way of resolving a NetBIOS name to an IP address in a TCP/IP environment, because TCP/IP requires IP addresses for any communication to occur. Expecting TCP/IP to use a NetBIOS name is a bit like expecting the postal service to deliver your mail if you use latitude and longitude coordinates on envelopes instead of street addresses. Now, in theory at least, the mailperson *could* deliver such mail if she had a book that related latitude and longitude pairs to traditional street addresses. The WINS database functions much like that hypothetical book.

WINS is a relational database-oriented service, like DNS (see Chapter 4). Its job, in a small nutshell, is to keep track of the changing mappings between NetBIOS names and IP addresses for all computers on the network. In a larger nutshell, here's what WINS does:

- ✔ Dynamically updates the database with a NetBIOS-name-to-IP-address mapping whenever a computer or service starts on the network.

- ✔ Answers queries from computers needing to know the IP address of a computer for which the NetBIOS name is known.

- ✔ Exchanges database updates with other WINS servers, if they exist.

The exam may use the abbreviation *NBNS,* which is short for *NetBIOS Name Server,* of which WINS is an example. So if you see NBNS, think WINS.

WINS has these key advantages:

- ✔ It enables applications running on older versions of Windows, which don't understand DNS host names but which use NetBIOS names instead, to access resources on a modern TCP/IP network. It also enables Windows 2000 systems to connect to older Windows clients.

- ✔ WINS reduces broadcast traffic by providing a single computer with which clients can communicate for both name registration and name querying. Clients can fall back on the broadcast method if WINS fails for some reason.

- ✔ WINS works across routers, permitting NetBIOS name resolution over subnet boundaries. (Routers must permit traffic on UDP port 137, which all WINS communications use.)

- ✔ By using a central, dynamic database that keeps itself up-to-date, WINS reduces the management overhead associated with maintaining static local text files on each network PC.

Incidentally, you can set DNS servers to perform WINS lookups by consulting WINS servers if the DNS servers can't resolve a name query any other way. You might also do so, for example, if you have clients that can use DNS but don't understand WINS and that need to resolve NetBIOS names. (Another approach to the latter problem is to use a *WINS proxy,* discussed later in this chapter.) Chapter 4 contains the details for configuring a DNS server to perform WINS lookups.

Alternatives to WINS

WINS isn't the only way to resolve NetBIOS names to IP addresses. In fact, WINS may not even be necessary on a given network, if alternatives to WINS are suitable. Other ways that computers can achieve NetBIOS name resolution include the following:

✔ Computers can *broadcast* (send a message to every computer on the network) name resolution queries. If a computer that owns the requested NetBIOS name exists on the network, that computer replies with its associated IP address. Broadcasts aren't very efficient, because every computer has to receive and evaluate them even though only one computer is going to respond. NetBIOS broadcast messages are also problematical in that most routers don't forward them between physical subnets. However, this method works okay on a single small subnet.

✔ Computers can use a static ASCII text file named *LMHOSTS* for resolving NetBIOS names. The default location on a Windows 2000 machine is C:\WINNT\SYSTEM32\DRIVERS\ETC. This file must exist on every PC, so using LMHOSTS can be a bit of a chore, even though you can centralize it to some extent with the #INCLUDE keyword. Table 6-1 lists the keywords that you can use in an LMHOSTS file, and Figure 6-1 shows a sample file that Microsoft provides (C:\WINNT\SYSTEM32\DRIVERS\ETC\LMHOSTS.SAM).

Table 6-1	LMHOSTS Keywords
Keyword	*What It Means*
#BEGIN_ALTERNATE	Indicates the beginning of a list of external LMHOSTS files referenced with the #INCLUDE keyword
#DOM:*<domainname>*	Identifies one or more remote domain controllers that the client can use for logon if the local domain controller is down, or if no local domain controller exists
#END_ALTERNATE	Indicates the end of a list of external LMHOSTS files referenced with the #INCLUDE keyword
#INCLUDE	Tells Windows to look at a remote LMHOSTS file (usually on a server, specified with a Universal Naming Convention path) and include its mappings for the benefit of the local computer; a way of reducing the administrative burden of decentralized LMHOSTS files

(continued)

Table 6-1 (continued)

Keyword	What It Means
#MH	Indicates multiple entries (for a multihomed computer having more than one network card)
#PRE	Indicates an entry to preload into the memory-resident NetBIOS name cache when TCP/IP initializes, so that the client need not query the network; the most significant feature of LMHOSTS in the Windows 2000 environment

```
# Specifying "#INCLUDE <filename>" will force the RFC NetBIOS (NBT)
# software to seek the specified <filename> and parse it as if it were
# local. <filename> is generally a UNC-based name, allowing a
# centralized lmhosts file to be maintained on a server.
# It is ALWAYS necessary to provide a mapping for the IP address of the
# server prior to the #INCLUDE. This mapping must use the #PRE directive.
# In addtion the share "public" in the example below must be in the
# LanManServer list of "NullSessionShares" in order for client machines to
# be able to read the lmhosts file successfully. This key is under
# \machine\system\currentcontrolset\services\lanmanserver\parameters\nullsessionshares
# in the registry. Simply add "public" to the list found there.
#
# The #BEGIN_ and #END_ALTERNATE keywords allow multiple #INCLUDE
# statements to be grouped together. Any single successful include
# will cause the group to succeed.
#
# Finally, non-printing characters can be embedded in mappings by
# first surrounding the NetBIOS name in quotations, then using the
# \0xnn notation to specify a hex value for a non-printing character.
#
# The following example illustrates all of these extensions:
#
# 102.54.94.97     rhino        #PRE #DOM:networking  #net group's DC
# 102.54.94.102    "appname  \0x14"                   #special app server
# 102.54.94.123    popular      #PRE                  #source server
# 102.54.94.117    localsrv     #PRE                  #needed for the include
#
# #BEGIN_ALTERNATE
# #INCLUDE \\localsrv\public\lmhosts
# #INCLUDE \\rhino\public\lmhosts
# #END_ALTERNATE
#
# In the above example, the "appname" server contains a special
# character in its name, the "popular" and "localsrv" server names are
# preloaded, and the "rhino" server name is specified so it can be used
# to later #INCLUDE a centrally maintained lmhosts file if the "localsrv"
# system is unavailable.
```

Figure 6-1: A sample LMHOSTS file.

You can force TCP/IP to reload #PRE entries in LMHOSTS by typing the following command at a command prompt:

```
NBTSTAT -R
```

Put often-used servers near the top of LMHOSTS, as Windows parses the file from top to bottom. Put #PRE entries at the bottom, because Windows typically processes them only once, at TCP/IP initialization.

Table 6-2 describes the different ways that a NetBIOS computer can be set up for NetBIOS name resolution behavior (the lingo is *node type*). Memorize the table and the following key facts:

✓ Windows 2000 clients use MS B-node if you don't configure WINS.

✓ Windows 2000 clients use H-node if you do configure WINS.

✓ You can set up DHCP to set the client's NetBIOS node type.

✓ You can also modify a client's Registry to force a node type.

✓ H-node is the reverse of M-node.

Table 6-2	NetBIOS Nodes	
Type	*Meaning*	*Behavior*
B-node	B is for broadcast.	Clients send a broadcast message to register and resolve NetBIOS names.
MS B-node	Microsoft enhanced.	Clients preload #PRE entries in the LMHOSTS file, then send a broadcast if necessary, and then check non-#PRE entries in LMHOSTS if broadcast fails.
P-node	P is for peer-to-peer.	Clients send a directed message to an NBNS to register and resolve NetBIOS names. Clients must be configured with the address of the NBNS, and the NBNS must be available.
M-node	M is for mixed.	Clients act like B-nodes unless that fails, and then they act like P-nodes.
H-mode	H is for hybrid.	Clients act like P-nodes unless that fails, and then they act like B-nodes.

When do you need WINS?

You need WINS if all the following conditions hold true:

✓ You have a network that includes down-level Windows machines such as Windows NT, Windows 9*x*, and Windows for Workgroups.

✓ Your network includes more than one physical subnet, or has more than 50 or so clients on a single physical subnet.

✓ The idea of maintaining a whole bunch of LMHOSTS files manually does not appeal to you.

Most of the time, networks need WINS, which is why Microsoft enables
NetBIOS-over-TCP/IP (NetBT) by default on Windows 2000 computers, and
still includes the WINS service with Windows 2000 Server. In a pure Windows
2000 network, however, NetBIOS names are no longer necessary and therefore WINS is no longer necessary. Certainly one of the benefits of upgrading
an entire network to Windows 2000 is the ability to remove an entire namespace from the network, together with its associated resource and management requirements.

Even if you have down-level Windows clients on your network, they may not
all need to use NetBT. Some proxy servers and firewall computers don't need
it, for example. Removing unneeded protocols is always a smart idea for
improving performance and reducing hardware requirements.

Depending on which Microsoft document you read, one WINS server can
handle 5,000 to 10,000 network clients, 1,500 name registrations per minute,
and 4,500 name queries per minute — assuming the server isn't burdened
with other duties. In practice, most networks have a backup WINS server for
fault tolerance, even if those networks are much smaller than 5,000 clients.
(For more on fault tolerance, see the section "Replication (a WINS-WINS situation)" later in this chapter.)

How WINS Works

This section presents typical sequences of events for the following events
having to do with NetBIOS name resolution:

- ✔ **Registration** (updating the WINS database with newly active NetBIOS
  name mappings)
- ✔ **Renewal** (keeping a registration active)
- ✔ **Release** (ending a NetBIOS name mapping)
- ✔ **Query** (discovering the IP address for a NetBIOS name)

WINS name registration

When a WINS client computer logs on to the network, that computer *registers*
its NetBIOS name (or names, if multiple NetBIOS services are running) with
the central WINS database, along with the client computer's IP address. This
way, the WINS database reflects the current NetBIOS-to-IP name map for
every active NetBIOS service as of that moment in time.

The process goes like this, when it's successful:

1. **At startup, the client workstation sends a** *name registration request* **to the WINS server.**

   The WINS server address comes from the local workstation's TCP/IP property sheet or its DHCP configuration, if the client is a DHCP client.

2. **If the WINS server is up and running, it checks the NetBIOS name against the WINS database.**

3. **If the name isn't already registered, the WINS server sends the client a registration confirmation message and updates the database.**

   The confirmation message contains a time period for the registration, called the *Time To Live (TTL)*. NetBIOS name registrations are temporary. The client needs to know the TTL, so the client knows when to request a name renewal. The default TTL in Windows 2000 is six days.

The NetBIOS registration TTL isn't the same as the value of the same name in an IP packet header.

Here are two wrinkles that you should know:

✔ If the primary WINS server is unavailable on the first try, the client tries two more times. If all three tries fail, the client tries a secondary WINS server, if one is configured. The process continues until the last WINS server listed on the client's TCP/IP property sheet, at which point the client sends a broadcast message to everyone on the network.

✔ If the NetBIOS name is already registered in the WINS database, WINS sends three rapid-fire messages (half a second apart) to the existing registrant, basically saying "Are you there? Someone else wants to use your NetBIOS name." If the existing registrant responds "Yes, I'm here, so no, he can't," then WINS sends a "Sorry, no can do" message to the client who's trying to register. If the existing registrant doesn't respond, WINS sends a registration confirmation message to the client who's trying to register, and updates the database accordingly.

A Windows 2000 computer typically registers more than one NetBIOS name. Registrations usually include the following:

✔ Computer name

✔ Workstation service

✔ Server service

✔ Messenger service

✔ Workgroup or domain name

✔ Name of currently logged-on user

WINS registration renewal

If a WINS client is still using a NetBIOS name when 50 percent of the Time To Live duration has passed, the client needs to renew the name registration and reset the timer. The registration renewal process goes like this:

1. **The client sends a *name refresh request* to the WINS server.**

   If multiple WINS servers are configured for the client, it uses the primary WINS server.

2. **The WINS server sends the client a *name refresh response,* along with a new Time To Live, and updates the WINS database.**

If the normal process is not successful and the primary WINS server doesn't respond, the client repeats the name refresh request every 10 minutes for one hour. Then, the client starts bothering the secondary WINS server (if configured), again, every 10 minutes for an hour. This process goes on with every configured WINS server and then starts over again with the primary WINS server. If no WINS server responds by the time the original TTL has expired, the registration is released.

WINS name release

Releasing registered names is the process whereby a client computer asks the WINS server to remove the client's NetBIOS name (for the computer and for any services that it may have registered) and IP address from the WINS database:

1. **When a network client shuts down properly or a NetBIOS service stops in an orderly way, the client or service sends a *name release request* to the WINS server.**

2. **If the WINS server finds the client's entry or entries in the WINS database, the server sends a name release confirmation to the client and updates the WINS database.**

   The name release response includes a TTL value of zero.

WINS name resolution query

The most common type of WINS message is a *name resolution query,* also called a *discovery* operation, in which one computer needs to contact another computer but only knows the other computer's NetBIOS name. For example, one computer may want to connect to a shared resource on the other computer. Here's the usual procedure:

1. **The WINS client first checks the NetBIOS name cache.**

   The NetBIOS name cache consists of any NetBIOS mappings made in the LMHOSTS file with the #PRE keyword. Windows loads such mappings into memory when TCP/IP initializes.

   Check out the contents of the NetBIOS name cache by typing the following command in a command prompt window:

   ```
   NBTSTAT -C
   ```

2. **If the name cache doesn't contain an entry for the desired NetBIOS name, the WINS client sends a name query to the primary WINS server.**

3. **The WINS server checks its database, resolves the name, and sends a message back to the WINS client, providing the IP address of the destination computer.**

   This message is called a *positive name query response*.

Certain of these steps can go wrong for various reasons:

- ✔ If, in Step 2, the primary WINS server is not available, the WINS client tries two more times to reach it, and then switches to the secondary WINS server or servers (if configured).

- ✔ If, in Step 3, the WINS server doesn't find the requested NetBIOS name in its database, the server sends a *negative name query response* message to the client, which then generates a broadcast message. If no computer responds to the broadcast message, the client parses the entire LMHOSTS file in search of the NetBIOS name.

WINS name resolution requests are routable UDP messages, so you don't need to have a WINS server on every physical subnet. In other words, when a WINS client issues a name resolution query, that query can cross router interfaces to locate a WINS server on another subnet.

Installing and Activating WINS

If you determine that you need WINS on a given network, you must perform steps on both the server side and the client side to install and activate all the necessary software components.

If the exam poses a question about a "pure" Windows 2000 network — that is, one that includes only Windows 2000 Professional workstations and Windows 2000 Server servers, and no down-level Windows machines — you don't need WINS. All the computers can communicate using DNS. One less protocol to manage! Huzzah and kudos!

Installing and activating WINS on a server

The WINS service can run on a Windows 2000 Server or on a Windows NT Server computer. Use a Windows 2000 Server for full integration with DNS. WINS on Windows NT Server 4.0 also integrates with DNS if installed.

You don't have to install WINS on a domain controller. A member server is fine.

Any server running WINS should have a static IP address, subnet mask, and (optionally) default gateway.

Lab 6-1 presents the steps for installing WINS on a Windows 2000 Server.

Lab 6-1	Installing WINS on a Windows 2000 Server Computer

1. **Choose Start➪Settings➪Control Panel.**

2. **Double-click the Add/Remove Programs icon.**

3. **In the icon list at the left, click Add/Remove Windows Components.**

4. **In the Windows Components Wizard window, scroll down to Networking Services and double-click it.**

   The Networking Services list appears, as shown in Figure 6-2.

Figure 6-2: WINS is a "detail" component on the Networking Services list.

> **Networking Services** ⊠
>
> To add or remove a component, click the check box. A shaded box means that only part of the component will be installed. To see what's included in a component, click Details.
>
> Subcomponents of Networking Services:
>
> | ☑ Dynamic Host Configuration Protocol (DHCP) | 0.0 MB |
> | ☐ Internet Authentication Service | 0.0 MB |
> | ☐ QoS Admission Control Service | 0.0 MB |
> | ☐ Simple TCP/IP Services | 0.0 MB |
> | ☐ Site Server ILS Services | 1.5 MB |
> | ☐ Windows Internet Name Service (WINS) | 0.9 MB |
>
> Description: Enables DCOM (Distributed Component Object Model) to travel over HTTP via the Internet Information Server (IIS).
>
> Total disk space required: 0.8 MB
> Space available on disk: 3311.5 MB
>
> Details...
>
> OK   Cancel

5. **Check the box by Windows Internet Name Service (WINS) and click OK.**

6. **Click Next.**

7. **If prompted, insert the Windows 2000 Server CD-ROM and click OK.**

   Windows copies necessary files onto the hard disk.

8. **Click Finish to close the wizard.**

9. **Click Close to close the Add/Remove Programs window.**

For WINS to run properly on a Windows 2000 Server computer, the Server service, the TCP/IP NetBIOS Helper Service, and the Windows Internet Name Service (WINS) service should all be running. Check these using the Services console in the Administrative Tools folder.

Installing and activating WINS on a client

This part is easy. WINS client capabilities come preinstalled on Windows 2000 (Professional and Server), Windows NT 3.5 and later, and Windows 9x clients.

WINS also runs on the following clients:

- ✔ Windows for Workgroups 3.11 (with the 32-bit TCP/IP stack)

- ✔ MS-DOS (with the Microsoft Network Client v3.0)

- ✔ LAN Manager v2.2c for DOS (but *not* for OS/2)

- ✔ Some varieties of UNIX

All you have to do is activate WINS by making the appropriate settings on the TCP/IP protocol's property sheet. Those settings typically include

- ✔ Whether the client should rely on DHCP to provide the address of one or more WINS servers. (For example, in Windows 2000 Professional, simply click the radio button labeled Obtain An IP Address Automatically on the TCP/IP property sheet for the LAN connection.)

- ✔ If not, the address of a WINS server, and (optionally) one or more secondary WINS servers. (NT 4.0 systems only offer the choice of one secondary server.) Any locally-entered IP addresses for WINS servers take precedence over any addresses configured by DHCP.

Lab 6-2 takes a closer look at how to manually configure the address of a WINS server on a Windows 2000 Professional client.

Lab 6-2	Configuring WINS on a Windows 2000 Professional Client

1. **Choose Start➪Settings➪Network and Dial-Up Connections.**

2. **Right-click the Local Area Connection icon and choose Properties.**

3. **Scroll down the components list until you find Internet Protocol (TCP/IP). Click it and then click the Properties button.**

   You can also simply double-click the list entry. In the dialog box that appears, you can click the radio button labeled Obtain An IP Address Automatically, if you want to use DHCP. You could configure your DHCP server to assign the client one or more WINS server addresses. For this lab, assume that no DHCP server is available.

4. **Click the Advanced button.**

5. **Click the WINS tab to display the dialog box shown in Figure 6-3.**

6. **Click the Add button, enter the IP address of your primary WINS server, and then click Add.**

7. **Repeat Step 6 for as many WINS servers as you want to configure, up to a maximum of 12.**

8. **Click OK multiple times to close all open dialog boxes.**

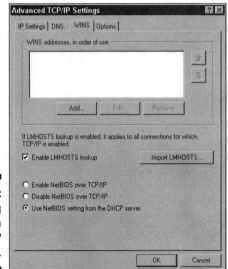

Figure 6-3: Configuring WINS on a non-DHCP client.

Another setting on the WINS tab deserves a comment. Note the three radio buttons at the bottom of the screen:

> ✔ **Enable NetBIOS Over TCP/IP:** This setting is the default when you choose to specify a WINS server address manually. It basically turns on NetBIOS and WINS support at the client. If the client is set up to use DHCP, this setting overrides whatever setting DHCP assigns.

✔ **Disable NetBIOS Over TCP/IP:** If you're absolutely, positively sure that no down-level Windows clients exist on your network, and that no applications on your network require NetBIOS support, then you can remove NetBT and WINS support with this choice.

✔ **Use NetBIOS Setting From the DHCP Server:** This setting is the default when you choose to obtain an IP address automatically via the main TCP/IP property sheet.

Make sure that you configure your DHCP server to provide correct values for WINS server addresses and the client node type (H-node). The DHCP codes are 044 (WINS/NBNS Servers) and 046 (WINS/NBT Node type), respectively.

For WINS to run properly on a Windows 2000 Professional computer, the TCP/IP NetBIOS Helper service, the Workstation service, and the Server service should all be running. Check these using the Services console in the Administrative Tools folder.

Configuring WINS

While the exam expects you to know how to install and activate WINS on both servers and clients, it also expects you to understand how to implement various manual configuration options. This section presents the key options for both WINS servers and clients.

Making the WINS server a client of itself

Right after installing WINS on a server, you should make the server a WINS client of itself. If you omit this step, the server does not have its own NetBIOS name in its WINS database.

Typically, a WINS server has a static IP address and is not a DHCP client. Therefore, the machine cannot receive a WINS server address via DHCP. In this situation, you would assign the WINS server its own IP address on the WINS tab of its TCP/IP property sheet, as I describe in Lab 6-2 (see the preceding section in this chapter).

Configuring LMHOSTS behavior at the client

You can control whether WINS clients use the LMHOSTS file. In Windows 2000, the setting is a checkbox (Enable LHMOSTS Lookup) on the WINS tab of the Advanced TCP/IP Properties dialog box. The default is for this checkbox to be selected (on), so that the system does use LMHOSTS if necessary.

Generally, you should leave this setting turned on, for two reasons:

> ✔ The #PRE values in the LMHOSTS file can preload the NetBIOS cache with frequently used mappings. Doing so can improve performance and reduce network traffic.

> ✔ Other mappings in the LMHOSTS file can function as a backup system in case problems occur with a WINS server.

The first reason is the more important one in a Windows 2000 network.

Configuring the network for non-WINS clients

What if you have one or more clients on the network that don't support WINS? Such computers may use NetBIOS names, but cannot register those names with the WINS server, nor can they obtain NetBIOS name resolution for computers on remote subnets. Different approaches solve different aspects of the non-WINS-client problem:

> ✔ Creating a *WINS proxy* enables non-WINS clients to obtain NetBIOS name resolution for computers on remote subnets.

> ✔ Creating a *static mapping* enables WINS clients to obtain NetBIOS name resolution for non-WINS clients.

The following sections elaborate.

Creating a WINS proxy

A *WINS proxy* is simply a computer on the network that listens for NetBIOS name registration, query, and release broadcasts, and then forwards the requests to a WINS server. (WINS servers don't respond to broadcasts, and so can't hear b-node clients that aren't WINS-capable.)

For example, if a non-WINS client broadcasts a name query, the WINS proxy first checks its NetBIOS name cache for a match. Failing that, the proxy forwards the query to a WINS server. The WINS server then returns the resolved IP address to the WINS proxy, which sends it to the non-WINS client.

A *proxy* in network infrastructure lingo is any computer or service that stands in for another computer or service, and acts as a relay agent or messenger. Thus, a WINS proxy isn't a WINS server, but it can get in touch with a WINS server on behalf of a non-WINS client. The concept is very similar to the DHCP Relay Agent; see Chapter 5.

What's the value of this method? Remember that NetBIOS broadcast messages typically don't cross routers. Therefore, if a non-WINS client is trying to locate a computer on a remote subnet, broadcasting alone doesn't work. With a WINS proxy on the same subnet as the non-WINS client, however, the proxy can send a directed message across the router to a WINS server in order to resolve the NetBIOS name.

Create a WINS proxy on a WINS-enabled Windows 2000 computer by setting the **Registry value** `EnableProxy` to 1 in the **Registry key** `HKEY_LOCAL_MACHINE\SYSTEM\CurrentControlSet\Services\NetBT\Parameters`. Add the value if it doesn't already exist. You must restart for the setting to take effect.

Microsoft recommends that you don't configure more than two WINS proxies on any given subnet, for traffic reasons. If you don't mind a little downtime when one WINS proxy fails, stick with one proxy per subnet.

Creating a static mapping

If a WINS client attempts to find a non-WINS client on the network, it obviously can't use WINS. The WINS client could send a broadcast message, but that doesn't help if the non-WINS client is on a separate subnet. The WINS client could use LMHOSTS, but that technique may involve some additional work in terms of administering distributed LMHOSTS files.

A network administrator can add a *static mapping* to the WINS database in order to permanently register a given computer's NetBIOS name and IP address. The static mapping method guarantees that WINS clients can always find the non-WINS computer, as long as the WINS server is available. Lab 6-3 shows how to set a static mapping on a Windows 2000 WINS server.

Lab 6-3	Setting a Static Mapping in WINS

1. **Choose Start⇨Settings⇨Control Panel and open Administrative Tools.**

2. **Double-click the WINS icon to open the WINS management console.**

3. **In the tree pane, click the + sign next to the server on which you want to configure the static mapping (see Figure 6-4).**

Figure 6-4:
The WINS management console.

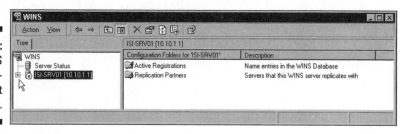

4. **Right-click the Active Registrations icon and choose New Static Mapping to open the dialog box shown in Figure 6-5.**

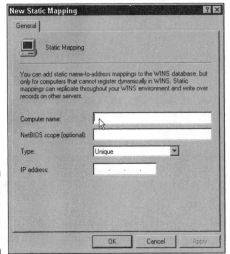

Figure 6-5:
Add a static mapping here.

5. **In the Computer Name field, type the computer name (NetBIOS name) for which you want to enter a static mapping.**

6. **Select the proper mapping type from the Type drop-down list.**

   For example, select Unique if you're mapping a computer name for a machine with a single network card.

7. **In the IP Address field, type the IP address for the computer named in Step 5.**

8. **If you want to add more mappings, click Apply. If you're done, click OK.**

   Windows updates the WINS database when you click Apply or OK.

You can make a WINS server import a bunch of static mappings contained in an LMOSTS file. Open the WINS console, right-click the Active Registrations icon, and choose Import LMHOSTS File. Browse to the LMHOSTS file containing the static mappings, and WINS will add its contents to the relational database.

If you're creating a static mapping for a DHCP client, you must create a *reservation* for that client on the DHCP server so the client's IP address doesn't change. See Chapter 5 for the procedure.

Replication (a WINS-WINS situation)

To provide fault tolerance on a single subnet, companies often allocate two WINS servers, so that if one goes down, the other can assume its function. Networks that have multiple subnets may have one WINS server on each subnet, to minimize traffic across WAN links.

Networks with multiple WINS servers can use *replication* to ensure that updates on one WINS server ultimately migrate to all other WINS servers on the network. That sort of replication is necessary, for example, if Bob on Subnet A with WINS server #1 wants to communicate with Janet on Subnet B with WINS server #2. WINS server #1 doesn't know about Janet, who registered with WINS server #2, unless WINS server #2 shares Janet's registration with WINS server #1.

Push me, pull you

To set up replication, you run the WINS console on one server and configure another WINS server as a replication partner. That partner can be a pull partner, a push partner, or a push-pull partner:

- ✔ A **pull partner** is a WINS server that asks replication partners for database updates at configurable intervals.

- ✔ A **push partner** is a WINS server that tells its replication partners when its database has logged a certain configurable number of change events. Then the replication partners respond with a request for database updates (not the whole database!), which the push partner supplies.

- ✔ A **push-pull partner** is a WINS server that performs both roles. Microsoft recommends using push-pull partners to ensure good bidirectional synchronization, and this is the default type when you create a new replication partner.

Why have different types of replication partners? The main reason is that some network links are slow and some are fast:

- ✔ Push partners let you configure WINS servers so that they never get very far out of synch. You can set them up so that as soon as a WINS server records as few as one event, it instigates a database replication. However, such a setup demands a fast link.

- ✔ Pull partners work better over slow links, because you set them up to request updates at a predefined time interval. This way, you can keep network traffic to a minimum, and even schedule replication to occur when the network is relatively idle. However, if a lot of WINS activity occurs between updates, the two WINS servers can get pretty far out of synch.

✔ Push-pull partners let you set both a time interval value and a number-of-events value as replication triggers. This way, you can be sure that the WINS servers update each other periodically even if not much WINS activity is going on, *and* that they update each other during periods of high WINS activity even if the time interval hasn't elapsed.

You normally configure the primary and secondary WINS servers as push-pull partners of each other. This requires configuration at each WINS server.

In addition to using the criteria specified in the replication scheme, WINS servers typically replicate databases when the WINS service starts, and when an administrator issues a Replicate Now command in the WINS management console.

The very first time a WINS server replicates its database, it includes all entries; subsequent replications consist only of new and changed entries.

Creating a replication partner

The process for creating and configuring a replication partner is fairly easy, and documented in Lab 6-4.

Lab 6-4	Creating and Configuring a WINS Replication Partner

1. **Choose Start⇨Settings⇨Control Panel and open Administrative Tools.**

2. **Double-click the WINS icon to open the WINS management console.**

3. **In the tree pane, click the + sign next to the server on which you want to configure the static mapping.**

4. **Right-click the Replication Partners icon and choose New Replication Partner.**

5. **Type an IP address or browse to specify the partner WINS server, and click OK.**

6. **In the Replication Partners list in the right window pane, right-click the WINS server you just added and choose Properties.**

   Note that the default type is Push-Pull.

7. **Click the Advanced tab, as shown in Figure 6-6.**

8. **Choose the Replication Partner Type you desire.**

   Note that your choice affects which areas in the property sheet are available for modification and which are grayed out. Nice design! Also notice the Use Persistent Connection For Replication checkboxes; make sure they're cleared if replication is to occur across a WAN link.

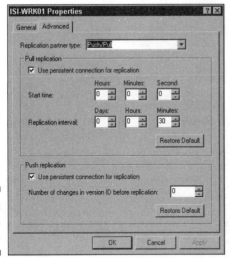

Figure 6-6:
Howdy,
partner.

9. **Fill in the replication start time and interval for pull replication, and/ or the database change threshold (Number Of Changes In Version ID Before Replication) for push replication, and click OK.**

The lower the database change threshold (for push replication), or the shorter the replication interval (for pull replication), the more network traffic you're going to see, but the more closely in synch your WINS servers will be, and the faster they will *converge* (achieve database consistency across the entire internetwork).

10. **If you're setting up a bidirectional replication, repeat Steps 1 through 9 for the partner server.**

Initiating replication manually

You can always force a replication by clicking the Replication Partners icon in the WINS console tree pane, right-clicking the server in the details pane, and choosing the appropriate command. For example, with a push-pull partner, you could choose Start Push Replication or Start Pull Replication.

Automatic discovery and WINS replication

WINS servers can perform automatic discovery of other WINS servers, as well as automatic configuration of replication partners. For traffic control, Microsoft recommends that you use this feature only on smaller networks with three or fewer WINS servers. Right-click the Replication Partners node, choose Properties, and click the Advanced tab. You can select the checkbox Enable Automatic Partner Configuration to turn on the automatic discovery feature; see Figure 6-7.

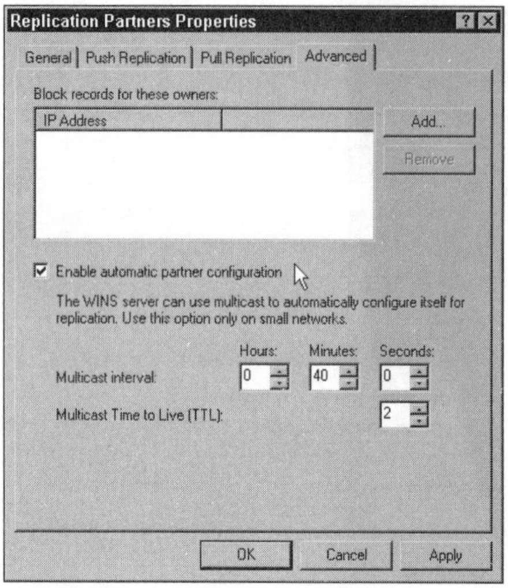

Replication Partners Properties

General | Push Replication | Pull Replication | Advanced

Block records for these owners:

IP Address		Add...
		Remove

☑ Enable automatic partner configuration

The WINS server can use multicast to automatically configure itself for replication. Use this option only on small networks.

	Hours:	Minutes:	Seconds:
Multicast interval:	0	40	0
Multicast Time to Live (TTL):			2

OK   Cancel   Apply

Figure 6-7:
Enabling
automatic
discovery
and
replication.

When you turn on automatic discovery and partner configuration, a WINS server sends an IGMP multicast at (by default) 40-minute intervals to address 224.0.1.24, looking for another WINS server. (You need routers that forward multicasts in order to find WINS servers on remote subnets.) If the sending WINS server finds another WINS machine, it makes the other server a push/pull replication partner and sets the pull interval to 2 hours.

Replication partners configured via this automatic mechanism are removed when WINS shuts down. If you want them to be activated again immediately at startup, you have to configure them manually as replication partners.

Managing and Monitoring WINS

Most of your WINS management and monitoring occurs at the WINS console — a Microsoft Management Console in the Administrative Tools folder. (Incidentally, the actual file is WINSMGMT.MSC in the *%SystemRoot%*\System32 folder, where *%SystemRoot%* is usually C:\WINNT.)

Backing up and restoring the database

You can back up the WINS database (WINS.MDB, normally in C:\WINNT\SYSTEM32\WINS) manually or automatically. The first time you perform a manual backup, WINS sets up automatic backups to occur at three-hour intervals.

Configuring WINS backup

To configure WINS backup:

1. **Open the WINS console.**

2. **Right-click the server in the tree pane and choose Properties.**

3. **On the General tab (see Figure 6-8), either enter a path or browse to a path in the Database Backup area.**

   WINS creates a new folder named WINS_BAK under the folder you identify, which must be on a local disk.

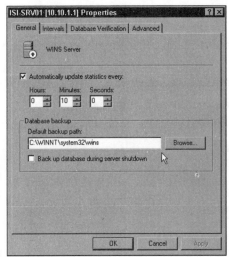

Figure 6-8:
Specifying
backup
options.

4. **Check Back Up Database During Server Shutdown if you desire this option.**

5. **Click OK.**

Performing WINS backup

To perform a manual backup after you've identified the backup folder:

1. **Open the WINS console.**

2. **Right-click the server in the tree pane, and choose Back Up Database.**

3. **Click the OK button to confirm the target folder.**

   The Browse For Folder dialog box is misleading. The highlighted folder is the one you named when configuring WINS backup. Do not choose the WINS_BAK folder underneath the folder you named.

4. **When you see the message notifying you of a successful backup, click OK.**

   To confuse things even more, WINS doesn't back up the files to the WINS_BAK folder, but to a subfolder of WINS_BAK named NEW.

You should also perform periodic backups of the Registry on the WINS server, because WINS maintains many configuration settings in the Registry.

Restoring a WINS backup

To restore a backed-up WINS database:

1. **Open the WINS console.**

2. **Right-click the server in the tree pane and choose All Tasks⇨Stop.**

3. **Choose Action⇨Refresh a few times until you see that the database is stopped.**

4. **Right-click the server in the tree pane and choose Properties.**

5. **Click the Advanced tab, as shown in Figure 6-9.**

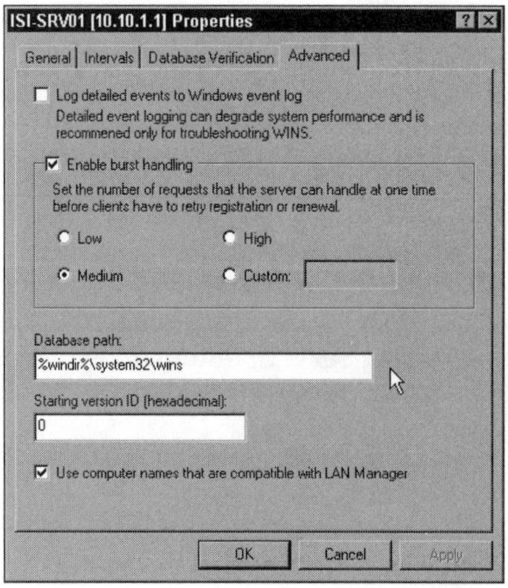

Figure 6-9: Finding the WINS database location.

ISI-SRV01 [10.10.1.1] Properties

General | Intervals | Database Verification | Advanced

☐ Log detailed events to Windows event log
  Detailed event logging can degrade system performance and is recommended only for troubleshooting WINS.

☑ Enable burst handling
  Set the number of requests that the server can handle at one time before clients have to retry registration or renewal.

  ○ Low   ○ High
  ◉ Medium   ○ Custom

Database path:
%windir%\system32\wins

Starting version ID (hexadecimal):
0

☑ Use computer names that are compatible with LAN Manager

OK   Cancel   Apply

6. **Note the database path specification.**

7. **In Windows Explorer, delete all files in the database path you discovered in Step 6.**

8. **Back in the WINS console, right-click the server in the tree pane and choose Restore Database.**

   If you don't see this command, WINS hasn't yet stopped. Wait some more.

9. **Specify the folder where the backup database resides and click OK.**

A faster way to perform a database restore may be to configure a replication with another WINS server, if one is available. Clever, eh?

Deleting database records

Occasionally, the WINS database may not delete registrations that are no longer valid. Also, released registrations do not instantly disappear from the database. You configure database cleanup on the Intervals tab in the server's Properties dialog box, as shown in Figure 6-10.

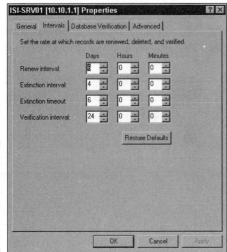

Figure 6-10:
Setting
database
house-
keeping
intervals.

Here's the least you must know about these housekeeping intervals:

✔ **Renew interval** is the NetBIOS name lease duration. The default is 6 days.

✔ **Extinction interval** is the delay between when WINS marks a registration as released and when WINS marks it extinct. The default is 4 days.

✔ **Extinction timeout** is the delay between when WINS marks a registration as extinct and when WINS deletes it from the database. The default is the renew interval; the minimum is 24 hours.

✔ **Verification interval** is the delay between when WINS registers names from another WINS server and when WINS verifies that those registrations are still valid. The default is 24 days; the minimum is also 24 days. Click the Database Verification tab to specify additional details about the verification process, such as the maximum number of records to verify each time. (You can manually initiate verification at any time by right-clicking the server and choosing Verify Database Consistency.)

You can clear the WINS database manually by opening the WINS console, right-clicking the server, and choosing Scavenge Database.

Compacting the database

Compacting a database essentially rebuilds it so that it occupies the least possible amount of disk space. According to Microsoft, compacting the WINS database is not an activity that you should need to perform under normal circumstances, which makes it an ideal subject for sick and twisted exam designers (the only kind, incidentally). Here's the procedure:

1. **Stop the WINS service in the WINS console by right-clicking the server and choosing All Tasks⇨Stop.**

2. **Wait until the console shows you that WINS has, indeed, stopped.**

3. **Open a command window by choosing Start⇨Run and then typing** CMD.

4. **Change to C:\WINNT\SYSTEM32\WINS (or wherever you have set as the WINS database path).**

5. **Run the following command, substituting whatever you want for ANYNAME:**

```
JETPACK WINS.MDB ANYNAME.MDB
```

   Windows copies WINS.MDB to the new file ANYNAME.MDB, compacting it in the process, and then copies ANYNAME.MDB back to WINS.MDB.

6. **Go back to the WINS console and restart the service.**

Viewing and logging WINS statistics

To view statistics for a given WINS server, right-click the server's icon in the tree pane of the WINS console and choose Display Server Statistics. You can see information about queries, releases, registrations, replications, and automatic scavenging. The refresh interval for this display is 10 minutes, but you can update it at any time by clicking Refresh.

You can also enable more-detailed-than-normal logging on the Advanced tab of the WINS server's Properties dialog box. (The checkbox is Log Detailed Events To Windows Event Log.) Use the Event Viewer to see the detailed entries that WINS pours into the System log. Only activate this detailed level of logging if you're troubleshooting a problem; it bogs down performance.

Prep Test

1 You manage a network with a fair number of down-level Windows clients running NT, 95, and 98. Your boss has asked you to take steps to minimize NetBIOS traffic on your overworked LAN. You have already implemented an NBNS on a Windows 2000 Server computer. What else can you do? (Choose the best answer.)

A ○ Set up a WINS server.

B ○ Set up DHCP to disable WINS on the client.

C ○ Configure LMHOSTS with #PRE entries.

D ○ Configure LMHOSTS with #POST entries.

2 You work with a network containing Windows 2000 Professional and OS/2 clients and Windows 2000 servers. The OS/2 clients need to be able to perform NetBIOS name resolution from the WINS database on one of the Windows 2000 Server machines. What should you do to achieve this result? (Choose the best answer.)

A ○ Set up a WINS proxy.

B ○ Set up a static mapping.

C ○ Configure the OS/2 client for the WINS server's IP address.

D ○ Assign the OS/2 client the WINS server's IP address using DHCP.

3 A WINS client issues a name query to the primary WINS server configured in its TCP/IP property sheet. The WINS server does not respond. What does the WINS client do now, before issuing a b-node query? (Choose all that apply.)

A ❑ Try the primary WINS server again.

B ❑ Try any secondary WINS servers.

C ❑ Check LMHOSTS.

D ❑ Check the NetBIOS name cache.

4 WINS replication is causing too much traffic across your WAN links. What should you do? (Choose the best answer.)

A ○ Set push replication to occur when the network is idle.

B ○ Set pull replication to occur when the network is idle.

C ○ Set push/pull replication to occur when the network is idle.

D ○ Fire half your employees.

5 Your WINS database seems to be occupying a lot of server disk space. You come in one Sunday evening and decide to compact it manually. Before you use the JETPACK command, what step must you take? (Choose the best answer.)

A ○ Boot the server to Safe Mode.

B ○ Stop the TCP/IP NetBIOS Helper service.

C ○ Stop the WINS service.

D ○ Make sure all network users are logged off.

6 You sign on as a new systems analyst for Gary's Gear Shift Knobs, Inc. You discover, to your shock, that the network has no WINS server, and that some clients are unable to connect to needed resources as a result. The employee you are replacing tells you that he created an LMHOSTS file containing static mappings for non-WINS-capable clients. How can you enter those mappings into your new WINS server most efficiently? (Choose the best answer.)

A ○ Open the WINS console. Right-click Replication Partners, choose Import LMHOSTS File, and then specify the file.

B ○ Open the TCP/IP property sheet. Click Advanced and then click the WINS tab. Click the Import LMHOSTS button and specify the file.

C ○ Open the WINS console. Right-click Active Registrations, choose Import LMHOSTS File, and then specify the file.

D ○ Open the WINS console. Right-click the WINS server, choose Properties, click the Advanced tab, and enter the file path in the Import LMHOSTS field.

7 Your boss says that the budget contains no money for a dedicated WINS server on your Windows network, and you're going to have to rely on LMHOSTS files for NetBIOS name resolution. What could you do to lessen the administrative burden of using LMHOSTS files? (Choose all that apply.)

A ❑ Use folder redirection to store a single copy of LMHOSTS for all network users.

B ❑ Use a shortcut where TCP/IP would expect to find the LMHOSTS file, and configure the shortcut to point to a network location.

C ❑ Use #DOM keywords to incorporate settings from a master LMHOSTS file that lives on a domain controller.

D ❑ Use #INCLUDE keywords to incorporate settings from a master LMHOSTS file that lives on a network server.

8 You're configuring a DHCP server to set up WINS on client machines. Which codes should you configure? (Choose all that apply.)

A ❑ 044

B ❑ 045

C ❑ 054

D ❑ 046

Answers

1 **C.** *Configure LMHOSTS with #PRE entries.* By configuring #PRE entries in LMHOSTS with NetBIOS-to-IP mappings for frequently accessed hosts, you can reduce the need for clients to go to the network to resolve NetBIOS names. Choice A is wrong because WINS is an NBNS server (NBNS means NetBIOS Name Service) and the question says you already have that. As for choice B, disabling WINS would increase traffic, not reduce it. In choice D, the #POST keyword doesn't exist. *See "Configuring LMHOSTS behavior at the client."*

2 **A.** *Set up a WINS proxy.* A WINS proxy can listen for NetBIOS name query broadcasts from the OS/2 client and forward them to the WINS server. Choice B is wrong because a static mapping is only used when WINS clients need to find non-WINS clients, the opposite of this situation. Neither C nor D can work, because WINS doesn't support OS/2 clients. *See "Creating a WINS proxy."*

3 **A and B.** The client goes through the list of WINS servers before issuing a broadcast message. C is wrong because the WINS client checks LMHOSTS only *after* it attempts a broadcast. Choice D is wrong because the WINS client checks the NetBIOS name cache *before* it tries to contact a WINS server. *See "WINS name resolution query."*

4 **B.** *Set pull replication to occur when the network is idle.* Pull replication means that you specify the start time and interval for database updates. It's used for slow links (such as many WAN links). Choices A and C are wrong because you can't schedule push replication or push-pull replication to occur only at specific times, and because these replication types are less suited to slow links. Choice D is just mean. *See "Push me, pull you."*

5 **C.** *Stop the WINS service.* Choice A isn't necessary and could take quite a while. Choices B and D aren't necessary, either. Stop the WINS service using the WINS management console. *See "Compacting the database."*

6 **C.** *Open the WINS console. Right-click Active Registrations, choose Import LMHOSTS File, and then specify the file.* Remember that static mappings are only for non-WINS clients, so you would not perform this operation if the LMHOSTS file given to you by your predecessor contained mappings for WINS-capable machines. *See "Creating a static mapping."*

7 **D.** *Use #INCLUDE keywords to incorporate settings from a master LMHOSTS file that lives on a network server.* In this scheme, you could make sure the centrally located LMHOSTS file reflects recent additions, deletions, and changes to NetBIOS-IP mappings, instead of running around to each machine. If you go with this method, you may want to set up a couple of servers with central LMHOSTS files and #INCLUDE them both, for fault tolerance. *See "Alternatives to WINS."*

8 **A and D.** The DHCP codes are 044 (WINS/NBNS Servers) and 046 (WINS/ NBT Node type). You should just memorize these. *See "Installing and activating WINS on a client."*

Part III

LAN/WAN
Infrastructure:
Connecting
the Dots

The 5th Wave   By Rich Tennant

"BETTER CALL MIS AND TELL THEM ONE OF OUR NETWORKS HAS GONE BAD."

In this part . . .

*W*hen I was a young lad in Houston, Texas, I had a schoolmate named Arun Jain, whose dad worked for IBM. We carpooled together, and Arun's dad once gave me a roll of black paper tape with thousands of holes punched in it. That roll of punched paper tape, its intricate and beautiful patterns hiding secret and important information, made me realize that a fascinating career lay ahead of me in the field of computing.

Not. That roll of tape actually made me think that computing was surely the most boring career possible, no offense to Arun or his father, and confirmed my decision to become a field biologist, preferably somewhere cool like Australia or Scotland. That didn't pan out — there were too many Latin words you had to memorize — but the world of business holds some of the same fascinations as the world of natural science. Helping organizations grow, and helping them develop their internal and external communications systems so that they can interact productively with other organizations and individuals, is a pursuit rich with ecological and biological parallels.

For example, wide-area network links are a little like global atmospheric or oceanic currents, affecting communities over remote distances but on a different time scale than local wind and water patterns. For another example, the Microsoft company is like an 800-pound gorilla, which is one reason why you want Microsoft certification. To that end, this Part deals with wide-area networking issues: remote access, routing, and Internet connectivity.

Chapter 7

Configuring and Supporting Remote Access

●●

Exam Objectives

▶ Configure inbound connections

▶ Configure a remote access profile

▶ Configure a virtual private network (VPN)

▶ Configure multilink connections

▶ Configure Routing and Remote Access for DHCP integration

▶ Manage and monitor remote access

▶ Configure authentication protocols

▶ Configure encryption protocols

▶ Create a remote access policy

●●●

*Y*ou can't turn on the TV or radio without hearing about all these great advances in communications technology. At social gatherings everywhere, Internet connection speed has replaced CPU speed as the basis for technological one-upmanship. The canonical authorities should ratify an eleventh commandment: Thou Shalt Not Covet Thy Neighbor's Fractional T-1 Line. What I want to know is, when are these advances going to make their way to my neck of the woods? On a good day, I can connect to the Net from home at 26Kbps. The phone and cable company salespeople just laugh and hang up when I call them about DSL and cable modems.

Exam 70-216 presumes that you work, or will work, in an organization with many more communications options than I have from my home office. This chapter explains the nuts and bolts of remote access connectivity. When I took the exam, it hit this subject hard, so this chapter is one of the longer ones. Get some coffee. (*Translation for UK readers:* Get some tea.)

Quick Assessment

Configure inbound connections	**1** To configure an inbound connection on a standalone Windows 2000 Server computer, you can use either _____ or _____.
Create a remote access profile	**2** To create or modify a dial-in profile, start with the _____ node in the Routing and Remote Access console's tree pane.
Configure a virtual private network (VPN)	**3** You want to use IPSec with a VPN. You should choose the _____ VPN protocol.
Configure multilink connections	**4** The protocol that adds and drops connections on demand is _____.
Configure Routing and Remote Access for DHCP integration	**5** RRAS gets _____ IP addresses at a time from a DHCP server for use configuring remote access clients.
Manage and monitor remote access	**6** The RRAS log file is stored in the _____ folder by default.
Configure authentica-tion protocols	**7** A smart-card user would most likely use the _____ authentication protocol.
Configure encryption protocols	**8** Your three choices for RRAS dial-in encryption are _____, _____, and _____.
Create a remote access policy	**9** A remote access policy's grant-or-deny permission setting is only effective if the Windows 2000 domain is running in _____ mode.
	10 You would configure a remote access profile to limit the duration of a RRAS session using the _____ tab of the profile property sheet.

Answers

1   *Network and Dial-Up Connections; Routing and Remote Access.* The section "A tale of two tools" elaborates.

2   *Remote Access Policies.* A remote access profile is part of a remote access policy. See "Remote access profiles" for more.

3   *L2TP.* "Remote access protocols" has the details.

4   *BAP.* "Bandwidth Allocation Protocol" would also be accepted by the judges. See the "Configuring multilink operation" section.

5   *10.* You can change the value in the Registry. For more, check out "Configuring DHCP integration" in this chapter.

6   *C:\WINNT\SYSTEM32\LOGFILES.* For this and other tender nuggets, see "Monitoring RRAS."

7   *EAP.* If you said "Extensible Authentication Protocol," give yourself extra credit for knowing the acronym. The "Authentication basics" section elaborates.

8   *No Encryption; Basic; Strong.* The "Remote access profiles" section offers details if you need them.

9   *Native.* That is, as opposed to "mixed." See "Dial-in permissions."

10   *Dial-in Constraints.* See "Remote access profiles" for more on the specific constraints you can configure.

Remote Access Basics

Remote access is a computer's ability to access another computer or network that is either distant or not connected by the usual permanent network adapter. (I have to add that last part because even a Direct Cable Connection, which may use a four-foot cable between two computers, is considered "remote" access.)

Servers, clients, and gateways — oh my

Every remote access connection has a *client* (the computer requesting the connection) and a *server* (the computer providing the connection). Windows 2000 software is not always available for both ends of a connection. For example, a Windows 2000 Server computer can act as a server for Apple Macintosh connections, but not as a client for such connections.

Normally, workstation-class machines running Windows 2000 Professional are remote access clients, and server-class machines running Windows 2000 Server are remote access servers. Windows 2000 Server ships with software designed specifically for hosting remote connections: Routing and Remote Access, or RRAS. However, a Windows 2000 Server can be a remote access client if it needs to, and a Windows 2000 Professional computer can host a communications session as a remote access server.

Outbound connections are those that you set up on the remote access client. *Inbound* connections are those that you set up on the remote access server.

Windows 2000 remote access servers typically act as *gateways* to the network where they live. That is to say, remote users connect to a remote access server, and through that server gain access to the entire network of which the remote access server is a part. The remote users can then work on the network as though they were physically present. The remote access server acts merely as a conduit through which the remote access clients access network resources — files, applications, printers, and so forth.

The gateway capability includes a routing capability, meaning that your connection to the remote access server doesn't even have to use the same LAN protocol that the remote access server uses to communicate with the central network. For example, you could connect to your company's network from your home PC, running NWLink, and gain access to network servers that run TCP/IP. (You may now begin to understand why Microsoft combined the routing and remote-access software modules into one utility in Windows 2000.)

You don't *have* to set up Windows 2000 Server as a routing and remote access server. For example, you can turn off the routing function of RRAS by clearing the Enable IP Routing checkbox on the server's IP property sheet. With that configuration, remote users can only access the RRAS server machine itself, not any other network resources.

When you set up a RRAS server as a routing gateway, and you use a public network (such as the Internet) to connect remote clients to the RRAS server, you have a Virtual Private Network (VPN). I discuss VPNs in more detail in the section "Remote access protocols," later in this chapter.

Remote access hardware

The exam doesn't spend much time dealing with hardware details. Know that Windows 2000 remote access can work across public dial-up lines, Integrated Services Digital Network (ISDN) lines, cable modems, X.25 adapters, parallel cables, serial cables, and infrared ports. That's about all you need to know about remote access hardware issues, aside from Windows 2000's *multilink* capability, which I discuss later in the chapter (see the section "Configuring multilink operation").

Remote access protocols

For remote access to work, a new protocol, called a *communications protocol* or a *remote access protocol,* is necessary — one that handles the establishment of the connection between the two communicating computers. (In a regular permanent LAN connection, the connection is permanent and needs no separate establishment.)

The choice you make for your remote access protocol is determined by the kind of computer (server) you're dialing into, for an outbound connection, and by the kind of computer (client) you're expecting to dial into your server, for an inbound connection. Choose a remote access protocol that the other computer doesn't support, and you won't connect. You have the following choices:

✔ **PPP:** *Point-to-Point Protocol* is the default choice for remote access connections because it's the most reliable, secure, and efficient connection protocol. Unlike SLIP, PPP supports error checking. It works with NetBEUI, IPX/SPX, and TCP/IP network protocols, and it works with non-Windows computers. Windows 2000 supports PPP on both the client and server sides.

✔ **RAS:** *Remote Access Server* (the strictly correct protocol name is *Asynchronous NetBEUI*) is supported in Windows 2000 on the server side of a remote access connection for interoperability with clients running NT 3.1, Windows for Workgroups, Windows 3.1, DOS, or LAN Manager. On the client side, Windows 2000 PCs running RAS can connect to servers running those same legacy operating systems.

✔ **ARAP:** Apple Remote Access Protocol permits Macintosh clients to dial into a Windows 2000 RRAS server. Microsoft does not supply a client-side ARAP component.

✔ **SLIP:** *Serial Line Interface Protocol,* or SLIP, is old, slow, and a bad choice unless you're calling up an old, slow UNIX server that doesn't work with PPP. No error correction, no encrypted passwords, no automatic IP address assignment. Windows 2000 only supports SLIP for the client side of a remote access connection.

A variation on the remote access theme is the *virtual private network,* or *VPN*. A VPN is a private network link that isn't really private and doesn't use a normal network connection (hence the *virtual*). A VPN creates a secure tunnel through an intermediary network, such as the public Internet, through which two computers can communicate privately and securely. The VPN bundles up IP, IPX, or NetBEUI packets inside PPP packets. VPNs are different from "normal" dial-up links in that they provide not only authentication, but also encryption and compression.

VPNs use special protocols, too, but they're a bit different from the remote access protocols mentioned earlier, like PPP. For one thing, a VPN link may use an existing permanent Internet connection, as opposed to a temporary dial-up link; all a VPN needs is IP connectivity of some kind between the communicating systems. For another, because VPN traffic may cross public networks, the VPN remote access protocols must provide some mechanism for encryption.

The remote access protocols that VPNs use are *PPTP,* or *Point-to-Point Tunneling Protocol,* and *L2TP,* or *Layer 2 Tunneling Protocol.* Here's what you must know about these communications protocols:

✔ Both PPTP and L2TP work over dial-up lines, local network links, wide-area network links, and public TCP/IP networks such as the Internet.

✔ PPTP requires an IP network connection. L2TP can work with an IP, ATM, frame relay, or X.25 connection. (You don't need to know the details of these connection types for the exam.)

✔ L2TP provides tunneling but not encryption. You would therefore normally use L2TP in combination with *IPsec* (Internet Protocol Security, a set of security protocols to protect the privacy of IP communications). PPTP provides encryption via PPP.

✔ L2TP uses header compression for lower overhead; PPTP doesn't.

After the remote access protocol sets up the connection, communication between computers takes place with "normal" LAN protocols. The LAN protocols, or transport protocols, that Windows 2000 supports include the following:

- ✔ TCP/IP
- ✔ NetBEUI
- ✔ NWLink
- ✔ AppleTalk (but not for VPNs)

Authentication basics

Obviously, remote access connections raise big-time security concerns. Just as the act of publishing your phone number makes you vulnerable to any idiot with a phone book, so the act of setting up a remote access server makes you vulnerable to any idiot with a modem — or, worse, any criminal with a modem. Therefore, Windows 2000 remote access tools come with lots of security features. One of those is the ability to authenticate remote users before letting 'em into the network.

Here's what you need to know about logon authentication protocols:

- ✔ **PAP (Password Authentication Protocol)** uses no password encryption (passwords travel in *cleartext*) and may be required for communicating with non-Windows systems. PAP is a low-security authentication protocol.

- ✔ **CHAP (Challenge Handshake Authentication Protocol)** authenticates the client and uses one-way encryption. This is a high-security authentication protocol that works with non-Windows systems. A synonym for CHAP is MD5 (Message Digest 5).

- ✔ **MS-CHAP (Microsoft Challenge-Handshake Authentication Protocol)** authenticates the client and uses one-way encryption. This is a high-security authentication protocol but requires Windows systems (NT 4, 95, 98, or 2000).

- ✔ **MS-CHAPv2** is another Microsoft protocol; this extension of MS-CHAP authenticates both client and server.

  MS-CHAPv2 is required over MS-CHAPv1 for encrypted PPP or PPTP connections and provides the strongest security available for a RRAS connection.

- ✔ **SPAP (Shiva Password Authentication Protocol)** is used for dialing into and out of Shiva (that's a brand name) communication products. It doesn't support data encryption but it does perform password encryption and is therefore a medium-security authentication protocol.

✔ **EAP (Extensible Authentication Protocol)** is an extension to PPP and evolved to support smart cards and other related devices. With EAP, client and server negotiate an authentication method — such as Transport Level Security (TLS), a smart-card authentication standard.

A tale of two tools

Windows 2000 offers two main tools for remote access: the Network and Dial-Up Connections folder, and the Routing and Remote Access service.

Here's when to use these tools to create or modify a remote access link:

✔ If you're using Windows 2000 Professional, use the Network and Dial-Up Connections folder for outbound and inbound connections. (Windows 2000 Professional doesn't come with RRAS.)

✔ If you're using Windows 2000 Server and it's not part of a domain, use Network and Dial-Up Connections for outbound and inbound connections.

✔ If you're using Windows 2000 Server and it *is* part of a domain, use Network and Dial-Up Connections for outbound connections, and use Routing and Remote Access for inbound connections.

Henceforth, in order to save time, space, and trees, I will abbreviate Network and Dial-Up Connections as NADUC (pronounced "nay-duck") and Routing and Remote Access Service as RRAS (pronounced "rrrrrrazz" to distinguish it from the old Windows NT RAS, pronounced "raz"). NADUC is my own abbreviation; Microsoft uses the RRAS abbreviation.

Network and Dial-Up Connections (NADUC)

The Network and Dial-Up Connections software (we used to call it DUN, for Dial-Up Networking, on the Windows 9x platform) lets you connect a Windows 2000 PC to a remote computer or to a remote network over a telephone line — be it regular analog or ISDN — or cable, or infrared link.

Central control

In Windows 2000, Microsoft decided to lump all connections — local and remote, regardless of media — into a single folder: Network and Dial-Up Connections, or NADUC. Get there by choosing Start⇨Programs⇨ Accessories⇨Communications⇨Network and Dial-Up Connections, or (more quickly) by choosing Start⇨Settings⇨Network and Dial-Up Connections, or (most quickly) by right-clicking My Network Places and choosing Properties. You see a window that looks something like the one in Figure 7-1. No more bouncing around between a Dial-Up Networking folder and a Network control panel; all connection settings are here in one place.

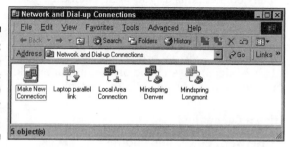

Figure 7-1: The Windows 2000 connectivity folder.

NADUC is where you configure both inbound and outbound connections, for Windows 2000 Professional can host incoming sessions as well as dial out to other networks.

The NADUC folder, which replaces the Network control panel you use in earlier versions of Windows, is very *deep* — that is, it has lots of settings and options. Thankfully, Microsoft has provided a Make New Connection wizard that gets you through most of the initial configuration.

Also, certain aspects of this folder's setup are automatic. For example, you can't manually create an icon for a LAN connection; Windows 2000 creates one for you automagically, when it detects a network interface card. (Windows 2000 does *not* automatically create an icon for a dial-up connection if the operating system detects a modem, however, for the good reason that a human being must supply a phone number to create a dial-up link.)

Connection independence

With some exceptions (such as dialing rules, rules for how Windows "fills in" partial DNS names, and so on), each connection that you create has its own communications settings. That is, two different connections can have different sets of DNS server addresses on their respective TCP/IP property sheets.

(I know, it sounds obvious, but it didn't work that way in Windows 95!) Generally, if a given setting isn't connection-specific but instead is global, the relevant property sheet advises you of the fact.

Creating an outbound connection with NADUC

A *connectoid* is Microspeak for a connection icon. You create connectoids on a Windows 2000 client by using the Network Connection wizard in the Network and Dial-Up Connections virtual folder, as Lab 7-1 demonstrates. You can create as many connections as you want; each time you create a new connection, a new connectoid appears in the NADUC folder.

The procedure for creating a dial-up connection is similar whether you're creating a regular dial-up link, a virtual private network link, or a direct cable connection. Lab 7-1 demonstrates the procedure for a plain-vanilla modem link and assumes that you've installed a modem.

Lab 7-1	**Creating a Connectoid**

1. **Right-click My Network Places and choose Properties.**

2. **Double-click the Make New Connection icon.**

   An explanatory screen appears. Note its title — Network Connection Wizard. The exam may refer to this program as the "Network Connection Wizard" *or* as the "Make New Connection" wizard; they mean the same thing. (User interface error #1,274.)

3. **Click Next to get past the verbiage.**

   The dialog box shown in Figure 7-2 appears.

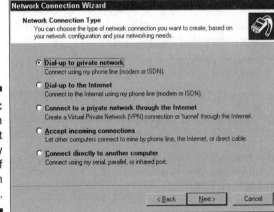

Figure 7-2:
You can create just about any kind of connection here.

Network Connection Wizard

Network Connection Type
You can choose the type of network connection you want to create, based on your network configuration and your networking needs.

○ **Dial-up to private network**
Connect using my phone line (modem or ISDN).

○ **Dial-up to the Internet**
Connect to the Internet using my phone line (modem or ISDN).

○ **Connect to a private network through the Internet**
Create a Virtual Private Network (VPN) connection or 'tunnel' through the Internet.

○ **Accept incoming connections**
Let other computers connect to mine by phone line, the Internet, or direct cable.

○ **Connect directly to another computer**
Connect using my serial, parallel, or infrared port.

< Back   Next >   Cancel

4. **Click the Dial-Up To Private Network button and click Next.**

   If you click Dial-Up To The Internet, Windows 2000 hands you off to the old *Internet Connection Wizard,* which is largely the same as it was in earlier Windows versions. You can create a new ISP account, move an existing account's settings to this PC, or specify details for a LAN-based Internet connection.

5. **If you have more than one dial-up device, choose the one you want for this connection and click Next.**

6. **Enter a phone number to dial and click the check box if you want this connection to follow the dialing rules you set in the Phone and Modem Options control panel. Click Next.**

7. **Specify whether you want all users of this PC to have access to the connection, or only you. Click Next.**

   This setting determines whether others that log on to the PC with different user accounts can use the icon that you are creating. Note that this is different from sharing the connection in the sense of Internet Connection Sharing (ICS), in which users of other physical computers can share the physical link you are configuring. Chapter 9 has more on ICS.

8. **Type a name for the new connection. Check the check box if you want Windows to add a shortcut icon to your desktop.**

9. **Click Finish, and marvel as Windows creates a new icon in the Network and Dial-Up Connections folder.**

   You're not really finished, of course. You probably need to configure your network protocol settings and modem settings, for example.

Creating an inbound connection with NADUC

The Network and Dial-Up Connections folder also contains icons for any inbound connections you may want to create. Lab 7-2 goes through the steps.

Lab 7-2	Creating an Inbound Connection with NADUC

1. **Log on as Administrator and start the Make New Connection wizard as usual.**

2. **In the Network Connection Type dialog box, select Accept Incoming Connections.**

3. **Choose the device (modem and parallel port are the usual choices) and configure it, if you want, by clicking the Properties button.**

4. **You can then tell Windows to accept incoming VPN connections, as long as your computer has a unique Internet domain name or IP address.**

5. **The rest of the process is straightforward: Specify who can have access to this inbound connection and set *callback* options for each user.**

   Callback simply means that your computer authenticates incoming callers, hangs up, and calls them back at a predefined phone number. This method increases security and localizes long distance or other carrier charges.

6. **Select the network components that you need for the inbound connection.**

   Choose only the minimum components (protocols, services, and clients) necessary to provide the required connectivity.

7. **Name your connection, and you're done.**

Routing and Remote Access

Routing and Remote Access (RRAS) is the tool to use for setting up inbound connections on a domain computer running Windows 2000 Server. The exam expects you to know this tool inside and out. (And I don't mean that you should read this section on your patio.)

Activating RRAS

When you install Windows 2000 Server, the setup program installs RRAS automatically; all you need to do is activate it. Lab 7-3 presents the procedure for activating RRAS to be a remote access server.

Before activating RRAS, install and test your communications hardware (modems, ISDN adapters, and so on). You should also install all network transport protocols you may want to use: TCP/IP, NWLink, and so on. Verify that your communications hardware and network protocols are all working correctly before you activate RRAS, and you won't have as much manual reconfiguration work to do later.

Lab 7-3	Activating a RRAS Remote Access Server

1. **Choose Start⇨Programs⇨Administrative Tools⇨Routing and Remote Access.**

2. **Right-click the server icon in the tree pane and choose Configure and Enable Routing and Remote Access.**

   The Routing and Remote Access Server Setup wizard starts.

3. **Click Next at the welcome window.**

You see the Common Configurations dialog box shown in Figure 7-3. You can set up an Internet connection server, which Chapter 9 examines in detail. You can set up a remote access server, which this lab illustrates. You can also choose to set up a VPN server. Chapter 8 deals with setting up a network router.

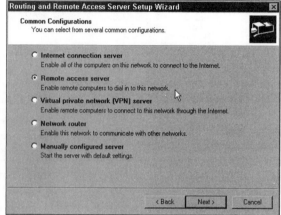

Figure 7-3:
From this
dialog box,
you can
create
several
different
server
types.

4. **Click Remote Access Server and then click the Next button.**

5. **In the Remote Client Protocols dialog box, click Yes, All Of The Required Protocols Are On This List and then click the Next button.**

If all the required LAN protocols aren't on the list displayed in this dialog box, you must quit the wizard and add protocols using the NADUC folder.

6. **If you have multiple network cards in the server, you see the Network Selection dialog box, where you should select the network to which Windows 2000 should funnel inbound connections, and click Next.**

7. **In the IP Address Assignment dialog box, click Automatically and then click the Next button.**

This is the most common setting. RRAS can use a DHCP server to assign IP addresses to client computers. The alternative is to specify a range of addresses for RRAS to assign, but that means more work for the network administrator. Using DHCP is easier if the service already exists on your network.

8. **In the Managing Multiple Remote Access Servers dialog box, choose No, I Don't Want To Set Up This Server To Use RADIUS Now and click Next.**

RADIUS is short for Remote Authentication Dial-In User Service, and it's a central database that handles authentication and accounting for several remote access servers.

9. **Click Finish to close the wizard.**

After a few moments, RRAS starts, and you see a console that looks like Figure 7-4. The server now has a green arrow indicating that it's up and running.

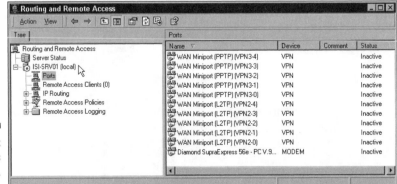

Figure 7-4:
RRAS is
rarin' to go.

Configuring RRAS ports and properties

After you've activated your remote access server, you have several other chores ahead of you before you can say the job is done. Setting up your RRAS ports and properties is the first order of business; later, you'll configure remote access policies and restrictions.

Configuring a RRAS port

RRAS normally autodetects installed serial modems, parallel ports, and other potential communications ports, when you install the service. However, you may need to change port settings if RRAS doesn't properly detect communication devices, or if you change your communications hardware after installing RRAS. Lab 7-4 explains the procedure.

Lab 7-4   Configuring a Communications Port in RRAS

1. **Choose Start⇨Programs⇨Administrative Tools⇨Routing and Remote Access.**

2. **In the tree pane, expand the tree if necessary, right-click Ports, and choose Properties.**

3. **Select a device in the Ports Properties dialog box (see Figure 7-5) and click the Configure button.**

You can configure a bunch of ports at once by holding down the Ctrl key while you click.

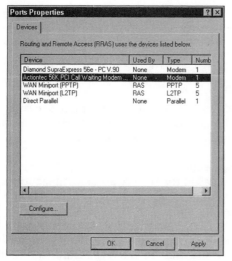

Figure 7-5:
Any port
in a storm.

4. **In the Configure Device dialog box, click applicable options, as shown in Figure 7-6.**

   Clicking Remote Access Connections (Inbound Only) enables the port for serving remote users. If you're just providing remote access, you can leave the Demand-Dial Routing Connections (Inbound And Outbound) setting cleared. If you're configuring a modem, fill in the Phone Number For This Device. Finally, if you're configuring a multiport device, set the Maximum Ports value to the number you want.

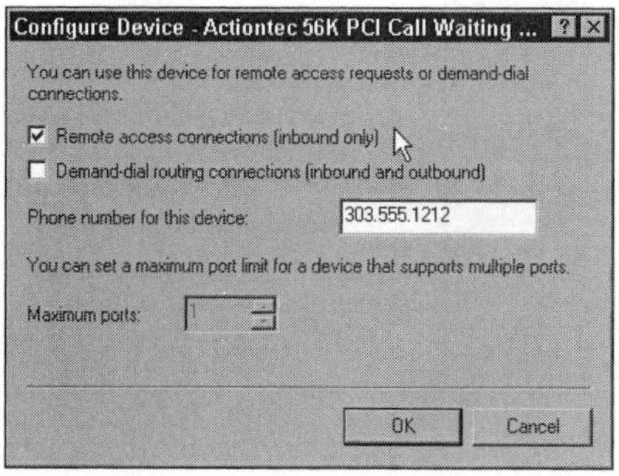

Figure 7-6:
Configuring
a port in
RRAS.

5. **Click OK, then click OK again, to get back to the RRAS console.**

   You should see your configuration changes reflected in the Ports detail pane of the RRAS console.

The procedure for configuring a VPN port is very similar to the procedure just described. RRAS automatically creates five PPTP ports and five L2TP ports for VPN use, but you can change that number without regard to the hardware in your PC: VPNs are logical connections, not physical connections.

Configuring multilink operation

One cool feature that Windows 2000 supports for remote access clients and servers is *multilink* operation — that is, combining two or more communications links to make them look and act like a single, faster link.

The Windows 2000 multilink feature uses a variation on the PPP theme called PPP multilink, which both sides of the remote access connection must support. This protocol works with modems, X.25 adapters, and ISDN lines (and you can mix and match devices, too).

Enable multilink PPP in the RRAS console by right-clicking the server, choosing Properties, and clicking the PPP tab (see Figure 7-7). Then, click the Multilink Connections check box. You must also enable multilink on the remote access client, typically on the connection's property sheet.

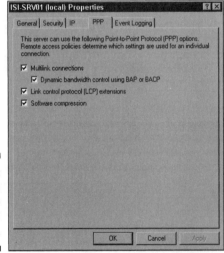

Figure 7-7:
Telling
RRAS to go
forth and
multiply.

Windows 2000 takes multilink operation further with something called *Bandwidth Allocation Protocol,* or *BAP.* BAP works behind the scenes to add or drop physical connections as necessary to meet user demand. For example, if a RRAS server is devoting two physical modems to a single multilink connection, but not much data transfer is going on, BAP tells RRAS to drop one of the modem connections so it's available for someone else.

In the opposite situation, if a client is using a single physical connection and needs more bandwidth, the client can ask the RRAS machine for another number to call. (That's why it's important to fill in the Phone Number For This Device field in the port configuration dialog box; see Lab 7-4, Step 4.) RRAS provides the phone number for any available port of the requested type, the client dials it, and both machines start using the additional link for increased throughput — all automatic.

Enable BAP globally by checking the Dynamic Bandwidth Control Using BAP Or BACP box on the PPP tab in the RRAS server's property sheet. Then, enable multilink on any relevant remote access profiles (see "Remote access profiles" later in this chapter).

About the only drawback of multilink PPP, aside from the fact that I can't always get it to work in my test network with different device types, is that it doesn't work well with callback authentication. That's when a remote user dials a RRAS machine, logs on, and then RRAS immediately hangs up and calls the user back at a predefined number. Note that I say "number," not "numbers," and you see why multilink and callback don't coexist, except in the case where two ISDN channels have the same phone number.

You can use multilink connections in the NADUC folder, too, as you would (for example) when configuring a Windows 2000 Professional machine as a remote access client. Just choose the connections you want to combine when you select your communications hardware in the Make New Connection wizard.

Configuring authentication

As I explain in the section on "Authentication basics," earlier in this chapter, Windows 2000 can use several methods for verifying that remote users are who they say they are: PAP, CHAP, MS-CHAP, and so on. In the RRAS console, you specify which authentication methods you want to allow RRAS to use on the Security tab in the server's Properties dialog box (see Figure 7-8).

On this tab, you specify whether you want to use Windows or a Remote Authentication Dial-In User Service (RADIUS) server, such as Internet Authentication Server (IAS), to provide authentication and accounting services for this RRAS machine. Some organizations with multiple remote access servers find it convenient to centralize authentication and accounting on a single server, such as an IAS server. A RADIUS server is an especially appealing solution for multivendor environments, as well as for organizations that want to outsource some of their remote access infrastructure.

If you use RADIUS, then RRAS forwards authentication requests to the IAS server. If you choose RADIUS authentication on the Security tab in the Properties dialog box for a RRAS server, you click the Configure button to add details about the RADIUS server (see Figure 7-9).

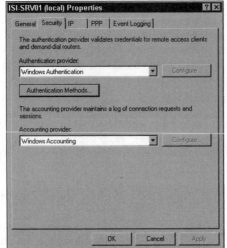

Figure 7-8:
Authentication settings, one of two.

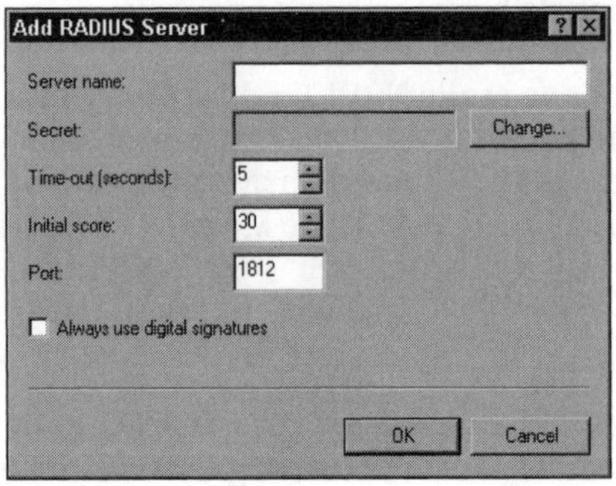

Figure 7-9:
Configuring RRAS to use a RADIUS server for authentication.

If you want fine-grained control over the authentication settings that your RRAS server can use, click the Authentication Methods button on the Security tab to display the Authentication Methods dialog box shown in Figure 7-10. Any protocol that has a cleared check box next to its name may not be used for authentication with this particular RRAS server.

If you don't want to require that remote access users supply a username and password, check the box labeled Allow Remote Systems To Connect Without Authentication.

EAP, or Extensible Authentication Protocol, is used mainly for smart-card authentication and other fancy technologies such as retinal scanners. If none of your remote access clients use such technologies, leave the EAP checkbox cleared.

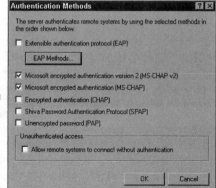

Figure 7-10:
Authenti-
cation
settings,
two of two.

RRAS attempts to authenticate remote users via the methods listed in order from top to bottom in the Authentication Methods dialog box. Note that the more secure authentication protocols are at the top. Makes sense.

Configuring DHCP integration

Exam 70-216 loves to ask questions about how the various network infra-structure components can interact. This little section provides a prime example, so listen up.

If you right-click a RRAS server, choose Properties, and select the IP tab, you see the dialog box shown in Figure 7-11. On this tab, you can change the IP addressing behavior that Windows made you specify when you originally activated the RRAS service. (Note on the figure: If your RRAS system has multiple network adapters, an additional field appears at the bottom of the IP tab asking you to pick the adapter that has a DHCP server. Windows 2000 just picks one at random by default.)

A remote access client running TCP/IP needs an IP address, subnet mask, and other TCP/IP configuration settings. A local access client typically gets this information from a Dynamic Host Control Protocol (DHCP) server on the local LAN. (See Chapter 5 for more than you ever wanted to know about DHCP.) But where and how can the poor remote access client get that information?

Configuring the client with a static IP address isn't a great solution, because the client may need to connect to different networks at different times, neces-sitating different IP addresses so that the network IDs match up. Also, static address assignment involves a lot of administrative overhead.

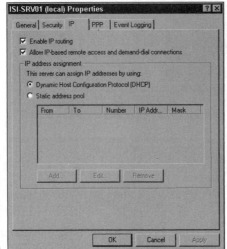

Windows 2000 presents two options:

✔ The RRAS server can assign IP addresses to remote access clients from a **predefined, static pool** of addresses. That's an okay method, and probably the one you'd use if your LAN doesn't have a DHCP server on board. However, you have some manual work to do in making sure that the address pool is neither too small nor too large, doesn't conflict with any other static or dynamic IP address assignments, and changes in size appropriately as RRAS usage traffic increases or decreases over time.

✔ The RRAS server can borrow IP addresses from an **existing DHCP server** on the LAN. This method is preferable if you have a DHCP server, because it's more of a set-it-and-forget-it approach. RRAS grabs ten IP addresses from DHCP to start with (taking the first one for its own server adapter), and grabs additional batches of ten addresses if and when needed. (You can change the number of addresses in a batch by editing the Registry.) When the RRAS service stops, it releases all the addresses that it borrowed from the DHCP server.

One drawback to the DHCP approach is that if the DHCP server is down, RRAS assigns IP addresses from the private network range of 169.254.0.1 through 169.254.255.254 — the same range Windows uses for Automatic Private IP Addressing (APIPA) in a TCP/IP LAN without DHCP. What can happen then is simple: Remote access clients may not be able to access the corporate network, although they could still access the RRAS machine.

As I explain in Chapter 5, DHCP typically provides a lot more information than just an IP address and subnet mask. It also provides the address of one or more DNS servers, WINS servers, and a DNS domain name. (Clients ask for this information with DHCPINFORM messages.)

Now, if a RRAS server uses DHCP for IP address assignment, the addresses of WINS and DNS servers get assigned along with the IP address. But how does the remote access client get this information if you've configured RRAS to assign IP addresses from a static pool? RRAS doesn't ask you for WINS and DNS server addresses; it just asks you for the IP address ranges in the static pool.

The answer is that RRAS uses the *DHCP Relay Agent* (a RRAS component) to forward those DHCPINFORM messages from a remote access client to a DHCP server on the network. (If you don't have a DHCP server, you have to configure the remote access clients with static addresses for DNS and WINS servers.)

RRAS sets up the DHCP Relay Agent automatically when you run the Routing and Remote Access Server Setup wizard, but you should double-check it manually, as follows:

✔ The DHCP Relay Agent node should contain the Internal interface, as shown in Figure 7-12. If it doesn't, right-click DHCP Relay Agent and choose New Interface.

✔ The DHCP Relay Agent needs the IP address of a DHCP server to use for processing DHCPINFORM messages. Right-click the DHCP Relay Agent node in the RRAS tree pane (it's under IP Routing), choose Properties, and enter one or more DHCP server addresses.

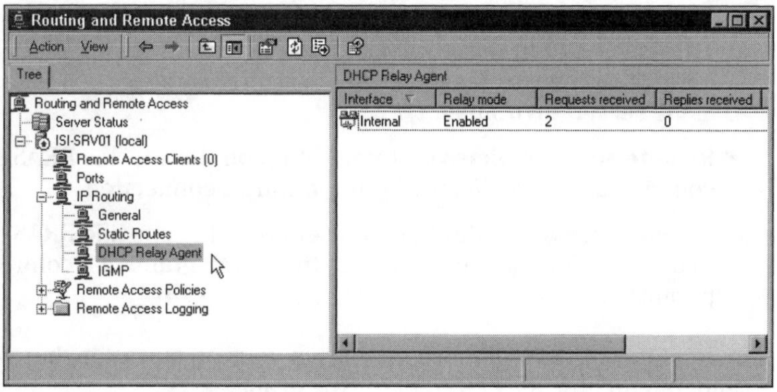

Figure 7-12: The DHCP Relay Agent handles non-IP-address DHCP chores.

Note that the DHCP Relay Agent is configured even if you choose to let RRAS use DHCP for IP address assignment. That doesn't hurt anything; if a remote access client issues a DHCPINFORM message after RRAS has already configured it with DNS and WINS server addresses, the DHCP Relay Agent simply processes the message and replies back to the client, most likely with the same address information that RRAS initially sent to the client. If the new information differs, however, then it takes precedence.

By using the Default Routing and Remote Access Class option class in DHCP, you can set remote access clients to have a shorter IP address lease duration than local LAN clients. That's a smart way to avoid tying up IP addresses excessively for remote users, who typically have short computing sessions. See Chapter 5 for details.

Configuring RRAS access

If you go through all the steps set forth in the previous sections, "Activating RRAS" and "Configuring RRAS ports and properties," then you try to dial up your newly activated and configured remote access server, you won't get in. This section deals with the very confusing subject of configuring RRAS access. Plan to read it twice, at least.

Access control overview

In many ways, Windows 2000 operates on a "need-to-know" basis, rather than a "need-to-withhold" basis. That is, access to network resources tends to be denied unless you explicitly enable it. RRAS is a good example: You must take explicit steps to allow users to gain access to your bright and shiny remote access server.

You also have to understand that a user's access to a RRAS machine is the result of a pretty complex combination of settings:

- The user's **dial-in permissions** (set in Active Directory Users and Groups for a domain environment, or in Local Users and Groups for a stand-alone server environment)

- **Remote access policies** that you set up on the specific RRAS server to contain various *conditions* for permitting a connection

- **Remote access profiles** that you set up on the specific RRAS server and that determine the type of access that RRAS grants if a connection is permitted

You don't have to use all these settings in your organization, but you do have to understand how they interact for the exam.

Dial-in permissions

You set a user's dial-in permissions via the Active Directory Users and Computers tool in a domain environment. Open the Users node in the tree pane, right-click the user in the details pane, and choose Properties. Then, click the Dial-In tab to see the dialog box shown in Figure 7-13.

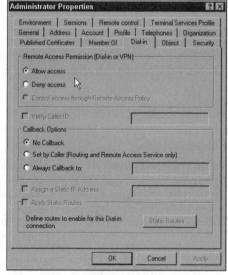

Figure 7-13:
Setting
dial-in
properties
for a user
account.

What you see in this dialog box depends on whether your Windows 2000 network runs in *native mode* (all servers run Windows 2000) or *mixed mode* (some servers run Windows NT Server). In native mode, or on a standalone server, all options are available; in mixed mode, only the Remote Access Permission and Callback Options areas are available.

Under Remote Access Permission (Dial-In Or VPN), you can make one of two or three choices:

✓ **Allow Access** means that the user passes the first hurdle, but may face other hurdles in the form of remote access policy conditions and profile restrictions (to be covered in a minute).

✓ **Deny Access** means that the user can't connect to a RRAS server, no matter what other conditions might be satisfied in a remote access policy.

✓ **Control Access Through Remote Access Policy** (only available for a standalone server or for a domain server in native mode) means that whether the user passes the first hurdle or not depends on the grant-or-deny permission setting in a remote access policy (see the next section).

The Callback Options let you add a healthy dollop of security in that the RRAS server authenticates the user, hangs up, and then dials the user back at a predetermined phone number. This feature is handy for employees who telecommute from home.

Remote access policies

Remote access policies are sets of conditions and restrictions on remote access connections. If a user gets past the hurdle of the account dial-in permissions (see the preceding section), the remote access policies take over in the decision process as to whether, and how, to allow the user access.

Here are three points to remember:

✔ At least one remote access policy must exist in order for anyone to access the RRAS computer remotely.

✔ If one or more remote access policies exist, the connection attempt must meet the conditions specified in at least one of those policies, or else Windows rejects the connection attempt.

✔ If multiple remote access policies exist, Windows chooses the first one in the list that matches, going from top to bottom. So, for example, if you want to grant access at any time of the day to everyone but members of the Temps group, who can only log on from 9:00 to 5:00, put the policy restricting the Temps group first and the policy granting access to the Everyone group second. Otherwise, members of Temps (who are also members of Everyone) could gain access at any time of day.

The best way to understand a remote access policy is to take a look at the automatically installed default remote access policy, whose properties you can view by right-clicking the policy in the details pane of the RRAS console's Remote Access Policies node. As shown in Figure 7-14, the name of this policy is Allow Access If Dial-In Permission Is Enabled.

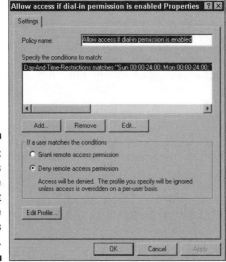

Figure 7-14:
Settings
for the
default
remote
access
policy.

Toward the top of the dialog box, you see a list named Specify The Conditions To Match. The default remote access profile has only one condition, a day-and-time condition, that covers the entire 24/7 time span. Every attempted RRAS connection meets that condition. So, this policy applies to everyone who tries to dial up this RRAS server.

Other conditions you can set include the following:

- ✔ Remote access protocol used by client (PPP, SLIP, and so on)
- ✔ Remote user's caller ID
- ✔ Membership to one or more Windows groups (the "Windows-Groups" condition)

Below the condition list is a box labeled If A User Matches The Conditions. Here, you tell the policy what it should do if all the conditions in the condition list are satisfied. The default remote access policy says "Deny Remote Access Permission," but you must remember that this denial only occurs if the user account's dial-in permission is set to Control Access Through Remote Access Policy. If the user account's dial-in permission is either Allow Access or Deny Access, this policy permission is irrelevant.

Remote access policies are stored on the local RRAS server (the file is IAS.MDB in the folder `C:\WINNT\SYSTEM32\IAS`), not in Active Directory. Makes sense, because some organizations want to use RRAS but don't use Active Directory. As a result, you can set different policies on different RRAS computers.

You can set up remote access policies from RRAS or from IAS, if you're using Internet Authentication Server. If you set them up on an IAS server, and point all your RRAS servers to IAS for authentication, you only have to create one set of remote access policies.

Remote access profiles

When you click the Edit Profile button on the remote access policy's Settings property sheet, you can create a set of constraints that determines what sort of access the user enjoys, after RRAS has already decided to permit a connection based on policy conditions and the user's dial-in permission. For example, you can make settings on the Dial-In Constraints tab (see Figure 7-15) that kill a connection after a predefined idle period, restrict a session's duration, restrict access to particular days and times, and permit a connection only if it comes in over a particular media type.

On the IP tab, you can set IP packet filters for the connection; Chapter 10 covers packet filters. The Multilink tab lets you explicitly allow or disallow multilink for the specific policy, or use the server's global default setting;

that's handy if you want to permit multilink operation for some groups but not others. Similarly, the Authentication tab lets you specify which authentication protocols to use for the policy (but be sure that the server's global settings also include the authentication methods you choose here).

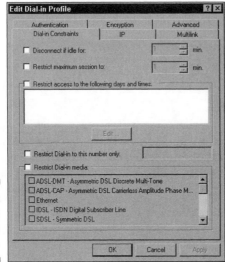

Figure 7-15:
Setting
dial-in
constraints.

The Encryption tab is worth an extra couple of minutes of your time. This tab offers three choices:

- ✔ **No Encryption** means that clients don't have to use any encryption method in order to connect to the RRAS server.
- ✔ **Basic** means that RRAS supports 40-bit encryption for IPSec (see Chapter 10) or MPPE (Microsoft Point-to-Point Encryption). (Careful, the Windows 2000 online help for the dialog box is wrong on this point.) Clients can connect with either encryption protocol.
- ✔ **Strong** means that RRAS supports 56-bit encryption for IPSec or MPPE.

Note that you can choose any combination depending on the possible encryption types you want to permit. For example, to require strong authentication for this profile, check its box and clear the other two checkboxes.

A remote access client must be using MS-CHAP (version 1 or 2) or EAP/TLS in order to use data encryption.

How everything interacts

Just plan on reading the following points over a few times until everything sinks in. I'm making this as simple as I can, believe me:

- ✔ If a user's dial-in permission is set to Deny Access, the user can't connect, period — even if the connection attempt meets the conditions specified in one or more remote access policies.

- ✔ If a user account's dial-in permission setting is either Allow Access or Deny Access, it overrides the remote access policy's similar permission setting. That's why the default remote access policy can say that it denies access to everyone, but you can change an individual user's dial-in permission to Allow Access and the user can gain access.

- ✔ It follows from the preceding point that the only time the remote access policy's permission (grant-or-deny) setting means anything is if the user's dial-in permission is set to Control Access Through Remote Access Policy. That's only possible in a pure, native-mode Windows 2000 network.

- ✔ A remote access policy's conditions list or profile can deny access even if the user's dial-in permission is set to grant access.

- ✔ All the conditions in a remote access policy must be satisfied, if multiple conditions exist for the policy.

A special problem

Remote user authentication can be a problem in a mixed-mode environment. Windows NT 4.0 servers running RAS but that are not domain controllers need to read user data from Active Directory in order to authenticate remote access clients. However, the servers are barred from doing so, because the NT RAS service has no credentials!

The problem can become evident if you have some non-domain-controller NT RAS servers and some Windows 2000 RRAS servers on the same network. Remote users can sometimes gain access to the network and sometimes can't, depending on whether they dial into an NT machine or a Windows 2000 machine.

Three solutions exist:

- ✔ Upgrade the NT server to Windows 2000 Server.

- ✔ Only use NT domain controllers for RAS. Domain controllers have the information needed to authenticate remote access users in the Registry.

- ✔ Loosen permissions for the Everyone group so that any member can read any property of any user object. The command is

```
net localgroup "Pre-Windows 2000 Compatible Access" Everyone
        /add
```

If you're just setting up a Windows 2000 Server to be a domain controller, you don't need to run the command at the end of the preceding list. Just run DCPROMO.EXE and, when prompted, select Permission Compatible with Pre-Windows 2000 Server.

Virtual Private Networking

Think of VPN as using the Internet as the communications medium instead of a traditional web of leased lines and wide-area network (WAN) carriers. The speed of a VPN is always subject to the speed of the various intervening Internet links, but if that's not a big deal, a VPN can save a company some money. A VPN can also increase the security of dial-up connections by providing encryption of the data stream.

I discuss remote access protocols for VPNs earlier in this chapter, in the section "Remote access protocols." Look that section over now, if you're not reading this chapter straight through.

Setting up a VPN link

Creating the VPN link on the server side follows very closely the sequence of steps in Lab 7-3, except in Step 5, you specify VPN Server instead of Remote Access Server, and follow the wizard from that point forward. You must also enable one or more inbound VPN connections in the Ports list of the RRAS console.

Create a VPN link in Windows 2000 on the client side by starting the Make New Connection wizard in the Network and Dial-Up Connections folder. Choose the Connect To A Private Network Through The Internet option.

Typically, to use the Internet to make a VPN connection, you use one icon to establish the Internet link, and another to establish the VPN tunnel. The first icon may already exist, in which case you should select it and click Automatically Dial This Initial Connection. If you don't need to create an ISP link (for example, because an always-on link already exists), click Do Not Dial The Initial Connection.

Follow the wizard and specify the domain name or IP address of the VPN server. As usual, you can also specify if you want the connection all to yourself or if you prefer to share it with other users of that PC. Name the connection and you're done.

Placing a VPN call

Establishing a VPN link via the Internet is easier than it is in Windows 98. Just double-click the connectoid that you created in the previous section. After Windows establishes the link, your PC behaves just as if it were logged on to the private network, rather than to the public Internet.

Monitoring RRAS

RRAS records its activities in three possible places: the System event log, the RRAS log on the local computer (if enabled), and the RADIUS IAS (Internet Authentication Server) machine (if present and enabled).

✔ RRAS manages logging to the System event log, but you can configure this function via the Event Logging tab in the RRAS server's Properties dialog box (see Figure 7-16); the default is Log The Maximum Amount Of Information. Use the Event Viewer console to view event log messages, which appear with a Source code of `RemoteAccess`. On a properly configured machine, most messages are informational, such as `The Remote Access Server acquired IP address 10.0.0.13 to be used on the Server Adapter`.

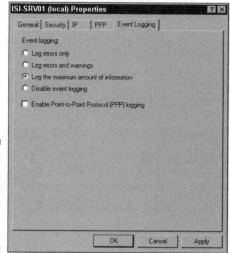

Figure 7-16:
Telling RRAS what to record in the System event log.

✔ Enable the RRAS log manually (it's off by default) on the local computer as shown in Lab 7-5. The default log file is `C:\WINNT\SYSTEM32\ LOGFILES\IASLOG.LOG`, but you can change the location. This log contains more detail than the System event log, typically storing accounting and authentication activities, but enabling it does have a performance impact so don't use it unless you need it.

✔ If you're using an IAS server to centralize authentication and accounting, run the IAS management console on that server and set your logging options just as you would for the RRAS log. (The IAS console looks and works a lot like the RRAS console.)

Lab 7-5   Enabling the RRAS Activity Log

1. **Choose Start➪Programs➪Administrative Tools➪Routing and Remote Access.**

2. **In the tree pane, expand the tree if necessary and click Remote Access Logging.**

3. **In the details pane, right-click Local File, and choose Properties.**

4. **Click the Settings tab.**

5. **Check boxes to enable logging categories as desired.**

   The checkboxes are three: Accounting Stop/Start Events, Authentication Requests, and Interim Accounting Requests.

6. **Click the Local File tab.**

7. **Choose a log file format.**

   IAS format is the default, but it doesn't use a fixed number of fields in each record; for that, choose Database Compatible File Format.

8. **Choose a log time period.**

   Your choices are Daily, Weekly, Monthly, Unlimited File Size, and When Log File Size Reaches X MB, where you specify X.

9. **Name or browse to a log file directory, if you want to change it.**

10. **Click OK and close the RRAS console.**

Prep Test

1 Your boss wants you to log as much activity detail as possible for your RRAS server. Which options should you enable? (Choose all that apply.)

A ❏ Check all three boxes on the Settings tab of the Local File Properties item in the Remote Access Logging node of the RRAS console.

B ❏ Check Unlimited File Size on the Local File tab of the Local File Properties item in the Remote Access Logging node of the RRAS console.

C ❏ Check Log Errors and Warnings on the Event Logging tab of the server's Properties dialog box in the RRAS console.

D ❏ Leave the RRAS server set up with its default logging options, which capture all possible detail.

2 You've set up a RRAS machine to provide IP addresses to dial-up clients from a predefined, static pool. What other steps should you take to ensure that the server properly configures TCP/IP on remote access clients? (Choose all that apply.)

A ❏ Verify that the address ranges you specified for RRAS do not overlap with any scopes on existing DHCP servers.

B ❏ Specify a DHCP server address on the property sheet for the DHCP Relay Agent in the RRAS console, if a DHCP server exists on the network.

C ❏ Configure the IP address of a DNS server and WINS server on the IP tab of the RRAS server's Properties dialog box in the RRAS console.

D ❏ Configure each remote access client to disable dynamic DNS.

3 You're managing a Windows 2000 network that runs in native mode. You decide to set the Active Directory properties for user objects to Control Access Through Remote Policy. You do not modify the default remote access policy. When you activate the server and users start trying to connect, none of them can access the network. Why? (Choose the best answer.)

A ○ RRAS is incompatible with native mode. You must use Network and Dial-Up Connections to configure an inbound connection in a pure Windows 2000 environment.

B ○ The Control Access Through Remote Policy setting only works on a standalone RRAS server.

C ○ The default remote access policy denies access to all users if Control Access Through Remote Policy is activated on a native mode network.

D ○ The Control Access Through Remote Policy setting only works in a mixed-mode network with NT 4.0 servers.

4 Dale dials up from home into your company's Windows 2000 remote access server. He connects okay, but can't access any shared resources on the network. He uses TCP/IP, which your company network also uses. What possible reasons could explain Dale's dilemma? (Choose all that apply.)

A ❑ IP routing has been disabled on the RRAS server.

B ❑ RRAS uses DHCP but the DHCP server is down.

C ❑ Dale's IP address lease has expired.

D ❑ Dale's user account has been set to Allow Access, but the default remote access policy is set to Deny Access.

5 You want to use encryption to protect the entire data stream for remote access clients connecting to your Windows 2000 Server RRAS computer. What authentication protocol choices do you have? (Choose all that apply.)

A ❑ PAP

B ❑ SPAP

C ❑ MS-CHAP

D ❑ EAP/TLS

E ❑ CHEAP

6 What has to be true for a user to be able to gain remote access to a RRAS machine in a Windows 2000 domain? (Choose all that apply.)

A ❑ The user's Active Directory account is not set to Deny Access on the Dial-In property sheet.

B ❑ The connection attempt meets at least one remote access policy's conditions.

C ❑ The constraints in the policy's profile are all satisfied.

D ❑ The client supports at least one authentication method that the RRAS server also supports.

E ❑ The moon is in the seventh house, and Jupiter aligns with Mars.

7 Where does a RRAS server store remote access policies? (Choose the best answer.)

A ○ In Active Directory.

B ○ On the RRAS server.

C ○ In the metabase.

D ○ In user profiles.

8 You've run the Routing and Remote Access Server Setup wizard and you've specified that you want the server to be a VPN host. You run a native-mode Windows 2000 network and you set the user dial-in permission for each user in the group TEMPS to use remote access policies for access control. You don't want anyone outside the TEMPS group to have a prayer of getting in to the VPN server. What should you do next? (Choose all that apply.)

A ❑ Create a profile and use the Limit To Groups field.

B ❑ Create a policy and set NTFS permissions on the .POL file.

C ❑ Create a policy using the condition Windows-Groups.

D ❑ Delete the default remote access policy.

Answers

1 **A** and **B.** Choice A is self-evident; choice B tells RRAS not to wipe the slate clean on a periodic basis, ensuring that you capture as much detail as you have room to store on the server's hard drive. Choice C isn't the best option for event logging; that would be Log The Maximum Amount Of Information, on the specified property sheet. *See "Monitoring RRAS."*

2 **A** and **B.** You must manually ensure the uniqueness of the IP address range that you specify for the RRAS server to use. You should specify a DHCP server for the DHCP Relay Agent to use in processing DHCPINFORM messages from clients needing the addresses of WINS and DNS servers. You can't specify WINS and DNS server addresses on the IP tab of the RRAS server's Properties dialog box, so C is wrong. Choice D is wrong because it's irrelevant to the question. *See "Configuring DHCP integration."*

3 **C.** *The default remote access policy denies access to all users if Control Access Through Remote Policy is activated on a native mode network.* Normally in this case, you would create at least one additional remote access policy that grants access based on an appropriate set of conditions. Choice A is wrong; RRAS is compatible with a native-mode network. Choice B is almost right; Control Access Through Remote Policy works on standalone servers and domain servers in a native mode network. Choice D is the opposite of the truth; you can't use the setting in a mixed-mode network. *See "Dial-in permissions" and "Remote access policies."*

4 **A** and **B.** If IP routing is disabled on the IP tab of the RRAS server's Properties dialog box in the RRAS console, then Dale can't see any resources other than those shared on the RRAS machine itself. If RRAS uses DHCP for address assignment, but the DHCP server goes down, RRAS reverts to using Automatic Private IP Addressing, and Dale's network ID won't match that of the network he's trying to use. Choice C isn't right because Dale hasn't been connected long enough for his IP address lease to expire. Choice D isn't the answer, either; Dale's Active Directory permission overrides the denial on the remote access policy. *See "Configuring DHCP integration."*

5 **C** and **D.** Only MS-CHAP and EAP/TLS support MPPE and IPSec, the two encryption technologies that RRAS uses. Choice E, CHEAP, doesn't support encryption, although it combines other characteristics of CHAP and EAP. (You all know I'm kidding here, right?) *See "Remote access profiles."*

6 **A, B, C,** and **D.** Remote access is strong evidence of Windows 2000's "need to know" security model; administrators have several ways to deny remote users access to the network, and to constrain that access once granted. If choice E reminds you of a song, I applaud you for rejecting the notion that you're too old to be taking exams. *See "Configuring RRAS access."*

7 **B.** *On the RRAS server.* If RRAS stored remote access policies in Active Directory, which sounds logical at first, you couldn't use RRAS in non-Active-Directory environments. The downside is that you have to configure multiple RRAS servers independently, unless you use an IAS RADIUS server to centralize authentication. *See "Remote access policies."*

8 **C** and **D.** If the only policy on the RRAS server has a condition that Windows-Groups equals TEMPS, then only members of TEMPS can get in. *See "Remote access policies."*

Chapter 8

Setting Up Windows 2000 as a Router

• •

Exam Objectives

▶ Update a Windows 2000-based routing table by means of static routes

▶ Implement demand-dial routing

▶ Manage and monitor border routing

▶ Manage and monitor internal routing

▶ Manage and monitor IP routing protocols

• •

*M*y wife and I went house-hunting a few years ago, before we fully understood how little money most computer authors make. We made an offer on one lovely home, but were outbid by a computer zillionaire who had designed software to optimize truck routes; he had just sold his company for big bucks. As it turns out, getting merchandise from A to B at the least possible cost is really big business.

Routing data packets from A to B is a big part of implementing a computer network's infrastructure. Like the trucking network, your computer network should perform the routing function efficiently, securely, and at low cost. You can set up a Windows 2000 Server PC to meet all those goals, and that's what this chapter's about. When I'm done writing it, I'm going to see if I can develop a handheld GPS device that truckers can use to determine the shortest route to a coffee shop. There's *money* in this routing business.

Quick Assessment

Update a Windows 2000-based routing table by means of static routes

1 You can add a permanent static route from a batch file with the command _____.

2 The destination part of a static route can be a network ID or a(n) _____.

Implement demand-dial routing

3 When you create a demand-dial link, you're configuring a(n) _____ type of network.

4 Configure security for a demand-dial link from the _____ node in the RRAS console.

5 When you set up authentication, the user account name for the dial-in credentials must be the same as the _____ name.

6 To restrict outgoing traffic to a particular IP protocol number, use a(n) _____.

Manage and monitor border routing

7 Use area border routers, or ABRs, with the _____ routing protocol.

Manage and monitor internal routing

8 You would use OSPF on an internetwork with more than _____ networks.

Manage and monitor IP routing protocols

9 The protocol that permits multicast forwarding is _____.

10 RIP broadcasts go out by default every _____ minutes.

Answers

1 *ROUTE –P ADD.* See "Adding a static route with the ROUTE command" if you didn't know this one.

2 *Host address.* "Adding a static route with the RRAS console" has more.

3 *WAN.* If you said "wide-area network," give yourself full credit. If you said "cool," give yourself no credit. See "IP Routing Basics."

4 *Routing interfaces.* The section "Configuring a demand-dial interface" has details.

5 *Demand-dial interface.* See "Adding network interfaces" for this tidbit.

6 *Packet filter.* "Configuring a demand-dial interface" explains.

7 *OSPF.* "Open Shortest Path First" would also get you one point. See the section titled (you guessed it) "OSPF."

8 *50.* "Fifty" is also acceptable. See "OSPF."

9 *IGMP.* Alternatively, Internet Group Message Protocol. See "IGMP" for details.

10 *0.5.* Yes, that's 30 seconds, and I know, it's a tricky question. You need to get used to them! See "RIP" for more.

IP Routing Basics

Routing is the process of deciding the path that a packet from a computer on Subnet 1 should take in order to reach a destination computer on Subnet 2. As long as your organization's network consists of one physical subnet, you probably don't need routing. However, as soon as you need to communicate with other computers, internal or external, on a different physical subnet, you need routing.

Routers may be dedicated, standalone devices (hardware routers), or they may be computers running a general-purpose operating system along with routing software (software routers). Windows 2000 Server supports Routing and Remote Access Server, or RRAS, which turns the computer into a multi-protocol software router. (Multiprotocol routers can route traffic between networks that use different network protocols.)

Routers do their job by consulting RAM-resident *routing tables* that contain details about interfaces to other networks. A routing table is just a collection of individual internetwork routes, each of which contains IP addresses, network IDs, and other information that helps the router map out the network and figure out how to get to a given destination.

Actually, every TCP/IP computer has its own routing table. (You can view it on a Windows 2000 computer by entering the **route print** command at a command prompt.) Windows 2000 Professional, for example, builds a routing table based on the settings in its TCP/IP property sheet.

Here's what happens when a computer needs to send a packet to another computer:

1. The sending computer looks at the destination address in order to figure out if the packet needs to be routed to a remote subnet.

2. If the packet needs routing, the sending computer looks in its own routing table to see if an entry exists that tells the sending computer how to send the packet.

3. If the sending computer's local routing table doesn't provide the necessary routing details, the sending computer sends the packet to a router, at the preconfigured default gateway address on the sending computer's TCP/IP property sheet.

4. The router consults its own routing table to see if an entry exists that tells the router how to send the packet.

5. If the router doesn't have the necessary details in its routing table, the router forwards the packet to its default gateway.

6. And so on and so on, up to a maximum number of *hops* (router crossings) before the packet either arrives or is discarded.

Routers, including RRAS routers, can be static or dynamic:

- ✔ A *static* router requires manual configuration and updating; static routers don't communicate with each other and don't update each other when routes change. An administrator must change the static router's routing table when a route changes or goes away. That's okay for a small network but a pain for a medium to large one.

- ✔ A *dynamic* router can build and update its routing table itself, by means of a routing protocol that specifies how dynamic routers can talk to each other and exchange information. When a route change has propagated to every router on the network, the network is said to have *converged*.

The Windows 2000 Server RRAS router

- ✔ Supports either static (manual) or dynamic (automatic) routing.

- ✔ Supports the dynamic router protocols RIP and OSPF (more on these later in the chapter).

- ✔ Can perform IPX routing and supports the RIP-over-IPX and SAP-over-IPX protocols for compatibility with Novell NetWare.

- ✔ Supports *demand-dial interfaces,* in which the server dials a remote connection automatically when necessary and hangs it up when the session's over, creating a wide-area network.

- ✔ Relays DHCP broadcast packets from one subnet to another (so you don't need a DHCP Relay Agent if one subnet doesn't have its own DHCP server; see Chapter 5).

- ✔ Can perform IP packet filtering to restrict traffic through the router based on source IP address, destination IP address, port number, or IP traffic type (see Chapter 10).

- ✔ Can perform IPX packet filtering based on source IPX address, destination IPX address, or IPX traffic type.

- ✔ Works with all the network adapters that Windows 2000 supports.

- ✔ Has a graphical management console (RRAS) and a command-line management tool (ROUTEMON.EXE).

Installing RRAS Routing

When you install Windows 2000 Server, the setup program installs RRAS automatically; all you need to do is activate it. You can activate the RRAS software router on a Windows 2000 Server two ways: by running the Routing and Remote Access Server Setup wizard (if RRAS hasn't been activated on the server before), or by enabling the routing feature on a machine already set up for remote access.

Installing routing with the wizard

Lab 8-1 sets forth the procedure for running the setup wizard to activate RRAS as a router. It's very similar to the procedure for activating RRAS as a remote access server (see Chapter 7).

Before activating the router, install and test your communications hardware (modems, ISDN adapters, and so on). You should also install all network transport protocols you may want to use: TCP/IP, NWLink, et cetera. Verify that your communications hardware and network protocols are all working correctly before you activate RRAS, and you won't have as much manual reconfiguration work to do later.

Lab 8-1	Activating a RRAS Router

1. **Choose Start⇨Programs⇨Administrative Tools⇨Routing and Remote Access.**

2. **Right-click the server icon in the tree pane, and choose Configure and Enable Routing and Remote Access.**

   The Routing and Remote Access Server Setup wizard starts.

3. **Click Next at the welcome window.**

   You see the Common Configurations dialog box. You can set up an Internet connection server, which Chapter 9 examines in detail. You can set up a remote access server, as Chapter 7 discusses. You can also choose to set up a VPN server.

4. **Click Network Router and then click the Next button.**

5. **In the Routed Protocols dialog box, click Yes, All Of The Required Protocols Are On This List, and click the Next button.**

   If all the required LAN protocols aren't on the list displayed in this dialog box, you must quit the wizard and add protocols using the Network and Dial-Up Connections folder.

6. **In the Demand-Dial Connections dialog box, choose Yes and click Next.**

   This step enables demand-dialing, whereby RRAS automatically dials a connection to establish a link when the router needs to communicate on the specified nonpermanent interface.

7. **Click Finish to close the wizard.**

   After a few moments, RRAS starts.

Installing by hand

If you're activating routing on a Windows 2000 Server computer that you've already configured as a remote access server, then the process is very simple, as Lab 8-2 demonstrates.

Lab 8-2	Activating Routing on an Existing RRAS Server

1. **Choose Start⇨Programs⇨Administrative Tools⇨Routing and Remote Access.**

2. **Right-click the server icon in the tree pane, and choose Properties.**

   The server's Properties dialog box appears, as shown in Figure 8-1.

3. **Click the Router checkbox.**

4. **Select LAN And Demand-Dial Routing to enable the router to use both permanent and temporary network interfaces.**

   Another way to put this is whether you want a LAN-only router, or a LAN-and-WAN router.

5. **Click OK.**

6. **Click Yes when Windows asks you if you want to restart RRAS.**

   Windows 2000 stops and restarts RRAS for you.

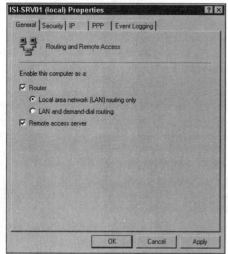

Figure 8-1:
Turning RAS
into RRAS.

Adding network interfaces

In the lingo of RRAS, a network *interface* is a device that connects the router to a network. The device may be permanently available, such as a traditional LAN network adapter, or available on demand, such as a dial-up modem or ISDN adapter (see Figure 8-2).

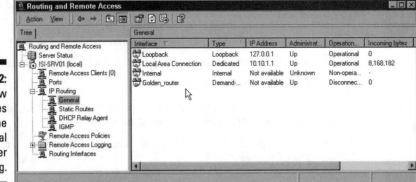

Figure 8-2:
View interfaces in the General node under IP Routing.

RRAS looks at all the communications devices on your computer at installation time, and automatically builds interfaces for them. However, if you add a communications device after activating RRAS, you must add it manually if you want to enable routing on the device. The process for adding an interface depends on the type of device, or port, as follows:

- ✔ If the device is a permanent network interface card, enable it for routing by right-clicking the General node under IP Routing in the RRAS console's tree pane and choosing New Interface.

- ✔ If the device is a modem or dial-up ISDN adapter (that is, a demand-dial device), enable it by right-clicking the Routing Interfaces node in the RRAS console's tree pane and choosing New Demand-Dial Interface.

If you try to add a demand-dial routing interface, and Windows complains that no ports are available, you must enable a port for routing. Right-click the Ports node in the RRAS console's tree pane and choose Properties. Click the port you want to enable for routing and click Configure. You'll see the dialog box shown in Figure 8-3. In this case, the port is a modem, so click the box labeled Demand-Dial Routing Connections (Inbound and Outbound) to enable the modem for routing.

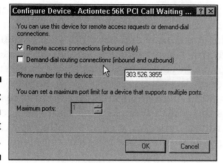

Figure 8-3:
Enabling a
modem port
for routing.

When you enable a dial-up port for routing, RRAS launches the Demand Dial Interface wizard. Here's the data you must provide when adding a demand-dial interface:

- ✔ Name of the interface (must match username account configured on a remote router's dial-out credentials if you permit that remote router to call in)

- ✔ Phone number of the dial-up server or router that you want to call (for example, a RRAS router modem on a remote subnetwork)

- ✔ Alternate phone numbers of the dial-up server or router that you want to call

- ✔ Protocol and security options, as follows:

  - • Route IP Packets On This Interface

  - • Route IPX Packets On This Interface (leave clear if you're not using IPX)

  - • Add A User Account So A Remote Router Can Dial In (the username is the interface name; you supply a password, and Windows 2000 creates the account on the router)

  - • Send A Plain-Text Password If That Is The Only Way To Connect

  - • Use Scripting To Complete The Connection With The Remote Router

- ✔ Dial-in password, if you enabled dial-in by another router

- ✔ Dial-out username, domain name, and password (this must match a domain account on the remote router)

Demand-dial authentication is a little confusing, so here's how it works. The simpler scenario is *one-way authentication,* in which your router can dial out, but other routers can't dial in. You supply dial-out credentials when you run the Demand Dial Interface wizard. Those credentials consist of a username, password, and domain name. When your router dials the remote Windows 2000 router, the remote router looks at the credentials you supply, and sees if they match an account configured on the remote router. The name of the account must be the same as the name of the demand-dial interface on the remote router. If the remote router finds that your credentials match the user account having the same name as the remote router's demand-dial interface, you're in!

Two-way authentication is necessary if your router can dial out, but you also want another router to be able to dial in. In addition to supplying the dial-out credentials, which authenticate your router when it calls the remote router, you must also supply dial-in credentials (basically a password), which your router uses to authenticate the remote router when it calls you. The dial-in account has a username that is the same as the name of the demand-dial interface on your router. So, two-way authentication just adds a mirror image of the one-way authentication setup.

Configuring a Windows 2000 Router

To configure a Windows 2000 router, you must complete the following tasks:

- ✔ Configure network interfaces.
- ✔ Configure routing tables (if you use static routing).
- ✔ Configure routing protocols (if you don't use static routing).

The following sections explore each task.

Configuring network interfaces

You can configure the network interfaces that your router uses by means of the interfaces' property sheets in the RRAS console.

The configuration procedures and options differ somewhat between demand-dial and permanent interfaces. In fact, the property sheets for the same demand-dial interface look quite different, depending on whether you select that interface under the console's Routing Interfaces node, or under the IP Routing/General node!

Starting with the simpler type of interface first, the following sections discuss configuration options for permanent and demand-dial interfaces.

Configuring a permanent interface

Under the IP Routing node in the RRAS console, click the General node. All the configured router interfaces appear in the details pane. Pick a permanent interface (that is, a network card with a name like Local Area Connection), right-click it, and choose Properties. You see a dialog box that looks like Figure 8-4.

The General tab contains some pretty important settings:

- ✔ **Enable IP Router Manager** determines whether the router enables TCP/IP on the specified interface.

- ✔ **Enable Router Discovery Advertisements** determines whether the router supports *ICMP router discovery*. If enabled, routers do two things. First, they periodically advertise their existence to network hosts, helping the hosts learn of malfunctioning routers. Second, they respond to hosts who send out a distress signal when their default gateway isn't working, helping the hosts use an alternate default gateway if one exists. Windows 2000 and Windows 98 are hosts that can use ICMP router discovery.

- ✔ **Input Filters** and **Output Filters** let you define packet filters for the routing interface. Chapter 10 discusses packet filters in more detail; it's enough to say here that you can use them to restrict the traffic that passes into or out of the interface, based on IP source address, destination address, IP protocol, source port, or destination port. I should also mention that you can set up packet filtering to either allow all traffic except that specified in a filter, or deny all traffic except that specified.

The Configuration tab is where you configure the interface's IP address, subnet mask, and default gateway.

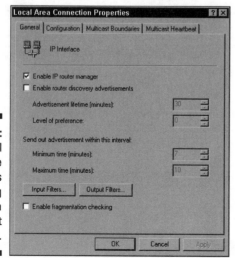

Figure 8-4:
The General tab in the Properties dialog box for a permanent interface.

The Multicast Boundaries tab lets you specify multicast scopes (that is, address ranges) that the router will *not* forward out the permanent interface. (You define one or more multicast scopes on the Multicast Scopes tab of the General node's property sheet.) See also the section later in this chapter titled "IGMP." (The Multicast Heartbeat tab gets a bit more obscure than the exam requires at this writing, so I'm omitting discussion of it here.)

Configuring a demand-dial interface

If you look at the property sheet for a demand-dial interface in the RRAS console's General node, you see all the settings that the preceding section describes. And they all work the same way.

Oddly, if you look at the property sheet for the very same demand-dial interface in the Routing Interfaces node, it looks entirely different. So, you have two property sheets to worry about when configuring a demand-dial interface, not one. The context menu is also different; see Figure 8-5.

I'll get to the property sheet in a minute, but first, look at the context menu in Figure 8-5. Two commands are worth your attention, as follows:

- ✔ Set IP Demand-Dial Filters lets you use packet filters to determine what type of IP traffic is allowed to trigger the demand-dial connection. (See Chapter 10 for more details on packet filters.)

- ✔ Dial-Out Hours (see Figure 8-6) lets you block out parts of the weekly timetable when you don't want to allow the demand-dial connection to initiate a link, even if the demand-dial filters are satisfied.

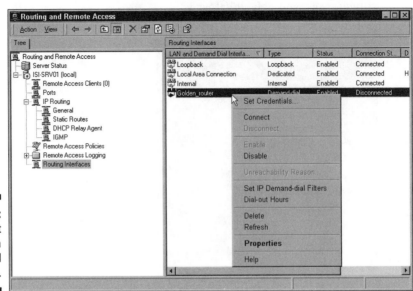

Figure 8-5:
The context menu of a demand-dial interface.

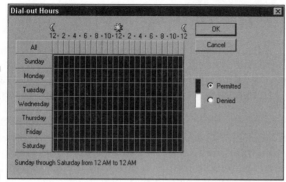

Figure 8-6:
You can limit
the hours a
demand-dial
connection
can call out.

The property sheet has four tabs:

- ✔ **General:** Configure the modem and specify the interface's phone
  number.

- ✔ **Options:** Specify dialing policy, such as how many times to retry and at
  what interval, and whether to use callback.

- ✔ **Security:** (This is the one the exam will ask you about; see Figure 8-7.)
  Define authentication and data encryption options for the interface.

- ✔ **Networking:** Configure the various network components (TCP/IP settings, and so on) for the interface.

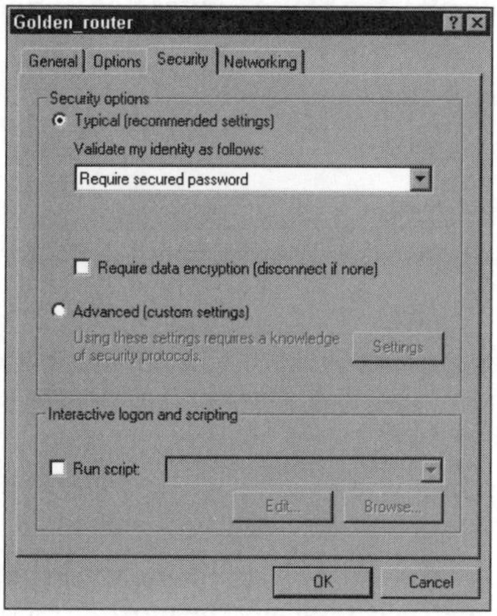

Figure 8-7:
Setting
security
for a
demand-dial
link.

Configuring the routing tables

You only have to configure the routing tables manually if you're using static routing. Most routers use dynamic routing, but dynamic routing often isn't practical or necessary with demand-dial interfaces. The exam expects you to know when you need to add a static route for a demand-dial connection.

Consider a simple example. Your company has two offices: one in Denver and one in Dallas. You have a RRAS router in both locations. Each router has a local area connection interface to the local subnet, and a demand-dial interface that connects to the remote router. In order for the routers to be able to pass traffic back and forth, you must do two things:

- ✔ Add a static route for the Dallas subnet on the Denver router's demand-dial interface.
- ✔ Add a static route for the Denver subnet on the Dallas router's demand-dial interface.

Adding a static route with the RRAS console

Lab 8-3 goes through the process of adding a static route.

Lab 8-3	Adding a Static Route

1. **Choose Start➪Programs➪Administrative Tools➪Routing and Remote Access.**

2. **Expand the tree pane to display the Static Routes node under IP Routing.**

3. **Right-click Static Routes and choose New Static Route.**

   The dialog box in Figure 8-8 appears.

4. **Fill out the fields and click OK.**

   Interface is the name of the network card or demand-dial interface.

   Destination is a network ID or host ID.

   Network mask is the destination network ID's subnet mask; the special network mask 255.255.255.255 specifies a route to a specific host, called (logically enough) a "host route."

   Gateway is the address of a router to which packets going to the destination should be sent; this setting isn't available for demand-dial interfaces.

   Finally, *Metric* is the "cost" of the route — for example, the hop count. The route with the lowest metric is typically the most attractive route.

If you create a static route with a network mask of 0.0.0.0, it's called a *default route,* and the router uses it when no other routes in the table apply.

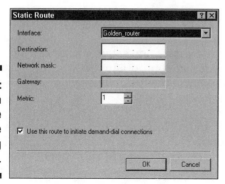

Figure 8-8:
Entering a
static route
into the
routing
table.

If the destination network for a packet connects to the router via a network interface card, the gateway address in the static route is the IP address of that interface.

If you want to see the contents of the current routing table, right-click the Static Routes node in the RRAS console's tree pane and choose Show IP Routing Table (see Figure 8-9).

Figure 8-9:
Viewing the
routing
table.

Destination	Network mask	Gateway	Interface	Metric	Protocol
10.0.0.0	255.0.0.0	10.10.1.1	Local Area Connection	1	Local
10.10.1.1	255.255.255.255	127.0.0.1	Loopback	1	Local
127.0.0.0	255.0.0.0	127.0.0.1	Loopback	1	Local
127.0.0.1	255.255.255.255	127.0.0.1	Loopback	1	Local
224.0.0.0	240.0.0.0	10.10.1.1	Local Area Connection	1	Local
255.255.255.255	255.255.255.255	10.10.1.1	Local Area Connection	1	Local

ISI-SRV01 - IP Routing Table

Adding a static route with the ROUTE command

Another way to add a static route is at the command prompt, using the ROUTE command. The syntax is

```
route add <destination> mask <network mask> <gateway>
```

Replace the values in angle brackets with the correct values for the route that you're adding.

Know the variations of the ROUTE command:

- ✓ The **route –p add** command indicates that you're adding a persistent route.

- ✓ The **route –f** command clears all routes.

- ✓ The **route delete** command . . . well, you can figure that one out.

- ✓ The **route print** command displays the machine's routing table.

Configuring routing protocols

If you get a bit fancier than static routes and set up Windows 2000 Server as a dynamic router, you must choose an appropriate routing protocol. Right-click the General node under IP Routing in the RRAS console and choose New Routing Protocol.

The protocols supplied for IP routing include Network Address Translation (NAT), DHCP Relay Agent, Routing Information Protocol (RIP) Version 2, Open Shortest Path First (OSPF), and Internet Group Management Protocol (IGMP). (If you don't see a protocol that you expect to see in this list, it's probably already installed on the server.)

This chapter doesn't discuss NAT, a special routing protocol (okay, it's really a service, but Microsoft lists it as a routing protocol) for sharing an Internet connection, but Chapter 9 does. Chapter 5 discusses the DHCP Relay Agent protocol.

RIP

Routing Information Protocol (RIP) is the most popular IP routing protocol, and it works well for networks having up to 50 or so subnetworks. A RIP router sends announcements on a regular basis to let other RIP routers know of any changes to the network topology. When a network gets really large, these announcements can create high traffic volume.

RIP is called a *distance vector* routing protocol, because a RIP router lets other routers know how many hops (router crossings) away a given network is. RIP announcements occur periodically regardless of whether the network configuration has actually changed. Further, no facility exists for the acknowledgement of RIP announcements. Still, RIP works well, and it supports both IP networks and IPX networks.

RIP broadcasts use UDP port 520. By default, a RIP router broadcasts routing information every 30 seconds over each configured network interface.

OSPF

OSPF is a more efficient but more complex routing protocol than RIP and is suited for networks with more than 50 or so subnetworks. OSPF routers maintain a network map (called the *link state database*) that enables them to figure out the shortest path from A to B. In a large network, that map becomes too big, so an OSPF router divides the network into *areas* and only memorizes that portion of the network map that contains the areas to which the router connects. When a change to the network map occurs, neighboring routers synchronize their link state databases and refigure the routing tables for their areas. In this scheme, routers exchange network map information instead of routing table information.

Here's some OSPF terminology that you may see on the exam:

- ✔ Areas connect to each other through a *backbone* area.
- ✔ Routers that connect the backbone area to other areas are called *area border routers* or *ABRs*.
- ✔ Routers that only connect to the backbone are called *internal routers*.

And here are a couple of configuration tips that may crop up:

- ✔ Routers should not connect two areas while bypassing the backbone. Such routers are called *backdoor routers*.
- ✔ If you set too much packet filtering on ABRs, the routers may not be able to pass network map information between each other.

Configuring RIP and OSPF routers can get mighty complicated. As I write this, the Network Infrastructure exam doesn't focus on the gory details. If Microsoft decides to include dynamic router protocol configuration topics on this test in the future, your best source of information is the Windows 2000 Server online help for RRAS (if you have access to it); second-best is `www.microsoft.com/technet`.

IGMP

Unicast routing is the sending of packets having a single source and a single destination. *Multicast* routing is the sending of network packets that have multiple recipients. Windows 2000 operating systems are multicast-capable. (Chapter 5 presents the basics of multicasting, and I won't repeat that material here, except the details that pertain to routing.)

A routing table entry for multicasting has the network address 224.0.0.0.

The *Internet Group Management Protocol,* or *IGMP,* is a routing protocol for the support of multicasting. Multicast routes exist, just as unicast routes do; RRAS can manage both. A multicast router is responsible for listening for multicast traffic and forwarding it to networks that have hosts who have registered their interest in receiving the multicast. Microsoft hastens to point out that IGMP isn't a "true" multicast router — it's more of a forwarder — and is only suitable in a one-router network.

If you look at the IGMP node under IP Routing in the RRAS console, the details pane contains two entries: one for a permanent interface (that is, network card), and one named Internal. The network card interface typically acts as an IGMP proxy, while the internal interface acts as an IGMP router.

The exam isn't likely to quiz you on the details of configuring an IGMP router, and Microsoft says that you shouldn't normally need to change the default settings for IGMP interfaces. However, you ought to be aware of the Multicast Boundaries tab on the property sheet of a permanent interface; see the "Configuring a permanent interface" section earlier in this chapter.

Managing Routers

You can add routers to the RRAS console by right-clicking the Server Status icon at the top of the tree pane and choosing Add Server. Figure 8-10 shows the various options for locating servers that you want to add to your Microsoft Management Console window.

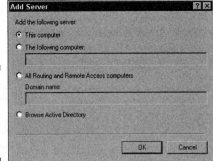

Figure 8-10:
Adding
servers to
the RRAS
console.

Prep Test

1 You want to inhibit multicast forwarding out a specific router interface for a specific IP address range. How can you do this? (Choose two.)

  A ❑ In the property sheet for the General node under IP Routing in the RRAS console, add a multicast scope defining the range you want to exclude.

  B ❑ Add the multicast scope that you want to exclude from forwarding to the list on the Multicast Boundaries tab of the interface's property sheet.

  C ❑ In the property sheet for the General node under IP Routing in the RRAS console, add one or more multicast scopes defining the range or ranges that you want to permit.

  D ❑ Add the multicast scope or scopes that you want to permit for forwarding to the list on the Multicast Boundaries tab of the interface's property sheet.

2 You're in charge of security for a specific Windows 2000 router. You only want to permit Web traffic on the demand-dial interface named Golden_Router. How can you do this? (Choose the best answer.)

  A ○ On the Golden_Router property sheet under the General node, set an input and output packet filter for TCP port 80.

  B ○ On the Golden-Router property sheet under the General node, set an input and output packet filter for TCP ports 20 and 21.

  C ○ On the Golden_Router property sheet under the Routing Interfaces node, set an input and output packet filter for TCP port 80.

  D ○ On the Golden-Router property sheet under the Routing Interfaces node, set an input and output packet filter for TCP ports 20 and 21.

3 Your network uses a demand-dial interface to connect to a branch office for exchanging operating data on a daily basis. The operating data exchange always occurs on a Friday afternoon at 3:00 pm. To your chagrin, you notice that the router seems to be connecting at other times, racking up costs on your expensive high-speed dial-up line. What should you do? (Choose the best answer.)

  A ○ Right-click the interface under the Routing Interfaces node, choose Properties, click Dial-Out Hours, and permit only Friday afternoon dialing.

  B ○ Right-click the interface under the Routing Interfaces node, choose Dial-Out Hours, and permit only Friday afternoon dialing.

  C ○ Define a remote access policy for the interface, and specify a condition that permits only Friday afternoon dialing.

  D ○ Define a remote access profile for the interface, and specify a condition that permits only Friday afternoon dialing.

4 Your network spans two locations: a central office downtown, and a suburban office. Each location has a Windows 2000 Server machine acting as a router. You use demand-dial interfaces to connect the two locations. You do not use a dynamic routing protocol.

What do you need to do in order to ensure that users at each location can use resources on the other location? (Choose two.)

A ❑ Add a static route for the suburban subnet on the demand-dial interface of the downtown router.

B ❑ Add a static route for the downtown subnet on the demand-dial interface of the suburban router.

C ❑ Configure the default gateway of the suburban server's demand-dial interface with the downtown server's IP address.

D ❑ Configure the default gateway of the downtown server's demand-dial interface with the suburban server's IP address.

5 In OSPF routing, what's the name for a contiguous subset of a large internetwork? (Choose the best answer.)

A ○ Border

B ○ Zone

C ○ Link

D ○ Area

6 You want to add a persistent route from a batch file. Which of the following commands would you use? (Choose the best answer.)

A ○ route –p add

B ○ route add

C ○ route add -p

D ○ iproute –p add

7 You've installed Routing and Remote Access on a Windows 2000 Server computer. This machine serves double duty as a router for the LAN and as a remote access server. You want to make sure that the router doesn't use any of the connected modems for routing purposes. Which setting should you make on the server's General property sheet? (Choose the best answer.)

A ○ Enable Permanent Interfaces Only

B ○ Disable Demand-Dial Access for Routing

C ○ Local Area Network (LAN) Routing Only

D ○ Enable Modems for Remote Access Only

8 When you configure an outbound-only demand-dial interface for one-way authentication, what username must you specify on the dial-out credentials for the interface? (Choose the best answer.)

A ○ Any valid domain user account.

B ○ Any valid domain user account that is enabled via the Dial-In tab of the user object for remote access.

C ○ The name of the local computer's demand-dial interface.

D ○ The name of the remote computer's demand-dial interface.

Answers

1 **A** and **B.** When you add a multicast scope to the list on the interface property sheet's Multicast Boundaries tab, you're telling RRAS that here's the IP address range you want to block from being forwarded out the designated interface. *See "IGMP."*

2 **A.** *On the Golden_Router property sheet under the General node, set an input and output packet filter for TCP port 80.* Web traffic uses HTTP, which is associated with TCP port 80. The property sheet where you can set packet filters is the one under the General node, not Routing Interfaces. *See "Configuring a demand-dial interface."*

3 **B.** *Right-click the interface under the Routing Interfaces node, choose Dial-Out Hours, and permit only Friday afternoon dialing.* Why this option lives on the context menu and not on a property sheet is a question only Microsoft designers can answer, but that's how it is. Notice that you only access the Dial-Out Hours option in the interface's property sheet under the Routing Interfaces node, not General. *See "Configuring a demand-dial interface."*

4 **A** and **B.** One of your clues on this one should be that you can't configure a default gateway on a demand-dial interface. As you don't have permanent connections or a dynamic routing protocol, you must manually add the static routes. *See "Configuring the routing tables."*

5 **D.** *Area.* The exam doesn't expect you to be able to configure OSPF, but it does expect you to understand the basic concepts. *See "OSPF."*

6 **A.** *route –p add.* You should be familiar with the ROUTE command's qualifiers and parameters for the test. *See "Adding a static route with the ROUTE command."*

7 **C.** *Local Area Network (LAN) Routing Only.* If you change your mind later and you do want to use modems or ISDN adapters for routing, select LAN And Demand-Dial Routing (it's a radio button, just like the setting in choice C). *See "Installing by hand."*

8 **D.** *The name of the remote computer's demand-dial interface.* When your router calls up the remote router and presents credentials, the remote router tries to match up the username your router presents with the name of the remote router's demand-dial interface. If they don't match, even if the credentials that your router provides specify a valid domain account, you ain't gonna connect. *See "Adding network interfaces."*

Chapter 9

Configuring the LAN for Internet Access

Exam Objectives

▶ Install Internet Connection Sharing

▶ Install NAT (Network Address Translation)

▶ Configure NAT properties

▶ Configure NAT interfaces

As the Internet has boomed, Internet addresses have become increasingly valuable — and not just domain names, but the numeric dotted-decimal IP addresses, too. On top of that, registering IP addresses isn't free. Fortunately, many computers that need Internet connectivity don't need their own globally unique IP address. They can use private IP addresses that everyone agrees never to use on the public Internet. Of course, some mechanism is required to convert between those private addresses and public ones — and that's the subject of this chapter. (If you read Chapters 5 and 8 first, this one should be easier.)

Quick Assessment

Install
Internet
Connection
Sharing

1 You can install ICS two ways: via the _____ folder and via the _____ management console.

2 ICS uses _____ public IP address(es) for Internet connectivity.

3 ICS runs on the following operating systems: _____, _____, and _____.

4 ICS should not run on networks that have _____ or _____ servers.

Install
NAT

5 The easiest way to install NAT is to run the _____ wizard.

6 The optional DHCP service for NAT goes by the name _____.

Configure
NAT
properties

7 You must set up client workstations in a NAT scheme to obtain an IP address _____.

8 Unlike ICS, NAT can use _____ public IP addresses.

Configure
NAT
interfaces

9 The NAT protocol requires two interfaces, typically: a network card interface for the local private network, and a(n) _____ interface for the dial-up Internet link.

10 When you create a default static route for a NAT demand-dial interface, use an IP destination address of _____.

Answers

1 *Network and Dial-Up Connections, Routing and Remote Access.* See "Enabling ICS on the translating computer" if you missed this one.

2 *One.* The section "Microsoft's IP address translators" fills in this and other details.

3 *Windows 2000 Professional, Windows 2000 Server, Windows 98.* Give yourself full credit if you named all three but in a different order. See "Microsoft's IP address translators."

4 *DHCP, DNS.* See the "Internet Connection Sharing (ICS)" section in this chapter.

5 *Routing and Remote Access Server Setup.* Catchy, eh? See "Configuring NAT using the wizard."

6 *DHCP allocator.* See "Turning on NAT addressing and name resolution" if this obscure question stymied you.

7 *Automatically.* See "Configuring NAT clients" for more.

8 *Multiple.* See "Using multiple public IP addresses" for more.

9 *Demand-Dial.* Always-on connections are legal, also. See "Configuring NAT using the wizard" for details.

10 *0.0.0.0.* See "Configuring NAT without the wizard" for the full procedure.

Connection Sharing Concepts

Consider a fictional company, Acme Cognac. Like many companies, Acme Cognac uses only a few published telephone numbers (for example, five). However, at its headquarters office, the company maintains 20 employees.

When Paulina needs to call out (for example, to tell her boyfriend Paul to remember to buy her flowers because it's her birthday), she does so by picking up her handset and using one of the published phone number lines. When Paul needs to return the call, he calls the main public number, and a receptionist routes the call to Paulina's phone. The private switching system uses an internal code (extension) to ring Paulina's handset. This system works great for Acme Cognac and for the community at large, because 1) published phone numbers are expensive, 2) all the employees need telephone connectivity occasionally, and 3) the local municipality only has X number of public phone numbers available.

Now consider Acme Cognac's Internet connectivity needs. As with the phone numbers, IP addresses are expensive. And, as with the phone numbers, the community has only so many IP addresses to give out. Why not use an "Internet switch" that works similarly to a private telephone switch? Most Acme Cognac employees don't need their own unique public IP address, any more than they need their own direct-dial phone line. Why not share a small number of public IP addresses, and use an internal coding system (like phone number extensions) for routing IP traffic inside the organization? The answer is, why not indeed, and Internet engineers developed the concept of network address translation.

If Acme Cognac doesn't need any connectivity to the public Internet, the company doesn't require any public IP addresses, and it could use whatever internal IP addressing scheme it wanted. However, if Acme Cognac doesn't connect to the Internet, its employees can't download MP3 audio files or e-mail jokes to friends and colleagues. So this is not a very practical solution in today's world.

Microsoft provides three Internet switches with Windows 2000: Internet Connection Sharing (ICS), Network Address Translation (NAT), and Proxy Server (soon to be replaced by Internet Security and Acceleration [ISA] Server 2000, as I write this). The next section looks at these products more closely.

Microsoft's IP address translators

All these products enable many network users to access the Internet while using only a small number of public Internet addresses:

✔ Small organizations and home offices are likely to use ICS, because it's the easiest of the three to configure. ICS runs mainly at the transport level of the U.S. Department of Defense networking model. (You can brush up on that model by turning to Chapter 3.)

✔ Medium-size organizations are likely to prefer NAT, because it permits greater configuration flexibility. NAT also runs mainly at the transport level.

✔ Medium to large organizations typically run Proxy Server, which is the only product of the three that Microsoft recommends for use in a domain environment where you already have one or more DNS servers, DHCP servers, gateways, or computers with static IP addresses. Proxy Server is a gateway that runs at the application layer of the networking model.

Exam 70-216 only covers ICS and NAT, so those are the two that this chapter explores. Table 9-1 lays out the key features of these two products.

Table 9-1	ICS and NAT
ICS	**NAT**
Comes with Windows 2000 Server, Windows 2000 Professional, and Windows 98 Second Edition	Comes with Windows 2000 Server
Works with one network card only	Works with multiple network cards
Set up with Network and Dial-Up Connections folder	Set up with Routing and Remote Access
Relatively simple, automatic setup	Relatively complex, manual setup
Uses DNS for name resolution	Uses either DNS or WINS for name resolution
Acts as a "mini" DHCP server	Acts as a "mini" DHCP server
Fixed address range for private machines	Customizable address range for private machines
Single public Internet address	Multiple public Internet addresses

ICS and NAT provide *translated* connections as opposed to traditional *routed* connections. Just as the Acme Cognac switchboard operator "translates" an incoming call from a published phone number into a private line by pushing a transfer button, ICS and NAT translate traffic between one or more public IP addresses and internal, private IP addresses. A traditional router setup, on the other hand, would require all of Acme Cognac's computers to have unique public IP addresses — for example, assigned by a DHCP server on your local network. You'd need to pay your ISP for the use of those public addresses. Your ISP would also tell you the address of a DNS server on the ISP's network to use for resolving public host names to IP addresses.

Traditional routing is faster than translating, but it requires more money, knowledge, and time to set up.

Just as a real-time simultaneous translator at the United Nations has two "network connections" (a headset to listen with, and a microphone to speak with), any computer running ICS or NAT must also have two connections: one to the internal private network, and one to the public Internet. The internal connection is typically a network card; the external connection can be a dial-up analog line, DSL, ISDN, cable modem, satellite link, and so on.

Both ICS and NAT increase network security, by hiding your private network addresses from the public Internet.

The main drawback of network address translators like ICS and NAT is that they can't accommodate the complete range of TCP/IP traffic that a traditional router can. With some types of TCP/IP traffic, the IP address appears in more than just the usual, expected places — meaning that the translator may not catch all the places in the data stream where it should perform translation. In such circumstances, you need a "NAT editor." Microsoft supplies a few with Windows 2000 (for FTP, ICMP, PPTP, and NetBT), but they don't cover every application. Also, ICS and NAT do not support the secure protocols Kerberos and IPsec.

ICS and NAT are specialized networking tools designed only for sharing an Internet connection. You would not use these technologies for general-purpose network-to-network links.

How translation works

ICS and NAT actually perform three main tasks:

- ✔ They assign private IP **addresses** to clients on the internal private network, using a "miniature" DHCP server called the *DHCP allocator.* The actual configuration data that ICS and NAT assign includes the IP address, subnet mask, default gateway (the ICS or NAT machine), and DNS server (also, the ICS or NAT machine). Note that for NAT, the DHCP allocator is an option, but for ICS, it is a requirement.

  The DHCP allocator is not a full-fledged DHCP server; for example, it does not support multiple scopes, superscopes, or multicast scopes. (See Chapter 5 for more on DHCP.)

- ✔ They **translate** between private and public IP addresses and port numbers, in both the outbound and inbound directions.

✔ They provide **name resolution.** For example, an ICS or NAT machine can receive DNS requests from internal private machines and forward those requests to an Internet-based DNS server. Then, when the Internet-based DNS server responds, the ICS or NAT machine receives the response and routes it back to the internal private machine that generated the initial request. Another way to say this is that ICS and NAT servers can act as *DNS proxies.* Again, for NAT, the DNS proxy behavior is an option, but for ICS, it is a requirement.

So how do ICS and NAT perform the magic of converting between private and public IP addresses? The key to it all is the use of TCP and UDP *ports* in addition to IP addresses. Ports are address qualifiers that normally specify a particular service; for example, TCP ports 20 and 21 specify the FTP service, port 80 specifies the World Wide Web service, and so on.

You can think of a port as loosely corresponding to the extension number in an office telephone system. Paul Price calls Acme Cognac employee Pauline at the company's published phone number (analogous to the IP address). The receptionist answers the phone, looks up Pauline's extension (analogous to the port), and forwards the call. Just as the extension number identifies Pauline's phone on the internal network, but is invisible to the caller who only has the public phone number, so does the port number identify a computer on the internal computer network, but is invisible to the "calling" Internet computer, which only has the public IP address of the ICS or NAT server.

In addition to the well-known ports such as 21 and 80 (which live in the range 0 to 1024), a class of *ephemeral ports* exists, in the range 1025 to 5000. ICS and NAT assign these ephemeral ports, normally on a dynamic basis, to identify machines on the private network. (Other ports exist beyond the ephemeral port range; their numbers go up to 65536.)

Outbound connections

Here's what happens when a private internal computer requests an Internet connection through NAT:

1. NAT checks to see if an address or port mapping exists for the internal client. If not, then NAT creates one, in order to uniquely identify the internal client. It either assigns the client an unused port number (if only one public IP address is available, as in ICS) or it assigns the client a mapping to a public IP address (if multiple public IP addresses are available).

   If multiple public IP addresses are available, they may run out at some point, in which case NAT begins assigning port numbers to identify internal network clients. Thus, you may have NAT set up with ten public IP addresses and twenty private computers. The first ten private computers would get mappings to the public IP addresses; the next ten private computers to come online would get port assignments.

2. NAT checks to see if the application requires a NAT editor (a program that handles IP address translation in other than the usual IP header location). If one is needed, NAT applies it.

3. NAT changes (translates) the packet headers.

4. NAT forwards the packet out through the Internet connection.

Inbound connections

Here's what happens when NAT receives an inbound packet from the public Internet:

1. NAT checks to see if an address or port mapping exists for the internal client. If not, NAT does nothing further, and the inbound packet dies a silent death.

   If inbound traffic is not in response to prior outbound traffic, and it is not addressed to a specific private client by means of a static mapping, the traffic can't get into the private network.

2. NAT checks to see if the application requires a NAT editor (a program that handles IP address translation in other than the usual IP header location). If one is needed, NAT applies it.

3. NAT changes (translates) the packet headers.

4. NAT forwards the packet into the internal network.

Private address ranges

The whole concept of network address translation depends on the use of designated private IP addresses that no one on the public Internet uses or ever will use. The Internet community has agreed on the following ranges of addresses:

- ✔ **192.168.0.1 through 192.168.255.254.** ICS uses this range exclusively, but NAT can use a different range.
- ✔ **172.16.0.1 through 172.31.255.254.**
- ✔ **10.0.0.1 through 10.255.255.254.**

Public IP addresses, which the InterNIC (Internet Network Information Center) assigns, are unique in the world. Private IP addresses, however, may occur over and over again, within private internal networks. That is, Acme Cognac may use 10.0.0.1 through 10.255.255.254 for its private internal network, and so may Classy Cordials, Inc., Larry's Liqueurs Limited, and a thousand other companies. No conflicts occur despite all this duplication, because these private IP addresses are never "seen" on the public Internet.

Internet Connection Sharing (ICS)

Internet Connection Sharing (ICS) made its debut in Windows 98 Second Edition, and it works similarly in Windows 2000 (both Professional and Server). If you don't need the configuration flexibility of NAT, you may prefer ICS because it offers an extremely simple setup procedure. Heck, you don't even have to get in touch with your ISP, because all the magic happens behind the curtain of your single Internet connection.

Microsoft warns against using ICS on networks that have Windows 2000 Server domain controllers, DHCP servers, DNS servers, or any computers with static IP addresses. Basically, ICS takes over the function of DHCP and DNS servers itself. ICS is a Small Office — Home Office (SOHO) application. On the other hand, you can use NAT on a network with DHCP servers and DNS servers, as long as you turn off NAT's own DHCP allocator and DNS proxy capabilities.

The Windows 2000 PC you configure to share an Internet connection must be the only computer on the network that provides an Internet gateway.

Enabling ICS on the translating computer

Enable ICS using the method in Lab 9-1. (On a Windows 2000 Server machine, you can also use the Routing and Remote Access Server Setup Wizard to enable ICS. However, the method I present in Lab 9-1 works on Windows 2000 Server and on Windows 2000 Professional.)

Lab 9-1   Enabling Internet Connection Sharing (ICS)

1. **Log on as an Administrator.**

2. **Choose Start⇨Settings⇨Network and Dial-Up Connections.**

3. **Right-click the external Internet connection that you want to share, and choose Properties.**

Choose the right connection — the external public Internet connection — when enabling ICS! If you erroneously select your *internal* network adapter for enabling ICS, then ICS works exactly backward. For example, your computer may try to assign IP addresses to outside computers on the public Internet, instead of to computers on your private internal network. You could create some serious problems for other Internet users this way.

4. **Click the Sharing tab.**

5. **Check the Enable Internet Connection Sharing For This Connection box, as shown in Figure 9-1.**

6. **If your connection isn't an "always-on" type (for example, if it uses an ISDN adapter or a dial-up modem), check Enable On-Demand Dialing so that the PC running ICS calls up the ISP when any networked PC tries to access the Internet.**

7. **Click OK.**

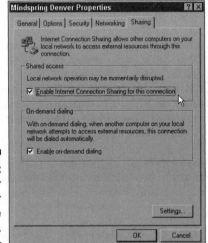

Figure 9-1:
Set up your
ICS server
machine
here.

When you create a shared Internet connection, Windows 2000 assigns your internal network card a static IP address (192.168.0.1, subnet mask 255.255.255.0). You can't change this address. All present TCP/IP connections between your PC and other network PCs are lost.

Configuring ICS clients

Other computers on the network that will use the ICS link must be set up to obtain IP addresses automatically in their Internet Protocol (TCP/IP) Properties dialog box, as shown in Figure 9-2. The ICS PC effectively becomes a DHCP server, allocating IP addresses to other PCs on the local network.

Those other computers must also configure their Internet Options control panel as follows (see Figure 9-3, which you reach by clicking the Connection tab and the LAN Settings button):

  ✔ Never dial a connection.

  ✔ Do not automatically detect LAN settings.

  ✔ Do not use an automatic configuration script.

  ✔ Do not use a proxy server.

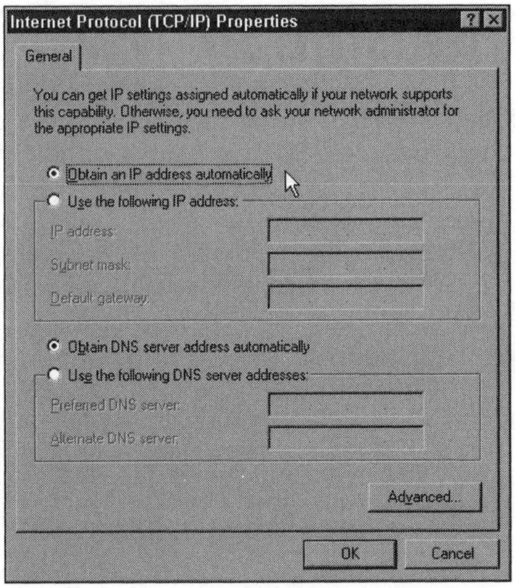

Internet Protocol (TCP/IP) Properties ? ☒

General

You can get IP settings assigned automatically if your network supports this capability. Otherwise, you need to ask your network administrator for the appropriate IP settings.

◉ Obtain an IP address automatically

○ Use the following IP address:

IP address:

Subnet mask:

Default gateway:

◉ Obtain DNS server address automatically

○ Use the following DNS server addresses:

Preferred DNS server:

Alternate DNS server:

Advanced...

OK   Cancel

Figure 9-2:
Setting
the ICS
client for
Windows
2000
Professional.

You aren't using a proxy server; you're using a network translator. That's why you must make the connection settings in the preceding list.

Local Area Network (LAN) Settings ? ☒

Automatic configuration

Automatic configuration may override manual settings. To ensure the use of manual settings, disable automatic configuration.

☐ Automatically detect settings

☐ Use automatic configuration script

Address

Proxy server

☐ Use a proxy server

Address: Port: Advanced...

☐ Bypass proxy server for local addresses

OK   Cancel

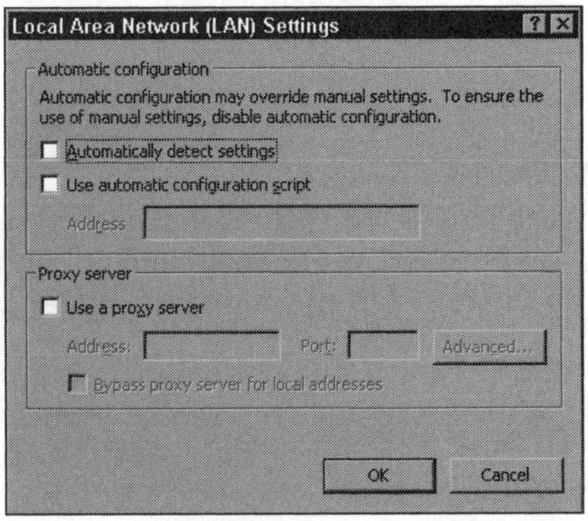

Figure 9-3:
Setting
other ICS
options.

If the Internet Connection Wizard has never been run before on the client workstation, you must run it by opening Internet Explorer and answering the wizard's prompts according to the settings in the preceding list. If you make a mistake, you can use the Internet Options control panel later to correct them.

Finally, configure any machines on the network that are not DHCP-enabled with static IP addresses.

Network Address Translation (NAT)

NAT gives you greater flexibility than ICS, but at the cost of some complexity in the setup and configuration processes. NAT's greater flexibility includes the following capabilities:

- Supporting multiple network cards
- Working with separate DHCP and DNS servers
- Using more than one public IP address
- Using a customizable range of private IP addresses

NAT is only available within the Windows 2000 Server family. If you run Windows 2000 Professional, you can only run ICS.

Enabling NAT on the translating computer

Unlike ICS, which you configure via the Network and Dial-Up Connections folder, you configure NAT via the Routing and Remote Access management console. You can set it up two ways: Using the Routing and Remote Access setup wizard, or manually, by making the various property sheet settings one by one.

Configuring NAT using the wizard

By far the easier way to configure NAT is using the setup wizard. You only have this option, however, if you have not yet enabled and configured Routing and Remote Access on the translating computer. Lab 9-2 presents the typical series of steps.

Lab 9-2   Setting Up NAT with the Wizard

1. **Choose Start➪Settings➪Control Panel.**

2. **Open the Administrative Tools folder.**

3. **Double-click the Routing and Remote Access icon.**

4. **In the tree window pane on the left side of the console, right-click the server you want to run NAT, and choose Configure and Enable Routing and Remote Access, as shown in Figure 9-4.**

5. **On the Routing and Remote Access Server Setup Wizard welcome screen, click the Next button.**

6. **Choose Internet Connection Server in the Common Configurations dialog box (see Figure 9-5) and click the Next button.**

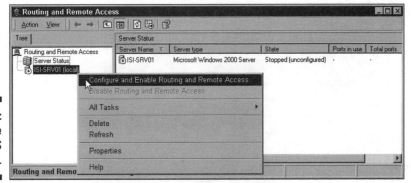

Figure 9-4:
Starting the
RRAS
wizard.

Figure 9-5:
The initials
say ICS, but
this is really
NAT.

7. **In the Internet Connection Server Setup dialog box (see Figure 9-6), select Set Up A Router With The Network Address Translation (NAT) Routing Protocol and click the Next button.**

   Note that your other option here is to choose ICS. So, on a Windows 2000 Server machine, you can set up ICS two ways: Here, and via the Network and Dial-Up Connections folder.

8. **Select your Internet link in the Internet Connection dialog box.**

   For example, if you use a dial-up device, click Create A New Demand-Dial Internet Connection, as shown in Figure 9-7.

9. **If you choose a demand-dial connection in Step 8, as this lab assumes, the RRAS wizard hands you off to the Demand Dial Interface Wizard. Click Next in the Applying Changes dialog box.**

10. **Click Next in the Welcome to the Demand Dial Interface Wizard window.**

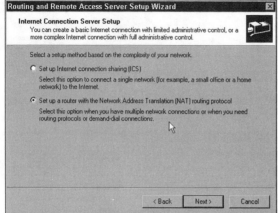

Figure 9-6:
NAT or ICS?

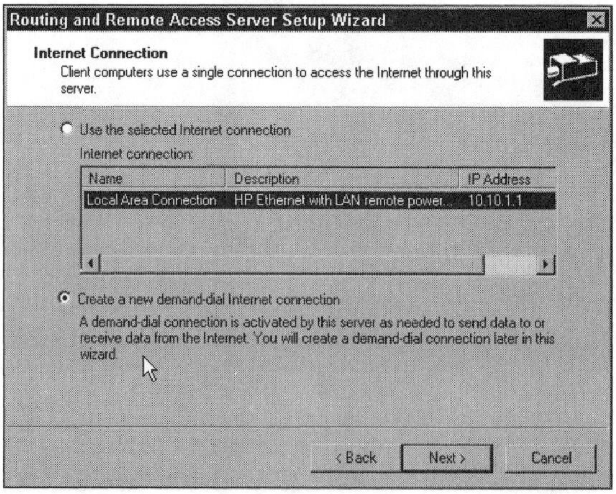

Figure 9-7:
Specify the
external
Internet link
here.

11. **Choose a name for the new interface, such as Public Internet Link. Click Next.**

12. **Choose a connection type: physical device, or Virtual Private Networking (VPN) connection. Click Next.**

13. **If you choose a physical device in Step 12, you must select one device out of a list in the Select A Device dialog box. Click Next.**

14. **In the Phone Number dialog box, enter the phone number of the dial-up server you need to dial to establish an Internet link.**

15. **In the Protocols and Security dialog box, check Route IP Packets On This Interface, as shown in Figure 9-8. (You may also need to check Send A Plain-Text Password If That Is The Only Way To Connect, if your ISP does not accept encrypted passwords.) Click Next.**

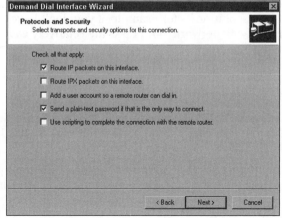

Figure 9-8:
Tell the
wizard how
to access
your ISP.

16. **In the Dial Out Credentials dialog box, specify your account name, domain (if applicable), and password for connecting to the remote router. Click Next.**

17. **In the Completing The Demand Dial Interface Wizard dialog box, click Finish.**

18. **In the Routing and Remote Access Server Setup Wizard completion dialog box, click Finish.**

    You should now see the Routing and Remote Access console with your newly activated NAT protocol, as in Figure 9-9.

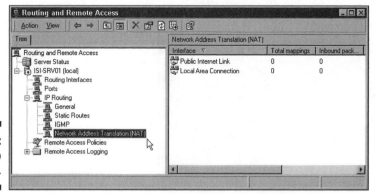

Figure 9-9:
NAT is up
and running.

Turning on NAT addressing and name resolution

In the default state after running the NAT wizard, NAT relies upon DHCP and DNS services if they're already running on the network. (This is a change from ICS, which Microsoft doesn't recommend if you already have DHCP or

DNS servers.) However, you may want to configure NAT to do its own addressing and name resolution — for example, if you don't have a DHCP or DNS server on your private network. Both tasks are relatively easy to do.

To activate the DHCP allocator, follow the steps in Lab 9-3.

Lab 9-3	Activating the NAT DHCP Allocator

1. **In the Network and Dial-Up Connections folder, configure the IP address of the network card on the private network to 192.168.0.1, subnet mask 255.255.255.0, and no default gateway.**

   You can use a different static IP address if you use a different private IP address range, but it's good practice to make the server the first address in the range.

2. **Open the Routing and Remote Access management console from the Administrative Tools folder.**

3. **In the tree pane, expand the icon for the server and then expand the IP Routing icon.**

4. **Again in the tree pane, right-click the icon for Network Address Translation (NAT) and choose Properties.**

5. **Click the Address Assignment tab, as shown in Figure 9-10.**

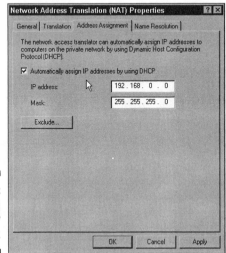

Figure 9-10:
Activating
NAT's DHCP
allocator.

6. **Check the Automatically Assign IP Addresses By Using DHCP box.**

7. **Fill in the IP address, mask, and any exclusions for IP addresses that are already assigned on the private network.**

8. **Click OK.**

To activate NAT's DNS proxy feature, follow the steps in Lab 9-4.

Lab 9-4   Activating the NAT DNS Proxy

1. **Open the Routing and Remote Access management console from the Administrative Tools folder.**

2. **In the tree pane, expand the icon for the server and then expand the IP Routing icon.**

3. **Again in the tree pane, right-click the icon for Network Address Translation (NAT) and choose Properties.**

4. **Click the Name Resolution tab.**

5. **Check the Resolve IP Addresses For Clients Using Domain Name System (DNS) box.**

6. **Check the Connect To The Public Network When A Name Needs To Be Resolved box.**

7. **Choose the demand-dial interface that connects you to the Internet.**

8. **Click OK to close the dialog box.**

Using multiple public IP addresses

In the simplest NAT configuration, your Internet interface uses a lone public IP address. However, you may have received a block of IP addresses from your ISP, in which case you can tell NAT to use 'em all. The procedure isn't too hard:

1. **Open the Routing and Remote Access console.**

2. **In the tree pane, navigate to the NAT icon and click it.**

   Your two interfaces — one to the Internet, one to your private network — appear in the details pane to the right.

3. **Right-click the Internet interface and choose Properties.**

4. **Click the Address Pool tab, as shown in Figure 9-11.**

5. **Click Add.**

6. **Specify a range of public IP addresses by using the starting and ending address fields.**

   If you don't mind doing some math, you can specify a single IP address and a mask, but I find the starting and ending addresses to be the easier way to go.

7. **Repeat Steps 5 and 6 for as many public IP address ranges as you have received from your ISP.**

8. **Click OK twice to get back to the RRAS console.**

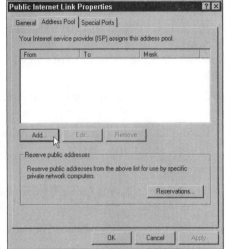

Figure 9-11:
Where to
add multiple
public IP
addresses.

Configuring NAT without the wizard

If Routing and Remote Access has already been enabled and configured on the PC where you want NAT to run, you must use the manual configuration method. Lab 9-5 assumes that you are using a dial-up link to connect to the Internet.

Lab 9-5	Setting Up NAT the Hard Way

1. **In the Network and Dial-Up Connections folder, configure the IP address of the network card on the private network to 192.168.0.1, subnet mask 255.255.255.0, and no default gateway.**

   You can use a different static IP address if you use a different private IP address range, but it's good practice to make the server the first address in the range.

2. **Open the Routing and Remote Access console, right-click the Ports icon in the tree window pane and choose Properties.**

3. **Click the Devices tab. Click the relevant dial-up device and click Configure.**

4. **Select the Demand-Dial Routing Connections (Inbound And Outbound) checkbox and click OK.**

   In Steps 2 through 4, you have enabled routing on the dial-up port.

5. **In the tree pane of the Routing and Remote Access console, right-click Routing Interfaces and choose New Demand-Dial Interface.**

   This action runs the Demand-Dial Interface wizard, which I describe in Steps 11 through 17 of Lab 9-2. I won't repeat those steps here.

6. **In the tree pane of the RRAS console, right-click the Static Routes icon under IP Routing and choose New Static Route to open the dialog box shown in Figure 9-12.**

7. **Select the Demand-Dial Interface you created in Step 5.**

8. **Set the destination as 0.0.0.0 and the network mask as 0.0.0.0.**

9. **Check the Use This Route To Initiate Demand-Dial Connections box and click OK.**

   In Steps 6 through 9, you have created a default static route that uses your interface to the Internet.

10. **In the tree pane of the RRAS console, right-click the General icon under IP Routing and choose New Routing Protocol.**

11. **Click Network Address Translation and click OK.**

    In Steps 10 and 11, you have installed NAT as a routing protocol.

12. **In the tree pane of the RRAS console, right-click Network Address Translation (NAT) and choose New Interface.**

13. **Add the Internet interface that you created in Step 5, checking the boxes labeled Public Interface Connected To The Internet and Translate TCP/UDP Headers (Recommended), as shown in Figure 9-13.**

14. **Repeat Step 12.**

15. **Add the interface to the local area connection (your network card), checking the box labeled Private Interface Connected To Private Network, as shown in Figure 9-14.**

    In Steps 12 through 15, you have added your Internet and private network interfaces to the NAT configuration.

16. **Lastly, if you want to enable NAT addressing and name resolution, follow the steps for these procedures described earlier in this chapter, in the section "Turning on NAT addressing and name resolution."**

    Phew. I *told* you the wizard was easier.

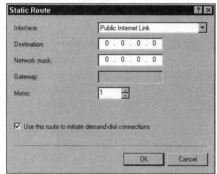

Figure 9-12:
Creating the
default
static route.

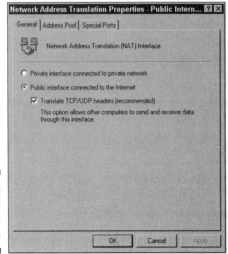

Figure 9-13:
Configuring
the public
Internet link.

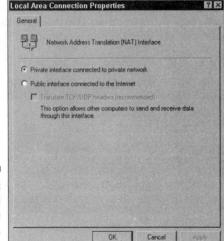

Figure 9-14:
Configuring
the private
intranet link.

Configuring NAT clients

I'll end this chapter with an easy part. Configure your Windows 2000
Professional private network clients just as I describe in the section
"Configuring ICS clients," earlier in this chapter. Hey, you made it this far;
you deserve a break.

Prep Test

1 You're using 172.16.0.1 through 172.31.255.254 as the address range for your internal private network. You use a single public IP address, 207.69.207.251, to connect to the Internet. What's the public IP address that NAT maps to the private internal address 172.16.0.2? (Choose one answer.)

A ○ 207.69.207.251

B ○ 207.69.207.252

C ○ 255.255.0.0

D ○ 172.16.0.3

2 What is the range of ephemeral ports? (Choose the best answer.)

A ○ 0 to 256

B ○ 257 to 512

C ○ 513 to 1024

D ○ 1024 to 5000

3 You decide to implement either NAT or ICS on your Windows 2000 network. Your network has an existing DNS server, but no DHCP server. Your company has a single public IP address assigned by your Internet Service Provider. All your network clients are on a single physical subnet.

Which of the following statements are true in this situation? (Choose all that apply.)

A ❑ You should use ICS, because you have only one public IP address.

B ❑ You should use ICS, because you have no DHCP server and ICS can fulfill that function.

C ❑ You should use NAT, because you already have a DNS server.

D ❑ You should use NAT, because you have only one subnet.

4 In a traditional routed network where all internal clients have IP addresses that are unique on the global Internet, certain types of traffic can flow that cannot flow across a translation interface such as ICS or NAT. Why is this? (Choose the best answer.)

A ○ Certain reserved IP addresses cannot be translated.

B ○ Translators such as ICS and NAT automatically perform packet filtering.

C ○ Some applications put address information in more than one header location.

D ○ ICS and NAT do not support Kerberos.

5 You have set up the NAT protocol on your Windows 2000 Server. The client systems on your private network all run Windows 2000 Professional. When your NAT router receives an inbound packet from the public Internet, and that packet does not correspond to an existing dynamic or static mapping at the translator, what happens next? (Choose the best answer.)

A ○ NAT creates a dynamic mapping by borrowing an unused ephemeral port number from the TCP/IP protocol stack.

B ○ NAT creates a static mapping by borrowing an unused ephemeral port number from the TCP/IP protocol stack.

C ○ NAT discards the packet and sends an error message to the network administrator via the Messenger service.

D ○ NAT discards the packet silently.

6 You need to create a NAT server on a Windows 2000 Professional computer. You have already configured a static IP address for the network adapter that connects the computer to the internal private network. You have also configured a dial-up icon to connect to your ISP. In order to add the necessary interfaces to the NAT protocol, what must you do? (Choose all that apply.)

A ❑ Run the Routing and Remote Access console, navigate to the NAT icon, right-click it, and choose New Interface. Do this twice: once for the private interface and once for the public interface.

B ❑ Run the Routing and Remote Access console, navigate to the IP Routing icon, right-click it, and choose New Interface. Do this twice: once for the private interface and once for the public interface.

C ❑ Run the Routing and Remote Access console, navigate to the Routing Interfaces icon, right-click it, and choose New Demand-Dial Interface. After creating the demand-dial interface, right-click the NAT icon and add it, as well as the private network interface.

D ❑ You cannot configure NAT in this situation. You must use ICS.

7 Which of the following IP addresses is a private address? (Choose all that apply.)

A ❑ 10.10.1.1

B ❑ 192.128.10.10

C ❑ 192.168.10.10

D ❑ 172.32.200.200

8 You have set up NAT on a Windows 2000 Server computer by running the Routing and Remote Access Server Setup wizard. What steps must you take on client machines on the internal private network? (Choose all that apply.)

A ❑ Configure the TCP/IP protocol on the local area connection to automatically obtain an IP address.

B ❑ Run the Internet Options control panel, click the Connections tab, and click Never Dial A Connection.

C ❑ Run the Internet Options control panel, click the Connections tab, click the LAN Settings button, and make sure that the checkbox that says Automatically Detect Settings is cleared.

D ❑ Run the Internet Options control panel, click the Connections tab, click the LAN Settings button, and make sure that the checkbox that says Use Automatic Configuration Script is cleared.

E ❑ Run the Internet Options control panel, click the Connections tab, click the LAN Settings button, and make sure that the checkbox that says Use A Proxy Server is cleared.

9 You're troubleshooting a NAT configuration that isn't working. You've set it up with a single public IP address. Which checkbox on the General tab of the interface for the public Internet link must be checked? (Choose one answer.)

A ○ Translate TCP/UDP Headers

B ○ Private Interface Connected To Private Network

C ○ Private Interface Connected To Public Network

D ○ Public Interface Connected To The Private Network

10 A particular Internet application works on the NAT computer, but not on any of the NAT clients. Other Internet applications work fine everywhere. What could be the problem? (Choose the best answer.)

A ○ No static routes have been configured in the Routing and Remote Acess console.

B ○ The application uses a nontranslatable payload.

C ○ The application uses both source and destination addresses in its IP headers.

D ○ The application requires the Windows 2000 Server version of the TCP/IP protocol stack.

Answers

1 **A.** *207.69.207.251.* NAT maps all internal private addresses to the single public IP address. Your organization doesn't have the address in choice B; choice C is a subnet mask; and choice D is another possible private IP address, not a public one. *See "Connection Sharing Concepts."*

2 **D.** *1024 to 5000.* ICS and NAT use port numbers from this range for dynamic port assignment to internal network clients, in order to uniquely identify them. *See "How translation works."*

3 **C.** *You should use NAT, because you already have a DNS server.* NAT can work with an existing DNS server, but ICS cannot, because you cannot separately disable the DHCP and DNS functions of ICS: It's an all-in-one package for Small Office — Home Office (SOHO) applications. Choice A is partly true in that ICS does work with a single public IP address, but ICS is still not the best choice here. Choice D doesn't apply, as both ICS and NAT work in a single-subnet environment. *See "Microsoft's IP address translators."*

4 **C.** *Some applications put address information in more than one header location.* When an application puts IP address data in a location that differs from the usual location, a translating router may not be able to translate the IP address everywhere it appears. NAT editors exist to provide compatibility for common applications such as FTP, however. Choice D is true, but it's not the best answer to this question. *See "Microsoft's IP address translators."*

5 **D.** *NAT discards the packet silently.* This is a security feature, in that incoming traffic can only reach the private network if it is: 1) in response to a request generated from within the private network, in which case a mapping of some kind must already exist; or 2) directed to a statically-mapped IP client such as a Web server, in which case a static mapping must already exist. Note that A and B are incorrect in the inbound case, but with an outbound packet, ICS and NAT do indeed create a dynamic mapping if a static mapping doesn't already exist. *See "How translation works."*

6 **D.** *You cannot configure NAT in this situation. You must use ICS.* Bit of a tricky question. Remember for the exam that NAT runs on Windows 2000 Server family operating systems only, not on Windows 2000 Professional. *See "Microsoft's IP address translators."*

7 **A** and **C.** Memorize the three ranges for private IP addresses. In particular, 192.168.x.x is the range that Microsoft uses by default for ICS and NAT. This differs from the 169.254.x.x range that Windows 2000 uses for Automatic Private IP Addressing (APIPA) when no DHCP server is available. *See "Private address ranges."*

8 **A, B, C, D,** and **E.** All these settings are required. Obtaining an IP address automatically ensures that NAT can allocate private IP addresses using DHCP. The Internet connection over the private network is via the LAN, not via any dial-up connections on workstations. The LAN checkbox settings ensure that the workstation doesn't try to find a proxy server. *See "Configuring NAT clients."*

9 **A.** *Translate TCP/UDP Headers.* Now, you can get away without TCP/UDP header translation if you have a bunch of public IP addresses, but the question states that you have only one. That means NAT must use port numbers with the single public IP address to generate mappings to the private network clients. Choices B, C, and D do not appear on the property sheet for the Internet interface. Choice B does appear on the property sheet for the private internal network interface. *See "Enabling NAT on the translating computer."*

10 **B.** *The application uses a nontranslatable payload.* That is, the application embeds the IP address in at least one nonstandard location, and no NAT editor for the application exists or has been applied. Note in choice C that all IP packets have a source and destination address. Regarding choice D, the TCP/IP protocol stack is essentially the same software code on all Windows 2000 products. *See "How translation works."*

Part IV

Security
Infrastructure

SURE, HE'S A LITTLE DIFFERENT, BUT HE WORKS HARD, AND KEEPS THE SYSTEM FREE OF BUGS.

In this part . . .

The Pretenders has always been one of my favorite bands, partly because of their name's irony: These musicians pretend to be pretenders, but they really know how to play. Many people in this world, however, are true pretenders, and they're trying to scam you. Computer technology has enabled such crooks to be crooked in new and different ways: setting up bogus Web-based universities with pay-in-advance tuitions, propagating damaging viruses, and so on.

Because networking puts us into electronic contact with so many people, we need to devote a big chunk of infrastructure to protecting ourselves from the pretenders — and from the eavesdroppers, data thieves with sinister sniffers, funneling trade secrets into the digital in-boxes of our competitors. Enter Part IV of this book, which concerns itself with certificates (helping prove that people are who they say and software is what you expect) and IPSec (helping ensure that your private conversations stay private, even across public network links).

Chapter 10

IPSec and Packet Filters

● ●

Exam Objectives

▶ Configure TCP/IP packet filters

▶ Configure and troubleshoot network protocol security

▶ Enable IPSec

▶ Configure IPSec for transport mode

▶ Configure IPSec for tunnel mode

▶ Customize IPSec policies and rules

▶ Manage and monitor IPSec

● ●

*A*s organizations become more reliant on their information systems, more confidential data buzzes across those network wires, increasing the need to secure transmitted data. (Windows 2000 facilitates security for *stored* data via the Encrypting File System.) Packet filtering and Internet Protocol Security (IPSec) can provide authentication and encryption for network communications. That, in turn, helps keep your network safe from the famous "disgruntled employee." (Ever hear of a *gruntled* employee? Me neither.)

Quick Assessment

1 TCP/IP packet filtering can restrict traffic based on _____, _____, and _____.

2 TCP port 80 corresponds to the _____ service.

3 Three types of network security are _____, _____, and _____.

4 Enable an IPSec policy by right-clicking it and choosing _____.

5 Transport mode IPSec is an example of the _____ security model.

6 Tunnel mode IPSec is most often used between two _____.

7 A total of _____ IPSec policy(ies) can be active at any one time for any given computer.

8 IPSec rules generally consist of five components. Three of those are _____, _____ , and _____.

9 Monitor active security associations using the utility _____.

10 Manage global IP filter lists and filter actions by right-clicking the _____ node in a Group Policy editor.

Answers

1 *TCP port; UDP port; IP protocol.* See "Basic TCP/IP packet filtering" for details.

2 *World Wide Web.* See "Basic TCP/IP packet filtering."

3 *Physical, perimeter, password, and stored-data* are all valid answers; you may use somewhat different terminology, which is okay. The "Network Security Overview" section covers this subject.

4 *Assign.* See "Enabling an IPSec policy" for more.

5 *End-to-end.* See "Configuring IPSec for transport mode" if you missed this one.

6 *Routers.* See "Configuring IPSec for tunnel mode" if this is news to you.

7 *One.* "Enabling an IPSec policy" contains this factoid.

8 *IP filter list, filter action, authentication method, tunnel setting, and connection type* are the valid answers. The section "Policies consist of rules" goes into detail.

9 *IPSECMON.EXE.* "Monitoring IPSec" has more on this program.

10 *IP Security Policies.* Actually, the node says either "IP Security Policies on Active Directory" or "IP Security Policies on Local Machine." See the "Fancy filtering" section.

Network Security Overview

A network's security infrastructure can have many levels, including

- **Perimeter security,** which deals with enforcing the private network's borders — that is, where the intranet meets the Internet or extranet

- **Physical security,** which deals with physical human access to machines and data (the combination lock on the server room door)

- **Stored data security,** such as the Encrypting File System (EFS) that comes with NTFS in Windows 2000

- **Password security,** such as that associated with Windows 2000 user accounts

Packet filters and IPSec deal with a very specific level: data in transit across network media. Why is securing data in transit important?

One reason is that the other security methods don't provide total security. Perimeter security doesn't protect against malice from within. Physical security has the same problem to some degree, and becomes impossible to enforce when networks connect to the Internet. Stored data security doesn't protect data in transit, and password security is only as good as the diligence with which users choose, keep, and use their passwords.

Another reason that transmission security is an important component of any network's infrastructure is that certain people have the technology and the motivation to perform various disruptive tasks with data in transit. These tasks can include

- **Eavesdropping,** or network monitoring. Heck, you even get a network monitor (or *sniffer*) with Windows 2000 Server (its name, appropriately, is Network Monitor). Anyone with a network monitor utility can view the innards of unencrypted IP packets and potentially recreate sensitive data files.

- **Counterfeiting,** in which an individual modifies data in transit.

- **Re-routing,** also known as "man in the middle," in which an individual captures a data stream to a destination other than its intended one.

- **Spoofing,** in which an individual generates packets that appear to come from a source other than their actual source.

In the United States' old West, when banks developed excellent security — safes and vaults — for stored money, bank robbers evolved into stagecoach (and, later, train) robbers. It was easier to steal money in transit than it was to steal money in bank vaults. Packet filters and IPSec are technologies that can help protect today's gold nuggets of information while they're en route from point A to B.

Packet Filters

Ever sort your mail near a garbage can, so you can route your junk mail into the "circular file?" Or divide the mail into stacks, based on which member of your family each piece of mail is addressed to? If so, you're performing packet filtering on your incoming mail traffic.

Packet filtering is a technique for restricting traffic or activating a security policy depending on a packet's source address, destination address, and/or traffic type. (Traffic type can be indicated by a TCP port number, UDP port number, or IP protocol number.)

You can use packet filtering on NetWare (IPX packets), but the exam focuses on its use in TCP/IP networks.

Basic TCP/IP packet filtering

Lab 10-1 demonstrates how to configure packet filtering on a Windows 2000 Server or Windows 2000 Professional computer running TCP/IP.

Lab 10-1	Enabling Packet Filtering on Windows 2000 Systems

1. **Choose Start➪Settings➪Network and Dial-Up Connections.**

2. **Right-click the Local Area Connection icon and choose Properties.**

3. **Double-click the listing for Internet Protocol (TCP/IP).**

4. **Click the Advanced button.**

5. **Click the Options tab.**

6. **Select TCP/IP Filtering in the list of optional settings and then click the Properties button.**

   Windows displays the TCP/IP Filtering dialog box, as shown in Figure 10-1.

7. **Check the box labeled Enable TCP/IP Filtering (All Adapters).**

8. **Click the Permit Only radio button in the category you want to restrict.**

   Your choices are TCP ports, UDP ports, and IP protocols. For example, TCP port 80 indicates Web traffic. UDP port 137 indicates WINS traffic.

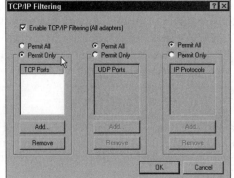

Figure 10-1:
Configuring
TCP/IP
packet
filtering.

9. **Click the Add button and then enter a port or protocol number to permit.**

   Windows 2000 filters out any ports or protocols other than the ones you expressly permit.

10. **Repeat Step 9 as necessary.**

11. **Click OK four times to close four dialog boxes.**

Packet filtering can have unintended consequences, especially if you choose to operate on a "permit only" basis. The most notorious example is that you can disable the PING command (essential for troubleshooting TCP/IP problems) if you permit only FTP or Web traffic and don't also explicitly permit ICMP traffic.

Although the most well-known application for packet filtering is in *firewalls* (computers that manage connections between a private, internal network and the public Internet), you can put packet filtering to use on a purely private internal network that does not connect to the "big I Internet." In fact, packet filtering is a key element of Microsoft's IPSec technology.

Fancy filtering

When you use packet filters with IPSec, you have a great deal more flexibility than you do when simply assigning filters at the TCP/IP transport layer. You can build and configure packet filters from a Microsoft Management Console that's equipped with the IP Security Policy snap-in. (See Lab 10-2 later in this chapter for details on creating such a console.) For now, you can simply run the Local Security Policy console from the Administrative tools folder.

Right-click the IP Security Policies On Local Machine node in the tree pane of the console and choose Manage IP Filter Lists and Filter Actions. You see the dialog box in Figure 10-2, which has two tabs: Manage IP Filter Lists, and Manage Filter Actions. This dialog box is global, by the way: It reflects all the filter lists and all the filter actions defined on the computer.

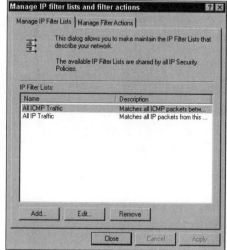

Figure 10-2:
Time to get
a little fancy
with the
filters.

Filter lists

A *filter list* is a list of filters (duh) that Windows treats as a single filter. A filter list doesn't *have* to include multiple filters — the two prefabricated lists, All IP Traffic and All ICMP Traffic, don't. But they can, which offers you some flexibility if you want to create (for example) a single filter list that covers traffic on two different physical subnets having different IP address ranges.

Take a look at the All IP Traffic filter by double-clicking its entry in the Manage IP Filter Lists dialog box. As shown in Figure 10-3, the list has a name, a description, and a list of filters.

Each filter has the following fields, which you can edit by clicking the filter in the list and then clicking Edit:

- ✔ **Mirror:** This is a shorthand way of telling Windows that you want the filter to apply bidirectionally, to outbound and inbound traffic, if the source and destination addresses are reversed.
- ✔ **Description:** Optional.

 ✔ **Protocol:** For example, TCP, UDP, and ICMP.

 ✔ **Source Port and Destination Port:** These are only available if the Protocol is TCP or UDP.

 ✔ **Source and Destination Addresses:** DNS name, IP address, and subnet mask.

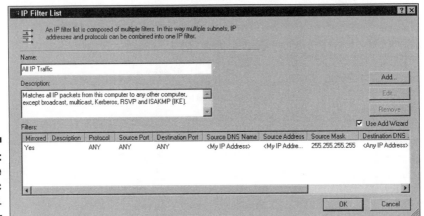

Figure 10-3:
Viewing the
All IP Traffic
filter list.

Filter actions

Now, all these details tell Windows what sort of traffic the filter should watch for, but you must also tell Windows what it's supposed to *do* when it encounters a match. That's the purpose of the Manage Filter Actions tab, shown in Figure 10-4.

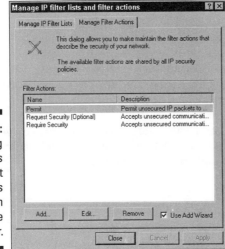

Figure 10-4:
Telling
Windows
what
actions
it can
associate
with a filter.

I should clarify that the list of filter actions is entirely independent of the filter lists. That is, you can associate any filter list with any defined filter action. You make that association later, when you create an IPSec rule. For now, just focus on what a filter action looks like.

If you double-click the action named Request Security (Optional), you see the filter action Properties dialog box shown in Figure 10-5. The "meat" of this dialog box is the Security Methods tab.

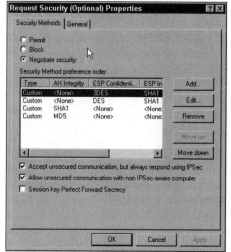

Figure 10-5:
Specifying a
filter action.

Note the radio buttons at the top of the dialog box. You can make a command decision to permit traffic or block traffic, without letting the two computers involved negotiate. Or, you can permit a negotiation in which the computers decide between themselves — based on the criteria you specify — whether to employ security, and if so, what kind.

The negotiations occur in the order specified in the list, from top to bottom. If you drill down even further by double-clicking one of the security methods in the list, you see the dialog box shown in Figure 10-6. Your choices are as follows:

- ✔ **High security (ESP, short for Encapsulating Security Payload):** This option ensures authentication (data address integrity) and encryption.

- ✔ **Medium security (AH, short for Authentication Header):** This option ensures authentication, but omits encrypting the data stream.

✔ **Custom:** You specify the algorithms to use for data address integrity and encryption:

> • For authentication purposes, SHA (Secure Hash Algorithm) is a high-security algorithm using a 160-bit key, while MD5 (Message Digest 5) is faster and uses a 128-bit key.

> • For encryption purposes, 3DES (where DES = Data Encryption Standard) is the most secure algorithm, using three 56-bit keys; 56-bit DES is next, using a single 56-bit key; and 40-bit DES is only for exports to France.

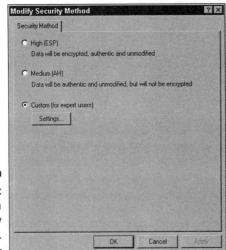

Figure 10-6:
Specifying a
security
method.

IPSec

This section explains how you can put all that nonsense in the previous section, about packet filters and filter actions, to productive use securing your network's data-in-transit.

What is IPSec?

IPSec is a set of software specifications designed to guarantee, through cryptographic means, the authenticity and confidentiality of data in transit across IP networks.

Windows 2000 installs IPSec components when you install TCP/IP onto the computer. Therefore, if an IPSec problem indicates file corruption (the IPSEC Policy Agent service doesn't start, for example), removing and reinstalling TCP/IP may fix the problem.

Here are some of the key features of IPSec:

✔ **IPSec operates at layer 3 (Network) of the seven-layer OSI model.**

Because it runs at a relatively low layer, and because it doesn't change the way Layer 3 interacts with higher layers in the modular networking stack, IPSec can provide security even for applications that aren't aware of its existence; any application that uses IP can enjoy the security benefits of IPSec. This is an advantage over Secure Sockets Layer (SSL), another cryptographic standard for transmitted data, which requires applications to be SSL-aware in order to provide security.

✔ **IPSec works between workstations, between workstations and servers, and between servers. IPSec also works with LAN, WAN (router-to-router), and dial-up connections.**

However, that's not to say that IPSec is compatible with *all* network connectivity situations. For example, it doesn't work with NAT (Network Address Translation) or ICS (Internet Connection Sharing) — methods for sharing an Internet connection with several users.

✔ **IPSec in Windows 2000 permits configuration through Group Policy and Active Directory utilities.**

In particular, support for policies reduces the administrative hassle of deploying IPSec, because you can create settings that apply to entire groups or domains at one fell swoop.

✔ **Users don't even have to be in the same domain to use IPSec, which is based on public key cryptography.**

✔ **Simple routers don't need any special tweaking to work with IPSec.**

Firewalls and other special-purpose routers may not be compatible with IPSec, but most simple traffic routers can move IPSec packets around just like regular IP packets. The only computers that have to "understand" IPSec are the sending and receiving computers, not the intermediary devices.

✔ **Time-coding prevents "replaying" data streams at a later time after capture.**

✔ **Administrators have some control over the degree of security enforced by IPSec, so they can balance performance versus encryption strength.**

You can use IPSec for secure *authentication* (verifying that a computer is who it says it is), *confidentiality* (encrypting the entire data stream), or both.

When do you use it?

Generally, use IPSec when the viewing, modification, or rerouting of transmitted data could be detrimental to your organization or to the public. The common applications of IPSec are two:

- ✔ When you need to encrypt communications between Windows 2000 computers, such as a workstation (or collection of workstations) and server

- ✔ When you need to encrypt communications between two Windows 2000 routers in a wide-area network tunnel, such as a Virtual Private Network (VPN)

Don't use IPSec unless you need it. The performance overhead of encrypting and decrypting packets is significant: the average packet size increases, network traffic increases, and CPU time increases.

How does IPSec work?

The best way to understand the workings of IPSec is to walk through a sample message transmission and consider the sequence of events that occurs. Before doing that, though, let me define the three main components of IPSec, so you can properly follow the sequence of events. Those components are

- ✔ **The IPSEC Policy Agent:** A system service (you can see it in the Services console of the Administrative Tools folder) that installs with TCP/IP on Windows 2000 computers. This component starts with the operating system. It retrieves the computer's IPSec policy, either from Active Directory (if present) or the local Registry. The policy agent then automatically starts the other two components and informs them of the active IPSec policy.

- ✔ **The IKE (Internet Key Exchange) service:** Formerly known as ISAKMP/Oakley Key Management Service. The IKE service has several responsibilities: It authenticates the computers about to participate in an IPSec exchange; it generates and distributes the keys that each computer will use for encryption and decryption; and it creates a Security Association (SA) between the two computers, consisting of all the possible security settings for that session (such as encryption method).

- ✔ **The IPSEC driver (IPSEC.SYS):** The watchdog in the whole scheme. It constantly checks all inbound and outbound IP traffic until a packet triggers a preset packet filter (here's where the packet filtering business comes in) specified by the active IPSec policy. The driver could trigger based on source IP address, destination IP address, or IP traffic type. If the data is outbound, the driver handles encryption; if inbound, the driver handles decryption.

In a nutshell, here's what happens in an IPSec communications scenario:

1. User A initiates a connection with User B.

2. The IPSEC driver detects outgoing traffic from User A's machine and checks to see if the traffic matches a filter in the currently active IPSec policy, which the Policy Agent set up when Computer A started.

3. The traffic does match a filter in the active policy, so the IPSEC driver tells the IKE service on Computer A that an IPSec session needs to be established for this communication.

4. The IKE service contacts User B's computer and sets up a security association, complete with shared keys.

5. The IKE service gives the shared keys and security association details to the IPSEC drivers on Computers A and B.

6. The IPSEC driver on Computer A encrypts the outgoing data and sends it on to Computer B.

7. Computer B gets the encrypted IPSec traffic and the IPSEC driver on that computer decrypts the traffic and forwards it to the appropriate application on the B machine.

All the preceding steps presume that no firewalls are in place, or that any firewalls between computers A and B are configured to forward IP traffic between the two.

Enabling IPSec with policies

You enable, configure, and edit IPSec parameters in Windows 2000 with *policies*. Windows 2000 uses policies to manage a wide variety of computer settings at various levels: computers (whether domain members or standalone), domains, organizational units, and so on.

Accessing policy consoles

Microsoft has provided several ways to access IPSec policies, as follows:

✔ Run the Local Security Settings console in the Administrative Tools folder, and click the node labeled IP Security Policies On Local Machine.

✔ Run the Local Group Policy tool (GPEDIT.MSC), and navigate to Computer Configuration\Windows Settings\Security Settings\IP Security Policies on Local Machine.

✔ On a domain controller, run the Active Directory Users and Computers console, and edit domain policies via the Group Policy tab of the domain property sheet. In this case, navigate to Computer Configuration\Windows Settings\Security Settings\IP Security Policies on Active Directory, as shown in Figure 10-7.

✔ Create your own custom Microsoft Management Console and add the IP Security Policy Management snap-in to it, or add the snap-in to an existing console. Lab 10-2 illustrates the technique.

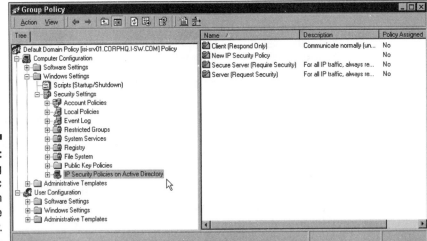

Figure 10-7: Modifying IPSec policies in Active Directory.

All these methods present a user interface that is essentially the same, although the first two methods restrict you to configuring IPSec on the local computer.

You must have administrator rights on the system to enable and configure IPSec policies.

Lab 10-2   Creating a Custom Management Console for IPSec

1. **At a Windows 2000 Server acting as a domain controller, choose Start⇨Run and type** MMC.

   This command runs the Microsoft Management Console.

2. **Choose Console⇨Add/Remove Snap-In.**

3. **On the Standalone tab in the Add/Remove Snap-In dialog box, click the Add button.**

   A list of available snap-ins appears.

4. **Scroll down to IP Security Policy Management, click it, and click the Add button (see Figure 10-8).**

Figure 10-8:
Adding the
IPSec Policy
Manage-
ment
snap-in.

5. In the Select Computer dialog box, choose Manage Domain Policy For This Computer's Domain (see Figure 10-9).

You can also choose to focus the snap-in on the local computer, another computer, or another domain.

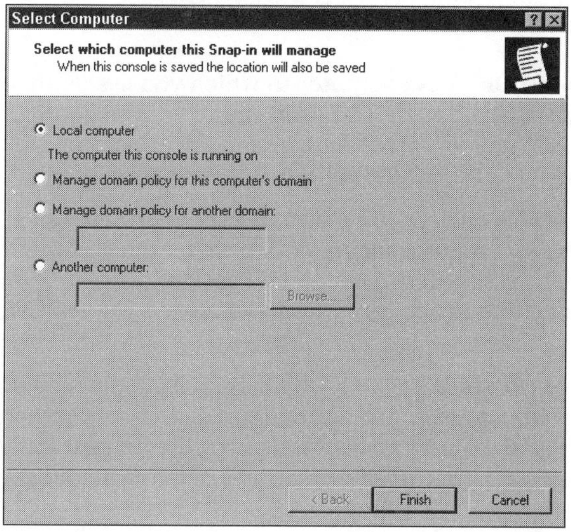

Figure 10-9:
Choosing
the
snap-in's
focus.

6. Click Finish.

7. Click Close to close the Add Standalone Snap-In dialog box.

8. Click OK to close the Add/Remove Snap-In dialog box.

You now have a custom console that looks like the one in Figure 10-10.

Figure 10-10:
The end
result: an
IPSec
manage-
ment
console.

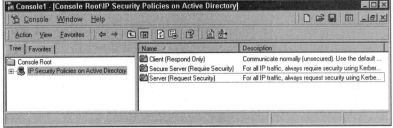

9. **Choose Console⇨Save As, choose a destination, and name your console.**

Although you can use the console you create in Lab 10-2 for viewing, adding, and editing IPSec policies, for some strange reason the standalone IP Security Policy snap-in doesn't allow you to actually assign policies. Add the Group Policy snap-in to your console for that purpose (you must navigate to Computer Configuration\Windows Settings\Security Settings).

Predefined IPSec policies

When you click the IP Security Policies On Active Directory node in the tree pane of the IPSec policy console that you created in Lab 10-2, three predefined policy templates appear in the details pane:

- ✔ **Client (Respond Only):** A computer to which you assign this policy only uses IPSec when asked to do so by another computer, but permits the use of cleartext (unencrypted) data communication. The computer defaults to using Kerberos for mutual authentication of identities.

- ✔ **Server (Request Security):** Microsoft defines this policy as applicable for computers that require secure data transfer most of the time, but not all the time. The computer to which you assign this policy can accept incoming traffic that is not encrypted, but always requests IPSec from the sender.

- ✔ **Secure Server (Require Security):** This is an example-only policy that you probably would never use as configured. A computer configured with this policy always rejects unsecured traffic (except ICMP, broadcast, multicast, and IKE traffic) and always secures all outgoing traffic.

Policies consist of rules

Each of these predefined policies uses one or more *rules* to define the behavior that the policy mandates. For example, if you right-click the Secure Server policy and choose Properties, you see the rules dialog box shown in Figure 10-11. This policy uses three rules: one that requires security for all IP traffic, one that permits unsecured ICMP traffic (such as PING commands), and one that uses the prebuilt "default response" rule.

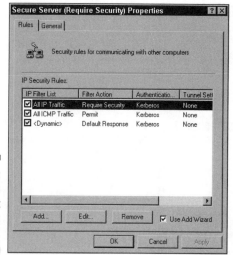

Figure 10-11:
An IPSec
policy is just
a collection
of rules.

The *default response rule* is one that Windows 2000 uses if another computer requests secure communications, and no other rule has been defined for the active IPSec policy to deal with such a request. You can include or exclude the default response rule when you create a new policy using the Add Policy wizard. This rule's property sheet looks a bit different from "normal" rule property sheets, and consists of the Security Methods, Authentication Methods, and Connection Type tabs.

Double-click any of the rules in the Secure Server (Require Security) Properties dialog box and you can see, from the Edit Rule Properties dialog box (see Figure 10-12), that an IPSec rule consists of the following components:

✔ An IP packet **filter list,** which can consist of a single packet filter definition or multiple filters

✔ A **filter action,** which defines how Windows should negotiate encryption security when a packet matches the criteria in the IP packet filter list

✔ An **authentication method,** which defines how Windows should verify the identity of the communicating computers

Kerberos is the default authentication method, but you can also use a certificate if a certificate authority exists on the network, or, failing that, a private preshared key known only to the two communicating computers.

✔ The IP address of a **tunnel endpoint,** if the policy is for a tunnel mode situation (router-to-router link)

✔ The **connection type** or types to which the rule applies (all connections, LAN connections, remote access connections)

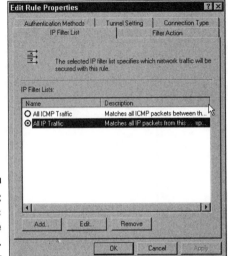

Figure 10-12:
Every IPSec
rule has five
components.

Enabling an IPSec policy

After you select or create the management console that's most convenient for you, enable an IPSec policy by right-clicking it and choosing Assign. IPSec policies do not take effect until you assign them.

You can assign only one IPSec policy at a time.

Configuring IPSec for transport mode

Transport mode is an end-to-end implementation of IPSec that you use to secure communications between two Windows 2000 computers. The computers don't have to be on the same subnet, because IPSec works across most routers. Unlike tunnel mode (see the next section), transport mode secures the data stream all the way from sender to receiver.

Transport mode is the default IPSec mode for Windows 2000.

Setting transport mode is one of the easier actions you can perform in IPSec management. Choose the policy you want to modify, drill down to the rule you want to modify, and edit its property sheet so that the Tunnel Setting tab states that This Rule Does Not Specify An IPSec Tunnel, as shown in Figure 10-13.

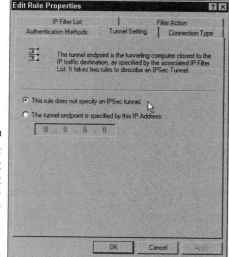

Figure 10-13:
Set
transport
mode by
turning off
tunnel
mode.

Configuring IPSec for tunnel mode

Tunnel mode is not an end-to-end implementation of IPSec. It's a router-to-router implementation. Two computers that communicate across a WAN link would only have the router-to-router portion of their communications stream protected by IPSec.

Such a configuration is useful if you have network clients on either end that don't run Windows 2000 and don't support IPSec, but your routers do. Encrypting one leg of a data stream's journey is better than encrypting none of it.

Set tunneling by choosing the policy you want to modify, drilling down to the rule you want to modify, and editing its property sheet so that the Tunnel Setting tab states The Tunnel Endpoint Is Specified By This IP Address (refer back to Figure 10-13).

You need to enter a valid IP address, so the computer at the tunnel endpoint must have a static IP configuration. You must do this on both ends of the tunnel.

Monitoring IPSec

Microsoft has provided a tool for monitoring active security associations. Start the IPSec Monitor from the Run dialog box by typing **IPSECMON**. If you want to run the tool and view statistics for a remote machine, type **IPSECMON <*computername*>**. You see a display such as that in Figure 10-14.

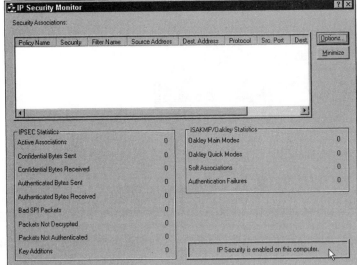

Figure 10-14: Monitor active security associations here.

The only configurable setting in this utility is the refresh period, which defaults to 15 seconds.

Even if no security associations are active, the message in IPSECMON's lower-right corner indicates whether the computer is IPSec-capable or not. According to Microsoft's documentation, if the message reads IP Security Is Enabled On This Computer, an IPSec policy must have been assigned to the computer. My own testing indicates otherwise, however, so maybe the safe assumption is that the message indicates IPSec capability — whether the capability has been assigned or not.

Microsoft tech note #Q231587 provides lots of gory details on IPSECMON statistics.

If you don't have quick access to IPSECMON, you can always open the LAN connection's Advanced TCP/IP Settings dialog box, click the Options tab, and double-click IP Security to see if IPSec is enabled and, if so, which IP security policy is active, as Figure 10-15 shows. You can also monitor IPSec by using the Event Viewer, as the next section mentions.

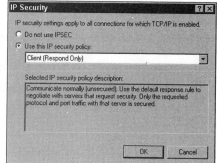

Figure 10-15:
Performing
a quick
IPSec status
check.

Troubleshooting IPSec

If IPSec isn't working, the following troubleshooting tips should help:

✔ **Turn off IPSec on both computers and then see if they can communicate.**

Do this by opening the Services console in Administrative Tools, right-clicking IPSEC Policy Agent, and choosing Stop. (You can also get to the Services console via the Computer Management console; it's under Services and Applications.)

If the computers still can't talk to each other, the problem is probably not with IPSec, but with some other network connectivity component. Re-enable the IPSEC Policy Agent. Try using PING to test low-level network connectivity.

The first time you run PING between two computers configured for IPSec communication, you typically see a message saying `Negotiating IP Security`. This is normal, and you may need to execute PING again in order to see the usual four success replies.

✔ **Run IPSECMON to see if a security association exists between the two computers.**

If not, check your IP Security Policies console to verify that you've assigned a policy to both computers.

✔ **Run Event Viewer to consult the Security and System event logs.**

Any logged events may point you in the right direction. Policy agent events appear in the System event log; security association events appear in the Security log (if auditing is enabled); and IKE messages appear in the Application log.

Prep Test

1 You want to set up IPSec on your mostly-Windows 2000 network. However, you have a few non-Windows clients that do not authenticate to the domain. What authentication method could you set up on the rule's property sheet in your IPSec policy? (Choose all that apply.)

A ❑ Use a certificate from a CA.

B ❑ Use Kerberos v5.

C ❑ Use a preshared key.

D ❑ Use Encapsulating Security Payload.

2 You have set up IPSec for a Windows 2000 network. One workstation cannot communicate with IPSec, although other workstations can do so. Upon reviewing the event log, you see that the IPSEC Policy Agent is not starting. You use the Services control panel to start it manually, without success. You decide to reinstall the files that relate to the IPSEC Policy Agent. What procedure should you follow? (Choose the best answer.)

A ◯ Run the Add/Remove Programs wizard, choose Add/Remove Windows Components, click Networking Components, and select IPSec. Remove it and then reinstall it.

B ◯ Run the Add/Remove Programs wizard, choose Add/Remove Windows Components, click Networking Services, and select Simple TCP/IP Services. Remove it and then reinstall it.

C ◯ Run the Add/Remove Programs wizard, choose Add/Remove Windows Components, and select Internet Protocol (TCP/IP). Remove it and then reinstall it.

D ◯ Open the Network and Dial-Up Connections folder and disable TCP/IP on each connection that uses it. On the final connection's property sheet, click Internet Protocol (TCP/IP) and Uninstall.

3 What two IPSec components does the IPSec Policy Agent automatically start? (Choose the two best answers.)

A ❑ ISAKMP/Oakley

B ❑ IKE

C ❑ IPSEC.SYS

D ❑ IPSEC.DRV

E ❑ IPSec Policy Management

4 Users on your network are reporting error messages in the event logs when they communicate using IPSec. You decide to try isolating the problem and seeing if the communication problems are IPSec-related, or more fundamental. You visit two computers and disable the IPSec service on both. What method can you use to stop IPSec? (Choose all that apply.)

A ❑ Right-click the Local Area Connection icon in the Network and Dial-Up Connections folder and choose Properties. Double-click Internet Protocol (TCP/IP) and click the Advanced button. On the Options tab, right-click IPSec and choose Stop.

B ❑ In the Computer Management console, open the Services and Applications node. Right-click IPSEC Policy Agent in the tree pane and choose Stop.

C ❑ Open the Administrative Tools folder and double-click Services. Right-click IPSEC Policy Agent and choose Stop.

D ❑ In the Computer Management console, open the Services and Applications node. Click Services in the tree pane. Right-click IPSEC Policy Agent in the details pane and choose Stop.

5 What information must you have in order to enable IPSec in tunnel mode? (Choose all that apply.)

A ❑ The DNS address of both tunnel endpoints.
B ❑ The IP address of both tunnel endpoints.
C ❑ The NetBIOS names of both tunnel endpoints.
D ❑ The computer names of both tunnel endpoints.

6 The first time you PING a computer with which you are configured to use encrypted TCP/IP communications, what message are you likely to see?

A ○ Negotiating IP security
B ○ Negotiating IPSec
C ○ Invalid response from *hostname*
D ○ Destination host not reachable

7 Which of the following acronyms identifies an encryption algorithm compatible with Encapsulating Security Payload? (Choose all that apply.)

A ❑ AH
B ❑ ISAKMP
C ❑ 3DES
D ❑ DES

8 **Which of the following network services are incompatible with IPSec? (Choose all that apply.)**

A ❑ NAT

B ❑ ICS

C ❑ DHCP

D ❑ RRAS

Answers

1 **A and C.** If a Certificate Authority (CA) is present, you can use that method to verify identity for non-Windows computers. Otherwise, you can set up a pre-shared secret key that both communicating computers know about, as long as the non-Windows computer permits such configuration. Kerberos is the authenticating protocol used by Windows 2000 domain clients; ESP is for encryption, not authentication. *See "Policies consist of rules."*

2 **D.** Windows 2000 doesn't let you install or remove IPSec as a separate component; you have to reinstall the whole TCP/IP protocol suite in order to guarantee a correct IPSec reinstallation. As with other network protocols, you install and remove TCP/IP via the property sheets for icons in the Network and Dial-Up Connections folder. *See "What is IPSec?"*

3 **B and C.** Answer A is sort of right, but the terminology is now outdated (although you still see it in the Windows 2000 user interface). Choice D is the wrong filename, and choice E is a management console snap-in that you must open yourself. *See "What is IPSec?"*

4 **C and D.** As usual with Windows operating systems, there's more than one way to skin a cat (or execute a command). The exam expects you to know your way around the various consoles. *See "Troubleshooting IPSec."*

5 **B.** The property sheet demands IP addresses; DNS and NetBIOS names don't work. Also remember to configure each tunnel computer for the other's IP address. *See "Configuring IPSec for tunnel mode."*

6 **A.** If you try the command again, it'll probably work, but the security negotiation process takes a bit of time. *See "Troubleshooting IPSec."*

7 **C and D.** 3DES is the most secure, and uses three 128-bit keys. DES comes in 40-bit and 56-bit flavors. AH stands for Authentication Header and is not an encryption algorithm. ISAKMP stands for Internet Standards Association Key Management Protocol, and is the older name for IKE (Internet Key Exchange). *See "Filter actions."*

8 **A and B.** Internet Connection Sharing and Network Address Translation don't work with IPSec, because those services need the ability to modify IP addresses inside unencrypted data packets. *See "What is IPSec?"*

Chapter 11

Certificates

. . . .

Exam Objectives

▶ Install and configure Certificate Authority (CA)

▶ Issue and revoke certificates

▶ Remove the Encrypting File System (EFS) recovery keys

. . . .

*I*n business, you earn you colleagues' trust, and they earn yours, over time and in increments. If events lead you to mistrust certain people, or if you find that they mistrust you, then you drop them like a hot coal. If certain other colleagues behave honorably even when it's inconvenient for them, you treasure those people. Sometimes the discovery process takes years, and most of us are in for at least one or two surprises along the way.

In computing, increasing connectivity means trust is more important than it used to be. Trust an anonymous e-mailer who professes love for you, and you catch a digital virus. The challenge is that in computing, you don't *have* years to develop and nurture a relationship with a particular Web site or ActiveX control. (Not that you would *want* to.) You need a fast method to decide whom and what you can trust. Digital certificates in your network infrastructure can provide a measure of assurance that X is, indeed, X and not Y — and that the message from X is just as X created it.

Quick Assessment

Install and configure Certificate Authority

1 If you want to set up a certificate server for internal use only, choose the _____ class server installation.

2 To install a standalone certificate server, you must have a(n) _____ account on the local server.

3 After installing the Certificate Server service, you may not change the server's _____ or its _____.

4 The default CSP for a Certificate Server is _____.

5 The usual recommended validity duration for an enterprise root CA is _____.

Issue and revoke certificates

6 If you want to support user certificate requests via the Web enrollment pages, install Certificate Services on a server that is already running _____.

7 If you want to grant access to an external user with no account in Active Directory, you can issue a certificate and create a(n) _____.

8 The URL for a user to request a certificate from a CA running IIS is _____.

Remove the EFS recovery keys

9 A local PC's Administrator has two EFS certificates: one for everyday encryption and decryption, and one for _____.

10 You can disable EFS on a given PC by deleting the EFS _____.

Answers

1   *Enterprise.* See "Types of certificate servers" for more.

2   *Administrator.* The "Installation requirements" section provides details.

3   *Computer name; domain membership.* If you specified these items in reverse order, give yourself full credit. (That's a joke, son.) See "The installation process" for this and other facts.

4   *Microsoft Base Cryptographic Provider.* A "CSP" is a Cryptography Service Provider. See "The installation process."

5   *Two years.* You can change it during installation; see "The installation process."

6   *Internet Information Services (IIS).* See "Installation requirements" for details.

7   *Mapping.* See "Mapping certificates to users" for more.

8   *http://<servername>/certsvr.* You get full credit if you said *http://<servername>/certsvr/default.asp*. See "Microsoft Certificate Services and Windows 2000."

9   *Recovery.* See "EFS, Certificates, and Recovery" if this is news to you.

10 *Policy.* The section "Removing the EFS recovery keys" explains.

Certificates Overview

This chapter may well be the most abstract one in the book, and the most difficult to grasp conceptually. The reason is partly that many of us have worked in organizations that never used digital certificates, and partly that Microsoft has effectively hidden certificate activity behind the user interface in Windows 2000 services that use certificates.

Public Key Infrastructure

Public Key Infrastructure, or *PKI,* is a network structure consisting of certificate authorities and certificates. The PKI verifies the identity of participants in an electronic exchange of information. The methods that a PKI uses to do this are collectively called *public key cryptography.*

Why not just passwords?

Now, wait a second. Isn't it enough that a user has to log on with an account name and password? Often, that's adequate verification of a user's identity, as long as that person is a member of your corporate network. But sometimes password protection isn't adequate — for example, when you interact electronically with someone who's *not* on your corporate network.

✔ Consider e-mail. "Spoofing" an e-mail address so that it appears to come from X, when it really comes from Y, isn't especially difficult. If you want truly secure e-mail, you probably want PKI.

✔ Consider a stolen notebook computer. A thief doesn't need your username and password to remove your hard drive, install it as a second disk on another machine, and gain access to its entire contents. The Windows 2000 Encrypting File System, or EFS, uses PKI in an effort to thwart such unauthorized access.

✔ Think about security for transmitted data. Windows 2000 uses PKI as the foundation for IPSec, which provides authentication and encryption for IP traffic between two users or between two routers (see Chapter 10). Encryption en route is a higher level of security than password protection alone.

What's public key cryptography?

Public key cryptography provides authentication and encryption functions in the context of a public key infrastructure.

The basis of both authentication and encryption is the *key pair.* A key is a random sequence of alphanumeric characters, and a key pair is just what it says: two keys. With public key cryptography, each user has a *public key,* which is published for the world to see, and a *private key,* known only to the user (or to the user's computer).

Public key encryption

Assume, for example, that Antonio is sending a message to Angelica, and the message is encrypted using public key cryptography. Before sending the message, Antonio gets Angelica's public key, which is published information that any user can obtain. Antonio's computer uses an *algorithm,* or mathematical formula, to encode his message using Angelica's public key. This algorithm is rather special: It's designed so that Angelica can use her private key to decode the message. Angelica's public key is therefore mathematically tied to her private key: Messages encrypted with her public key may be decrypted with her private key.

In other words, if some interloper eavesdrops on Antonio's message to Angelica, all the eavesdropper sees is a coded message (called *ciphertext*). That message means nothing unless the eavesdropper can decode it, and the eavesdropper can't decode it without Angelica's private key. (Her public key is fine for *en*crypting the message, as Antonio did, but no good for *de*crypting it. The public key encryption process is a one-way street, as it must be; otherwise, the eavesdropper could simply decrypt the ciphertext with the public key.)

This is a pretty slick system. All Antonio needs to know in order to send a coded message to Angelica is her public key, and which algorithm her computer uses. On the receiving end, she's the only one who can read that coded message, because the algorithm requires that her private key be used for decryption.

Public key authentication

That's fine for encryption, but how does the public/private key pair system handle authentication? In that scenario, say Angelica wants to put an ActiveX control on her company's public Web site, to perform some useful function in the context of a Web page. She uses a private key to create a *digital signature* (a sequence of bits in the ActiveX control's file).

Any Web visitor with access to the corresponding public key — available, for example, from a public Certification Authority (CA) — can verify that Angelica is the source of the ActiveX control, because if she didn't have the private key (which she got from the CA), she couldn't have created the digital signature. Here again, the public and private keys are mathematically related.

Of course, public key authentication relies on the diligence of the Certification Authority, who may take steps to verify Angelica's existence, address, phone number, articles of incorporation, and so forth, before issuing her the private key she'll use to create digital signatures.

If you use a public key first, and a private key afterward, you're performing a *key exchange operation* — for example, for message encryption. If you use a private key first, and a public key afterward, you're performing a *digital signature operation*.

Digital signatures not only vouch for the identity of a document's creator, they also vouch for the document's integrity — in the sense that the document is just as Angelica created it. The process of adding a digital signature uses a *hash algorithm* so that the signature is invalid if a single bit of the document's content is changed.

Certificates and what they do

A digital certificate is a file containing a digitally signed statement, issued by an authoritative (or trusted) source, that attests to the identity of the certificate holder. The certificate holder could be an individual, a computer, or a computer program (such as a service). Windows may use a certificate for encryption or authentication.

In terms of the public key cryptography discussion in the previous section, a certificate consists of the public key and certain characteristics of the key pair, such as an expiration date.

The relevant standard here is X.509, from the International Telecommunications Union (ITU). Windows 2000 certificates are compliant with the X.509 standard, and Windows 2000 can use certificates from other computers that also comply with this standard.

Certificate terminology

Here are a few terms to know for the exam:

> ✔ A **Certificate Authority (CA)** is a computer or organization that generates and assigns public and private keys, and their associated digital certificates, for encryption and authentication. CAs can also revoke certificates if and when necessary. Each CA can have a different set of criteria for issuing certificates. Each CA can also have a different set of attributes that it associates with a certificate. Certificate Authorities generally confirm their own identity with a certificate that another CA issued, although a CA may have a certificate that it gave to itself.
>
> > • Public CAs issue certificates on a paid basis — for example, to companies that want to provide authentication of their software products to their customers.

- Private CAs issue certificates on a private network. Windows 2000 Servers running Certificate Services typically act as private CAs.

✔ A **Certificate Store** is a group of certificates — not a place you go to buy certificates. (My theory is that the occasional bad joke wakes you up.)

✔ **Revoking** a certificate means marking the certificate as invalid and simultaneously moving it to the Revoked Certificates folder, actions an administrator takes (for example) when the validity of a certificate is called into question for some reason.

✔ A **Certificate Revocation List (CRL)** is a list of certificates that have been revoked. CAs publish CRLs to inform others that the revoked certificates should no longer be considered valid.

Microsoft Certificate Services and Windows 2000

In Windows 2000, various components enable, manage, and use Public Key Infrastructure. Components for enabling and managing PKI include the following:

✔ **Certificate Services** is the operating system service for Windows 2000 Server that underpins the entire Public Key Infrastructure.

✔ **The Certification database** contains certificate details; it usually lives in `C:\WINNT\SYSTEM32\CERTLOG`, although you can specify an alternative location when you install Certificate Services.

✔ **The Certification Authority management console** (CERTSRV.MSC) is the tool you use to manage Certificate Services on a Windows 2000 Server. Its icon resides in the Administrative Tools folder. Use this console to view certificates, revoke them, edit certificate-related policies, back up the database, and so on.

✔ **The Certification console snap-in** (CERTMGR.MSC) is the tool you use to view and manage existing certificates on a Windows 2000 Server or Windows 2000 Professional computer.

✔ **Certificate Services Web interface** is a Web server to which network users can connect (by pointing their browser to `http://<servername>//certsvr`) to request certificates.

This component only works if Internet Information Server is running on the Windows 2000 Server that's running Certification Services.

✔ **Active Directory,** the enterprise directory service, is one vehicle for publishing certificates and certificate revocation lists. (It's not the only vehicle; for example, Windows 2000 users can get certificates embedded in smart cards.)

Components that use PKI include the following:

- **IPSec,** a set of protocols for securing IP traffic between computers and between routers, uses certificates. You do not need to have Certificate Services running on a Windows 2000 machine for IPSec to work, however.

- **EFS,** the Encrypting File System, is another operating system feature that uses certificates. As with IPSec, EFS doesn't require the presence of a server running Certificate Services.

- Many Windows **applications,** including Internet Explorer, Internet Information Server, and Outlook Express, use certificates for authentication and encryption.

Installing Certificate Services

Before you install Certificate Services on a Windows 2000 machine, you should have a good understanding of the different types of certificate servers. You should also be aware of the prerequisites for the different types. This section presents all that information, plus a sample procedure for installing one particular type of Certificate Authority, the enterprise root CA.

Types of certificate servers

You can classify certificate servers two ways: enterprise versus standalone, and root versus subordinate:

- An **enterprise** certificate authority (CA) is suitable for providing certificates inside a private Windows 2000 network. Enterprise CAs require the presence of Active Directory, and any entity requesting a certificate must have an Active Directory account as well as appropriate security permissions within Active Directory. Because Active Directory requires DNS, enterprise CAs also require DNS.

- A **standalone** CA is suitable for providing certificates outside a private Windows 2000 network. Standalone CAs do not require Active Directory and don't have to be part of a domain.

- A **root** CA is the most trusted CA in an organization. In big companies, root CAs typically issue certificates to subordinate CAs, although root CAs can also issue certificates to network clients.

- A **subordinate** CA is simply a CA that some other CA (called its *parent*) has certified. Every subordinate CA must have a parent CA. In big companies, subordinate CAs typically issue certificates to network clients for specific applications (such as smart cards or secured e-mail). Subordinate CAs can also issue certificates to even-more-subordinate CAs.

A hierarchy of certificate servers provides scalability for large or growing organizations. Having said that, not all organizations need to use all types of certificate servers, and smaller organizations may not need a certificate server at all.

An enterprise CA can be a root CA or a subordinate CA. A standalone CA can be a root CA or a subordinate CA. So, you really have four types of certificate servers: enterprise root, enterprise subordinate, standalone root, and standalone subordinate.

Some other terminology you may see on the exam presumes a three-tiered CA structure instead of a two-tiered structure. In such a hierarchy, you have a *root* CA, an *intermediate* CA, and an *issuing* CA.

Installation requirements

To install an enterprise CA, you must have administrator privileges in Active Directory. To install a standalone CA, you must have administrator privileges on the local server.

Windows expects you to have your Server CD-ROM handy so that it can copy the necessary files to the server computer's hard drive. Although Windows 2000 Server ships with Certificate Services, the service doesn't install itself by default during a server installation.

You must have Internet Information Server (IIS) installed on the computer if you want the Certificate Authority to permit users to request certificates via the Web enrollment pages.

The installation process

After you know what type of CA you want to install, the actual installation is fairly straightforward. Lab 11-1 goes through a typical procedure.

Installing Certificate Services is more than a casual act; it requires a certain commitment. As shown in Figure 11-1, Windows doesn't let you change the computer's name or its domain membership after you perform the installation — unless you uninstall Certificate Services first.

Figure 11-1:
A
preliminary
caution.

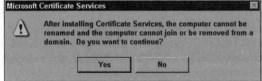

Microsoft Certificate Services

After installing Certificate Services, the computer cannot be renamed and the computer cannot join or be removed from a domain. Do you want to continue?

[Yes]   [No]

Lab 11-1   Installing an Enterprise Root CA

1. **Choose Start➪Settings➪Control Panel.**

   By the way, you must be logged on as an Administrator on a server that belongs to an Active Directory domain.

2. **Double-click Add/Remove Programs.**

3. **Click the Add/Remove Windows Components button along the left edge of the window.**

4. **Check the Certificate Services box in the Windows Components dialog box and then click the Next button.**

5. **Click the Yes button in the warning message dialog box.**

6. **In the Certification Authority Type dialog box, click Enterprise Root CA (see Figure 11-2).**

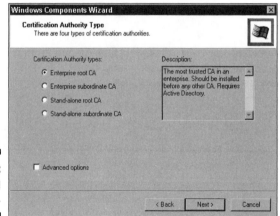

Figure 11-2:
Selecting
the CA type.

7. **Click the Advanced options checkbox and click the Next button.**

   This action lets you view and modify the cryptography options.

8. **View the cryptography settings in the Public and Private Key Pair dialog box (see Figure 11-3) and click the Next button.**

   You may not need to change these settings. Microsoft Base Cryptographic Provider is the default Cryptographic Service Provider (CSP), which handles key creation, and SHA-1 is the default hash algorithm, which Windows uses for digital signatures. You may want to use a longer key length for a root CA; the default is 512 bits, but Microsoft recommends 2,048 bits or greater. The Use Existing Keys setting only applies if you're reinstalling a CA on a machine that already had one installed.

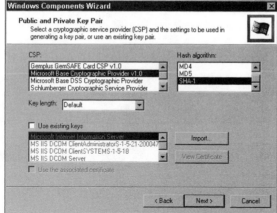

Windows Components Wizard

Public and Private Key Pair
Select a cryptographic service provider (CSP) and the settings to be used in
generating a key pair, or use an existing key pair.

CSP:
Gemplus GemSAFE Card CSP v1.0
Microsoft Base Cryptographic Provider v1.0
Microsoft Base DSS Cryptographic Provider
Schlumberger Cryptographic Service Provider

Hash algorithm:
MD4
MD5
SHA-1

Key length: Default

☐ Use existing keys
Microsoft Internet Information Server
MS IIS DCOM ClientAdministratorS-1-5-21-200047
MS IIS DCOM ClientSYSTEMS-1-5-18
MS IIS DCOM Server

Import...

View Certificate

☐ Use the associated certificate

< Back   Next >   Cancel

Figure 11-3:
Viewing
crypto-
graphy
settings for
the CA.

9. **In the CA Identifying Information dialog box (see Figure 11-4), fill in the fields and click the Next button.**

   The fields on this form include CA name (64 characters maximum), organization, description, and validity duration (the CA's lifetime, typically two years).

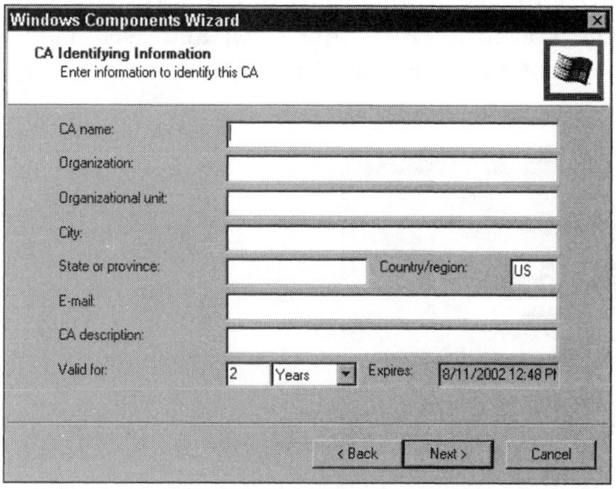

Windows Components Wizard

CA Identifying Information
Enter information to identify this CA

CA name:
Organization:
Organizational unit:
City:
State or province: Country/region: US
E-mail:
CA description:
Valid for: 2 Years ▼ Expires: 8/11/2002 12:48 PM

< Back   Next >   Cancel

Figure 11-4:
Identifying
the CA and
specifying
its tour of
duty.

10. **Tell Windows where you want it to put the certification database, log, and configuration data, as shown in Figure 11-5.**

    The default location for the database is C:\WINNT\SYSTEM32\CERTLOG. The default location for the configuration data is C:\WINNT\CACONFIG.

11. **If IIS is running, Windows asks you to stop the service; click OK.**

    Windows restarts it at the end of the procedure.

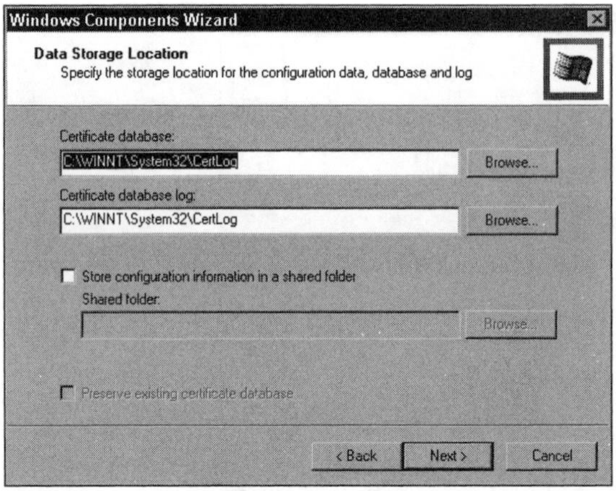

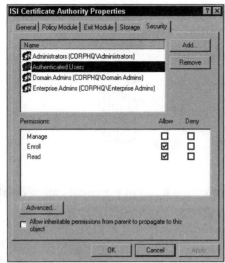

Figure 11-5:
Everything
in its place.

After the installation of an enterprise CA, you can check Active Directory Users and Computers to see that Windows 2000 has made the computer a member of the Cert Publishers group. That membership confers onto the CA the right to publish certificates to other domains.

You can also view the CA's Properties dialog box to confirm details such as database location (the Storage tab) and access controls (the Security tab). By default, Administrators, Domain Admins, and Enterprise Admins have the permissions Manage, Enroll, and Read. Authenticated Users have the permissions Enroll and Read, as shown in Figure 11-6.

Figure 11-6:
Security for
Certificate
Authority.

Issuing and Revoking Certificates

This section looks at the details of certificate issuance and revocation.

Issuing a new certificate

The certificate issuance process (called *enrollment*) may occur behind the scenes or explicitly. The generic process has the following steps:

1. A user, computer, or service issues a certificate request along with a set of authenticating credentials determined by the Certificate Authority (CA).

2. The CA receives the request and confirms the credentials.

3. If the credentials check out, the CA creates a certificate document using its private key. That is, the CA either generates the certificate, or denies the request.

4. Assuming the CA grants the request and generates the certificate in Step 3, the CA then publishes the certificate (for example, via Active Directory) so the requester can retrieve it.

The methods for initiating a certificate issuance request, assuming a CA is present, include the following:

✔ A Windows 2000 user, computer, or service can run the Certificate Request wizard (see Lab 11-2). This method is *only* for requesting a certificate from an enterprise CA in an Active Directory environment.

✔ A Windows 2000 user can connect to the Certificate Services Web page and fill in the forms. You can use this method for an enterprise CA *or* a standalone CA, but the CA must be running IIS, and the user must have *execute script* permission on the `C:\WINNT\SYSTEM32\CERTSRV` folder of the Web site.

Lab 11-2	Running the Certificate Request Wizard

1. **Log on to a domain that has an enterprise CA.**

2. **Open a management console containing the standalone Certificates snap-in.**

Create the console if one does not already exist.

3. **Expand the tree pane, right-click the Personal folder, and choose All Tasks⇨Request New Certificate.**

4. **Click Next after reading the boring message.**

5. **Choose a template and click Next.**

Only enterprise CAs use templates, which are predefined certificate types set by Group Policy. After a default installation, an enterprise CA can issue the *Administrator, Basic EFS, EFS Recovery Agent,* and *User* templates for users, and the *Domain Controller, Computer,* and *Web Server* templates for computers. The types of certificate a user can choose from depend on that user's account access rights.

If you click the Advanced Options checkbox, you can modify the cryptographic settings in the next dialog box. You can also choose to enable *strong* protection, meaning that Windows prompts you every time it uses the private key.

6. **Pick a name for your certificate and click Next.**

7. **Click Install Certificate.**

If you're administering a standalone CA, then (depending on how the CA was originally configured) you may need to approve pending certificate requests before Windows 2000 issues the certificates. (Enterprise CAs generally either issue or deny certificates immediately, based on Group Policy settings.) Use the Certification Authority management console and click the Pending Requests folder to view pending requests and review the credentials submitted by users. Right-click a specific request, choose All Tasks, and choose either Deny or Issue, depending on what you want to do.

Checking out existing certificates

You can see which certificates you already have on your PC by using one of two interfaces:

✔ The Certificates snap-in to a management console (see Figure 11-7), which you create by running MMC.EXE and adding Certificates as a standalone snap-in.

✔ The Certificates dialog box (see Figure 11-8), which you open by clicking the Certificates button on the Content tab in the Internet Options control panel. This dialog box presents the same information and functionality as the Certificates snap-in, but in a different layout.

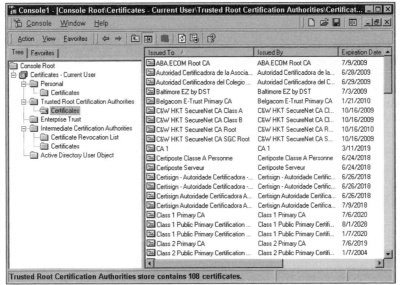

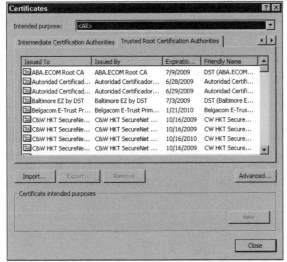

Note that in the Certificates snap-in, you can view certificates by logical certificate stores (the default view), or by certificate purpose. Choose the view by right-clicking Certificates – Current User and choosing View⇨Options (see Figure 11-9).

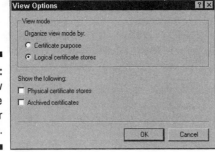

Figure 11-9:
Pick a view
to browse
your
certificates.

Certificates in the Certificate snap-in's Personal folder are just that: certificates for which you have access to the private key. *Trusted Root Certification Authorities* are CAs (both internal and external) which you, and programs you run, trust. Windows 2000 installs a prebuilt list of trusted root CAs.

If you supply code to the public (for example, via a Web site) and you obtain a "code signing" certificate (also called a *software publisher certificate*) from a trusted external commercial CA, users are more likely to trust your code and install it onto their machines. You can use Certificate Server to issue code-signing certificates to internal software developers who sign the code that you publish on your Web sites.

Mapping certificates to users

You can use certificates as a replacement for the traditional Ctrl+Alt+Del logon mechanism. For example, a smart card can contain a certificate that automatically authenticates an Active Directory user. For another example, you can grant an external (non-AD) user a certificate and then *map* that certificate to a generic AD account. The external user can then gain access to your intranet, using his browser's SSL (Secure Sockets Layer) capability, by presenting the authenticating certificate (which happens automatically).

The procedure for mapping a certificate is as follows:

1. **In Active Directory Users and Computers, create the account you want to support the external user.**

   One account can support many users.

2. **In Active Directory Users and Computers, click Active Directory Users and Computers in the tree pane, and choose View⇨Advanced Features.**

3. **In the tree pane, click the Users folder in the relevant domain.**

4. **In the details pane, right-click the user Account for mapping, and choose Name Mappings.**

5. **Click the X.509 Certificates tab in the Security Identity Mapping dialog box, as shown in Figure 11-10.**

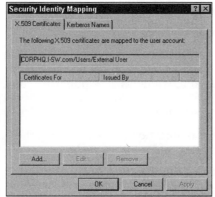

Figure 11-10:
Mapping a
certificate
to an
account.

6. **Click the Add button.**

7. **Type the name and location of the certificate file (*.CER) you want to map to the user account, and click OK.**

8. **In the Add Certificate dialog box, map the certificate by checking or clearing the Identity Mapping boxes.**

   Check both Use Issuer For Alternate Security Identity and Use Subject For Alternate Security Identity if you want a one-to-one mapping.

   Check only Use Issuer For Alternate Security Identity if you want to map any certificate having the same issuer to the specified AD account.

   Check only Use Subject For Alternate Security Identity if you want to map any certificate having the same subject to the specified AD account.

Revoking a certificate

Certificates have a lifetime and they expire at some predetermined date. However, some certificates may lose their validity before their expiration date, for any number of reasons: a private key becomes lost, a new certificate supersedes the older one, a CA has a security breach and is no longer trusted, and so on.

A full certificate revocation cycle requires three steps:

1. **An administrator revokes the certificate.**

   For example, in the Certification Authority console, highlight the Issues Certificates folder, right-click the certificate to revoke, and choose All Tasks⇨Revoke Certificate. You can then enter a reason code (key compromise, CA compromise, and so on).

2. **The CA publishes a Certificate Revocation List (CRL).**

   CRL publication happens automatically at an interval specified on the Revoked Certificates property sheet (typically one week, but you can change the period). By default, Windows 2000 publishes the CRL to `C:\WINNT\SYSTEM32\CERTSRV\CERTENROLL` and (in the case of an enterprise CA) to the Active Directory database.

   An administrator can force publication by right-clicking the Revoked Certificates icon and choosing All Tasks⇨Publish.

3. **The relevant clients need to retrieve the CRL.**

   Typically, clients cache a copy of the CRL and don't retrieve a new one until the CRL's validity period has expired. A client can manually retrieve a CRL using the CA's Web page interface. Connect to `http://<servername>/certsrv` and click Retrieve The CA Certificate Or Certificate Revocation List (CRL). Save the CRL as a disk file. In Windows Explorer, right-click the CRL file and choose Install CRL.

To verify a certificate, then, all that's necessary is the public key of the CA and a check against the CRL published by that CA.

Managing a Certificate Server

As with just about any Windows 2000 service, Certificate Service requires some administration and management. Typical chores include backing up and restoring the certificate database and starting and stopping the service.

Backing up and restoring the database

The certificate database is a key component (pun intended) to protect with a backup program. If you have a program in place that includes regularly backing up all the hard drives on your Windows 2000 Server machines, you don't need to back up and restore the certificate database separately. The certificate database is part of the *system state,* which Windows backs up as part of a full system backup. (The system state also contains the Registry and, on a domain controller, the Active Directory database.)

However, you can back up the certificate database separately by following the steps in Lab 11-3.

The certification service relies not only upon its own database, but also upon the Registry and (in the case of a Web server) the Internet Information Server *metabase*. The various interdependencies explain why Microsoft recommends a full backup for a server running as a CA. If you back up the CA database separately, consider backing up the Registry and metabase separately at the same time.

Lab 11-3	Backing Up the Certificate Database

1. **Log on to the server as a member of Backup Operators or Administrators.**

2. **Choose Start⇨Programs⇨Administrative Tools⇨Certification Authority.**

If the Administrative Tools menu entry is not present, you can enable it by choosing Start⇨Settings⇨Taskbar & Start Menu, clicking Advanced, and checking the Display Administrative Tools box.

3. **Right-click the server CA in the tree pane to the left, and choose All Tasks⇨Backup CA.**

The Certification Authority Backup wizard starts.

4. **Click Next.**

The Items to Back Up dialog box appears, as shown in Figure 11-11.

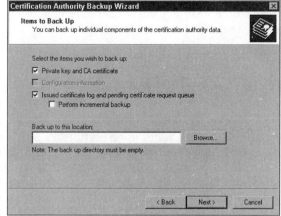

Figure 11-11: Selecting parts of the certification database to back up.

5. **Check Private Key And CA Certificate.**

6. **Optionally, check Issued Certificate Log And Pending Certificate Request Queue.**

   If you choose this option, you can also choose whether to perform a full backup of the issued certificate log and pending request queue, or just back up data that has changed or been added since the last backup.

7. **Type or browse to a backup location, which must be an empty folder.**

8. **Specify a password to secure the private key backup.**

   You'll need this password if you must ever restore the CA using the Certificate Authority console. Windows asks you to enter it twice, for confirmation.

9. **Click Finish.**

Restoring the database is pretty much the mirror image of backing it up, with the exception that you must stop the Certificate Services service before performing the restore. (The restore wizard can perform this action for you.) Windows will also want the password you created in Step 8 of the backup procedure.

Starting and stopping Certificate Service

Piece of cake. Open the Certification Authority console and right-click the CA in the tree pane. Choose All Tasks⇨Stop Service to stop the CA, or All Tasks⇨Start Service to start it.

You can also start and stop the service via the Services console, by right-clicking Certificate Services and choosing Start or Stop.

EFS, Certificates, and Recovery

The Windows 2000 Encrypting File System (EFS), a new feature of the NTFS file system (now in Version 5), relies upon certificates for its operation (although you don't have to have a server running Certificate Service). A user can designate a file for encryption by simply checking a box on the file's property sheet. After that, only the user who encrypted the file can read, modify, or delete it.

EFS is a great security tool for users of portable computers because you have to log on with the correct username and password in order to see the contents of an encrypted file. Having the computer does you no good unless you also have the user's credentials — even if you have a low-level disk scanning utility.

When a user designates a file for encryption, Windows encodes it using a symmetric key that's uniquely associated with that file. Then, Windows uses the user's public key (associated with the user's EFS certificate) to encrypt the symmetric key. If the user wants to modify the file later, Windows uses the user's private key (again, associated with the user's EFS certificate) to decrypt the file's symmetric key. All this activity occurs transparently to the user. You don't even need to enable a certificate server for EFS to work.

Well and good so far, but what if a user forgets his or her account name or password? Or quits the company suddenly? That could be a single point of failure in the system. Microsoft provides a contingency plan in the form of the EFS *recovery agent.*

In a non-domain environment, the default EFS recovery agent account is the local Administrator account. In a domain environment, the default EFS recovery agent is the local Administrator account of the first domain controller for that domain. In Figure 11-12, the PC's local administrator has two certificates: a regular EFS certificate for daily encryption and decryption, and a file recovery certificate.

Figure 11-12:
The local administrator is both an EFS user and a recovery agent.

The recovery agent has a special EFS recovery certificate. So if Bob encrypted a bunch of files and then left the country suddenly and permanently, a tech support person could log on to Bob's computer and copy the encrypted files over to the domain administrator's PC. The domain administrator could then decrypt them by clearing the property sheet checkbox. The domain administrator's file recovery certificate works for recovering any encrypted file on the domain.

You can back up your own EFS certificate to a diskette, thereby removing the need for you to contact a recovery agent if your local hard disk suffers file damage and your private key becomes corrupted. Lab 11-4 demonstrates one procedure; another would be to start with the Internet Options control panel's Content tab, where you click the Certificates button. Note that many certificates are not exportable, but all EFS certificates (except the ones for Recovery Agents) are.

Lab 11-4   Backing up (Exporting) a Certificate

1. **Open a management console equipped with the Certificates stand-alone snap-in.**

   If you don't already have such a console defined, create and save one with the MMC.EXE program. Choose Certificates as the standalone snap-in, and My User Account as the snap-in's focus.

2. **In the tree pane, navigate to** `Certificates - Current User\ Personal\Certificates` **and click it to highlight it.**

3. **In the details pane, right-click the EFS certificate and choose All Tasks⇨Export.**

   The EFS certificate lists Encrypting File System as the certificate's purpose.

4. **Click Next after reading the boring text.**

5. **In the Export Private Key dialog box, click the radio button labeled Yes, Export The Private Key.**

6. **Click Next.**

7. **In the Export File Format dialog box, accept the default settings and click Next.**

   The default file format is *PKCS #12,* which uses the suffix *.PFX.

   Other formats you should know for the exam are *PKCS #7,* which you can use for a group of certificates in the same path; *DER Encoded Binary X.509,* which uses the *.CER suffix and supports non-Windows clients; and *Base64 Encoded X.509,* which also uses the *.CER suffix and supports non-Windows clients.

8. **Enter and confirm a password to protect the backed-up certificate and click Next.**

9. **Specify the filename and destination folder and click Next.**

   If you back up the certificate to a diskette, plan a safe place for the diskette.

10. **Click Finish.**

Adding a Recovery Agent

You may want to change the default Recovery Agent setup. For example, you may want a designated security guru, Al, to handle all EFS recovery problems, even though Al is not a domain administrator. You can confer that capability upon Al by means of one of the various Group Policy editing tools. For example, a domain administrator can open a Group Policy editing console on the first domain controller in a domain (only members of Domain Admins can confer EFS Recovery Agent status). For a local computer, Lab 11-5 illustrates the process.

You need at least one Certificate Authority on the local network in order to designate additional EFS Recovery Agents.

Lab 11-5	Adding an EFS Recovery Agent

1. **Log on using the PC's local Administrator account.**

2. **Choose Start⇨Settings⇨Control Panel.**

3. **Double-click the Administrative Tools folder.**

4. **Double-click the Local Security Policy icon.**

5. **In the tree pane, navigate to** `Security Settings\Public Key Policies\Encrypted Data Recovery Agents` **and right-click that node.**

   In the context of an Active Directory domain policy window, the node would be `Computer Configuration\Windows Settings\Security Settings\Public Key Policies\Encrypted Data Recovery Agents`.

6. **Choose Add.**

   The Add Recovery Agent wizard starts.

7. **Click Next.**

8. **Choose a user to add, either by locating the user's certificate file (*.CER) or browsing the Active Directory.**

9. **Follow the remaining wizard screens to completion and click Finish.**

Removing the EFS recovery keys

To disable EFS on a given computer, follow Steps 1 through 5 of Lab 11-5, and then, instead of choosing Add in Step 6, choose Delete Policy. Deleting the policy also deletes the recovery agent list. If EFS doesn't see at least one recovery agent, it won't run.

Prep Test

1 James is trying to connect to the Web-based certificate enrollment page of an enterprise root Certificate Authority running Windows 2000 Server. However, he cannot connect. What should you check? (Choose all that apply.)

A ❑ Make sure the CA is running DHCP.

B ❑ Make sure the CA is running IIS.

C ❑ Make sure the CA is running PWS.

D ❑ Check permissions on the CERTSRV folder.

2 Jeanette is trying to request a user certificate by running the Certificate Request wizard from a management console containing the Certificates snap-in. However, she gets a message stating that `Windows cannot find a certification authority that will process the request`. What could be the problem? (Choose two answers.)

A ❑ Jeanette is logging on to the local computer, not the domain.

B ❑ Jeanette doesn't have execute script permissions on the CA's folder `C:\WINNT\SYSTEM32\CERTSRV`.

C ❑ The CA is an enterprise CA, not a standalone CA.

D ❑ The CA is a standalone CA, not an enterprise CA.

3 Which of the following sequences describes a digital certificate? (Choose the best answer.)

A ○ A private key is used first, and then a public key.

B ○ A public key is used first, and then a private key.

C ○ Two private keys related by a cryptographic algorithm are used in succession.

D ○ Two public keys related by a cryptographic algorithm are used in succession.

4 You discover that a particular certificate has been compromised, so you revoke it at the CA. What else must you do in order to make the revocation take effect as quickly as possible? (Choose two answers.)

A ❑ Publish the CSP.

B ❑ Publish the CRL.

C ❑ Have the affected clients import the CSP.

D ❑ Have the affected clients import the CRL.

E ❑ Have the affected clients log off the domain and log back on, to clear the revocation cache.

5 You perform a backup of the certification database using the Certification Authority console. What other structures should you back up, due to data dependencies, in order to ensure recoverability of the CA in the event of disk failure? (Choose all that apply.)

A ❑ The Registry metabase

B ❑ The IIS metabase

C ❑ The Registry

D ❑ NTDS.DBF

6 For a Certificate Authority to be able to issue certificates in a particular domain, the CA server must belong to what group in that domain? (Choose the best answer.)

A ○ Certificate Publishers

B ○ Cert Publishers

C ○ Cert Pubs

D ○ CPs

7 Vicky has left the company, but she has left some encrypted files on her Windows 2000 Professional workstation. You are a domain administrator for acmecognac.com, the domain to which Vicky belonged, which is a pure Windows 2000 network. How should you recover the encrypted files? (Choose the best answer.)

A ○ Export your EFS recovery certificate to diskette. Go to Vicky's computer and log on. Import the recovery certificate. Unlock the files.

B ○ Go to Vicky's computer and copy the encrypted files to the first domain controller on acmecognac.com. Go back to that computer and unlock the files.

C ○ Go to Vicky's computer and copy the encrypted files to the Primary Domain Controller (PDC) for acmecognac.com. Go back to that computer and unlock the files.

D ○ Remove the hard drive from Vicky's computer and install it on any other Windows 2000 Professional computer. Log on as the local PC Administrator and unlock the files.

8 What types of CA use certificate templates? (Choose all that apply.)

A ❑ Enterprise root

B ❑ Enterprise subordinate

C ❑ Standalone root

D ❑ Standalone subordinate

E ❑ Enterprise subordinate standalone root

Answers

1 **B** and **D.** The CA must be running Internet Information Services, Microsoft's Web server product, in order to handle client certificate enrollment requests by means of a browser interface. Also, the CERTSRV folder needs to have the execute script permission for at least one group to which James belongs. *See "Issuing a new certificate."*

2 **A** and **D.** If Jeanette didn't log on to the domain, but logged on to her PC locally, she would not be using Active Directory, and Windows 2000 would not have a basis for locating the Certificate Authority. Also, the Certificate Request wizard only works for enterprise CAs, not for standalone CAs. *See "Issuing a new certificate."*

3 **A.** *A private key is used first, and then a public key.* Choice B describes a key exchange operation characteristic of a data encryption operation. Choices C and D ignore the fact that public key encryption always uses one private key and one public key. *See "What's public key cryptography?"*

4 **B** and **D.** A CSP is a Cryptography Security Provider, which doesn't figure into the situation here. The CRL, or Certificate Revocation List, is of interest here. As for Choice E, merely rebooting a PC would not induce the PC to request and import a new CRL; the client must perform that action manually in order to clear its existing CRL cache. *See "Revoking a certificate."*

5 **B** and **C.** The metabase is the configuration database for Internet Information Server (IIS). The Registry contains a number of PKI-related settings. The "Registry metabase" does not exist, and NTDS.DBF doesn't, either (the Active Directory database lives in NTDS.DIT). *See "Backing up and restoring the database."*

6 **B.** *Cert Publishers.* When you install a CA, it makes itself a member of Cert Publishers for existing domains. If you subsequently add domains that you want the CA to serve, you must add the CA server to the Cert Publishers group for the new domain using Active Directory Users and Computers. *See "The installation process."*

7 **B.** *Go to Vicky's computer and copy the encrypted files to the first domain controller on acmecognac.com. Go back to that computer and unlock the files.* Choice A is technically feasible, but I don't like it, because it involves putting a domain administrator's private key on a workstation computer — not the most secure action in the world, especially if you forget to remove the key. As for Choice C, Windows 2000 Server doesn't use Primary Domain Controllers. And as for D, hey, the fact that it doesn't work is a big reason for the existence of EFS. *See "EFS, Certificates, and Recovery."*

8 **A** and **B.** The reason that standalone CAs don't use certificate templates is that standalone CAs don't use Active Directory, and Active Directory Group Policy controls the use of certificate templates. If you chose E, please re-read this chapter, twice. *See "Issuing a new certificate."*

Part V
The Part of Tens

The 5th Wave   By Rich Tennant

"I guess you could say this is the hub of our network."

In this part . . .

A few months ago, I was a little late with the last section of a book I was writing on the Windows Registry, and I was trying to come up with a creative way to lessen my workload. Because digital computing is a world of ones and zeroes, I suggested to Dummies Press that we rename the final section "The Part of Twos" instead of "The Part of Tens." My editor countered with the suggestion that, because book writing is a world of alphabetical characters, maybe my last couple of chapters should be in a Part of Twenty-Sixes, at which point I remember muttering that maybe ten was not such a bad number after all.

Anyway, the Part of Tens is a traditional and much beloved feature of Dummies titles. I like it particularly because it lets me sneak in some stuff that doesn't fit neatly anywhere else. This Part contains ten test-taking tips to help you succeed with the exam, and ten places to get information that can supplement, stretch, and re-inforce the material in these pages. And now that I'm done writing this book, I am going to smoke ten Dunhill cigarettes, take ten sips of a chilled perfect Manhattan, kiss my wife ten times, and sleep for ten days. When I wake up, I'll jog ten miles. (Or maybe ten minutes — a man's got to know his limitations.)

Chapter 12

Ten Test-Taking Tips

*T*he best single tip I can give you for passing the exam, and the only one you really need, is to learn the subject matter — and that takes time and effort. However, knowing a few test-preparation tricks can give you a bit of an edge, and I want to give you every advantage I can. So here are ten suggestions, any one of which may help vault you to a passing grade after you've already studied the core material. Good luck!

Use Windows 2000

No better way exists to understand a computer product inside and out than to study a book like this one while forcing yourself to use the product day in and day out. Think immersion.

Even if you normally work with Windows 3.*x* or NT 4 at work and/or at home, consider the benefits of switching to Windows 2000 for the weeks prior to the MCSE test. Set up a dual-boot machine if you need to; use an alternate PC if one is available. Whenever you have a few minutes to kill during the day or night, experiment with the Windows 2000 control panels, management consoles, property sheets, and system utilities. Many of you know Windows NT Server 4.0 inside and out by virtue of working with it every day, but Windows 2000 is a different animal in many important respects.

You can install and run Windows 2000 Server on most desktop (and even notebook) PCs. The Server product is more useful for you to study in preparation for exam 70-216. (The online help alone is a great resource, even if you never connect the PC to any other machines.)

Although most MCSE candidates are networking professionals, sometimes students pursue certification to help land that first networking job. If you're in that boat, you should be able to get your hands on an academic version of Windows 2000 for substantially less money than us working stiffs. If you're nervous about trashing your C: drive, buy an "el cheapo" IDE drive and swap it out. When you're a bona fide MCSE, you can restore your original drive and go back to Windows 9*x*, Linux (the "L-word"), or whatever you had before.

Leverage Your Biorhythms

The medical establishment will tell you (if you ask it) that most people experience a lull in alertness in mid-afternoon, anywhere between 1:30 p.m. and 3:30 p.m. You probably don't need the medical establishment to know that little factoid, however. Don't schedule the exam to fall during this time period! For most people, a mid-morning time is best.

You know your own body; if you're an evening person rather than a morning person, slate the exam for as late in the day as you can arrange it. The point is to take the test at a time of day when you normally feel productive and energized.

Prepare to Focus

When taking the timed exam, you don't have the luxury of taking breaks, making a phone call or two to interrupt the tedium, or walking around the building in mid-test to get the blood flowing. So you should put yourself in a good position to sit down for a couple of hours and focus like a laser beam the entire time.

What helps you focus? Different people are different, but here are some suggestions from which you can choose:

- ✔ **Plenty of sleep the night before.** Don't party hearty on Exam Eve. You know how much sleep you need to be at your peak; for most people, the amount is between seven and eight hours.

- ✔ **Exercise.** Run a mile or two the morning of the test day to oxygenate your brain cells. Or swim, walk, pump iron, or just do some jumping jacks and running in place. For most people, a little exercise improves alertness.

- ✔ **Light food.** Don't chow down on heavy food before the exam. A full stomach means naptime. Eat a light breakfast or lunch — something that won't weigh you down. And avoid fast food burgers. They contain chemicals that induce drowsiness.

✔ **Caffeine.** If a cup of joe or a can of soda revs your engine, go for it. The test center may even let you bring a beverage in with you. (If you're a practicing Mormon, on the other hand, see the next suggestion.)

✔ **Cinnamon.** Cinnamon seems to be an energizing spice. No one seems to know why, but it works for me. A suitably sinful cinnamon roll half an hour before the test may be your tasty ticket to alertness. If that would weigh you down too much, just sprinkle some in your coffee.

One substance you *don't* want swimming through your veins on test day is alcohol. If you're taking an afternoon exam, the lunchtime glass of wine or beer will slow you down. Celebrate after you pass, not before.

Warm Up

"Cramming" isn't necessarily a great idea, although I must say it works for some people. *Warming up* shortly before the test, on the other hand, seems to help most people I've talked with about the exams, and I always do it. The difference between cramming and warming up is one of degree. You don't want to be exhausted before you even start the exam, but you do want to get your brain going so you don't have to shift from first gear into fifth as you enter the testing room.

So, spend some time right before you head to the test center getting your mental momentum going. You can do this several ways: with the CD-based material in this book, with the sample tests, by running through some of the labs, or simply by flipping through the book looking for points that you highlighted and making sure you understand them.

My advice is to spend between one and two hours on your warm-up. Too little time, and you don't do yourself any good; too much, and you make yourself tired.

Part of your warm-up should be to re-read Chapter 1 of this book. It will remind you of what to expect regarding the mechanics of the exam.

Get LOTS of Paper

The testing centers I've visited are strangely stingy about the amount of scratch paper they provide. (When I took the Network Infrastructure exam, I got three, count 'em three, sheets. How parsimonious.) Some don't even give you paper, but rather a small whiteboard.

If you don't get at least a dozen sheets of paper, ask for more. If you aren't comfortable with the whiteboard, ask for paper. (Bring your own pad just in case. I did that once, and after the administrator looked it over to be sure I hadn't written notes on a tiny sheet tucked up by the adhesive strip, or scratched answers onto the pages with a leadless mechanical pencil, I was allowed to use my pad. Good thing, too, as all the center had was the markerboard, which I can't stand. Why waste time erasing that thing every 20 seconds?)

Drawing your own mini-diagrams can be a great help, especially in the "scenario" questions that tell a rather long story. The last thing you want to get between you and a successful exam is a problem as mundane and easily avoidable as not having enough paper.

Jump the Gun, Legally

Following on the previous suggestion, and remembering that neither the exam clock nor the new "total elapsed time for everything" clock start running until you "log on" to the computer, here's a clever trick: Write down any charts, mnemonic devices (such as the OSI model), or other memory-joggers (like the address ranges of different IP address classes) on your scratch paper before starting the exam. Why use up valuable exam time for this sort of thing if you don't have to? (See, buying this book really *was* a good idea!)

True, you may not use all the bits and pieces that you jot down ahead of time, but, on the other hand, it doesn't cost you anything, and it can't hurt.

Don't take too much time on the pre-exam brain dump onto the scratch pages if the meter is running. The time I took the test, I had only a half-hour beyond the actual exam for answering the questionnaire, commenting on the exam, and jotting down pre-exam notes. My test administrator "logged me on" so I didn't have the luxury of making those notes before the "total elapsed time for everything" clock started ticking. Still, I figured I had at least ten or fifteen minutes, and I put 'em to good use.

Don't Reinvent Wheels

When I take a multiple-choice certification test, I mark off a half-page on the first sheet of scratch paper to keep track of eliminations: answers I know are wrong on questions I plan to review later. If you study question #19, for example, and you're not quite sure what the answer is but you know it isn't B or C, you would mark "19. A B C D" on the scratch paper and X out the B and C. This way, when you review those tough questions after making your first pass through the exam, you don't waste time or brain cells figuring out all over again that B and C aren't correct answers to problem #19.

Putting this "record of eliminations" on the first sheet of your scratch paper means that you don't have to hunt around several pages for these notes.

Trust Your Gut

Although the exam questions can be tricky on occasion, many of them are fairly straightforward, which means that you should give some extra weight to your first reaction.

By all means, review questions that you have doubts about, and check your reasoning twice on every question if you have the time. (Remember, in a non-adaptive test — and 70-216 is non-adaptive as I write this — you can mark questions for review as you go along, and then go back and study them after you reach the end of the test.) All I'm saying here is that if you're tempted to change an answer, be sure you have a compelling reason for doing so. I've found from taking lots of MCSE assessment tests that my gut reaction is more often right than wrong. That should be true for you, too, if you've read much of this book.

Check the Numbers

Perhaps the most frustrating missed answers of all are those in which you click one answer when the question really calls for two or three or "as many as apply." One of the things I do on every exam, therefore, is to go back through each question and double-check whether it's asking for a single answer or multiple ones. Even though I'm aware of the pitfall, I still usually catch one or two questions on which I didn't pay enough attention and omitted a relevant answer.

Of course, in order to have the time to make this check (and to review any questions you've marked because you're unsure about your answer), you must make it all the way through the test on your first pass with some time to spare. Remember to check your time periodically to make sure you lay eyes on every single question in your allotted 90 minutes. You will be able to answer many questions fairly quickly; save the tough ones for last in order to maximize your percentage of correct answers in case time becomes a crucial factor at the end.

Keep Your Perspective

Yes, you'd like to pass the test on the first try. However, passing is nothing remotely like a do-or-die situation. Those who don't get terribly worked up about the exam are less likely to waste valuable exam time worrying about not passing.

Worry can become a self-fulfilling prophecy: If you agonize over whether you're answering enough questions right instead of focus on the questions themselves and what you know, you're likely to create cause for worry! Just remind yourself of the following points, and you're more likely to cruise to a passing grade:

- A hundred bucks is more than lunch money but less than a nice night on the town for two. The exam fee is the rough equivalent of six good pizzas; don't obsess over it. Recognize that even if you do have to retake the exam, your $200 investment will come back to you many times as you progress in your career. (If your company is paying, come up with the second $100 out of your own pocket if you'd feel awkward asking the boss a second time.)

- The exam is *not* a measure of how smart you are! It's a measure of how well you know the things about Windows 2000 that Microsoft thinks you need to know, how well you take tests, and how sharp you're feeling on exam day.

- Microsoft, the testing center, the test, and this book are not going anywhere anytime soon. Your window of opportunity is very large here. If you don't pass today, you can pass next week or next month or whenever you feel ready.

- You're just not going to get a 99 percent score. These MCSE tests are designed so that almost nobody gets a perfect score, and darn few people get an "A" (90 percent or above). Make up your mind that you will be content with 63 percent or whatever the exam requires when you take it, and the blood pressure drops considerably. Remember, an MCSE with a 63 percent average across seven exams gets the same letters after his or her name as an MCSE with a 95 percent average.

- You're already at a great advantage over most exam-takers by virtue of having read this book. You can feel justifiably confident because of that edge. (I said "confident" and not "cocky," by the way; the difference between those two words is at least ten percentage points on the exam, because cocky test-takers don't pay enough attention to the questions.)

One last tip along these lines: Don't tell everyone you know that you're taking the exam. The fewer people who know that you're taking it, the less you'll worry about things like "What will Bob think of me when I tell him I didn't pass?" and "Will my date still want to go out with me this weekend if I didn't get my MCP?" and so forth. Of course, it's probably really none of Bob's business whether you pass, and if your date doesn't like you without your MCP, then I venture to say that you're with the wrong person anyway. Nevertheless, if you want to minimize exam-time stress, don't make the test into a bigger deal than it should be by telling the world about it ahead of time. No sense putting more pressure on yourself than Microsoft is already putting on you!

Chapter 13

Ten Places to Get More Information

● ●

In This Chapter

▶ Books

▶ CD-ROMs

▶ Internet Web sites

▶ Internet newsgroups

● ●

*W*ith plenty of hands-on experience and careful study of this book, you have the tools you need to pass exam 70-216. Of course, you never know when Microsoft will change the content or the format of an exam, and you can count on facing a steady stream of fresh challenges throughout your career as a network administrator. So, far be it from me to discourage you from exploring other resources that could help fill in your knowledge gaps.

So far, in fact, that I've assembled ten suggestions for places where you could profitably spend some study time. These will be especially valuable if you're unable to wangle access to a Windows 2000 network for study purposes.

Many of the resources in this chapter will help you with other MCSE tests besides the Windows 2000 network infrastructure exam.

Windows 2000 Server Resource Kit

Yes, it's expensive. Yes, a lot of the documentation really should come with the operating system CDs, especially for what Microsoft is charging for the software. And yes, it's still not a bad idea to go out and buy it, especially if you plan to use Windows 2000 after you take the exam.

You're not going to read all 7,296 pages cover to cover (at least I hope not), and you really don't need it to pass the exam. However, for dipping in and out of various technical subjects that you may need to understand more thoroughly, this massive box o' books is a smart addition to your bookshelf.

As I write this, the best price on this product is at `www.provantage.com`, but you may want to check other online bookstores as well; the list price is US$299.99, which is fairly appalling. The ISBN number is 1-57231-805-8.

Here's some happy news for those who aren't independently wealthy: You get a subset of the full Resource Kit product "free" on the Windows 2000 Server CD. Install the Resource Kit tools, which take about 20MB of disk space, as follows:

1. **Log on as a member of the Administrators group.**

2. **Run SETUP.EXE from the** `\SUPPORT\TOOLS` **folder of your setup CD.**

3. **Restart the system.**

The tools install onto your local hard drive, typically `C:\Program Files\ Support Tools`. The tools appear on the taskbar as Start⇨Programs⇨ Windows 2000 Support Tools. Be aware that although most of the softwa re resides in a cabinet file (SUPPORT.CAB), merely extracting the files from the cabinet file does not perform a complete installation of the Resource Kit tools.

You can also install the tools from the command prompt. Microsoft has packaged them using the Windows Installer methodology, so you can use MSIEXEC.EXE with the appropriate options. For example, if H: is your local CD-ROM drive, you could use a command such as the following:

```
MSIEXEC /I H:\SUPPORT\TOOLS\2000RKST.MSI
```

The Resource Kit Tools consist of two categories of software: documentation and utilities. The documentation files include

- ✔ **The Deployment Planning Guide** (DEPLOY.CHM): A compiled HTML file with a fair amount of information on rolling out Windows 2000.

- ✔ **Error and Event Messages** (W2000MSGS.CHM): A compiled HTML file listing Windows 2000 messages that may appear in the event logs, in dialog boxes displayed by the operating system itself, in control panels, in utilities, during installation, and so on.

✔ **Tools Help** (W2RKSUPP.CHM): A compiled HTML file detailing functions and command-line qualifiers for the utilities. This well-designed module is your most convenient single point of reference for all the support tools, both GUI and command-line varieties. It provides syntax and (even better) examples.

✔ **Release Notes** (SREADME.DOC): A Word/WordPad file providing the most current details on installing the support tools software.

The Resource Kit Support Tools package contains GUI-mode utilities and command-line utilities:

✔ You can view the list of GUI-mode utilities in the menu structure at Start⇨Programs⇨Windows 2000 Support Tools⇨Tools.

✔ You can view information about the command-line utilities in the Tools Help file (Start⇨Programs⇨Windows 2000 Support Tools⇨ Tools Help).

Many of the utilities are holdovers from the Windows NT 4.0 resource kit. In fact, some have not even been modified from their NT 4.0 versions. Note also that some of the support tools pertain to specific environments. For example, Active Directory Administration Tool, Active Directory Replication Monitor, and ADSI Edit are not relevant for an environment that does not use AD.

Finally, you should also know that some of the support tools duplicate functions that already exist in the user interface. KILL.EXE and MEMSNAP.EXE, for example, overlap with the Windows Task Manager display (Ctrl+Alt+Del⇨ Task Manager).

Windows 2000 Professional Resource Kit

Not as relevant for exam 70-216 as the Server resource kit (see the preceding section), but not a bad choice for those of you on a budget, this book (ISBN number 1-57231-808-2) from Microsoft Press costs US$69.99 as I write this.

Focus on Chapters 7 (Introduction to Configuration and Management), 13 (Security), 21 (Local and Remote Network Connections), 22 (TCP/IP in Windows 2000 Professional), 23 (Windows 2000 Professional on Microsoft Networks), and 24 (Interoperability with NetWare).

IDG Books Worldwide

IDG Books Worldwide has some great Windows 2000 books at reasonable prices (in contrast to Microsoft Press). The list is evolving as I write this, so check out www.idgbooks.com and www.dummies.com to see the most current listing. One in particular that I can vouch for (shameless plug ahead) is my own *Windows 2000 Registry For Dummies.*

Microsoft TechNet

Whether you subscribe to the CD-ROMs (recommended; $295/year) or simply patronize the Web site shown in Figure 13-1 (www.microsoft.com/technet), TechNet is a good reference for common problems and their solutions. However, it has expanded considerably beyond its early scope of presenting the Microsoft knowledge base in CD format. Now it includes selected resource kits, service packs, online seminars, white papers, walkthroughs, and client and server utilities.

As I write this, you get a 50 percent discount on a year's subscription to TechNet when you get your MCSE.

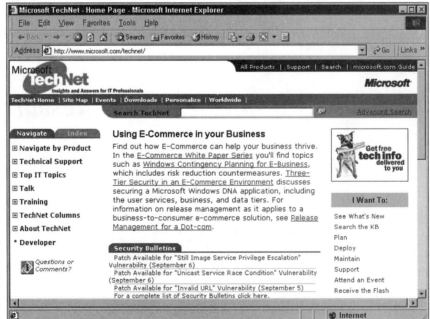

Figure 13-1: TechNet is handy when studying for the exam and even handier later on.

Internet Search Engines

Internet search engines are great for finding Windows 2000 information; choose "Windows 2000" as a search phrase and go wild, or get more specific with a query such as ("Windows 2000 Server" and "DHCP"). Here are some of the more popular search services, in alphabetical order:

- ✔ All the Web (www.alltheweb.com)
- ✔ Altavista (www.av.com)
- ✔ Excite (www.excite.com)
- ✔ HotBot (www.hotbot.com)
- ✔ Lycos (www.lycos.com)
- ✔ Northern Light (www.northernlight.com)
- ✔ Yahoo! (www.yahoo.com)

If you do lots of Internet searching, you may want to check out Copernic 2000, a program that consults many popular search engines in one fell swoop. Point your browser to www.copernic.com to download the software.

Usenet Newsgroups

Usenet newsgroups are like Internet bulletin boards. Some contain lots of information about Windows 2000. These groups can also be good places to post a question when you can't get an answer anywhere else, or when you just want to read what other Windows 2000 users are saying. Newsgroups also often post FAQs (Frequently Asked Questions documents) within the newsgroups themselves and on related Web sites; such FAQs can be good sources of distilled information on specific subjects.

Newsgroups are public. Any sloppy, lazy, uninformed or even malicious bozo can post to them. Use newsgroups for clues, ideas, and potential problem solutions, but check every tip yourself before you use it or pass it along to others.

Newsgroups of interest include

- ✔ alt.certification.mcse
- ✔ comp.os.ms-windows.misc
- ✔ microsoft.public.cert.exam.mcse
- ✔ microsoft.public.certification.mcse

- microsoft.public.win2000.enable
- microsoft.public.win2000.activedirectory
- microsoft.public.win2000.applications
- microsoft.public.win2000.dns
- microsoft.public.win2000.filesystem
- microsoft.public.win2000.general
- microsoft.public.win2000.group_policy
- microsoft.public.win2000.hardware
- microsoft.public.win2000.msi
- microsoft.public.win2000.multimedia
- microsoft.public.win2000.netware
- microsoft.public.win2000.networking
- microsoft.public.win2000.printing
- microsoft.public.win2000.registry
- microsoft.public.win2000.security
- microsoft.public.win2000.setup
- microsoft.public.win2000.setup_deployment
- microsoft.public.windows.inetexplorer.ie5.browser

Software is required to read postings from these newsgroups. Windows 2000 comes with Outlook Express 5, formerly Microsoft Internet Mail and News. If you use America Online to access the Internet, you can't use Outlook Express, but you can use AOL's built-in newsreader. Just choose keyword *newsgroups,* click the Expert Add button, and type in the newsgroup name.

Exam Simulations

A number of companies are in the business of providing exam simulations. The fees for these tests have gone down somewhat in recent years, and you can often download demos from the Web before shelling out actual cash. A couple to check out are as follows:

- Transcender (www.transcender.com) — A Transcender demo accompanies this book, on the CD-ROM.
- Self-Test Software (www.stsware.com/microsts.htm)

Microsoft Web Sites

Microsoft has hundreds of particular pages on its own Web site that pertain to Windows 2000. Here are a few to get you started:

- ✔ www.microsoft.com/mcp/certstep/mcse.htm
- ✔ www.microsoft.com/windows/professional/default.asp
- ✔ www.microsoft.com/windows/server/default.asp
- ✔ http://resourcelink.mspress.microsoft.com/reslink
- ✔ ftp://ftp.microsoft.com/bussys/winnt/winnt-public/reskit
- ✔ www.microsoft.com/mcp
- ✔ www.microsoft.com/technet
- ✔ www.microsoft.com/trainingandservices/default.asp
- ✔ www.microsoft.com/windows2000/default.asp
- ✔ http://support.microsoft.com/support

Third-Party Exam Information Sites

Dozens of non-Microsoft sites out there offer aid and sustenance to the MCP-seeker. Here is but a small sample:

- ✔ www.certificationshack.com (that's Certification Shack, not Certifications Hack) is a pretty useful site with details on most Microsoft exams.
- ✔ www.cramsession.com has some good overview pages for review the day or two before you take the exam, just to make sure you have all the important bases covered.
- ✔ www.mcsedirectory.com is an all-you-can-eat MCSE smorgasbord, featuring everything from sample exams to online books. Very useful.

Magazine Web Sites

Here are a few "webzine" sites that are worth a visit. Most have their own keyword search facilities:

- ✔ *PC World* (www.pcworld.com/pcmag)
- ✔ *InfoWorld* (www.infoworld.com)

- *PC Magazine* (www.zdnet.com/pcmag)
- *PC Computing* (www.zdnet.com/pccomp)
- *PC Week* (www.zdnet.com/pcweek)
- *Windows* 2000 Magazine (www.winntmag.com)

For ongoing technical education, I recommend a print subscription to that last one. Call 800-621-1544 or 970-663-4700, or write P.O. Box 447, Loveland, CO 80539-0447 USA.

Part VI
Appendixes

The 5th Wave   By Rich Tennant

"You the guy having trouble staying connected to the network?"

In this part . . .

*T*his book has four (count 'em, four) appendixes: a practice exam, a description of the MCSE certification program, a glossary of techie terms, and a look at what's on the CD-ROM that comes with this book.

Unlike a human appendix, these appendixes have considerable value. The practice exam is an absolute must before you take the real thing. The appendix on certification is helpful if you're planning your MCSE exam sequence and curriculum. The glossary will be useful to you as you read through chapters in the main body of the text, and the CD-ROM has many more practice and review questions (they're different from the ones in the practice exam). Perhaps best of all, and also unlike a human appendix, these are guaranteed not to rupture and send you to the hospital.

Appendix A

Practice Exam

● ●

Exam Objectives

▶ Allow yourself 90 minutes to answer the 50 questions

▶ Consider 84 percent a passing score

▶ Treat this test as closed book; don't look ahead (to the answers) or behind (to the chapters)

● ●

A few quick words before you dive in to this sample test, which will help you prepare for the real deal.

First off, exam 70-216 is a tough test. If you've taken any Windows NT exams, you know that they're no walk in the park, and the Windows 2000 core exams are certainly more difficult. Microsoft may be trying to limit the number of "paper MCSEs" in the industry by making the exams more difficult to pass if you don't have hands-on experience and beaucoup knowledge. That strategy is hard on you in the short term, but good for you in the long run, because it protects the value of your certification. If you've taken other exams, and this book and these questions seem more difficult than what you've seen before, that's a reflection of today's harder exams.

The actual passing grade is 62 percent as I write this, but Microsoft can change it at any time. (FYI, the number of questions is 55, and the time limit is 2 hours and 20 minutes; you should use every minute.) Also, the passing percentage is likely to change if and when Microsoft makes the exam adaptive (it's not right now). If you get 84 percent or better on this sample exam, you should be in good shape for the real thing. If you get above 90 percent, then you should take the real test right away, before you forget anything.

This book covers the same topics that the Microsoft exam covers, but none of the questions in this practice exam appear verbatim on the Microsoft exam. If you miss a question on the practice exam, rather than memorize it, re-read the section in the book that covers that topic. The answers guide you to the correct chapter and objective. Of course, you should also take advantage of any additional information sources you may have, such as the Windows 2000 online help, Microsoft's Web-based TechNet knowledge base, and Windows 2000 resource kits. You may not understand the way I explain a topic, but you may understand how someone else explains it. (I hope that the reverse is more often the case!)

The real exam includes a number of graphical exhibits. I dispense with these here, partly so that we have enough room to include 50 sample questions, and partly because if you can understand the word questions, the graphical exhibits will actually be easier for you.

When you take the real exam, use the Tile button so that you can read the exam question while looking at a graphical exhibit. This technique saves you some time clicking back and forth between the question window and the exhibit window. Many test centers even now still have only plain old 15-inch VGA monitors running at 640x480 resolution, but the tiling technique even works under those conditions (although you have to adjust the window sizes carefully).

Last point: You may spot a detail or two from these questions that the main body of the text does not cover. I've tried to make sure the text includes enough information to answer all these sample questions. If you run across a fact that you didn't see in the main text, *don't let it distract you.* Try to answer the question based on what you know. The Microsoft exams do this sort of thing all the time — tossing in a fact that you have no earthly way of knowing ahead of time, just to throw you off balance. Similarly, if I explain something in the Answers section that you don't remember reading earlier, I'm probably just taking the opportunity to dispense another network knowledge nugget that may help you pass the test. After all, a good test is one that not only measures your knowledge, but increases it a little, too.

And now, ladies and gentlemen, it's time to see how well you can work your net and structure your infra. Good luck.

Questions

1 You manage a mixed-mode network containing Windows 2000 Server machines and Windows NT Server 4.0 machines. The NT machines are running Service Pack 5. One of the NT servers is running Remote Access Service (RAS); it is not a domain controller.

Users complain that when they dial in to the network from home, they sometimes gain access to the network and sometimes don't. What two steps could you perform to correct this situation? (Choose two.)

A ❑ Promote the NT server to domain controller status using DCPROMO.EXE.

B ❑ Upgrade the NT server to Windows 2000 Server.

C ❑ Use the **net localgroup** command to add the Everyone group to the Pre-Windows 2000 Compatible Access group.

D ❑ Use the **net group** command to add the Pre-Windows 2000 Compatible Access group to the Everyone group.

2 You've been running a WINS server for several months, and you decide to do some housekeeping. What command should you use to compact the WINS database? (Choose the best answer.)

A ◯ PACK

B ◯ JETPACK

C ◯ COMPACT

D ◯ EXTRACT

E ◯ CRUNCH

3 You're using Windows 2000 Professional on a network, and your system uses DHCP for IP addressing. A network administrator calls you up and says she's doing some testing of server traffic with Network Monitor. She needs to know the IP address and MAC address of your computer's network card. What's the quickest way for you to look up this information? (Choose the best answer.)

A ◯ Run a command prompt session and type **IPCONFIG**.

B ◯ Run a command prompt session and type **IPCONFIG /FULL**.

C ◯ Run a command prompt session and type **IPCONFIG /ALL**.

D ◯ Run WINIPCFG.

E ◯ Run WINIPCFG /ALL.

4 **You've just been hired as an Information Technology planner for Acme Cognac, Inc., which has 60 offices all over Europe and North America. Each office runs its own standalone TCP/IP network. One of your jobs is to help in the planning process for tying those networks together into a wide-area network. Acme Cognac's management wants to use Windows 2000 Server computers at each office as routers.**

What routing protocol would you be inclined to recommend? (Choose the best answer.)

A ○ RIP v1

B ○ RIP v2

C ○ RIP v3

D ○ OSPF

E ○ OPSF

F ○ Static routing

5 **Your network has grown in such a way that your DHCP server, Calvin, would be better placed on a different subnet in order to reduce WAN traffic. You determine that you should move the DHCP service from Calvin to another Windows 2000 server computer named Hobbes, which is on a different (and larger) subnet that connects to Calvin's subnet via routers that forward DHCP broadcasts. You want to perform the operation with as little disruption as possible. With the help of Microsoft Technet article Q130642, you proceed as follows:**

You stop the DHCP service on Calvin.

You back up the Registry key HKLM\SOFTWARE\Microsoft\DhcpServer\ Configuration.

You install DHCP onto Hobbes.

You stop the DHCP service on Hobbes.

You restore the Registry key from Calvin onto Hobbes.

You delete the contents of C:\WINNT\SYSTEM32\DHCP on Hobbes.

You copy DHCP.MDB from Calvin onto Hobbes.

You start the DHCP service on Hobbes.

What else must you do in order to synchronize the database with the Registry on the Hobbes machine, and see all active leases in the DHCP console? (Choose the best answer.)

A ○ Reconcile All Scopes.

B ○ Reconcile Database.

C ○ Run JETPACK.

D ○ Type **net reconcile dhcp** at a command prompt.

6 **As manager of Acme Cognac's headquarters network, you install WINS onto a Windows 2000 Server computer for NetBIOS name resolution. Brad and Janet run UNIX workstations on the network. Windows 2000 users complain that they can't seem to access either Brad's machine or Janet's using NetBIOS names. What should you do? (Choose all that apply.)**

A ❑ Open the WINS console, right-click the server, and choose New Static Mapping.

B ❑ Open the WINS console, right-click Active Registrations, and choose New Static Mapping.

C ❑ Open a Registry Editor. Set the DWORD value `EnableProxy` to 1 in the key `HKLM\SYSTEM\CurrentControlSet\Services\Netbt\Parameters` to install a WINS proxy.

D ❑ Open the WINS console, right-click the server, and choose New WINS Proxy.

7 **How do you set up a caching-only DNS server? (Choose the best answer.)**

A ○ Set up a regular DNS server but don't configure a reverse lookup zone.

B ○ Set up a regular DNS server but don't configure a forward lookup zone or a reverse lookup zone.

C ○ Set up a regular DNS server but don't configure a forward lookup zone, reverse lookup zone, or diagonal lookup zone.

D ○ Set up a regular DNS server but don't configure any subdomains.

E ○ When running the DNS Server Setup wizard, choose Caching-Only in the Select a Server Type dialog box.

8 **Acme Cognac is developing a Web site and testing it in two different locations. You have deployed one IIS Windows 2000 Server at each location to host the site. You want employees to be able to access the Web site on both subnets by entering the domain name of the Web server, `www.acmecognac.com`. However, you want to minimize traffic across the WAN link, so you do not want a user on subnet A to be accessing the Web server on subnet B.**

What must you do in order to achieve your goals? (Choose all that apply.)

A ❑ Enter multiple A resource records into your DNS database, each of which associates the two IIS server IP addresses with the same domain name.

B ❑ Enter one A resource record into your DNS database associating the first IIS server IP address with the domain name and then enter a CNAME resource record using an alias.

C ❑ Activate the round robin feature on your DNS clients and server.

D ❑ Activate subnet optimization in the Registry.

9 Your boss has asked you to minimize WINS traffic on your network, which contains a single WINS server and 50 client computers on a single subnet. You aren't getting paid much, so your boss tells you that even if you have to spend extra time administering your network, that's all right with her as long as you achieve your goal. Which of the following actions could you take to minimize WINS traffic? (Choose the best answer.)

A ○ Add another WINS server.

B ○ Add #DOM entries to LMHOSTS on each client.

C ○ Add #PRE entries to LMHOSTS on each client.

D ○ Delete LMHOSTS on each client.

10 The network you troubleshoot has a variety of Microsoft and Novell servers on it. You need your Windows 2000 Professional clients to be able to access NetWare 3.*x* servers as well as NetWare 4.*x* servers. What step can you take to meet this goal? (Choose the best answer.)

A ○ Edit the REG_MULTI_SZ value `PktType` in the Registry to contain two values, one for each frame type.

B ○ Modify the REG_SZ value `PktType` in the Registry to contain the single value "802.2,802.3".

C ○ Open the CSNW control panel on each client, click the Advanced tab, and check the box labeled Enable Legacy NetWare Server Support.

D ○ Enable the Group Policy Enable Legacy NetWare Server Support for the domain.

11 You're opening Acme Cognac's London branch and you've set up two subnets in your new building. You put a WINS server on each subnet and your goal is that the two servers are as closely synchronized as possible. You anticipate network traffic to be light for the first couple of years. How would you configure your WINS servers to meet your goal? (Choose all that apply.)

A ❑ Configure both servers for push/pull replication.

B ❑ Configure one server for pull replication and the other for push replication.

C ❑ On the Advanced tab of the replication partner property sheet in the WINS console, set Number Of Changes In Version ID Before Replication to 1 on both servers.

D ❑ On the Advanced tab of the server property sheet in the WINS console, choose Configure Replication, and set Number Of Changes In Version ID Before Replication to 1 on both servers.

E ❑ On the Advanced tab of the server property sheet in the WINS console, choose Configure Replication, and set Replication Trigger Threshold to 1 on both servers.

12 You're setting up several remote access servers on your internetwork, and they're all running Windows 2000 Server and Routing and Remote Access. You don't want to bother configuring authentication options separately at each server. By the same token, you don't want to go out and buy any more software. What technology can you use to achieve your goal? (Choose all that apply.)

A ❑ SNMP

B ❑ IAS

C ❑ RADIUS

D ❑ BAP

13 You want to set up DNS on your Windows 2000 network but you want to spend the least possible amount of time administering the service. What type of zones would you create? (Choose the best answer.)

A ○ Standard primary

B ○ Standard secondary

C ○ Active Directory-integrated

D ○ Auto-replicating

E ○ Enterprise root

14 You set up Routing and Remote Access on a Windows 2000 Server PC. You configure it to use DHCP to assign IP addresses to clients. Dilbert, Acme Cognac's Director of Distillation, calls you up and complains that his group members cannot access network resources when they dial in to the server that you've configured. Dilbert confirms that his people can connect to the RRAS server. What steps should you take to correct this problem? (Choose all that apply.)

A ❑ Make sure the RRAS console has the DHCP Relay Agent installed as a routing protocol.

B ❑ Make sure the RRAS console is configured with the proper DHCP scope.

C ❑ Set the RRAS console so that the DNS and WINS server addresses are correct on the scope property sheet.

D ❑ Set the RRAS console so that the DHCP Relay Agent points to an active DHCP server.

15 You're at a Windows 2000 Server command prompt and you want to add a persistent static route. What's the proper syntax, assuming that angle brackets indicate an actual IP address? (Choose the best answer.)

A ○ **route add persistent** *<gateway> <destination>*

B ○ **route add** *<destination>* **mask** *<mask> <gateway>* **-p**

C ○ **route –p add** *<destination>* **mask** *<mask> <gateway>*

D ○ **route –f add** *<destination>* **mask** *<mask> <gateway>*

E ○ **route –s add** *<destination> <mask> <gateway>*

16 Internet Connection Sharing seems so much simpler to implement than NAT (Network Address Translation). Your manager asks you why you would ever consider using NAT over ICS. Which of the following answers would be correct? (Choose all that apply.)

A ❑ ICS doesn't work with Windows 2000 Server, only Windows 2000 Professional.

B ❑ ICS doesn't enable you to configure the private IP address range, but NAT does.

C ❑ NAT performs faster than ICS because it uses the Simple TCP/IP Protocol.

D ❑ Microsoft recommends using NAT rather than ICS if you already have separate DHCP and DNS servers.

E ❑ "NAT" is more fun to pronounce than "ICS."

17 Your WAN uses a demand-dial ISDN line that costs money every time it's used. Your boss wants you to find out why the line is being used so much, when it's supposed to be used only once a week for inventory reconciliation. You suspect that certain broadcasts are triggering the demand-dial link, which you have configured using Windows 2000 Server's Routing and Remote Access console. What should you do to nip this problem in the bud? (Choose the best answer.)

A ○ In the RRAS console, open the Routing Interfaces node, right-click the demand-dial interface, and choose Dial-Out Hours.

B ○ In the RRAS console, open the Routing Interfaces node, right-click the demand-dial interface, choose Properties, click the Options tab, and click Dial-Out Hours.

C ○ In the RRAS console, open the Routing Interfaces node, right-click the demand-dial interface, choose Set IP Demand-Dial Filters, and click Dial-Out Hours.

D ○ In the RRAS console, open the IP Routing node, click General, right-click the demand-dial interface, and choose Dial-Out Hours.

18 The economy is good, and Acme Cognac (your employer) is expanding. Your headquarters is in New York, but you're opening new branches in San Francisco and Dallas. Your boss has asked you to improve the performance of your DNS implementation, taking the new branches into account. Right now, you have only a single Windows 2000 DNS server in New York. However, your boss has also asked you to make sure that administration responsibility for DNS resides in New York. What should you do? (Choose all that apply.)

A ❑ Install a DNS server for San Francisco, and another one for Dallas.

B ❑ Create subdomains and delegated zones for the new branches.

C ❑ Create secondary servers for the new branches.

D ❑ Set push/pull replication between New York and San Francisco, and do the same between New York and Dallas.

E ❑ Configure San Francisco and Dallas clients to consult the local DNS server first and the New York DNS server next.

19 You've set up Routing and Remote Access on a Windows 2000 Server to provide dial-in access for telecommuters. You need to meet the following goals:

Initially, you only want remote users to be able to access a shared folder on the RRAS machine itself.

You must be able to administer the server remotely.

How can you accomplish these goals? (Choose the best answer.)

A ○ Remove any network interface cards from the server.

B ○ Clear the Enable IP Routing checkbox on the RRAS server's property sheet.

C ○ Configure the dial-in port's property sheet for Remote Access Connections (Inbound, This Server Only).

D ○ Remove the TCP/IP Protocol from all connections in the Network and Dial-Up Connections folder.

20 Your company just bought another company, and 40 new employees are joining your network. Their PCs are configured as NetWare clients. The new employees need access to shared folders and printers. You will migrate them to your Windows 2000 network at some point; for the meantime, you want to provide the access necessary with a minimum amount of administrative work. What software should you use? (Choose the best answer.)

A ○ Gateway Service for NetWare

B ○ Client Service for NetWare

C ○ File and Print Services for NetWare

D ○ Windows 2000 Services for NetWare Clients

21 You're setting up the NAT service on a Windows 2000 Server computer. Your network doesn't have a DHCP server. You want NAT to assign IP addresses to local workstations when those workstations connect to the Internet through the NAT router. You want to define the pool of addresses from the private IP address network 10.0.0.0. What action do you need to take in the RRAS console? (Choose the best answer.)

A ○ Configure the NAT DHCP allocator.

B ○ Configure the NAT DHCP proxy.

C ○ Activate Automatic Private IP Addressing.

D ○ Specify the address of an Internet-based DHCP server.

E ○ Install the DHCP Relay Agent.

22 Which of the following IP addresses can never be used on the public Internet? (Choose all that apply.)

A ❑ 10.0.0.3

B ❑ 172.16.1.1

C ❑ 127.0.0.1

D ❑ 192.168.0.50

23 Your Windows network includes some non-Windows clients that can only issue b-node NetBIOS name resolution queries. Your WINS server runs on a Windows 2000 Server machine that resides on a remote subnet. What can you do to permit the non-Windows clients to resolve NetBIOS names? (Choose the best answer.)

A ○ Convert one of the Windows 2000 clients into a WINS proxy.

B ○ Enable b-node listening on the WINS server.

C ○ Enable h-node listening on the WINS server.

D ○ Enable m-mode listening on the WINS server.

24 Your 20-person software company has developed a fancy public Web site that uses downloadable ActiveX programs and the IIS server software. You've decided to make it easier for visitors to your site to download those ActiveX controls. What type of certificate should you use for your digital signatures? (Choose the best answer.)

A ○ One issued by an enterprise root CA within your company.

B ○ One issued by a standalone root CA within your company.

C ○ One issued by a standalone subordinate CA within your company.

D ○ One issued by a large external commercial CA.

25 A network administrator has just manually changed an A resource record for Hans' workstation on a Windows 2000 DNS server to reflect a change in Hans' static IP address. Franz is unable to connect to Hans' computer. He tries pinging Hans' computer by host name, but gets an unknown host error. What can Franz do to fix the problem immediately? (Choose the best answer.)

A ○ Open a command prompt and type **ipconfig /release**.

B ○ Open a command prompt and type **ipconfig /renew**.

C ○ Open a command prompt and type **ipconfig /flushdns**.

D ○ Open a command prompt and type **ipconfig /flush**.

E ○ Choose Start⇨Run and type **winipcfg**. On the General property sheet, click Reset DNS Cache.

26 Your DNS server runs on a Windows 2000 member server, and you've decided that the convenience of Active Directory-integrated zoned is a great idea. Which of the following DNS zone types can you upgrade to the Active Directory-integrated type, using the DNS management console on your server? (Choose all that apply.)

A ❑ Standard primary

B ❑ Standard secondary

C ❑ Standard tertiary

D ❑ Replicated primary

E ❑ None of the above

27 You've set up a Certificate Services computer on Windows 2000. Windows 2000 Professional users try to request certificates by connecting to `http://<servername>/certsrv`, but they cannot complete the procedure. These users can PING the certificate server without error, and they can access other Web pages on the server through their browsers. Oh dear, what can the matter be? (Choose the best answer.)

A ○ A packet filter is restricting TCP port 80 on the IIS computer.

B ○ The CA has not been authorized in Active Directory.

C ○ The users do not have the Execute privilege on the CERTSRV folder.

D ○ The users do not have the Execute Script privilege on the CERTSRV folder.

28 You just installed the DHCP service on a Windows 2000 Server computer, using the Network Components dialog box in the Add/Remove Programs wizard. The software installed without error. You have configured scopes and scope options. You have configured Windows 2000 Professional clients to obtain an IP address automatically. However, DHCP is still not working. What should you do next? (Choose the best answer.)

A ○ Stop and restart the DHCP service.

B ○ Stop and restart the Windows 2000 Server computer.

C ○ Right-click the DHCP server in the DHCP console and choose Start.

D ○ Right-click the DHCP server in the DHCP console and choose Authorize.

E ○ Open Active Directory Users and Computers. Navigate to the DHCP server in the computers folder, right-click it, and choose Authorize.

29 You're setting up a remote access server using Windows 2000. You discover that some cybervandals have been trying to eavesdrop on network com-muni-cations in order to obtain the secret recipe for your new product, Acme Cognac Coolers. So, you decide to perform data encryption as well as authen-tication on the RRAS machine. You create a remote access profile and then click the Encryption tab.

What must you do in order to enforce 56-bit encryption on all communications sessions that use this profile? (Choose all that apply.)

A ❏ Check the No Encryption box.
B ❏ Clear the No Encryption box.
C ❏ Check the Basic box.
D ❏ Clear the Basic box.
E ❏ Check the Strong box.
F ❏ Clear the Strong box.

30 You've set up a remote access server but you have a limited number of devices in your modem pool. You need to provide the highest-speed access possible to members of the Management group, many of whom have two phone lines at home; but you do not need to provide greater than 50Kbps dial-up access to members of the Accounting group. You want to ensure that mem-bers of the Management group don't tie up bandwidth needlessly.

How can you configure a remote access policy that meets these needs? (Choose all that apply.)

A ❏ Create a single remote access policy.
B ❏ Create two remote access policies.
C ❏ Use Windows-Groups as a condition in the remote access profile.
D ❏ Use Windows-Groups as a condition in the remote access policy.
E ❏ Select the Allow Multilink radio button for Management users.
F ❏ Check the box labeled Require BAP For Dynamic Multilink Requests.

31 You've been advised by your local Windows 2000 MCSE (you're not one yet, or you wouldn't be reading this) that you should use MS-CHAP version 2 for the most secure possible authentication with remote access clients.

Which of the following must be true in order for MS-CHAPv2 authentication to take place? (Choose all that apply.)

A ❏ The MS-CHAPv2 checkbox must be selected in the Authentication Methods dialog box for the RRAS server's property sheet.
B ❏ Windows Authentication must be selected as the Authentication Provider on the Security tab of the RRAS server's property sheet.

C ❑ The MS-CHAPv2 checkbox must be selected on the Authentication tab of the dial-in profile for the remote access policy.

D ❑ The MS-CHAPv2 checkbox must be selected on the property sheet for the remote user's connection icon in the Network and Dial-Up Connections folder.

E ❑ The MS-CHAP (v1 and v2) checkbox must be selected on the property sheet for the remote user's connection icon in the Network and Dial-Up Connections folder.

32 What NetBIOS name resolution node type performs a p-node query first, followed by a b-node query if the p-node query fails? (Choose the best answer.)

A ○ h-node

B ○ m-node

C ○ pb-node

D ○ mixed-node

E ○ x-node

F ○ arpa-node

33 **You're running Network Monitor to capture all IP traffic on a Windows 2000 Server computer with 96MB of RAM. You set the capture buffer to 96MB. The utility reports a high number of dropped frames. What could you do to reduce the number of dropped frames? (Choose all that apply.)**

A ❑ Set a capture filter.

B ❑ Add RAM.

C ❑ Increase the pagefile size.

D ❑ Upgrade to the full version of Network Monitor.

34 **Windows NT 4.0 Server computers require Service Pack 4 or higher in order to run the DNS service in an Active Directory environment. Why? (Choose all that apply.)**

A ❑ SP4 includes support for NTFS Version 5.

B ❑ SP4 includes support for SRV resource records.

C ❑ SP4 includes support for Dynamic DNS.

D ❑ SP4 fixes bugs in earlier versions of DNS.

35 **What kind of resource record would you add to a Reverse Lookup zone in the DNS console? (Choose the best answer.)**

A ○ CNAME

B ○ A

C ○ B

D ○ PTR

E ○ b-node

36 **You're setting up a DHCP server and you want to configure integration with DDNS. Your network consists of Windows 2000 Professional clients and Windows NT 4.0 Workstation clients. You need to make sure that all DHCP clients have both A and PTR records updated in the DNS database, but you want to keep network traffic and DNS database traffic as low as you can.**

What setting would you make on the DNS tab of the DHCP scope in order to achieve these goals? (Choose all that apply.)

A ❑ Automatically Update DHCP Client Information In DNS

B ❑ Update DNS Only If DHCP Client Requests

C ❑ Always Update DNS

D ❑ Enable Updates For DNS Clients That Do Not Support Dynamic Update

37 **You're running Windows 2000 Routing and Remote Access on an Active Directory domain controller. Your network runs in native mode, nary a Windows NT 4.0 server in sight. You decide to configure Active Directory so that the Dial-In property sheet for each of the four users whom you want to enable for remote access says** `Control Access Through Remote Access Policy`**. You are distressed to discover that none of the four users can access the RRAS server. What should you do? (Choose the best answer.)**

A ○ Add a remote access policy that specifies one or more conditions that apply to all four users (for example, group membership). Set that policy to allow access. Place that policy first in the list of Remote Access Policies.

B ○ Add a remote access policy that specifies one or more conditions that apply to all four users. Set that policy to allow access. Place that policy last in the list of Remote Access Policies.

C ○ Delete the default remote access policy.

D ○ Delete the default remote access profile.

38 **You want to link Acme Cognac's Denver office with its Vancouver office. The Denver office consists exclusively of Windows 2000 computers, both Server and Professional. The Vancouver office consists of Windows 2000, NT, and Windows 95 computers.**

You decide to implement IPSec for encrypted traffic between the two networks. How would you configure the Windows 2000 routers at each office? (Choose all that apply.)

A ❑ On the Denver and Vancouver routers, select This Rule Does Not Specify An IPSec Tunnel, on the rule's property sheet.

B ❑ On the Denver router, select The Tunnel Endpoint Is Specified By This IP Address, and enter the address of the Vancouver router, on the rule's property sheet.

C ❏ On the Vancouver router, select The Tunnel Endpoint Is Specified By This IP Address, and enter the address of the Denver router, on the rule's property sheet.

D ❏ On each router, right-click the server icon in the Routing and Remote Access console and choose Enable IPSec For Encrypted Communications.

39 **You want to set an IP packet filter for a router interface to block all FTP traffic. What ports should you block? (Choose all that apply.)**

A ❏ TCP 10

B ❏ TCP 20

C ❏ TCP 21

D ❏ TCP 80

E ❏ UDP 20

40 **What's the strongest encryption algorithm you can specify for a Windows 2000 IPSec transport mode connection? (Choose the best answer.)**

A ○ MD5

B ○ PKI

C ○ SHA

D ○ 3DES

E ○ FYI

41 **Your organization uses three subnets: A, B, and C. Subnet A connects to subnet B via router AB. Subnet A connects to subnet C via router AC.**

Due to a series of reorganizations at your company, all Subnet A users, with two exceptions, spend most of their time accessing shared resources that reside on Subnet C. The two exceptions, Damon and Pythias, spend most of their time accessing shared resources that reside on Subnet B.

You want to set up DHCP for Subnet A users to enjoy the best possible performance when accessing resources over the network. What should you do? (Choose all that apply.)

A ❏ Create a scope for subnet A users.

B ❏ Set a scope option for subnet A users that specifies router AC in the Router (003) field.

C ❏ Set a scope option for subnet A users that specifies router AB in the Router (003) field.

D ❏ Create reservations for Damon and Pythias.

E ❏ Create static mappings for Damon and Pythias.

F ❏ Set a DHCP option for Damon and Pythias that specifies router AB in the Router (003) field.

42 **How do you calculate WINS convergence? (Choose the best answer.)**

A ○ Average the replication times for each WINS server on the internetwork.

B ○ Sum the replication times for each WINS server on the network.

C ○ For each possible WINS server pairing, calculate the worst-case propagation time. The highest number is the convergence time.

D ○ Right-click the WINS server in the WINS management console and choose Convergence. Click the Calculate Now button.

43 **Your company uses two DNS servers: a Windows 2000 machine as the master server, and a UNIX machine as a secondary server. When the master server went down for maintenance last weekend, DNS did not appear to be working at all. What could the problem be? (Choose all that apply.)**

A ❑ The Windows 2000 machine could be using reverse-encrypted zone delegations.

B ❑ The Windows 2000 machine could be using fast zone transfers.

C ❑ The Windows 2000 machine could be using round robin record sequencing.

D ❑ The Windows 2000 machine could be using WINS forward lookups.

44 **Your Active Directory network consists of Windows 2000 Professional clients and Windows 2000 Server servers. Your network includes servers running DHCP, DNS, and WINS, but not RRAS. What is the default behavior of dynamic DNS updates? (Choose the best answer.)**

A ○ Clients update the A record; DHCP updates the B record.

B ○ Clients update the A record; DHCP updates the PTR record.

C ○ Clients update the A record and the PTR record.

D ○ DHCP updates the A record and the PTR record.

45 **What setting enables you to use Access Control Lists for precise control of which users and groups can and cannot perform dynamic updates to an Active Directory-integrated DNS zone? (Choose the best answer.)**

A ○ Only Secure Updates, on the zone property sheet

B ○ Only Secure Updates, on the server property sheet

C ○ Use ACLs, on the zone property sheet

D ○ Use ACLs, on the server property sheet

E ○ No Windows 2000 setting enables you to do this.

46 **When you set up Internet Connection Sharing, the IP address of the local network interface is reset. To which value? (Choose the best answer.)**

A ○ 192.168.255.255

B ○ 172.16.0.1

C ○ 10.1.1.1

D ○ 192.168.0.1

47 Your boss has charged you with maximizing security of your LAN infrastructure. You consider implementing IPSec. Why would you probably not want to assign the Server (Require Security) policy to your entire domain? (Choose all that apply.)

A ❑ You can only apply this policy to servers. It is incompatible with Windows 2000 Professional.

B ❑ Such an approach could prevent communications with other Windows and non-Windows computers on the network.

C ❑ The processor and traffic overhead could burden the network and cause performance problems.

D ❑ The policy is only a sample and is not intended for application in real-world networks.

48 Frank has used the Encrypting File System to encrypt various files and folders on his networked Windows 2000 Professional PC. However, he has just left the company to take a job with Larry's Liqueurs. By default, who is the designated Recovery Agent for Frank's encrypted files? (Choose the best answer.)

A ○ Anyone in the Power Users group.

B ○ The administrator of the first domain controller in the domain.

C ○ The administrator of the last domain controller in the domain.

D ○ Anyone in the Backup Operators group.

49 You're using the Network Monitor tool that came with Windows 2000 Server in order to analyze IP traffic on your network. You discover that the Tools⇨Find Routers command does not work. What can you do to correct this problem? (Choose the best answer.)

A ○ Install Network Monitor again and specify Full Installation in the Networking Components dialog box.

B ○ Invoke Network Monitor from a command prompt, with the /FULL qualifier.

C ○ You don't have any routers on your network. Add one.

D ○ Upgrade to the full version of Network Monitor.

50 You're setting up a small home network for yourself and your family. Which network transport protocol should you use for LAN communications? (Choose the best answer.)

A ○ TCP/IP

B ○ NWLink

C ○ NetBEUI

D ○ IPX/SPX

Answers

1 **B** and **C.** Access is intermittent because the NT server can't gain access to Active Directory in order to validate the remote user. You can either upgrade the RAS server to Windows 2000, or relax the security restrictions on the Everyone group in the Windows 2000 domain so that anyone (including the RAS server) can read any property of any Active Directory object. You can't promote an NT server to domain controller status with DCPROMO; that's a Windows 2000 tool. Remember for the exam that you don't run into this problem if the NT server is a domain controller, because then it doesn't have to go to an Active Directory DC for the account information; the server gets the account information from its local Registry. *Objective: Configure inbound connections (Chapter 7).*

2 **B.** In practice, you rarely have to do this with Windows 2000, which performs dynamic compaction online, but it's the sort of obscure question that exam writers love. The command is JETPACK (although personally I like CRUNCH). The syntax, which you may also need to know, is JETPACK WINS.MDB TEMP.MDB, where you can use whatever you want in place of TEMP.MDB because it's just an intermediate file that the JETPACK command uses during the compaction. (You can use the same command for DHCP.MDB, by the way; it works with any Jet database.) Don't forget to take the database offline first, by stopping the service. *Objective: Manage and monitor WINS (Chapter 6).*

3 **C.** If you just run IPCONFIG by itself, you get your DNS suffix, IP address, subnet mask, and default gateway address. To see the MAC address (the hardware ID of your network card), however, you need to run IPCONFIG with the /ALL qualifier. Sadly, the graphical WINIPCFG utility is available to Windows 9x users but not Windows 2000 users. *Objective: Install and configure TCP/IP (Chapter 3).*

4 **D.** Open Shortest Path First (OSPF) is the dynamic routing protocol that Microsoft recommends when you must connect more than 50 physical networks. Windows 2000's router software, RRAS, also supports RIP (Routing Information Protocol), but it puts more traffic onto the network and therefore would probably not be Acme Cognac's best choice. Using static routes would work, but would require more manual administration than using a dynamic routing protocol. *Objective: Manage and monitor IP routing protocols (Chapter 8).*

5 **A.** The Reconcile All Scopes command for the new DHCP server synchronizes the Registry data on Hobbes with the DHCP database. You would choose Verify, see if any leases need reconciliation, and if so, click Reconcile. *Objective: Manage and monitor DHCP (Chapter 5).*

6 **B.** When you have clients on a subnet that other Windows users can't find because their NetBIOS-to-IP mappings aren't present in the WINS database, you have to create static mappings in the WINS database. Use a WINS proxy (for which, FYI, choice C is the correct procedure) when a non-WINS client can't find other hosts on the network using NetBIOS names — that is, the mirror image of this situation. *Objective: Configure NetBIOS name resolution (Chapter 6).*

7 **B.** A caching-only DNS server is not authoritative on any zone and has no local zone database. It only knows what it learns over time by doing lookups (therefore, its usefulness is zero at first, but grows as it builds up its cache). FYI, choice C is wrong because there's no such thing as a diagonal lookup zone. *Objective: Configure a caching-only server (Chapter 4).*

8 **A.** All you have to do is create the multiple resource records. (They can both be normal A records; you don't need an alias because you're only dealing with one host name.) Windows 2000 automatically performs subnet optimization, so when a client receives two associations for www.acmecognac.com, it automatically uses the server on the same subnet. The round robin method would not meet your goals because it disables subnet optimization. *Objective: Manually create DNS resource records (Chapter 4).*

9 **C.** By adding #PRE entries to LMHOSTS, you instruct Windows clients to pre-load the IP addresses of commonly accessed hosts on the network. This pre-loading occurs when TCP/IP is initialized on the client computers (that is, when they boot). If a client finds an address mapping in the preloaded name cache, the client doesn't have to send a query to the WINS server. *Objective: Install, configure, and troubleshoot WINS (Chapter 6).*

10 **A.** You would think the people at Microsoft would have put this into the user interface by now, but they haven't. REG_MULTI_SZ is Registry-speak for a multistring value; you need one string specifying the 802.2 frame type for the NetWare 4 server, and one specifying the 802.3 frame type for the older NetWare 3 server. *Objective: Install the NWLink protocol (Chapter 3).*

11 **A and C.** By setting the replication update threshold to 1, you ensure that each server lets the other one know whenever the WINS database changes, so the other server can then request an update. You wouldn't take this approach over a slow and expensive WAN link, because of the traffic it would generate. *Objective: Configure WINS replication (Chapter 6).*

12 **B and C.** Internet Authentication Service comes with Windows 2000 Server. It's an implementation of Remote Authentication Dial-In User Service, or RADIUS. You can set up your remote access policies once, on a single RADIUS machine, and then tell all your RRAS servers to use that machine for authentication. *Objective: Manage and monitor remote access (Chapter 7).*

13 **C.** When you set up Active Directory-integrated zones, Windows 2000 manages the replication of the DNS database as part of Active Directory replication. One less chore for you to worry about. *Objective: Configure a root name server (Chapter 4).*

14 **A** and **D.** What's happening, most likely, is that the dial-up clients are issuing DHCPINFORM messages querying for the location of DNS and WINS servers, but RRAS doesn't know how to provide them. The DHCP Relay Agent protocol relays such requests to an active DHCP server on the network. You don't configure scopes in RRAS when you're using DHCP to provide IP addresses; RRAS gets addresses from a DHCP server, ten at a time. *Objective: Configure Routing and Remote Access for DHCP integration (Chapter 7).*

15 **C.** The –f command qualifier clears the routing table, which you don't want to do here. The –s command qualifier does not exist. You may as well just memorize a few examples of the route command, because Microsoft always puts it on this sort of exam. *Objective: Update a Windows 2000-based routing table by means of static routes (Chapter 8).*

16 **B** and **D.** Microsoft designed ICS for small office and home office environments, NAT for medium-sized organizations, and Proxy Server for larger firms. You can see evidence of the design intention in that you configure ICS via the Network and Dial-Up Connections folder, which exists on Windows 2000 Professional, whereas you configure NAT via the Routing and Remote Access console, which only exists on Windows 2000 Server. *Objective: Install NAT (Chapter 9).*

17 **A.** The Dial-Out Hours option appears on the demand-dial interface's property sheet under Routing Interfaces, but not under the General node. You would set a demand-dial filter to restrict traffic based on source address, destination address, or traffic type. *Objective: Implement demand-dial routing (Chapter 8).*

18 **C** and **E.** Secondary DNS servers at the new locations will periodically replicate data from the master server in New York. Microsoft recommends having one DNS server on each subnet for performance, so that DNS queries don't always have to cross WAN links. If you created delegated subdomains, you don't meet the goal of maintaining central administration of the zone. *Objective: Configure zones (Chapter 4).*

19 **B.** The checkbox is on the IP tab of the property sheet. If you remove the network interface cards, you don't have LAN access to the server in order to administer it from other computers. If you remove TCP/IP, remote access clients won't even be able to access the RRAS server itself. *Objective: Configure inbound connections (Chapter 7).*

20 **C.** File and Print Services for NetWare is a separate product that runs on Windows 2000 Server. It makes the Windows server appear just like a Novell server to the clients, minimizing the amount of configuration work necessary for the 40 new employees. Generally, configuring one server is easier than configuring 40 workstations. The Gateway Service for NetWare does just the opposite: It enables Windows clients to access resources on NetWare servers. *Objective: Install the NWLink protocol (Chapter 3).*

21 **A.** The NAT DHCP allocator is part of the NAT protocol that doles out IP addresses to clients requesting Internet access. You configure it on the Address Assignment tab of the NAT protocol's property sheet in the Routing and Remote Access Server management console. *Objective: Configure NAT properties (Chapter 9).*

22 **A, B, C,** and **D.** The addresses in A, B, and D are from private IP address ranges that organizations may use internally as long as their networks don't connect to the Internet, or connect to the Internet through a translator or proxy server. Note that Internet Connection Sharing, or ICS, uses addresses with the network ID 192.168.x.x. The address in C is the loopback address, specifying the local machine; it's used for diagnostic purposes. *Objective: Install Internet Connection Sharing (Chapter 9).*

23 **A.** In order for the non-WINS clients to resolve NetBIOS names of computers on the remote subnet, a WINS proxy must listen for the b-node broadcasts and forward them to the remote WINS server when necessary. The proxy computer receives the address mapping from the WINS server and then relays it back to the originating b-node client. You can configure a Windows 2000 machine to act as a WINS proxy by modifying the Registry. *Objective: Configure NetBIOS name resolution (Chapter 6).*

24 **D.** By obtaining a certificate from a large external Certificate Authority, you make it easier for visitors to your Web site to trust the code you're asking them to download. You may also want to set up a CA and a policy that lets software developers request a code-signing certificate. *Objective: Issue and revoke certificates (Chapter 11).*

25 **C.** Windows clients maintain a local cache of DNS data; you can view the local cache with the command ipconfig /displaydns. Cached data hangs around until the Time To Live value has expired, so the cache may not reflect recently changed data. Note that Windows 2000 doesn't come with the graphical WINIPCFG utility that comes with Windows 98. *Objective: Configure a DNS client (Chapter 4).*

26 **E.** Now, admittedly, you have to read carefully to get this one right. The question says that your DNS server is a member server — that is to say, not a domain controller. You can't change an existing DNS standard zone to an Active Directory-integrated zone if you aren't running the DNS service on a domain controller. (If you got this one right, and for the right reason, pat yourself on the back.) There's no such thing as a tertiary server, by the way, although you can have secondary servers pointing to other secondary servers. *Objective: Configure a root name server (Chapter 4).*

27 **D.** What's happening is that the users can't run the script that performs the certificate request. An IP packet filter on port 80 would prevent users from accessing any Web pages on the server. *Objective: Issue and revoke certificates (Chapter 11).*

28 **D.** You have to authorize a DHCP server in Active Directory before it starts working. You have to be a member of the Enterprise Administrators group in order to perform this action. Why? Well, considering the importance of IP configuration details to client connectivity, you don't want just any Tom, Dick, or Harry firing up DHCP servers. *Objective: Authorize a DHCP server in Active Directory (Chapter 5).*

29 **B, D,** and **E.** By clearing the No Encryption box, you're telling Windows that this remote access profile will not permit unencrypted sessions. By clearing the Basic box, you're specifying that 40-bit encryption just isn't good enough. Leave the Strong box checked so clients can actually connect with 56-bit encryption. *Objective: Configure encryption protocols (Chapter 7).*

30 **B, C, E,** and **F.** You're going to need two remote access policies, because you have to create two different profiles based on group membership: a multilink-capable policy for Management, and a non-multilink-capable policy for Accounting. Windows-Groups is a profile setting rather than a policy setting, so choice D is out. The Bandwidth Allocation Protocol, BAP, ensures that additional devices on multilink connections can be dropped if throughput is low. *Objective: Configure multilink connections (Chapter 7).*

31 **A, C,** and **D.** The RRAS server has to support the protocol globally, and the remote access policy has to support it as well. If the client doesn't support MS-CHAPv2, then everything else is moot. Note that B is incorrect because an IAS (Internet Authentication Server) can be set up very similarly to a RRAS server, including MS-CHAPv2 authentication. Note also that MS-CHAPv2 has a number of security enhancements compared to MS-CHAPv1, just in case the exam asks you which is better *Objective: Configure authentication protocols (Chapter 7).*

32 **A.** The h-node, or hybrid node, behavior is the default for a Windows 2000 WINS client. The m-node type is just the opposite: broadcast first, point-to-point query second. Choices C, D, E, and F do not exist. *Objective: Install, configure, and troubleshoot WINS (Chapter 6).*

33 **A** and **B.** You're dropping frames because Windows 2000 Server probably doesn't have much, if any, free RAM on a 96MB computer. (Believe me — I'm using just such a machine on my test network.) As a result, Network Monitor must use the pagefile to buffer the captured information, and the slow speed of the disk-based pagefile compared to semiconductor RAM means that something's got to give. A capture filter would reduce the number of packets captured and therefore ease up on the free RAM requirement. *Objective: Manage and monitor network traffic (Chapter 3).*

34 **B.** Active Directory requires support for SRV resource records, as well as CNAME and A (host) resource records, to use as locators. That support is not present in versions of Windows NT 4.0 Server earlier than Service Pack 4. Choice A is correct as far as it goes, but isn't really relevant. Choice C is emphatically not true; Dynamic DNS is one of the cool new features of Windows 2000. *Objective: Install the DNS Server service (Chapter 4).*

35 **D.** The PTR, or pointer, resource record performs IP-address-to-host name mapping. Certain applications and utilities (for example, NSLOOKUP and TRACERT) can fail if a PTR RR doesn't exist for a particular host. *Objective: Manually create DNS resource records (Chapter 4).*

36 **A, B,** and **D.** The checkbox in choice A is a prerequisite for DHCP to update DNS at all. You can choose either B or C in the dialog box; if you choose C, the DHCP server updates both A and PTR records even though Windows 2000 clients update their A records by default. So B is a better choice for keeping needless traffic down. Choice D instructs the server to update both A and PTR records for clients (such as NT 4.0) that don't support dynamic DNS at all. *Objective: Configure DHCP for DNS integration (Chapter 5).*

37 **A.** For the exam, know that the order in which remote access policies appear is critical to how RRAS behaves in terms of allowing or denying access. The default remote access policy denies access to everybody at all times of day, if Active Directory is set to let the remote access policies govern the decision (as is the case here). So if you create a policy to grant access to a specific group, that policy must appear first in the list. As soon as a policy matches, RRAS acts on it; if the default policy (deny everyone) is first in the list, nobody ever gets in to connect. *Objective: Create a remote access policy (Chapter 7).*

38 **B** and **C.** You need to use tunnel mode because transport mode really only works with Windows 2000 computers. You can't do point-to-point transport mode IPSec with the down-level Windows clients in Vancouver. When setting up tunnel mode IPSec, you must configure each server with the other's IP address. *Objective: Configure IPSec for tunnel mode (Chapter 10).*

39 **B** and **C.** TCP port 20 is the FTP data channel, while TCP port 21 is the FTP control channel. Other well-known ports you should memorize are 23 (telnet traffic), 25 (Simple Mail Transport Protocol, or SMTP), and 80 (Web server or http traffic). *Objective: Configure TCP/IP packet filters (Chapter 10).*

40 **D.** The possible encryption protocols for IPSec are 40-bit DES, 56-bit DES, and 3DES; the latter uses three 56-bit keys for high security (and unfortunately, also high overhead). Note that SHA and MD5 are authentication algorithms, not packet encryption algorithms; that is, SHA and MD5 are used during the authentication process only, and not to encrypt and decrypt the data stream. *Objective: Customize IPSec policies and rules (Chapter 10).*

41 **A, B, D,** and **F.** The general approach to a situation like this is to set the main scope to specify the most often used router as the primary one, and create exceptions (reservations) for clients needing scope options that vary from the herd. You can set DHCP options for each individual reservation that you make. A reservation is sort of like a static mapping, but that's not the proper terminology in the context of DHCP. *Objective: Create and manage DHCP scopes, superscopes, and multicast scopes (Chapter 5).*

42 **C.** An internetwork is said to have **converged** when a change that occurs on one part of the network — in this case, to a WINS server — has propagated throughout the network. With WINS servers that use push and pull replication, you should assume that only a single event occurs, and that the database replicates by pull replication only (unless you've set an update threshold of one event). In reality, multiple events may trigger the update threshold, causing convergence to occur more rapidly than you would predict using worst-case analysis. ***Objective: Manage and monitor WINS (Chapter 6).***

43 **B** and **D.** Older UNIX servers don't support the fast zone transfers that Windows 2000 uses by default; right-click the server and select the checkbox BIND Secondaries, on the Advanced tab, to disable fast zone transfers. If you've configured DNS to perform WINS lookups when DNS can't resolve a host name, the Windows 2000 DNS server includes special WINS resource records that could confuse a secondary server. Select the relevant records and choose Do Not Replicate This Record if that's the case. *Objective: Manage and monitor DNS (Chapter 4).*

44 **B.** You can modify this behavior at the client; for example, on the TCP/IP property sheet for the LAN connection, clearing the checkbox labeled Register This Connection's Address In DNS effectively disables A resource record updating by the client. *Objective: Configure a DNS client (Chapter 4).*

45 **A.** It makes sense that this setting should be on the zone property sheet rather than the server property sheet, because you can change the setting on a per-zone basis. For example, a zone that is not Active Directory-integrated does not provide this option. *Objective: Configure zones for dynamic updates (Chapter 4).*

46 **D.** This is the first address in the range that ICS uses. If the computer had been using a different IP address on that network interface, all existing TCP/IP connections would be lost. *Objective: Install Internet Connection Sharing (Chapter 9).*

47 **B, C,** and **D.** You can apply the policy to Windows 2000 Professional computers, but the other objections are valid. Use IPSec only where truly necessary to ensure security for data in transit. *Objective: Enable IPSec (Chapter 10).*

48 **B.** The administrator of the first domain controller in Frank's domain has a certificate that will enable him or her to decrypt Frank's files after they've been copied to the domain controller. *Objective: Remove the Encrypting File System recovery keys (Chapter 11).*

49 **D.** The version of Network Monitor that comes with Windows 2000 Server is a "lite" version that's missing many useful commands. The full version comes with Microsoft's Systems Management Server (SMS) product. *Objective: Manage and monitor network traffic (Chapter 3).*

50 **C.** That way you don't have to mess with any of the complicated stuff in this book. *Objective: Stay sane (No chapter reference).*

Appendix B

MCSE Certification and You

● ●

In This Chapter

▶ Understanding the different types of Microsoft certification

▶ Figuring out the best MCP or MCSE road map for you

▶ Discovering certification benefits

● ●

*M*icrosoft certification has great value for individual consultants, who can gain client confidence through accreditation. Certification can be great for techies in all sizes of organizations, too. Almost any technical professional who works with Microsoft products should look at getting certified.

The MCSE (Microsoft Certified Systems Engineer) certification represents a significant commitment to mastering Microsoft's desktop and server software products. On the other hand, the MCP (Microsoft Certified Professional) certification may be all that you want or need. In either case, you can use this book and exam 70-216 to help you obtain the credentials you desire.

This chapter lays out the details of Microsoft's certification program so that you can plan the route that makes most sense for you. You may discover some certification options that you didn't know about before.

In Chapter 1, I provide more details on where, how, and when to take the exams. Chapter 1 also provides more information on the Windows 2000 Network Infrastructure test that is the subject of the rest of this book.

Types of Certification

This section aims to clear up the different certifications available and their requirements.

Everything in this chapter is accurate as I'm writing it, but Microsoft can change its certification requirements whenever it wants to. Check the certification Web site at (www.microsoft.com/train_cert) for the latest requirements.

Always take the newest exams that fulfill the various certification requirements. I never recommend that you take older exams, even if you're more familiar with the older products that they cover. The earlier Microsoft retires the exams you take, the sooner you'll have to pony up more time and money to freshen your certification.

Unlike a typical college degree, Microsoft certification doesn't require you to take any particular exams before others; that is, none of the exams have pre-requisites. You can turn this exam sequencing flexibility to your advantage by taking the tests in order from easiest to hardest, based on your own product knowledge and experience. In this way, by the time you get to the more challenging exams, you're comfortable with the testing format and you're less likely to be tripped up by procedural errors (such as forgetting to choose multiple answers in questions that call for them).

MCP

You can become a Microsoft Certified Professional, or MCP, by passing any Microsoft certification exam *except* the following:

- **Networking Essentials (70-058).** As I write this, Microsoft plans to retire this exam on December 31, 2000.

- **Microsoft Windows 2000 Accelerated Exam for MCPs Certified on Microsoft Windows NT 4.0 (70-240).** If you're a candidate to take this exam, you're already an MCP. This exam is due for retirement on December 31, 2001.

The MCP certification, which Microsoft also calls "Microsoft Certified Product Specialist," lets you put the letters "MCP" or "MCPS" after your name. It also bestows the benefits listed under the "Benefits and Responsibilities" section later in this chapter.

Despite the title of this book, you can use it to become an MCP, whether or not you choose to go on to get your MCSE.

MCP+Internet

This certification is an MCP with Internet focus. It's a little harder to squeeze onto your business card, so use one of the abbreviated forms: *MCP+I* or *MCPI*. You have to pass the following three exams:

✔ **Implementing and Supporting Windows NT Server 4.0 (70-067)**

✔ **Internetworking with Microsoft TCP/IP on Windows NT 4.0 (70-059)**

✔ **Implementing and Supporting Internet Information Server 4.0 (70-087)** — the earlier test, 70-077, covers IIS 3.0 and also qualifies at this writing

Microsoft is retiring the MCP+I certification on December 31, 2000, and recommending that those who are considering MCP+I consider Windows 2000 MCSE or MCSE+I instead.

MCP+Site Building

Here's another variation on the MCP theme. The MCP+Site Building certification (MCP+SB) indicates that you can use Microsoft tools to create a Web site, even one with e-commerce and database features. To get this certification, pick two exams from the following three:

✔ **Designing and Implementing Web Sites with FrontPage 98 (70-055)**

✔ **Designing and Implementing Commerce Solutions with Site Server 3.0, Commerce Edition (70-057)**

✔ **Designing and Implementing Web Solutions with Visual InterDev 6.0 (70-152)**

MCSE

The Microsoft Certified Systems Engineer (MCSE) certification has three tracks: Windows 2000, Windows NT 4.0, and Windows NT 3.51.

I strongly recommend not pursuing the NT 3.51 track. The tests are either retired or soon to be retired as I write this, and more importantly, virtually no one is deploying Windows NT 3.5x anymore.

Microsoft is retiring the Windows NT 4.0 track on December 31, 2000. However, if you have already made some headway toward your MCSE on this track and have completed all three NT 4.0 exams, you can maintain your MCSE certification past December 31, 2000 by taking the "Microsoft Windows 2000 Accelerated Exam for MCPs Certified on Microsoft Windows NT 4.0" (70-240). That exam will be available until December 31, 2001. It's a one-shot deal, though; no retakes if you fail. On the positive side, Microsoft is saying that it will be free to all MCPs — huzzah and kudos!

At the end of the MCSE process, you're knowledgeable and qualified to plan, deploy, and manage Microsoft information systems on both the client and the server side. The inclusion of the BackOffice tests puts the MCSE designation on a higher plane than certifications such as MCP that don't necessarily indicate mastery of server products.

NT 4.0 track

Microsoft is retiring the NT 4.0 MCSE track on December 31, 2000.

This track requires that you pass six tests: four core tests covering operating systems, and two electives, most of which cover BackOffice products.

NT 4.0 track core exams

The four core MCSE tests in the NT 4.0 track include one software-and-hardware test (Networking Essentials) and three operating system tests, as follows:

- **Networking Essentials (70-058).** You can receive credit from Microsoft for this test if you have one of the following certifications: a Novell CNE (Certified NetWare Engineer) or CNI (Certified NetWare Instructor), a Banyan CBS (Certified Banyan Specialist) or CBE (Certified Banyan Engineer), or a Sun CAN (Certified Network Administrator) for Solaris. This exam is due for retirement on December 31, 2000.

- **A desktop operating system.** You can choose one exam from the following: Implementing and Supporting Microsoft Windows 98 (70-098), Implementing and Supporting Microsoft Windows NT Workstation 4.0 (70-073), or Implementing and Supporting Microsoft Windows 95 (70-064).

- **Implementing and Supporting Windows NT Server 4.0 (70-067).** This test is the more basic of the two Windows NT Server tests. This exam is due for retirement on December 31, 2000.

- **Implementing and Supporting Windows NT Server 4.0 in the Enterprise (70-068).** And this one's more advanced. This exam is due for retirement on December 31, 2000.

NT 4.0 track elective exams

The two electives must be exams from the following list, most of which cover the Microsoft BackOffice product family.

It's smart to pick products that you expect to work with in your daily job, so that you can leverage your training to the greatest possible degree. Taking the most recent test in any product category is also smart.

You may choose from any of the following tests:

- **Implementing and Supporting Microsoft Internet Explorer 5.0 by Using the Internet Explorer Administration Kit (70-080).** This exam wins the award for longest title. It also counts toward the MCSE+I certification (see the next section). The earlier version of this test (70-079) covers IE 4.0.

- **Implementing and Supporting Internet Information Server 4.0 (70-087).** This test also counts toward the MCSE+I certification (see the next section). The earlier version of this test (70-077) covers IIS 3.0. Exam 70-087 is scheduled for retirement on December 31, 2000.

- **Implementing and Supporting Proxy Server 2.0 (70-088).** The earlier version of this test (70-078) covers Proxy Server 1.0.

- **Implementing and Supporting Web Sites Using Site Server 3.0 (70-056).**

- **Internetworking with TCP/IP on Windows NT 4.0 (70-059).** This test also counts toward the MCSE+I certification (see the next section). The earlier version of this test (70-053) covers NT 3.5*x*.

- **Implementing and Supporting Microsoft Exchange Server 5.5 (70-081).** The earlier version of this test (70-076) covers Exchange Server 5.0.

- **Implementing and Supporting Microsoft SNA Server 4.0 (70-085).** The earlier version of this test (70-013) covers SNA Server 3.0.

- **Administering Microsoft SQL Server 7.0 (70-028).** The earlier version of this test (70-026) covers SQL Server 6.5.

- **Designing and Implementing Databases with Microsoft SQL Server 7.0 (70-029).** The earlier version of this test (70-027) covers SQL Server 6.5.

- **Designing and Implementing Data Warehouses with Microsoft SQL Server 7.0 (70-019).**

- **Implementing and Supporting Microsoft Systems Management Server 2.0 (70-086).** The earlier version of this test (70-018) covers SMS 1.2.

- **Designing a Microsoft Windows 2000 Directory Services Infrastructure (70-219).** Yes, this and the three that follow are Windows 2000 exams, but they count as electives toward the NT 4.0 track. You can't apply these tests to both tracks simultaneously, however.

- **Designing Security for a Microsoft Windows 2000 Network (70-220).**

- **Designing a Microsoft Windows 2000 Network Infrastructure (70-221).**

- **Upgrading from Microsoft Windows NT 4.0 to Microsoft Windows 2000 (70-222).**

You can probably tell by scanning the list of electives that it's easy to take two tests that deal with overlapping subject matter. For example, if you're into database development, tests 70-028 and 70-029 both deal with SQL Server 7.0. If you expect to be setting up Web servers using Microsoft products, tests 70-087, 70-088, 70-056, and 70-059 all contain a certain amount of overlap. If you're interested in getting your MCSE as soon as you can, give some consideration to taking two elective tests covering similar subject matter; you'll do less studying.

Windows 2000 track

The Windows 2000 MCSE track typically requires that you pass *seven* tests: four core operating system tests, one core network design test, and two electives, most of which cover BackOffice products.

Windows 2000 track core operating system exams

The four core operating system MCSE tests in the Windows 2000 track are as follows:

- ✔ **Installing, Configuring and Administering Microsoft Windows 2000 Professional (70-210).**

- ✔ **Installing, Configuring and Administering Microsoft Windows 2000 Server (70-215).**

- ✔ **Implementing and Administering a Microsoft Windows 2000 Network Infrastructure (70-216).** This book!

- ✔ **Implementing and Administering a Microsoft Windows 2000 Directory Services Infrastructure (70-217).**

Note that the Networking Essentials test no longer appears, as its material now appears in exams 70-216 and 70-221. Also note the conspicuous absence of the Windows 98 and 95 exams. Microsoft states that it has removed the Windows 9*x* tests from the new MCSE track because it expects businesses to use Windows 2000 Professional rather than Windows 9*x*. Well, okay, that may become true eventually; but for quite a while, many organizations will continue using Windows 9*x* on the desktop. To omit that operating system from the new MCSE track makes little sense to me, but that's the way it is.

If you've already taken the three Windows NT 4.0 exams from the core group in the Windows NT 4.0 MCSE track (that is, 70-067, 70-068, and 70-073), you can skip taking the four core Windows 2000 exams and just take the free exam 70-240 (Microsoft Windows 2000 Accelerated Exam for MCPs Certified on Microsoft Windows NT 4.0). But remember, you can only take that exam one time! So study hard!

Windows 2000 track core network design exams

To fulfill the network design exam requirement, you must choose one from the following three exams:

- ✔ **Designing a Microsoft Windows 2000 Directory Services Infrastructure (70-219).**

- ✔ **Designing Security for a Microsoft Windows 2000 Network (70-220).**

- ✔ **Designing a Microsoft Windows 2000 Network Infrastructure (70-221).**

Windows 2000 track elective exams

You must take two elective exams for Windows 2000 track MCSE certification. As I write this, the list of exams is the same as for the Windows 4.0 track (see the earlier section in this chapter, "NT 4.0 track elective exams").

MCSE+Internet

The MCSE+Internet certification indicates that you're an MCSE who has some extra knowledge about intranet/Internet software: browsers, Web servers, proxy servers, database links, and electronic commerce. To achieve MCSE+I status, you must pass seven core exams and two elective exams.

As with the MCP+I designation, MCSE+I pertains mainly to the Windows NT 4.0 track. The Windows 2000 track already has a heavy emphasis on Internet technologies. At this time, Microsoft hasn't yet announced the retirement of MCSE+I as it has for MCP+I, but I expect it's only a matter of time.

Core exams

The core exams are the same as the four core exams for MCSE status in the Windows NT 4.0 track, plus the following:

- ✔ **Implementing and Supporting Microsoft Internet Explorer 5.0 by Using the Internet Explorer Administration Kit (70-080).** The earlier version of this test (70-079) covers IE 4.

- ✔ **Implementing and Supporting Internet Information Server 4.0 (70-087).** The earlier version of this test (70-077) covers IIS 3.0.

- ✔ **Internetworking with TCP/IP on Windows NT 4.0 (70-059).** The earlier version of this test (70-053) covers NT 3.5*x*.

Astute readers will notice that these three "added" core exams also appear as electives for the MCSE test. So, if you're planning your MCSE curriculum and thinking about MCSE+I for later, be sure to choose MCSE electives that count toward MCSE+I.

Elective exams

The elective exams for MCSE+I must include two from the following list:

- ✔ **Implementing and Supporting Proxy Server 2.0 (70-088).** The earlier version of this test (70-078) covers Proxy Server 1.0, but I suggest you take the more recent exam.

- ✔ **Implementing and Supporting Web Sites Using Site Server 3.0 (70-056).**

- ✔ **Implementing and Supporting Microsoft SNA Server 4.0 (70-085).** The earlier version of this test (70-013) covers SNA Server 3.0.

- ✔ **Administering Microsoft SQL Server 7.0 (70-028).** The earlier version of this test (70-026) covers SQL Server 6.5.

- ✔ **Designing and Implementing Databases with Microsoft SQL Server 7.0 (70-029).** The earlier version of this test (70-027) covers SQL Server 6.5.

- ✔ **Implementing and Supporting Microsoft Exchange Server 5.5 (70-081).** The earlier version of this test (70-076) covers Exchange Server 5.0.

MCSD

The Microsoft Certified Solution Developer (MCSD) certification indicates your qualification to develop applications using Microsoft products. This four-test certification consists of three core exams and one elective exam. The tests revolve around Microsoft's Visual C++, Visual Basic, and Visual FoxPro programming environments. I don't offer details of MCSD certification requirements here because very little overlap exists with the MCP and MCSE programs; if you need the skinny on MCSD, point your Web browser to www.microsoft.com/mcp/certstep/mcsd.htm.

MCT

The Microsoft Certified Trainer (MCT) certification indicates your qualification to teach official Microsoft courses at an Authorized Technical Education Center (ATEC). You get an MCT certification for each course you qualify to teach. You have to pass the course (one would hope so!) plus demonstrate presentation skills, either by producing a relevant certificate or by attending a Microsoft-approved "train the trainer" course. The details of becoming an MCT are too involved to include in their entirety here; check out www.microsoft.com/train_cert/mct/ for more information.

MCDBA

The Microsoft Certified Database Administrator (MCDBA) targets those professionals who need to create and manage databases using Microsoft's flagship database manager, SQL Server. This program, like the MCSE program, has both a Windows 2000 track and a Windows NT 4.0 track. You should know about MCDBA if you're thinking of pursuing MCSE, because you could very well achieve both certifications at the same time.

Windows 2000 track

This track requires three core exams and one elective exam, so it's one exam easier than the Windows NT 4.0 track (see the next section). The core exams are as follows:

- ✔ **Administering Microsoft SQL Server 7.0 (70-028) or Installing, Configuring, and Administering Microsoft SQL Server 2000 Enterprise Edition (70-228)**

- ✔ **Designing and Implementing Databases with Microsoft SQL Server 7.0 (70-029) or Designing and Implementing Databases with Microsoft SQL Server 2000 Enterprise Edition (70-229)**

- ✔ **Installing, Configuring, and Administering Microsoft Windows 2000 Server (70-215)** or, if you've already passed three Windows NT 4.0 exams, **Microsoft Windows 2000 Accelerated Exam for MCPs Certified on Microsoft Windows NT 4.0 (70-240)**

You must also choose one elective test from the following:

- ✔ **Implementing and Administering a Microsoft Windows 2000 Network Infrastructure (70-216)** or, if you've already passed three Windows NT 4.0 exams, **Microsoft Windows 2000 Accelerated Exam for MCPs Certified on Microsoft Windows NT 4.0 (70-240)**

- ✔ **Designing and Implementing Distributed Applications with Visual C++ 6.0 (70-015)**

- ✔ **Designing and Implementing Data Warehouses with SQL Server 7.0 and Decision Support Services 1.0 (70-019)**

- ✔ **Implementing and Supporting Internet Information Server 4.0 (70-087)** (scheduled for retirement on December 31, 2000)

- ✔ **Designing and Implementing Distributed Applications with Visual FoxPro 6.0 (70-155)**

- ✔ **Designing and Implementing Distributed Applications with Visual Basic 6.0 (70-175)**

Windows NT 4.0 track

This track requires four core exams and one elective exam. The core exams are as follows:

- ✓ **Administering Microsoft SQL Server 7.0 (70-028)**
- ✓ **Designing and Implementing Databases with Microsoft SQL Server 7.0 (70-029)**
- ✓ **Implementing and Supporting Windows NT Server 4.0 (70-067)** (scheduled for retirement on December 31, 2000)
- ✓ **Implementing and Supporting Windows NT Server 4.0 in the Enterprise (70-068))** (scheduled for retirement on December 31, 2000)

You must also choose one elective test from the following:

- ✓ **Designing and Implementing Distributed Applications with Visual C++ 6.0 (70-015)**
- ✓ **Designing and Implementing Data Warehouses with SQL Server 7.0 and Decision Support Services 1.0 (70-019)**
- ✓ **Internetworking with TCP/IP on Windows NT 4.0 (70-059)** (scheduled for retirement on December 31, 2000)
- ✓ **Implementing and Supporting Internet Information Server 4.0 (70-087)** (scheduled for retirement on December 31, 2000)
- ✓ **Designing and Implementing Distributed Applications with Visual FoxPro 6.0 (70-155)**
- ✓ **Designing and Implementing Distributed Applications with Visual Basic 6.0 (70-175)**

Benefits and Responsibilities

What are some of the benefits and responsibilities of becoming an MCP or MCSE?

The benefits include the following:

- ✓ You have the right to put letters after your name that inform your colleagues, managers, and/or clients that you know your stuff and that you're worth more money than you're currently getting. Lots of studies show that Microsoft certification can help your career. (As long as you stay in the industry, of course. If you become a rock musician, your MCSE won't help much. "Glenn and the MCSEs" would be a bad name for a band.)

✔ You can use the appropriate logo on your business card and letterhead, too. Microsoft sends you photo-ready art after you pass.

✔ You get to connect to Microsoft Web resources, such as downloadable training modules, that are only available to certified pros. As I write this, you can find the secured MCP sites at `partnering.one.microsoft.com`. You can get to them by pointing to the main certification site, `www.microsoft.com/train_cert`, and clicking MCP only. I recommend that you do go through the mildly tedious signup process; you can find some cool stuff on the MCP-only Web site.

✔ If you live in North America, you receive free of charge *Microsoft Certified Professional Magazine.* This periodical includes information about new exams and exams that are about to be retired, to help you stay current with your certification.

✔ If you get your MCSE, you also receive a 50-percent discount on a one-year subscription to the Microsoft TechNet CD-ROM database of technical information. This benefit is great, because TechNet contains the Microsoft knowledge base of common problems and solutions. (Well, at least it contains the part of that knowledge base that's reasonably current — the entire database can't fit on a single CD-ROM anymore.)

✔ Another MCSE benefit is a one-year membership, updated monthly, in the Beta Evaluation program. For example, you can tinker with pre-release software to help your company evaluate an upcoming product.

✔ A special benefit goes to Microsoft Certified Trainers: a free subscription to *Microsoft Education Forum Newsletter.*

You have only one real responsibility as an MCP or MCSE: *Stay current.* If you take an exam that Microsoft retires, you may have to take a newer exam to retain your certification.

How do you hear about recertification requirements? Glance over *Microsoft Certified Professional Magazine* periodically (pun intended), read your mail (Microsoft generally mails notices if your certification needs renewing), and check the certification Web site from time to time. It's at `www.microsoft.com/train_cert` — make it a bookmark in your Web browser.

Appendix C

Glossary

● ●

*T*he following glossary defines most of the technical terms that appear in this book. Terms that have acronyms appear under the acronym's listing.

ACL. Access Control List, a data structure containing access information for a file or folder on an NTFS disk (that is, who can do what with the file or folder).

ACPI. Advanced Configuration and Power Interface, an updated power management standard that lets Windows 2000 have more control over system board power-saving hardware features. See also **APM.**

Active Desktop. A collection of Windows 2000 user interface features that makes the desktop into a layered Web page that can include Java and ActiveX programs as well as HTML files. As used by Microsoft, the term includes other enhancements, such as a more customizable taskbar and the ability to preview certain types of data files.

Active Directory. Windows 2000 Server's directory service, which organizes all network resources (users, printers, computers, and so on).

ActiveX. ActiveX lets programmers create programs (called "controls") that run in the same window space as other programs, and that share program modules across disks and even networks, whether or not those programs are written in the same language. ActiveX also includes the file type associations that govern how the computer treats files with specific suffixes.

Adapter. A circuit board, such as a network interface card, that plugs into a computer's motherboard.

Administrator. A special user account on a Windows 2000 system that has the rights to perform just about any action on that system. Administrators can partition disks, create user accounts, assign security restrictions to other users and groups, install and remove software, and so on. Many operations in Windows 2000 require that the user log on as Administrator.

ADSL. Asynchronous Digital Subscriber Line, technology that uses regular old twisted-pair phone wire for fast connections (up to 8Mbps to the user and up to 1Mbps from the user). Also called *DSL.*

AGP. Accelerated Graphics Port, a bus specification designed to enhance 3D graphics performance for display adapters. An AGP display adapter isn't necessarily fast, though! Windows 2000 uses AGP and PCI display adapters for its multiple display feature.

Answer file. A text file (usually named UNATTEND.TXT) that provides answers to questions that Windows 2000 setup would normally pose of a user during an interactive installation.

API. Application programming interface; a defined set of commands or "calls" that application programs use to communicate with underlying services, software, or devices. A programmer uses API calls when creating a program. TAPI, for example, enables applications to interact with modems without using Hayes AT commands. Because each operating system has its own distinct API, programs written for the Mac won't run on a Windows 2000 PC unless the programmer rewrites them to use the Windows API.

APM. Advanced Power Management, an earlier standard that Windows 2000 supports if the APM tab appears in the Power Options control panel. See also **ACPI**.

Applet. A small application, such as the Windows 2000 calculator; in the context of the Internet or intranets, a downloadable program that can run within a Web browser.

AppleTalk. Apple's network protocol suite, which Windows 2000 Server supports.

Application program. Software that enables users to perform useful tasks with the computer. Word processors and spreadsheets are examples.

Application server. A network server that provides specialized functions such as communications, database management, or file backup. Application servers typically have their own dedicated computer.

ARP. Address Resolution Protocol, which relates IP addresses to the MAC (Media Access Control) addresses burned into a network adapter's read-only memory.

ATM. Asynchronous Transfer Mode, a packet-switching network protocol designed to guarantee a certain high throughput rate for the duration of a session, and to permit traffic prioritization; useful for digital video, audio, and other demanding needs.

Attachment. A data file or program sent along with a mail message. Attachments may be in any form, text or binary.

Attribute. See **File attribute**.

Audit. To track activity on a computer system, by username or service name. Windows 2000 disables auditing by default, but you can activate the feature to track logons, file and folder accesses, and even Registry accesses, among other activities. See also **Event log.**

Authentication. The process of checking that a user who supplies a given name and password is, in fact, a legitimate user and allowed to log on at a particular time.

Autorun. A feature that permits properly configured CD-ROMs to automatically run programs and install drivers when the CD-ROM is inserted into the drive.

B Channel. A bidirectional data-carrying channel in an ISDN connection, capable of moving information at 64 kilobits per second. B channels can carry data, voice, audio, or video information. See also **ISDN, BRI, PRI.**

Backup. 1) To create a copy of files on a computer, either for long-term storage or to provide a way to recover from hardware failure. 2) The tapes or disks created by a backup operation, also called a "backup set."

Backup agent. A program that runs on a computer (usually a workstation) with files to be backed up and that communicates over the network with the computer running the main backup program (usually a server). Backup agents enable a server to back up a workstation on the same network. The agent determines which files need to be backed up and feeds them to the main backup program when requested.

Bandwidth. The data-carrying capacity of a data communications channel.

Basic disk. A Windows 2000 disk organization method that uses partitions, basic disks work much like the disk organization structure in previous versions of Windows and DOS. See also **Dynamic disk.**

Batch file. A file that contains a sequence of commands that run one after the other. Batch files have the suffix *.BAT.

Baud rate. A term on its way out. Technically not the same as the bit-per-second rate, the baud rate represents signal modulations over a serial link (how often frequencies change). Advanced modems can send more than one bit for each modulation, so the bps rate exceeds the baud rate.

Binary file. A data file that a user can't read or modify without a particular software application, in contrast to a text file.

Bindery. In NetWare 2.*x* and 3.*x,* the files that contain user, group, and print server information. NetWare Directory Services (NDS) takes over bindery functionality in NetWare 4.*x* and 5.*x*.

Bindery emulation. A feature of newer NetWare servers that permits applications to interact with users and groups in the same manner they did under NetWare 3.*x*.

Binding. The process of logically connecting a network card driver to a transport protocol, a transport protocol to a network client, or a transport protocol to a network service. Windows 2000 handles bindings via the Network and Dial-Up Connections control panel's Advanced menu.

BIOS. Short for Basic Input-Output System. ROM-based software that loads before the operating system and handles low-level data transfer between disk drives, printers, keyboards, monitors, and memory; also includes Power-On Self Test code. Devices such as video adapters and disk controllers typically have their own BIOS in addition to the main PC BIOS.

Bit. Short for binary digit. The smallest unit of computer data, consisting of a zero or one. It usually takes eight bits to make a byte, which represents one alphanumeric character, although a byte may contain seven or nine bits.

Boot. The process a computer goes through when it starts and loads the operating system into memory.

Branch. One of the six main Registry keys. See also **HKCC, HKCR, HKCU, HKLM,** and **HKU.**

BRI. Basic Rate Interface, the most common type of ISDN connection, consisting of two 64Kbps digital voice-and-data channels ("B" channels) and one digital signaling channel ("D" channel). The BRI is designed for an individual line connection over standard copper telephone lines. See also **PRI.**

Bridge. A device that connects one network to another, usually the same type (for example, Ethernet to Ethernet), and passes data between the two. Usually, a bridge is simply a computer with two network interface cards in it, but they don't necessarily use the same cable type.

Broadcast. To send information to all networked clients. For example, servers typically broadcast their availability periodically to let workstations know they're online.

Browser. The application program used to view Web pages (either on the public Internet or on a private intranet) in a graphical user interface, navigate among them, link from one to another, and ensure security and performance. The Internet Explorer browser comes with Windows 2000.

Buffer. An interim storage location for data in transit; usually used to smooth out data transfer between devices capable of operating at different speeds.

Built-in group. A local or network group account already defined by Windows 2000 to have a convenient set of rights. Examples include Everyone, Authenticated Users, Administrators, Power Users, Guests, and Users.

Bus. An internal and usually standardized data communications channel that links components to each other. Traffic flows on buses between all the computer's component parts: processor, memory, storage devices, keyboard, screen, and network interface card. Modern PCs typically have more than one bus.

Bus mastering. A feature of high-performance computer circuit boards that enables them to temporarily take control of the computer and shuttle data around without CPU intervention. Bus mastering is generally used by disk controllers, network adapters, and video cards.

Bus topology. A network layout in which a single cable, terminated at each end by an electrical component called a resistor, connects all workstations. Inexpensive for very small networks, but cable failure renders the whole segment inoperable.

Byte. A data unit corresponding to one alphanumeric character; composed usually of eight bits.

CA. Certificate Authority, an organization or program that can issue, revoke, and/or verify digital certificates that (like birth certificates or passports) guarantee the identity of users, computers, and organizations.

CAB (or cabinet) file. A Microsoft format for combining multiple files into a single compressed container with its own filename. For example, Windows 2000 stores a collection of often-used drivers in the file DRIVER.CAB.

Cache. (Pronounced "cash.") An intermediary memory storage location, usually to help smooth over speed differences between devices. A *disk cache* is a memory region that stores disk data recently read or considered likely to be read again soon. A *CPU cache* is usually high-speed chip memory that caches main memory in the same way. Web browsers such as Internet Explorer use a special cache to store recently accessed Web sites and graphics for faster performance.

Callback modem. A security modem that returns a call. You first call the callback modem, and then it calls you back at a predetermined number, based on a password you enter on the first call.

Capture. To associate a network printer location with a logical local port (such as LPT3:). Performed via a printer's property sheet; necessary only for older DOS programs.

CardBus. A 32-bit-capable PCMCIA card.

Certificate. A data group that authenticates a user, computer, or service.

Channel. In the SCSI specification, a host adapter and its connected peripherals. Some definitions of "channel" also include the power supply.

CHAP. Short for Challenge Handshake Authentication Protocol, supported by Windows 2000 Dial-Up Networking for establishing a serial communications link with encrypted passwords so that picking the password off the data stream is virtually impossible.

Child domain. Also known as a *subdomain*. A domain located beneath another domain in a DNS hierarchy.

Client. 1) A workstation that connects to a shared resource on a server (in a client/server network). An intranet client, for example, can be running Windows 2000 Professional, Windows 98, OS/2, UNIX, or MacOS software. 2) An application running on a client workstation, such as a Web browser. 3) The layer of network software that enables a computer to connect to a particular kind of Network Operating System. 4) The combination of client hardware and software.

Client/server network. A network (such as NetWare or Windows 2000 Server) in which a dedicated computer handles resource-sharing responsibilities, such as file and printer sharing, for client computers (user workstations). More recently, client/server has come to emphasize cooperative processing environments in which a front-end process executes on the client and a back-end process executes on the server.

CLSID. Short for "Class ID," a unique 16-byte object identifier under Windows 2000 that consists of a 32-character hexadecimal string. The bytes in a CLSID are expressed by two-digit numbers arranged in a 4-2-2-2-6 pattern, like {25336920-03f9-11cf-8fd0-00aa00686f13}. See also **Object.**

Codec. An algorithm, or formula, for compressing and decompressing a digital video or audio file.

Command prompt. The Windows 2000 command prompt, which you can activate by choosing Start⇨Programs⇨Accessories⇨Command Prompt, or by choosing Start⇨Run and typing **CMD** followed by Enter.

Communications server. A LAN server that shares modems or fax modems for inbound access, outbound access, or both. Communications servers manage queues and assign devices much like print servers do; they may be dedicated or non-dedicated. Windows 2000 can function as a communications server via the Network and Dial-Up Connections control panel's Make New Connection wizard (specify that you want to create an "incoming" connection).

Compound document. In Windows, a document containing data created by more than one application; the result of a link or embedding operation.

Context menu. In Windows 2000, the pop-up menu of choices that appears when a user right-clicks an object; defined by Registry settings.

Control panel. A Windows 2000 program that lets you change various system settings. Clicking Start⇨Settings⇨Control Panel displays all the available control panels in a single window. Control panels typically modify the Registry in a safer way than the Registry Editor. See also **MMC.**

Controller. 1) A circuit board that controls a computer device. For example, a SCSI host adapter can act as a hard drive controller. 2) The person in your company who tells you that you'd better pass the Windows 2000 Network Infrastructure exam on the first try.

Cookies. Disk files that reside on a user's PC during an Internet or intranet browsing session in order to maintain user information (identity, preferences, visiting history, "shopping cart" items, and so on) as the user navigates from page to page.

Cooperative multitasking. A type of multitasking in which programs must periodically relinquish control to other programs and be "good citizens" to avoid hangups; used in Windows 3.*x,* and with Windows 3.*x* programs running under Windows 98 and 95. See also **Preemptive multitasking.**

Crash. The event that causes a computer system or application to stop working suddenly, immediately, and irreversibly.

D Channel. A control and signaling channel in an ISDN connection. See also **ISDN, BRI, PRI.**

Daisy chain. A string of two or more computer devices connected together in a row (A to B, B to C, and so on). SCSI hard drives, USB devices, and FireWire devices can connect in a daisy chain, and so can many hubs.

Database. A collection of related, structured information that you can search, edit, add to, delete from, and print. Some databases, however, are for Windows 2000's private internal use, such as the Logical Disk Manager database on dynamic disks.

Dedicated. Said of a computer devoted to one specific task exclusively. For example, a network server that cannot or does not double as a user workstation is a dedicated server.

Defragment. Generally, to reorganize a file so that all its sectors are physically contiguous, or adjacent. Improves performance of disks and disk caches. The Windows 2000 defragment command is less sophisticated than the Windows 98 defragmenter, but better than nothing (which was what Microsoft supplied with Windows NT 4.0).

DES. Data Encryption Standard, a strong encryption algorithm developed by the United States federal government.

Device driver. Software that enables a PC to communicate productively with a particular input or output device (for example, mice, networks). Windows 2000 loads device drivers into memory via the Registry. Device drivers interpret computer data and provide the commands or signals needed by the device. They can be considered as "add-ons" that, when loaded, become an extended part of the operating system.

DFS. Distributed File System, a method in Windows networks for grouping shared directories on different computers into a single logical structure for ease of user navigation.

DHCP. Dynamic Host Configuration Protocol, a software utility common in Windows-based TCP/IP networks that allows a server to make on-the-fly IP address assignments, and other TCP/IP configuration settings, from a predefined pool of addresses as users connect to the network. DHCP servers can also manage static IP address assignments. Windows 2000 Server includes the DHCP service, and Windows 2000 Professional can be a DHCP client.

Differential backup. A backup scheduling method calling for periodic backups of all files that have changed since the last full backup. A file restore requires two backup sets: the last full backup and the last differential backup.

Digital signature. A code that is part of a computer file or message and that guarantees authenticity by encoding information about the file's originator; used by Windows 2000 for device drivers, for example.

Directory. An organizing structure that a computer operating system uses to group files and, optionally, other directories together; synonymous with folder.

Directory services. Network software that makes resource information (such as usernames and addresses, user groups, and printers) available to everyone on the network in an organized way. NDS (NetWare Directory Services) and Microsoft Active Directory are examples.

Distribution server. A network server with a complete set of Windows 2000 installation files. A user can connect to a distribution server in order to install Windows 2000, instead of using a CD-ROM. See also **RIS**.

DLC. Data Link Control, a networking protocol for communicating with IBM minicomputers and mainframes, and Hewlett-Packard network laser printers.

DLL. Dynamic Link Library; in Windows and OS/2, basically a group of program subroutines collected together that perform related functions. Code modules in DLLs can be loaded and unloaded as needed at runtime, instead of at compile time (when the program is created). Much of the Windows 2000 operating system consists of DLLs. A DLL can also contain an icon library.

DMA. Direct Memory Access, wherein data transfers between devices do not require the direct involvement of the PC's CPU but rather are managed by a separate processor (for example, on a disk controller). Hard disk backup programs often use DMA for better performance.

DMI. Desktop Management Interface, a network management system offered by the Desktop Management Task Force (DMTF). Similar in concept to SNMP; memory-resident "agents" can report on PC configurations and problems.

DNS. Domain Name System, also known as Domain Name Service; a software program for matching up computer IP addresses such as 207.68.137.40 with easier-to-remember "host names," such as acme.pub.com.

Domain. A uniquely named group of computers (possibly containing multiple servers) and users that share a single security database. Windows 2000 and Windows NT Server 4.0 use domain-based security. Relations between domains are called *trusts*.

Domain controller. A server that maintains the security database and authenticates network users. Windows 2000 Server does away with the NT concept of primary and backup domain controllers. See also **Domain.**

Driver. See **Device driver.**

DVD. Short for Digital Versatile Disc or Digital Video Disc, an optical storage medium capable of storing computer, audio, and video data on the same disc.

DWORD (double-word) **value.** A Registry value consisting of a sequence of four two-digit hexadecimal numbers, not separated by spaces, introduced by "0x" and usually followed by the equivalent decimal number in parentheses. For example, 0x000001c4 (452).

Dynamic disk. A Windows 2000-specific type of disk organization that permits the creation of volumes rather than partitions, and that allows greater flexibility in how space from multiple hard drives is combined. See also **Basic disk.**

Dynamic HTML. Variously interpreted by different companies, Dynamic HTML extends "regular" HTML — for example, by permitting precise pixel-level positioning of elements on a Web page. Internet Explorer 5 supports Microsoft's implementation of Dynamic HTML.

EAP. Extensible Authentication Protocol, which lets two computers connecting over a dial-up link with PPP, PPTP, or L2TP decide between themselves which authentication method to use in order to permit a connection to proceed.

ECP. Extended Capabilities Port. See **IEEE 1284.**

Effective permissions. The "net" total of a given user's NTFS permissions on a file or folder, based on that user's individual permissions plus any permissions connected with groups to which the user belongs. Generally, NTFS permissions are additive, with the proviso that negative permissions ("no access") always hold sway.

EFS. Encrypting File System, the new encryption feature in Windows 2000's NTFS 5. You must log on as the user who encrypted a file or folder, or as a Recovery Agent, in order to be able to use the file or folder.

EIDE. Enhanced Integrated Drive Electronics, a popular type of disk drive interface permitting larger drive sizes, more connected devices per chain, and speed enhancements compared to IDE.

EMF. Enhanced MetaFile print spooling, which creates a high-level metafile to be processed in the background, returning application control to the user more quickly. Only for PCL printers, not PostScript ones.

Encapsulation. Wrapping one communications packet inside another.

Encryption. Coding information so that only authorized users can see it. Most encryption schemes rely on keys to decode encrypted data at the receiving end.

Enhanced Parallel Port. See **IEEE 1284.**

Environment. The operating system's "corkboard," where information (such as where to store temporary files) can be posted for all programs to see. Windows 2000 still uses the environment for information such as the current PATH; view environment variables via the System control panel's Advanced tab.

EPP. Enhanced Parallel Port (see **IEEE 1284**).

Ethernet. A very popular 10MBps networking standard using either thick coaxial, thin coaxial, or twisted-pair cable, which handles network traffic using a collision-detection technology.

Event log. A file (usually with the extension EVT and residing in the folder C:\WINNT\SYSTEM32\CONFIG) in which Windows 2000 records events of note, including application events, system events, and security events (auditing).

Explorer. 1) The Windows 2000 file management utility, EXPLORER.EXE. 2) The Windows 2000 shell, or graphical user interface.

Export. 1) To make a full or partial Registry backup, in the form of a REG file, with the Registry Editor's Registry⇨Export Registry File command. 2) Generally, to save a file in a format other than the application's usual format.

Fast Ethernet. 100Mbps Ethernet that can run on standard twisted-pair cables, but requires updated NICs. Multimedia application programs run better over Fast Ethernet.

FAT. File Allocation Table, a data structure that keeps track of which disk clusters are in use and where the "next" cluster is in a file. DOS, Windows 3.*x,* and Windows 95/98 use a 16-bit FAT for hard disks by default, meaning that larger cluster sizes must be used for larger capacity disks. Windows 2000 works with FAT, although Microsoft recommends NTFS, and NTFS is required for Windows 2000 Server domain controllers. See also **FAT32, NTFS.**

FAT32. An enhanced File Allocation Table with support for large drives and small clusters. Windows 2000 provides a one-way conversion utility. Not readable by MS-DOS, the original version of Windows 95, or Windows NT.

Fault tolerance. A computer system's ability to weather potentially damaging events, such as hardware failures, with either no damage or easily repairable damage.

File association. A connection between a file suffix (such as .REG) and an application program (such as REGEDIT), so that double-clicking the file runs the associated application program. The Registry maintains all file association information in Windows 2000, specifically in the key HKCR.

File attribute. Characteristics of a stored computer file that determine under what conditions that file can be copied, deleted, modified, or viewed. For example, the Read-only attribute means that you can't modify or delete the file. Windows 2000 file attributes also include System, Hidden, Archive, Indexing, Compression, and Encryption; not all attributes are available on FAT or FAT32 disks.

File Replication Service. A Windows 2000 Server service that manages the synchronization of replicated data structures, such as DFS trees, on NTFS volumes.

File server. A network server that shares files, as opposed to a print server (which shares printers), application server (which shares programs), or Web server (which shares Web pages).

File type. A category of files all having a particular file association.

Firewall. Any system or group of systems that implements and enforces an access control policy between two networks. Firewalls can run on their own special computer, or on the same computer as a Web server. Firewalls can be software-only or a combination of software and hardware. Many firewalls offer auditing capabilities as well.

FireWire. A high-speed serial bus (faster than USB) that supports daisy-chaining, FireWire is intended for use with high-bandwidth devices such as digital video cameras. Supported by Windows 2000 to the extent that contemporaneous standards allow. Also known as IEEE 1394.

Firmware. Software in hardware; that is, nonvolatile memory that keeps its software contents when powered off.

Flash memory. Nonvolatile memory such as that used in software-updatable "Flash BIOS" chips.

Flow control. See **Handshaking.**

Flush. To move any delayed writes (for example, with a read/write disk cache) to the physical disk.

Folder. Windows 2000-speak for "directory."

Font. A set of character definitions for a specific typeface and a specific style (normal, bold, italic). TrueType and OpenType fonts have the extension .TTF; PostScript fonts have the extensions .PFM and .PFB; bitmap fonts under Windows have the extension .FON. Scalable fonts are synonymous with "typefaces."

FQDN. Fully Qualified Domain Name, a DNS name stated "in full" instead of relative to another domain name.

Frame. The envelope of control, addressing, and error-correcting information around a packet. Ethernet frame types include ETHERNET_II, ETHERNET_SNAP, ETHERNET_802.2, and ETHERNET_802.3.

Frame relay. A packet-switching point-to-point networking system known for comparatively high speeds and high data-carrying capacities.

FTP. File Transfer Protocol, a TCP/IP program designed for copying files of various types between local and remote computers. Most Internet browsers and servers support FTP for downloading, and FTP runs as a service on IIS (Internet Information Server). Windows 2000 provides a command-line version of FTP as well.

Full backup. A backup of all the files on a computer's hard drive or drives, bar none. See also **Differential backup** and **Incremental backup.**

Full duplex. A method of communication that lets both sides send information in opposite directions at the same time. For example, good speakerphones are full duplex; bad ones are *half duplex* (one person can't speak while the other one speaks).

Gateway. A computer that connects to two or more networks and can deliver traffic between them. A Windows 2000 PC with an incoming connection set up can act as a gateway as long as the remote protocol (such as IPX/SPX) is the same as the local network protocol. The "default gateway" in a PC's TCP/IP property sheet lets that PC connect to other networks beyond the local corporate network.

GDI. Graphical Device Interface, the Windows standard language for creating graphics on displays and printers.

Gigabyte (abbreviated GB). A data storage unit equaling 1,024 megabytes, or about one billion bytes, a byte being equivalent to one letter or number.

Group. A collection of network users sharing the same set of rights and restrictions regarding shared resources such as files, programs, and printers. In Windows 2000, a *global group* works at the domain level, whereas a *local group* is specific to a particular client PC.

GUI. Graphical User Interface, a method of presenting information to a computer user wherein each pixel may vary, as opposed to a text-mode interface, such as the DOS command line or a mainframe terminal.

HAL. Hardware Abstraction Layer, the part of Windows 2000 that communicates with the underlying hardware (CPU, motherboard, and so on). Windows 2000 installs an appropriate HAL during setup, and you can't change it thereafter without reinstalling the operating system.

Half duplex. A method of communication in which one participant must listen when the other one is sending information — that is, both cannot send information at once.

Handshaking. A communications protocol that prevents data overrun between two devices operating at different speeds, such as a computer and printer or computer and modem. *Hardware* handshaking (ready/busy) uses a dedicated wire for this purpose and is more reliable at high speeds, while *software* handshaking (XON/XOFF) uses control codes over standard data lines. In the context of modems, handshaking is a complex negotiation to determine the best speed, error-correction, and compression options to use.

Hardware profile. A Windows 2000 hardware setup specification. Windows 2000 permits multiple hardware profiles; for example, a docked notebook and an undocked notebook. The Registry stores hardware profiles.

Hardware tree. The hierarchical representation of a PC's hardware setup, used by Plug and Play and viewable from the System control panel's Hardware tab, Device Manager button.

HCL. Hardware Compatibility List, the master reference listing devices known by Microsoft to be compatible with Windows 2000. HCL.TXT appears on the Windows 2000 CD-ROM, and updated versions live on Microsoft's Web site.

Header. The "front part" of a network packet, typically including both source and destination addresses as well as a time stamp.

Hexadecimal. A base-16 number system in which digits go from 0 to F instead of from 0 to 9; often used to identify memory addresses, to specify numbers in the Registry, and to identify a Windows 2000 software object class. Hexadecimal numbers may be followed by the letter "H" or "h" to differentiate them from base-10 numbers. Hex is useful to programmers because, unlike decimal numbers, it reduces directly to binary.

HKCC. Short for HKEY_CURRENT_CONFIG; the Registry branch concerned with the current hardware configuration.

HKCR. Short for HKEY_CLASSES_ROOT; the Registry branch concerned with file associations and drag-and-drop behavior. HKCR is an alias to HKLM\Software\Classes.

HKCU. Short for HKEY_CURRENT_USER; the Registry branch concerned with the current user logged on to Windows 2000, including individual preferences and settings. HKCU is an alias to a subkey of HKU.

HKLM. Short for HKEY_LOCAL_MACHINE; the Registry branch concerned with settings that don't vary from user to user or reflect individual user preferences.

HKU. Short for HKEY_USERS; the Registry branch concerned with settings for all persons who can use the computer. This branch includes the contents of HKCU.

Hop. A data packet's jump across a router. The total number of traversed routers over a packet's entire journey is called the *hop count.*

Host. In the lingo of TCP/IP, a computer.

Host adapter. The controller card on a SCSI device chain.

Hot swapping. The ability to replace a component without powering it or its host computer down; a feature of some PC Cards and an inherent part of the USB hardware standard.

HTML. Hypertext Markup Language, a specification describing the layout and content of a World Wide Web page, including links to other pages, via a plain text file. HTML documents can be used to customize the display of the Windows 2000 desktop and of individual folders.

HTML Help. A Microsoft technology for providing online help using HTML as the base page makeup language, relying on an ActiveX control to provide features such as an index, table of contents, and pop-up windows.

HTTP. Hypertext Transfer Protocol, the connectionless communications protocol used to manage links between pages on the World Wide Web and Web-based intranets.

Hub. Most generally, a device at a common location to which two or more cables connect in a star topology. In a typical PC network, the hub is a necessary component from which twisted-pair cables radiate to individual workstations. Hubs may be separate devices or plug-in circuit boards; they may be powered or unpowered; they may include network management software ("intelligent" hubs); or they may not.

Hyperlink. A highlighted text area or graphic that takes the user to a different place in the same document, or to another document, when clicked with a mouse.

IDE. Integrated Drive Electronics, a popular hard drive interface standard in which the controller is integrated with the drive unit and typically plugs into a motherboard connector.

IEAK. Internet Explorer Administration Kit, a free software package from Microsoft for giving administrators and installers greater control over Internet Explorer browser configurations.

IEEE. Institute of Electrical and Electronic Engineers, a computer and telecommunications standards-setting body with over a quarter of a million members.

IEEE 802.2. The Ethernet standard to which NetWare 4.*x* and 5.*x* default. A modification of 802.2 called Ethernet_SNAP adds a header extension for AppleTalk compatibility.

IEEE 802.3. The formal name for the "raw frame" Ethernet standard (also StarLAN) and the version of Ethernet to which NetWare 3.11 defaults. See **Ethernet.**

IEEE 802.5. The formal name for the Token Ring standard. See **Token Ring.**

IEEE 1284. A parallel port standard providing for higher data transfer rates and better bidirectional communication compared to the traditional Centronics standard. The PC port type should be set to ECP or EPP in the BIOS configuration program to support this standard.

IEEE 1394. See **FireWire.**

IIS. Internet Information Server, the WWW and FTP server bundled with both Windows 2000 Server and Windows 2000 Professional.

Import. To merge a REG file Registry backup into the current Registry with REGEDIT's Registry⇨Import Registry File command, or by simply double-clicking the REG file.

Incremental backup. A backup scheduling method calling for periodic back-ups of all files that have changed since the previous backup. Less convenient for file restores than differential backups, incremental backups require less space on backup media.

INF file. A text file with a predefined format that specifies how a device driver, other operating system component, or application should install. INF files typically include details about which files should copy where, and which Registry modifications are required to support the new hardware or software. In Windows 2000, MSI (Microsoft Software Installer) files are taking the place of INF files, but the transition is incomplete.

INI file. A text file, such as BOOT.INI, that contains operating system or application program configuration details. Windows 2000 depends on INI files to a much lesser extent than earlier Windows versions, having moved nearly all of their settings to the Registry.

Internet. The world's largest computer network, the Internet was originally just for military and academic use but has now grown to include all manner of private, public, and commercial uses. Physically, the Internet is a collection of millions of computers that each has its own unique network address to identify itself to other computers. Each computer on the Internet speaks the same basic communications language — TCP/IP. These computers connect to each other via a complex network of communication links managed by computerized traffic routers.

Internet Explorer. The Web browser that comes with Windows 2000 and enables users to view Internet and intranet documents and to navigate between them via hyperlinks.

Interrupt. A signal to the CPU from a device that needs attention, usually to service an input or output demand. When the CPU receives an interrupt, it may pause what it's doing and give control to an *interrupt handler* program that will take it from there. View interrupt assignments with the Device Manager on the System control panel.

Intranet. A "company-wide Web" network based on Internet technologies such as TCP/IP, HTTP, and HTML, but run within a private organization — for example, to publish human resources information that employees can view with a Web browser like Internet Explorer. Intranets often forbid, or restrict, access to the public Internet. Windows 2000 (both Professional and Server) comes with Internet Information Server to permit PCs to host, as well as view, intranet pages.

IP. Internet Protocol, the part of the TCP/IP networking protocol set that handles addressing and routing. See also **TCP/IP**.

IP address. The numerical address of a particular computer on the Internet or an intranet, consisting of four numbers (called *octets*) separated by periods. Each computer on a TCP/IP network needs a unique IP address. See also **IP, DHCP, DNS,** and **WINS.**

IPCONFIG. A Windows 2000 command-line utility for checking TCP/IP settings, such as IP address, subnet mask, and default gateway, on the local machine.

IPsec. A set of standards for securing communications over IP-based networks.

IPX. Internet Packet eXchange, a message routing protocol that runs on the Network layer of the OSI model; used by NetWare LANs. IPX by itself does not guarantee message delivery. See also **SPX, NWLink.**

IrDA. Infrared Data Association, which standardizes infrared communication device characteristics. Windows 2000 supports IrDA ports, which operate using invisible, long-wavelength light.

IRQ. Interrupt ReQuest line, basically a hardware "hot line" that devices (such as network boards) use to snag the attention of the CPU. No two devices in an ISA-bus PC may share the same IRQ simultaneously, though PCI, MCA, and EISA machines permit interrupt sharing under specific circumstances. Windows 2000 supports PCI interrupt sharing, as does Windows 98 and Windows 95 OSR2.

ISDN. Integrated Services Digital Network; enables voice, fax, data, and video on the same network. Telephone companies in major metropolitan areas offer ISDN connectivity, although ADSL often offers more for your money. Windows 2000 supports ISDN and comes with drivers for ISDN "terminal adapters." (It isn't technically proper to call these modems, as ISDN is all digital.) See also **Multilink PPP.**

ISO. International Standards Organization, headquartered in Geneva and produces the OSI (Open Systems Interconnect) network model, among other standards.

ISP. Internet Service Provider, an organization that offers Internet connectivity, usually for a monthly fee. ISPs offer Web hosting services for both Internet and intranet use.

Java. A programming language, developed by Sun Microsystems and derived from the C++ programming language, that is known for its portability, platform independence, and security. Java programs run on any computer that provides a Java "virtual machine." Windows 2000 includes Microsoft's Java virtual machine.

JavaScript. A programming language that uses "scripts" embedded in an HTML document. The browser code reads (interprets) the script and acts on it when it encounters a Web page that includes a script. JavaScript is not the same as Java; JavaScript is both easier and more limited.

Kerberos. A security protocol developed at MIT that permits authentication of user or computer identity using encrypted passwords. Windows 2000 includes support for Kerberos.

Kernel. The part of an operating system concerned with CPU multitasking, memory management, and other low-level functions.

Key. A Registry data storage location; a container for Registry information, either values or other keys. Keys appear like folders in the Registry Editor window's left (key) pane.

Kilobit. 1,024 bits, where a bit is a zero or one.

Kilobyte (abbreviated K). 1,024 bytes, where a byte is a character equivalent to one letter or number.

L2TP. Layer 2 Tunneling Protocol, a communications protocol that enables a secure communications session to take place "inside" an Internet, intranet, or other network connection. Unlike PPTP, L2TP doesn't provide encryption services, so it should be used together with a protocol such as IPsec for best security. Also unlike PPTP, L2TP doesn't require IP. Windows 2000 dial-up connections support L2TP. See also **Virtual Private Networking** and **PPTP.**

LAN. Local Area Network, a network containing servers, workstations, cable, and software all linked together, within a relatively small geographical area.

Leased line. A telephone line leased from a common carrier and dedicated for exclusive, round-the-clock service between two locations; also called "dedicated circuit." May be conditioned for better data capability.

Legacy (Device, Application). A nice way of saying "old."

Link. See **Hyperlink.**

Load balancing. Generally, a performance improvement technique in which relatively busy devices offload work to relatively idle ones.

Local bus. A bus, such as AGP or PCI, running at higher speeds (often at the CPU's clock rate) and possibly wider data pathways than the PC's standard bus; useful for video, disk, and network adapters.

Logical. As distinct from "physical," in computer systems, a high-level view independent of underlying detail. For example, a logical connection between two PCs might navigate several physical network devices, or a single physical disk drive might contain several logical drives.

Log on. To identify oneself to the network, usually by keying in a username and password, in order to use shared network resources such as files, printers, and programs.

Logon script. A text file containing a sequence of commands that run when a user logs on to the network. Some networks permit different logon scripts for different groups of users or even individual users.

Lost cluster. A data cluster that has lost its link to the original file.

LPT port. See **Parallel port.**

Map. To associate a network resource (such as a printer or directory) with a logical name (such as a local port or drive letter). For example, the LPT2: device on a PC may map to a shared network printer instead of corresponding to a printer that's physically connected to the workstation's second parallel port. Mapping has become less necessary now that many operating systems understand UNC paths.

MBR. The Master Boot Record of a disk.

Megabit (Mb). About one million bits, a bit being a one or a zero. Usually used in speed measurements, such as megabits per second (Mbps).

Megabyte (MB). A measure of data storage capacity equaling 1,024 kilobytes, or roughly a million bytes, a byte being equivalent to one letter or number.

Megahertz (MHz). One million cycles per second, or, more meaningfully, a comparative way to rate CPU speeds. A 400 MHz CPU isn't necessarily twice as fast as a 200MHz CPU, though, so the comparison is only approximate.

Memory. See **RAM.**

MIME. Multipurpose Internet Mail Extensions, a set of extensions to the original Internet e-mail standards so that users can send and receive data types other than text.

Minidriver. A driver usually supplied by a device manufacturer that includes code specific to that device's unique characteristics. Minidrivers work together with universal drivers, which contain code common to an entire class of devices, to provide complete device driver functionality.

Mixed mode network. In Windows 2000, a mode of networking in which Windows NT Server domain controllers coexist with Windows 2000 domain controllers. You cannot nest groups on a mixed mode network. This mode is the default. See also **Native mode network.**

MMC. Microsoft Management Console, a new sort of control panel that brings a minimal level of consistency and a high level of customizability to administrative tools. The host program is MMC.EXE, and actual consoles have the extension .MSC. Windows 2000's administrative tools are provided using MMC. See also **Snap-in.**

Modem. Short for **mo**dulator-**dem**odulator, a modem converts digital computer signals to analog signals that phone lines can handle, and vice versa.

Motherboard. A computer's main circuit board; also called the system board. If you try to be politically correct and call this a parentboard, nobody will know what you're talking about.

MRU list. A list of "most recently used" documents, programs, or Internet locations, maintained by Windows 2000 in the Registry or on disk.

MS-CHAP. A Windows-centric spin on the CHAP authentication protocol, supported by Windows 2000. See **CHAP.**

MSI. Microsoft Software Installer, a new method of packaging applications for greater consistency and recoverability. Also called Windows Installer.

Multilink PPP. A feature of Windows 2000 dial-up connections that enables the combining of two communications ports (such as two modems, or one modem and one ISDN terminal adapter) in order to create a single virtual port with a higher effective speed.

Multitasking. When a computer manages two or more simultaneous tasks, it multitasks. Various techniques (for example, timeslicing) exist for single CPUs to appear to be doing two or three things at once. *Cooperative* multitasking relies on well-behaved applications; *preemptive* multitasking (as featured in Windows 2000) enables the operating system to play traffic cop and "preempt" a program that hogs PC resources.

Multithreading. When a program manages two or more simultaneous tasks. Thread creation is known as "spawning." Windows 2000 tracks computer resources on a per-thread basis so that it can free up memory when a thread terminates.

Name resolution. The process of translating one sort of identifying characteristic with another; for example, translating a NetBIOS name to an IP address. See also **DNS, WINS.**

Native mode network. In Windows 2000, a mode of networking in which no Windows NT Server domain controllers exist. This mode permits nesting of groups. See also **mixed mode network.**

NCP. NetWare Core Protocol, a set of procedures NetWare uses to deal with all network-related client requests. See also **SMB.**

NDIS (pronounced EN-dis). Network Driver Interface Specification, developed by Microsoft and 3Com in 1989; a standard for network drivers, enabling any OSI Level 3 and 4 software to communicate with any NDIS-compliant network card driver at OSI Level 2. NDIS 3.1 and higher support Plug and Play.

NDS. NetWare Directory Services, a domain naming system for NetWare 4 and 5 and also available for Windows NT Server that includes all network resources in a tree-structured hierarchy.

NetBEUI (pronounced NET-booie). NetBIOS Extended User Interface, a high-speed, non-routable network transport protocol that controls access to file and print sharing. Often used for small, informal networks not expected to grow large. Originally introduced by IBM in 1985.

NetBIOS. Network Basic Input/Output System, network software residing in OSI Level 5 on DOS or UNIX machines, which handles redirection of I/O requests to network resources. Made popular by IBM and Microsoft; used by application developers.

NetBIOS name. The name of a computer or workgroup in the Microsoft networking scheme. A "pure" Windows 2000 network uses DNS to identify computers, instead of NetBIOS names.

NetWare. A popular Network Operating System from Novell. Version 5.0 removes NetWare's traditional dependence on the IPX/SPX protocol and can run TCP/IP as a native language, although Windows 2000 clients can only communicate with NetWare servers running IPX/SPX. Other available versions include NetWare 4.2 and NetWare for Small Business 4.12.

Network. Two or more computer systems connected to enable communication or resource sharing; the sum total of clients, servers, and interconnecting infrastructure. Often informally used as a synonym for **LAN.**

Network adapter. See **NIC.**

Network drive. A disk drive shared with other network users.

Network Interface Card. See **NIC.**

Network modem. A modem (such as those made by Shiva) that connects directly to a network, rather than indirectly through a PC.

NIC (pronounced "nick"). Network Interface Card, the circuit board that plugs into a PC expansion slot and a network cabling system and manages the physical data transfer between the PC and the network.

Node. A device that connects to a network, be it a workstation, printer, network modem, or what have you.

Nonvolatile. Said of computer memory that retains its contents without power.

NOS (pronounced "noss"). Network Operating System, the core system software running on a network server — for example, Novell NetWare or Windows NT Server.

Notebook. A portable computer, the size of a large paper notebook.

NT. See **Windows NT Server 4.0, Windows NT Workstation 4.0, Windows 2000 Server, Windows 2000 Professional.**

NTFS. The NT File System, in Version 5 as of Windows 2000. NTFS is not compatible with DOS or Windows 98/95. Further, NTFS 5 is not fully compatible with NTFS 4, used in Windows NT 4.0. Advantages of NTFS include file- and folder-level access control, auditing, and error recovery, among others.

NWLink. Microsoft's implementation of IPX/SPX. See **IPX** and **SPX.**

Object. 1) A named network resource in Active Directory. 2) An entity that a user or programmer can manipulate in Windows 2000. Objects include data files, such as an Excel spreadsheet; programs, such as Excel; and program modules, such as the code that displays and processes dialog box radio buttons, that software developers can call from their programs. See also **ActiveX** and **CLSID.**

OLE. (pronounced "oh-LAY") Object Linking and Embedding, a Windows technology that permits the creation of compound documents (using data from more than one program) and the editing of pasted data using its originating application and within the same window as the host application. OLE also encompasses file association information such as that stored by the Registry's HKCR branch.

OpenType. A new extension to TrueType font technology, supported by Windows 2000; these fonts appear in the Fonts folder with an "O" icon.

Operating system. The basic software that enables a computer to interact with users, manage files and devices, and communicate at a basic level over computer-to-computer connections, the operating system also provides APIs to which application software developers write their programs. Operating systems are considered to provide the basic computer software services that every user needs, as opposed to applications, which provide software services that only certain users require. Windows 2000, UNIX, MacOS, and OS/2 are operating systems. An operating system designed for network servers, such as NetWare and Windows NT Server, is called a Network Operating System, or NOS.

Organizational Unit. In Windows 2000 Active Directory, an organizing structure that lets you group objects within a given domain.

OSI. Open Systems Interconnect, a seven-layer network model established in 1984 by the ISO (International Standards Organization) to help enable network software developers to create programs at each level independently. The layers are (from bottom to top) Physical, Data Link, Network, Transport, Session, Presentation, and Application. Remember them with the mnemonic device Please Do Not Throw Sausage Pizza Away (bottom up) or All People Seem To Need Data Processing (top down).

OSR2. OEM Service Release 2, a version of Windows 95 sold only on new PCs, having the version number 4.00.950B or 4.00.950C on the System control panel.

Packet. The unit of data transfer on a LAN; a chunk of data packaged for transmission in a way specific to the network protocol being used, but generally containing both address information, data to be transmitted, and error control information.

Pagefile. Also called *paging file* or *swapfile*. An area of hard drive space used as a supplement to main memory. The pagefile (PAGEFILE.SYS in Windows 2000) runs much more slowly than RAM but avoids an `out of memory` error. Windows 2000 dynamically resizes the pagefile to adapt to system needs, although you can override this behavior via the System control panel.

PAP. Password Authentication Protocol, which permits the creation of a remote communications link.

Parallel port. A microcomputer connection, used typically for printers, in which each bit of a byte has its own wire. Eight bits travel simultaneously, like traffic on an eight-lane freeway. See also **IEEE 1284.**

Partition. A portion of a Windows 2000 basic disk set aside as a separate and distinct logical device. A *primary partition* may be used as a boot device; an *extended partition* may host several logical drives. You manage partitions with the Disk Management snap-in to the Computer Management console.

Patch. A modification to an operating system or application program to correct a problem.

PC Card. Personal Computer Memory Card Industry Association, a group that created a set of standards for the 68-pin "credit-card" devices popular in portable computers. Types I, II, and III differ in the thickness dimension only, but share connector specifications.

PCL. Printer Control Language, a standard developed by Hewlett-Packard for controlling its line of laser printers. Originally more oriented to text processing than PostScript, PCL levels 5 and 6 offer many of PostScript's capabilities.

PDL. Page Description Language, a set of device-independent commands for printers. See **PostScript** and **PCL.**

Peer-to-peer network. Synonymous with "workgroup," a type of network in which no dedicated PC acts as a central server, but in which every PC may share attached printers and local files, with network processing occurring in the background. These are suitable for small groups with limited or no security requirements.

Peripheral. A computer device outside a computer's system unit. Peripherals include keyboards, mice, printers, and modems.

Permission. Also called "access permission." An attribute of a shared object that controls who may do what with it. Permissions apply to objects, while rights apply to users. See also **ACL.**

PING. Short for Packet Internet Groper, an IP utility that troubleshooters use to confirm a network connection between two computers.

Plug and Play. Often abbreviated PnP. A set of standards developed by Microsoft, Intel, Compaq, and Phoenix (among others) to ease the configuration of hardware devices through autodetection of device characteristics, resource allocation, and conflict arbitration. A full implementation requires PnP compatibility at all levels, including BIOS, motherboard, operating system (such as Windows 2000), adapter, device, and driver.

Policy file. A file (usually with the suffix .POL) that applies restrictions and customizations to the information in the Registry. The tools for creating policy files in Windows 2000 are the Local Group Policy utility for workstation policies, and the Active Directory Users and Groups utility (on Windows 2000 Server) for network policies. See also **Template.**

Port. A socket on the back of a computer or peripheral used to connect it to some other computer or peripheral.

POST. The Power-On Self Test residing in a PC's BIOS that runs on power-up and checks the computer's vital signs.

PostScript. An interpreted, device-independent page description language from Adobe Systems, used to control printers and (on some workstations) displays; known for sophisticated graphics-handling. Windows 2000 does not support EMF spooling on PostScript printers.

PPP. Short for Point-to-Point Protocol, a standard for communications across relatively slow links (such as dial-up phone lines). The default protocol for Windows 2000 dial-up connections.

PPTP. Point-to-Point Tunneling Protocol, a communications protocol that enables a secure communications session to take place "inside" an Internet, intranet, or other network connection. Windows 2000 dial-up connections support PPTP. See also **VPN** and **L2TP.**

Preemptive multitasking. A type of multitasking in which the operating system can manage allocation of CPU and other resources to multiple simultaneous processes. Available in Windows 2000, Windows NT, OS/2, and (with 32-bit programs only) Windows 95/98.

PRI. Primary Rate Interface, a commercial ISDN installation consisting of 24 digital channels in the U.S. and 31 in Europe. In the U.S. version, 23 of the channels carry data and the 24th is used for commands. See also **BRI**.

Print device. Microsoft's name for what the rest of the world simply calls a "printer."

Print server. 1) The part of a NOS that manages the queuing and printing of documents over the network. 2) A computer, or specialized single-purpose device, that links to the network and handles print requests from other computers. In Microspeak, "printers" reside on "print servers."

Printer. In Microspeak, the software interface between Windows 2000 and a physical print device, rather than the print device itself.

Printer pool. A Windows 2000 "printer" (see separate definition) that can submit documents to multiple physical print devices, preferably identical ones.

Property sheet. A window that displays information about a file or control panel and usually lets you change some or all of the information it contains. Windows 2000 typically serves up a property sheet when you right-click an icon and choose Properties.

Protocol. Rules or standards that control and manage the creation, maintenance, and termination of data transfer on a network or across modems.

Proxy server. A server that permits no direct traffic between one network and another, but, for security reasons, acts as a store-and-forward device for data or messages meeting predefined criteria. If you're on a network with a proxy server and you browse to an Internet Web page, the proxy server picks up the Web page, checks it to see whether it meets security needs, and then sends it down the network to you. Proxy servers may forward permitted data or messages automatically, or only on request from another computer. See also **firewall.**

Queue. Any kind of waiting or holding location; typically, the list of documents waiting to be printed on a print server.

RAM. Random Access Memory, chip-based memory in a computer that is both faster and more expensive than disk-based memory. A computer's RAM contains the currently active programs and data files, and its contents start empty every time the computer restarts.

RRAS. Routing and Remote Access Service, Microsoft's remote node software that enables remote PCs to access NetBIOS, TCP/IP, and IPX networks over phone lines.

Redirector. Workstation software that routes read/write requests to network devices as appropriate — for example, Microsoft's 32-bit Client Service for NetWare (CSNW).

Registry. The Windows 2000 evolution of Windows 3.*x*'s REG.DAT file, the Registry is a central database of PC configuration information; it stores hardware information in SYSTEM.DAT and user information in USER.DAT. Microsoft considers the optional system policy file to be a third component of the Registry, although I prefer to think of it as a filter or mask.

Registry Editor. You get two of them with Windows 2000. REGEDIT.EXE hails from the Windows 9*x* side of the family, while REGEDT32.EXE traces its lineage to Windows NT. Both tools enable you to view, edit, print, export, and import the Registry. REGEDIT has better search facilities, whereas REGEDT32 can handle security restrictions.

Remote node. A remote PC linked directly into a LAN via modem. Remote node PCs function just as if they were logged in on-site. This technique for remote access requires high-speed modems to handle the traffic. Windows 2000 dial-up connections are remote node connections.

Repeater. A simple network device that boosts incoming signals so that they can be sent a longer distance. Repeaters do not look at packets or protocols; they just amplify and recondition every bit they receive and then retransmit.

Resource. Any computer drive, directory, printer, or other peripheral that can be shared among network users.

Restore. To copy previously backed up files to your PC's hard disk — for example, with the Microsoft Backup utility. The reverse of **backup.**

Reverse lookup. The process in which a computer determines a computer's domain name by providing an IP address; the reverse of the usual DNS forward lookup, in which the domain name is known but the IP address is not.

Right. A user's ability to do something on the computer, such as back up its files. Users have rights, while objects have permissions.

Ring topology. A network layout in which computers connect via a closed loop of NICs. In Token Ring networks, the ring topology may reside entirely inside the hub, with the actual cabling in a star topology radiating from the hub.

RIP. Router Information Protocol, a method of determining packet routes in which routers communicate with each other and update each other's routing tables with the goal of minimize the average hop count for packets traversing the network.

RIS. Remote Installation Service, software that runs on a Windows 2000 Server machine to permit installation of Windows 2000 Professional on client PCs that may not even have an operating system installed.

ROM. Read-Only Memory, a computer memory chip or storage device that permits reading information, but not changing or deleting it. See also **BIOS.**

Root directory. The top-level directory on a disk, below which all other directories exist.

Router. A network device, more sophisticated than a bridge, that can send or redirect data traffic to the least crowded routes by examining data packet destination addresses. Multiple networks connected by routers form internetworks.

RPC. Remote Procedure Call, a technique for computer-to-computer program execution across a network wherein one computer issues a function call that is processed by another computer. Windows 2000 uses RPC for services such as remote Registry editing.

Safe mode. A Windows 2000 startup option that you activate by pressing the F8 key at startup and choosing either "Safe Mode" or "Safe Mode, Command Prompt Only." Windows 2000 loads a minimal set of drivers in safe mode, so it's handy for troubleshooting recently installed (and misbehaving) drivers.

SAP. Service Advertising Protocol, a method by which servers "advertise" their existence, location, and services.

Scope. A pool of IP addresses from which a DHCP server can choose for assigning IP addresses to DHCP clients on a TCP/IP network.

SCSI (pronounced "scuzzy"). Small Computer Systems Interface, a separate, internal or external, terminated bus that can support multiple connected devices; usually used for high-performance, high-capacity server hard drives and CD-ROM drives. Variants include Fast SCSI, Ultra SCSI, and Ultra Wide SCSI.

Sector. The smallest unit of storage readable or writable to a disk drive; usually 512 bytes for hard drives.

Segment. A discrete portion of a network.

Serial port. A microcomputer connection, used typically for modems but also occasionally for printers and mice, in which each bit of a byte travels sequentially down a single wire. Serial ports are slower than parallel ports.

Server. 1) A computer that provides network services, such as Web, file, print, communication, namespace, directory, security, or application services. In peer-to-peer networks, a server is any computer that is sharing a local resource over the network, and any given computer may be both a server and a client for different resources. 2) A program providing services to a client application — for example, a database server. 3) The combination of server hardware and programs.

Shell. The operating system component that presents computer resources to the user and facilitates human/machine interaction, as opposed to the component that talks to devices or software. In Windows 2000, the usual shell is Explorer, although Program Manager is an alternative (and unsupported) shell.

Shortcut. In Windows 2000, a file (with the extension LNK) that points to a local or network file, folder, program, control panel, disk drive, or printer normally tucked away where it may not be as easily accessible. Shortcuts are identified by a small "jump" arrow in the lower-left corner.

SID. Security ID, in Windows 2000 (and Windows NT 4.0), a unique number identifying computers, users, and other objects in a network.

SLIP. Serial Line Interface Protocol, a communications standard similar to PPP but less efficient. Windows 2000's Dial-Up Connections feature supports SLIP.

SMB. Server Message Block, a network protocol for handling workstation requests on Microsoft networks. See also **NCP.**

Snap-in. A program that provides one or more administrative functions when loaded into a management console. For example, Disk Management is a snap-in to the Computer Management console. See also **MMC.**

SNMP. Simple Network Management Protocol, a popular standard that grew out of the UNIX world for managing LANs. SNMP specifies a protocol for communication between a management "console" and network devices.

Spanned volume. A Windows 2000 dynamic disk volume that incorporates space from 2 to 32 drives and that fills each chunk of space sequentially; spanned volumes offer space efficiency and conservation of drive letters. See also **Striped volume.**

Spool. Actually an acronym for Simultaneous Peripheral Operations On Line, a spooler is a program that re-routes print output to a disk file before allowing it to go to a printer. Spooling at a server lets multiple users print multiple documents that go to a common directory to wait their turn at the printer. Spooling at a workstation lets the user regain control of the computer more quickly after submitting a print job and aids in reprinting a document if the printer is busy or hangs. See also **EMF.**

SPX. Sequenced Packet Exchange. Runs over IPX and provides error checking and flow control to make sure packets reach their intended destination and reach it accurately; a "connection-oriented" protocol. Used instead of NetBIOS and commonly required by data backup and communications applications. See also **IPX** and **NetWare.**

SQL. Structured Query Language, a set of commands for interrogating databases; very popular among database management system vendors in client/server networks.

SSL. Secure Sockets Layer, a standard method of providing encrypted data transmission between a browser and Web server.

Star topology. A network layout in which network connections extend in a star from a central point, like spokes on a wheel. See also **Bus topology** and **ring topology.**

Stream. To begin playing as soon as a download operation begins, instead of only after it's completed. For example, streaming audio starts playing as soon as the user opens a Web page containing a sound file.

String value. A value in the Windows 2000 Registry whose data field consists of a sequence of alphanumeric characters. String values appear in the Registry Editor bracketed by double quotes and next to an icon with the letters "ab."

Striped volume. A Windows 2000 dynamic disk volume that incorporates space from 2 to 32 drives and that fills each chunk of space at the same rate, providing a speed benefit because multiple disk controllers can be brought to bear on a single read or write operation. See also **Spanned volume.**

Subnet mask. A 32-bit value that lets computers figure out where the network ID part of an IP address ends and the host ID part begins.

Subscribe. To specify that you want Internet Explorer to periodically download updates to a Web site's content.

Switch. Also called "parameter" or "qualifier," a switch is a command modifier, usually beginning with a forward slash. In the command SCANREG /RESTORE, which restores an earlier version of the Registry, the switch is the "/RESTORE" part.

Sysprep. A tool for automating Windows 2000 installation, Sysprep is run before "cloning" a disk image and it avoids the problem of having multiple machines with identical security identifiers.

TAPI. Windows 2000's Telephony API, which provides a standard way for programs to use the services of data and voice modems.

Taskbar. In Windows 2000, the graphical on-screen bar containing buttons for access to the Start menu and all executing programs.

TCP/IP. Transport Control Protocol/Internet Protocol, a set of network protocols for file transfer, network management, and messaging. It was developed in the early '70s by DARPA (Defense Advanced Research Projects Agency) for the Arpanet research network and is becoming the most popular protocol for LANs as well as WANs. TCP breaks apart and reassembles packets in the correct order, and resends if errors occur; IP handles routing and transmission.

Template. A file having the extension .ADM that the Group Policy utility consults for details as to how to modify particular Registry entries for Windows 2000, Internet Explorer, Microsoft Office, and so on.

Terabyte (abbreviated TB). A measure of data storage capacity equaling 1,024 gigabytes, or roughly a trillion bytes, a byte being equivalent to one letter or number.

Thread. An execution path. In Windows 2000, programs can "spawn" multiple concurrent threads, each of which shares code, data, and window structures with the parent program.

Timeout. Said to occur when a device or program fails to perform an action within a predetermined maximum time limit. For example, Windows 2000 sets printer timeouts via printer property sheets.

Token. A unique sequence of (typically) 24 bits that confers the right to access a token-ring LAN and includes origin and destination data. In a token-ring network, a transmitting station waits for an empty token to circulate to its location, where the station fills the token with destination and message information. All stations monitor circulating tokens to determine whether any are targeted to them; if so, the station retrieves the token data and resets the token to an empty state.

Token Ring. A 4- to 16-MBps network standard promulgated by IBM and noted for predictable response and fault tolerance, as well as somewhat higher cost than Ethernet. See also **Token.**

Topology. The shape or layout of a network cabling and/or signaling scheme; common topologies include **Bus topology, Ring topology,** and **Star topology.**

TRACERT. A Windows 2000 command-line program that "traces the route" that a TCP/IP packet takes on its journey across routers.

Transport protocol. The "language" of a network, typically NetBEUI, TCP/IP, or IPX/SPX. Computers in a network must speak the same transport protocol to communicate.

Trust. A relationship between domains in which one domain recognizes, and permits access to, a user who is authenticated by another domain. In Windows 2000, trusts are *transitive,* meaning that if domain A trusts domain B, and domain B trusts domain C, then A trusts C. This is a departure from Windows NT networking.

TTL. Time To Live, an attribute of TCP/IP packets that determines how many times the packet may be forwarded or cached, and still be considered valid.

Tunneling. Running one network protocol inside another. See **PPTP** and **Virtual Private Networking.**

UDP. User Datagram Protocol, a "connectionless" protocol with relatively low overhead but no guaranteed delivery confirmation.

UNC path. The Universal Naming Convention format for a network file or print resource, in the format \\server\queue or \\server\volume\directory. Windows 2000 supports UNC paths for many network types, including Microsoft and Novell servers.

Universal Naming Convention. See **UNC path.**

UNIX. A computer operating system originally developed at AT&T Bell Labs. Most Internet and intranet technologies were developed in the UNIX world, and it's still a popular operating system for high-performance servers.

URL. Uniform Resource Locator, the address (such as http://www.adobe.com) that points to a specific location on the Internet or an intranet. For example, that location may be a Web page or a file to download.

USB. Universal Serial Bus, a Windows 2000-supported PC external bus for connecting computer devices, such as mice and keyboards, in a daisy-chain of cables that plugs into a single computer port. You can connect and disconnect USB devices without rebooting the PC; USB is a Plug-and-Play bus. USB hubs are required in order to support more than a few devices.

User profiles. The Windows 2000 mechanism for keeping individual desktop settings and preferences distinct from other users' by storing multiple copies of the Registry's NTUSER.DAT file as well as of other files. For example, multiple users share a single PC and still see their own settings and preferences. User profiles also let network users log on to any networked PC and still see their settings and preferences. The location for user profiles has moved from C:\WINNT\PROFILES to C:\Documents and Settings.

Value. A data element contained in a Registry key. Values have a name field and a data field, and have one of several types, the most common being binary, DWORD, and string. A single Registry key can contain multiple values.

VBScript. A programming language, based on Microsoft's Visual Basic for Applications, that uses "scripts" (little programs) embedded in an HTML document. The browser reads (interprets) the script and acts on it when it encounters a Web page that includes a script.

Virtual drive. A drive letter to which a remote drive or directory is logically connected.

Virtual memory. A technique for enabling programs to access memory addresses that correspond to disk space instead of RAM. Windows' pagefiles are virtual memory constructs.

Virtual port. A parallel port to which a remote printer is logically connected. It's not necessary to actually have a local port corresponding to the virtual port.

Virtual Private Networking. See **VPN.**

Virus. A computer program intended by its creator to cause mischief or outright damage. Usually, a virus is designed to spread from one computer to another, something a network usually makes very easy. Most viruses take various steps to conceal their existence until they can fulfill their creator's evil intent. Viruses usually attach to other program files.

Volume. A chunk of disk space, or collection of such chunks, that appears to users as a single drive — even though an actual hard drive may contain multiple volumes, and a volume may span multiple actual hard drives. A feature of Windows 2000 dynamic disks. See also **Spanned volume** and **Striped volume.**

VPN. Virtual Private Networking creates a secure, private Wide Area Network by "tunneling" a network protocol inside a communication link on the public Internet. Windows 2000 comes with VPN support. See also **PPTP** and **L2TP.**

WAN. Wide Area Network, LANs linked over large distances, usually via serial line protocols running on satellite, microwave, or public data network links. See also **VPN.**

Web. See **WWW.**

Web browser. See **browser.**

Windows. A family of Microsoft operating systems that present a graphical user interface, enable you to run multiple programs at once, and facilitate the copying and pasting of data among programs.

Windows 2000 Professional. The follow-on to Windows NT 4.0 Workstation, originally called Windows NT 5.0 Workstation, offering Plug and Play and ACPI power management.

Windows 2000 Server. The follow-on to Windows NT 4.0 Server, originally called Windows NT 5.0 Server, with new features such as Active Directory (a network directory service). The "Advanced" version supports four or more processors, up to 8GB of RAM, and server clustering, while the "Datacenter" version supports up to 32 processors, up to 64GB of RAM, and online transaction processing applications.

Windows 95. A popular PC operating system from Microsoft that succeeds Windows 3.*x* and presents a very different user interface. Microsoft released several versions, including OSR2. Windows 98 is greatly similar to OSR2.5 running Internet Explorer 4.

Windows 98. An evolutionary upgrade to Windows 95, including bug fixes, new utilities, new device drivers, support for new hardware types, a user interface that can present the desktop as a Web page, and Internet Explorer. A "Second Edition" is available that fixes bugs and adds Internet Connection Sharing.

Windows NT Server 4.0. The predecessor to Windows 2000 Server. A network operating system offering relatively easy installation and management (for small networks) and strong security. Windows NT Server 4.0 shares the same GUI as Windows 95, and Windows 2000 Server shares the same GUI as Windows 98.

Windows NT Workstation 4.0. The predecessor to Windows 2000 Professional. A workstation operating system for PCs requiring high performance, security, or reliability. NT4 is more expensive than Windows 98, more demanding in its hardware requirements, and more restrictive in its list of compatible hardware and software.

Windows Update. A Windows 2000 command (by default, on the Start menu) that connects to the Internet and downloads an ActiveX program that scans the PC for outdated DLLs and device drivers, and then presents a list of suggested updates from which the user can choose. You can disable Windows Update with Group Policy tools.

WINS (Windows Internet Name Service). Software that matches up IP addresses with computer names, called *NetBIOS names,* in a routed Microsoft network. NetBIOS names are easier for users to remember than IP addresses.

Workgroup. 1) A network with no centralized security provider. Windows 98 and 95 have built-in workgroup networking. Windows 2000 offers a different sort of workgroup in that each Windows 2000 machine has its own local security database. 2) A team of individuals who commonly work together and need to share programs and files and printers.

Workstation. Generally, a user computer. So-called scientific or engineering workstations are higher-powered computers capable of handling powerful, demanding software such as Computer-Aided Design.

WWW. (pronounced "dub-dub-dub" by those in the industry.) The World Wide Web, born in 1993, an Internet service in which "pages" can include color graphics, sound, video, and hyperlinks to other Web pages. Windows 2000 lets you view your desktop, and individual desktop folders, as Web pages. The Web is based on the TCP/IP, HTTP, and HTML standards.

XON/XOFF. See **Handshaking.**

Zone. A separately managed branch of a DNS tree for which at least one DNS server is configured.

Appendix D

About the CD

On the CD-ROM:

▶ The QuickLearn game, a fun way to study for the test

▶ Practice and Self-Assessment tests, to make sure you are ready for the real thing

▶ Practice test demos from Transcender, QuickCert, and Self Test Software

System Requirements

Make sure that your computer meets the minimum system requirements listed in this section. If your computer doesn't match up to most of these requirements, you may have problems using the contents of the CD:

- ✔ A PC with a 486 or faster processor.

- ✔ Microsoft Windows 95 or later.

- ✔ At least 16MB of total RAM installed on your computer. For best performance, we recommend at least 32MB of RAM installed.

- ✔ A CD-ROM drive — double-speed (2x) or faster.

- ✔ A sound card.

- ✔ A monitor capable of displaying at least 256 colors or grayscale.

- ✔ A modem with a speed of at least 14,400 bps.

Important Note: To play the QuickLearn game, you must have a 166 or faster computer running Windows 95, 98, or 2000 (Server or Professional), with SVGA graphics. You must also have Microsoft DirectX 5.0 or later installed. If you do not have DirectX, you can install it from the CD. Just run D:\Directx\ dxinstall.exe. Unfortunately, DirectX 5.0 does not run on Windows NT 4.0, so you cannot play the QuickLearn Game on a Windows NT 4.0 or earlier machine.

Using the CD

To install the items from the CD to your hard drive, follow these steps.

1. **Insert the CD into your computer's CD-ROM drive.**

2. **Click Start➪Run.**

3. **In the dialog box that appears, type** D:\IDG.EXE.

   Replace *D* with the proper drive letter if your CD-ROM drive uses a different letter. (If you don't know the letter, see how your CD-ROM drive is listed under My Computer.)

4. **Click OK.**

   A license agreement window appears.

5. **Read through the license agreement, nod your head, and then click the Accept button if you want to use the CD — after you click Accept, you'll never be bothered by the License Agreement window again.**

   The CD interface Welcome screen appears. The interface is a little program that shows you what's on the CD and coordinates installing the programs and running the demos. The interface basically enables you to click a button or two to make things happen.

6. **Click anywhere on the Welcome screen to enter the interface.**

   Now you are getting to the action. This next screen lists categories for the software on the CD.

7. **To view the items within a category, just click the category's name.**

   A list of programs in the category appears.

8. **For more information about a program, click the program's name.**

   Be sure to read the information that appears. Sometimes a program has its own system requirements or requires you to do a few tricks on your computer before you can install or run the program, and this screen tells you what you might need to do, if necessary.

9. **If you don't want to install the program, click the Back button to return to the previous screen.**

   You can always return to the previous screen by clicking the Back button. This feature enables you to browse the different categories and products and decide what you want to install.

10. **To install a program, click the appropriate Install button.**

    The CD interface drops to the background while the CD installs the program you chose.

11. **To install other items, repeat Steps 7–10.**

12. **When you've finished installing programs, click the Quit button to close the interface.**

    You can eject the CD now. Carefully place it back in the plastic jacket of the book for safekeeping.

In order to run some of the programs on this *MCSE Windows 2000 Network Infrastructure For Dummies* CD-ROM, you may need to keep the CD inside your CD-ROM drive. This is a Good Thing. Otherwise, the installed program would have required you to install a very large chunk of the program to your hard drive, which may have kept you from installing other software.

What You'll Find

Shareware programs are fully functional, free trial versions of copyrighted programs. If you like particular programs, register with their authors for a nominal fee and receive licenses, enhanced versions, and technical support. Freeware programs are free, copyrighted games, applications, and utilities. You can copy them to as many PCs as you like — free — but they have no technical support. GNU software is governed by its own license, which is included inside the folder of the GNU software. There are no restrictions on distribution of this software. See the GNU license for more details. Trial, demo, or evaluation versions are usually limited either by time or functionality (such as being unable to save projects).

Here's a summary of the software on this CD.

Dummies test prep tools

This CD contains questions related to implementing and administering a Windows 2000 network infrastructure. Here at IDG, we've tried to include questions that will help you prepare for the exam, but please understand that we can't know exactly what subjects you'll see the day you take the test. Also, if you find some CD questions that don't receive explicit treatment in the main body of the book (and it's bound to happen), we try to provide enough information in the question explanation for you to understand what you need to know on that subject. Be sure to access TechNet on the Web (www.microsoft.com/technet) if you need more details. Finally, taking the CD test is no substitute for taking the practice exam in Appendix A. If you only have time to do one or the other, go through the practice exam in Appendix A.

QuickLearn Game

The QuickLearn Game is the ...*For Dummies* way of making studying for the Certification exam fun. Well, okay, less painful. OutPost is a DirectX, high-resolution, fast-paced arcade game.

Answer questions to defuse dimensional disrupters and save the universe from a rift in space-time. (The questions come from the same set of questions that the Self-Assessment and Practice Test use, but isn't this way more fun?) Missing a few questions on the real exam almost never results in a rip in the fabric of the universe, so just think how easy it'll be when you get there!

Please note: QUIKLERN.EXE on the CD is just a self-extractor, to simplify the process of copying the game files to your computer. It will not create any shortcuts on your computer's desktop or Start menu.

You need to have DirectX 5.0 or later installed to play the QuickLearn game; and it does not run on Windows NT 4.0.

Practice Test

The Practice test is designed to help you get comfortable with the certification-testing situation and pinpoint your strengths and weaknesses on the topic. You can accept the default setting of 60 questions in 60 minutes, or you can customize the settings. You can choose the number of questions, the amount of time, and even decide which objectives you want to focus on.

After you answer the questions, the Practice test gives you plenty of feedback. You can find out which questions you answered correctly and incorrectly and get statistics on how you did, broken down by objective. Then you can review the questions — all of them, all the ones you missed, all the ones you marked, or a combination of the ones you marked and the ones you missed.

Self-Assessment Test

The Self-Assessment test is designed to simulate the actual certification-testing situation. You must answer 60 questions in 60 minutes. After you answer all the questions, you find out your score and whether you pass or fail — but that's all the feedback you get. If you can pass the Self-Assessment test regularly, you're ready to tackle the real thing.

Links Page

I've also created a Links Page — a handy starting place for accessing the huge amounts of information on the Internet about the certification tests. You can find the page at D:\Links.htm.

Screen Saver

Here's a spiffy little screen saver that the Dummies team created. Maybe, like sleeping with the book under your pillow, this can help you learn subliminally! Screen shots of test questions will fill your screen, so when your computer is not doing anything else, it can still be quizzing you! And if you'd like to visit the *Certification ...For Dummies* Web site, all you have to do is press the space bar while the screen saver is running — your default browser will be launched and send you there! (You might want to keep this in mind if you're the kind of person who hits the space bar to get rid of your screen saver. . . .)

Commercial demos

QuickCert, from Specialized Solutions

This package from Specialized Solutions offers QuickCert practice tests for several Certification exams. Run the QuickCert IDG Demo to choose the practice test you want to work on. For more information about QuickCert, visit the Specialized Solutions Web site at www.specializedsolutions.com.

Self Test for MCSE Windows 2000 Network Infrastructure Demo, from Self Test Software

This demo gives you practice questions to help you prepare for the Network Infrastructure exam. For more information about Self Test Software, visit www.selftestsoftware.com.

Transcender Certification Sampler, from Transcender Corporation

Transcender's demo tests are some of the more popular practice tests available. The Certification Sampler offers demos of many of the exams that Transcender offers. Visit www.transcender.com for more information.

Transcender Windows 2000 Network Infrastructure Flash, from Transcender Corporation

Another demo from the good folks at Transcender, this one is designed to help you learn the fundamental concepts and terminology behind Windows 2000 network infrastructure. You provide short answer-type explanations to questions presented in a flash card format, and grade yourself as you go.

If You've Got Problems (of the CD Kind)

I tried my best to compile programs that work on most computers with the minimum system requirements. Alas, your computer may differ, and some programs may not work properly for some reason.

The two likeliest problems are that you don't have enough memory (RAM) for the programs you want to use, or you have other programs running that are affecting installation or running of a program. If you get error messages like `Not enough memory` or `Setup cannot continue,` try one or more of these methods and then try using the software again:

- ✔ **Turn off any antivirus software that you have on your computer.** Installers sometimes mimic virus activity and may make your computer incorrectly believe that it is being infected by a virus.

- ✔ **Close all running programs.** The more programs you're running, the less memory is available to other programs. Installers also typically update files and programs; if you keep other programs running, installation may not work properly.

- ✔ **In Windows, close the CD interface and run demos or installations directly from Windows Explorer.** The interface itself can tie up system memory, or even conflict with certain kinds of interactive demos. Use Windows Explorer to browse the files on the CD and launch installers or demos.

- ✔ **Have your local computer store add more RAM to your computer.** This is, admittedly, a drastic and somewhat expensive step. However, adding more memory can really help the speed of your computer and enable more programs to run at the same time.

If you still have trouble installing the items from the CD, please call the IDG Books Worldwide Customer Service phone number: 800-762-2974 (outside the U.S.: 317-572-3342).

Index

• **E** •

• Q •

• R •

• T •

• Z •

Notes

IDG Books Worldwide, Inc., End-User License Agreement

READ THIS. You should carefully read these terms and conditions before opening the software packet(s) included with this book ("Book"). This is a license agreement ("Agreement") between you and IDG Books Worldwide, Inc. ("IDGB"). By opening the accompanying software packet(s), you acknowledge that you have read and accept the following terms and conditions. If you do not agree and do not want to be bound by such terms and conditions, promptly return the Book and the unopened software packet(s) to the place you obtained them for a full refund.

1. **License Grant.** IDGB grants to you (either an individual or entity) a nonexclusive license to use one copy of the enclosed software program(s) (collectively, the "Software") solely for your own personal or business purposes on a single computer (whether a standard computer or a workstation component of a multiuser network). The Software is in use on a computer when it is loaded into temporary memory (RAM) or installed into permanent memory (hard disk, CD-ROM, or other storage device). IDGB reserves all rights not expressly granted herein.

2. **Ownership.** IDGB is the owner of all right, title, and interest, including copyright, in and to the compilation of the Software recorded on the disk(s) or CD-ROM ("Software Media"). Copyright to the individual programs recorded on the Software Media is owned by the author or other authorized copyright owner of each program. Ownership of the Software and all proprietary rights relating thereto remain with IDGB and its licensers.

3. **Restrictions on Use and Transfer.**

   (a) You may only (i) make one copy of the Software for backup or archival purposes, or (ii) transfer the Software to a single hard disk, provided that you keep the original for backup or archival purposes. You may not (i) rent or lease the Software, (ii) copy or reproduce the Software through a LAN or other network system or through any computer subscriber system or bulletin-board system, or (iii) modify, adapt, or create derivative works based on the Software.

   (b) You may not reverse engineer, decompile, or disassemble the Software. You may transfer the Software and user documentation on a permanent basis, provided that the transferee agrees to accept the terms and conditions of this Agreement and you retain no copies. If the Software is an update or has been updated, any transfer must include the most recent update and all prior versions.

4. **Restrictions on Use of Individual Programs.** You must follow the individual requirements and restrictions detailed for each individual program in the "About the CD" section of this Book. These limitations are also contained in the individual license agreements recorded on the Software Media. These limitations may include a requirement that after using the program for a specified period of time, the user must pay a registration fee or discontinue use. By opening the Software packet(s), you will be agreeing to abide by the licenses and restrictions for these individual programs that are detailed in the "About the CD" section and on the Software Media. None of the material on this Software Media or listed in this Book may ever be redistributed, in original or modified form, for commercial purposes.

Installation Instructions

To install the items from the CD to your hard drive, follow these steps.

1. **Insert the CD into your computer's CD-ROM drive.**

2. **Click Start⇨Run.**

3. **In the dialog box that appears, type** D:\IDG.EXE.

   Replace *D* with the proper drive letter if your CD-ROM drive uses a different letter.

4. **Click OK.**

5. **Read through the license agreement that's displayed and then click the Accept button.**

   The CD interface Welcome screen appears.

6. **Click anywhere on the Welcome screen to enter the interface.**

   The interface displays a list of categories for the software on the CD.

7. **To view the items within a category, just click the category's name.**

   A list of programs in the category appears.

8. **For more information about a program, click the program's name.**

9. **To install a program, click the appropriate Install button. If you don't want to install the program, click the Back button to return to the previous screen.**

   The CD interface drops to the background while the CD installs the program you chose.

10. **After you install the programs you want, click the Quit button and then eject the CD.**

For more information, see the "About the CD" appendix.

IDG BOOKS WORLDWIDE BOOK REGISTRATION

We want to hear from you

Register This Book and Win!

Visit **http://my2cents.dummies.com** to register this book and tell us how you liked it!

- ✔ Get entered in our monthly prize giveaway.

- ✔ Give us feedback about this book — tell us what you like best, what you like least, or maybe what you'd like to ask the author and us to change!

- ✔ Let us know any other *For Dummies*® topics that interest you.

Your feedback helps us determine what books to publish, tells us what coverage to add as we revise our books, and lets us know whether we're meeting your needs as a *For Dummies* reader. You're our most valuable resource, and what you have to say is important to us!

Not on the Web yet? It's easy to get started with *Dummies 101*®: *The Internet For Windows*® 98 or *The Internet For Dummies*® at local retailers everywhere.

Or let us know what you think by sending us a letter at the following address:

For Dummies Book Registration
Dummies Press
10475 Crosspoint Blvd.
Indianapolis, IN 46256

BESTSELLING BOOK SERIES